Mother

Maxim Gorky

RUPA

Published by
Rupa Publications India Pvt. Ltd 2023
7/16, Ansari Road, Daryaganj
New Delhi 110002

Sales Centres:
Allahabad Bengaluru Chennai
Hyderabad Jaipur Kathmandu
Kolkata Mumbai

Edition copyright © Rupa Publications India Pvt. Ltd. 2023

All rights reserved.
No part of this publication may be reproduced, transmitted,
or stored in a retrieval system, in any form or by any means, electronic,
mechanical, photocopying, recording or otherwise, without the prior
permission of the publisher.

P-ISBN: 978-93-5520-998-6
E-ISBN: 978-93-5520-999-3

First impression 2023

10 9 8 7 6 5 4 3 2 1

Printed in India

This book is sold subject to the condition that it shall not, by way of
trade or otherwise, be lent, resold, hired out, or otherwise circulated,
without the publisher's prior consent, in any form of binding or
cover other than that in which it is published.

Mother

Alexei Maximovich Peshkov, more commonly known as **Maxim Gorky**, was a Russian writer, socialist political thinker and voice for the proletariat. Born on 28 March, 1868, Gorky was a member of the growing Marxist communist movement, as well as the Bolshevik movement. Famed for his short stories, novels and plays, he was nominated for the Nobel Prize in Literature five times. Some of his famous works include big titles such as *The Lower Depths* (1902) and *Mother* (1906).

He was exiled from Russia and later the Soviet Union for a large portion of his life and only returned on Joseph Stalin's personal invitation, after which he was officially dubbed the 'founder of Socialist Realism'. There is an air of mystery surrounding the cause of his death, which occured on June 14, 1936.

CONTENTS

Introduction 7

PART I

Chapter I	11
Chapter II	17
Chapter III	26
Chapter IV	38
Chapter V	45
Chapter VI	53
Chapter VII	60
Chapter VIII	67
Chapter IX	77
Chapter X	83
Chapter XI	92
Chapter XII	99
Chapter XIII	104
Chapter XIV	122
Chapter XV	130
Chapter XVI	140
Chapter XVII	149
Chapter XVIII	160
Chapter XIX	169
Chapter XX	175

PART II

Chapter I	187
Chapter II	196
Chapter III	211
Chapter IV	223
Chapter V	232
Chapter VI	238
Chapter VII	249
Chapter VIII	255
Chapter IX	262
Chapter X	272
Chapter XI	284
Chapter XII	300
Chapter XIII	309
Chapter XIV	323
Chapter XV	333
Chapter XVI	348
Chapter XVII	358
Chapter XVIII	364
Chapter XIX	373

INTRODUCTION

Mother is a groundbreaking piece of Russian socialist realism that is loosely based on events that occurred on the eve of the 1905 revolution. The symbol of the 'enduring mother' of the title is Pelagueya Nilovna Vlasova. After learning to read, her son Pavel adopts a revolutionary socialist stance and converts the local factory workers in his village. Pelagueya had been leading a miserable and ignorant life, represented by Gorky to be the lifestyle of the oppressed and illiterate proletariat, but her son's socialist awakening transforms both of their lives as their rented working-class shack becomes a buzzing hub of revolutionary activity.

The mother–son bond, which consists of a unique kind of love—that can at times verge on being unhealthy—is one of the fundamental relationships in society. The relationship between a mother and her son is examined in this book.

Mother is a tale told from the viewpoint of a mother, and it centres on how she observes the development of her one and only child. The protagonist of this motivational story, Pavel, is central in the narrative, and the entire plot—including that of his mother—circles around him.

Being the only significant novel by Gorky about the Russian revolution doesn't take away from the fact that it may also be the least popular. Despite this, compared to the author's other novels, it continues to be his most well-known work. Because it paints such a vivid picture of his 'God-Builder' ideas, contemporary critics believe it to be Gorky's most significant pre-revolutionary novel.

First published by Appleton Magazine in the United States, the book was later published by Ivan Ladyzhnikov Publishers in

Germany. Due to tsarist censorship, it wasn't published in Russia until after the February Revolution. Gorky wrote the book in 1906 during a visit to the United States. The novel's political agenda was obvious. After the first Russian revolution was put down in 1905, he attempted to revive the proletarian movement by promoting his political views among his readers. Gorky was attempting to boost morale among the revolutionaries in order to combat their dejected attitude. Because the book is based on actual events involving Anna Zalomova and her son Pyotr Zalomov, he felt a personal connection to it. Gorky had a stronger connection to the tale because he was a distant relative of Anna Zalomova, who had visited Gorky's family when he was a child. The incident happened in Sormovo in 1902 during a May Day protest.

The book was adapted into a number of films and translated into numerous languages. *The Mother*, a play written in 1932 by the German playwright Bertolt Brecht and his collaborators, was inspired by this book. Though it may not be Gorky's most popular book, contemporary critics still cite it as his most significant pre-revolution work.

Gorky's writing style gradually improved over time, but it still had the same flaws, including an excessive desire for effect, a tendency to overstate things and a knack for making the reader uncomfortable with excessive use of adjectives. In addition to his propensity for philosophical tangents, Gorky also has some flaws, including a lack of refinement of emotional intelligence. However, his attention to tangible detail, ability to give his characters life and unmatched understanding of the Russian 'lower depths' are significant factors that works in favour of making him stand out from other authors. Even though Gorky is not in the same league as Chekhov, Tolstoy and other prominent Russian authors, he is still one of the most significant writers of his time, because he was the only Soviet author whose work encompassed both the pre- and post-revolutionary periods so thoroughly.

PART I

CHAPTER I

Every day the factory whistle bellowed forth its shrill, roaring, trembling noises into the smoke-begrimed and greasy atmosphere of the workingmen's suburb; and obedient to the summons of the power of steam, people poured out of little gray houses into the street. With somber faces they hastened forward like frightened roaches, their muscles stiff from insufficient sleep. In the chill morning twilight they walked through the narrow, unpaved street to the tall stone cage that waited for them with cold assurance, illumining their muddy road with scores of greasy, yellow, square eyes. The mud plashed under their feet as if in mocking commiseration. Hoarse exclamations of sleepy voices were heard; irritated, peevish, abusive language rent the air with malice; and, to welcome the people, deafening sounds floated about—the heavy whir of machinery, the dissatisfied snort of steam. Stern and somber, the black chimneys stretched their huge, thick sticks high above the village.

In the evening, when the sun was setting, and red rays languidly glimmered upon the windows of the houses, the factory ejected its people like burned-out ashes, and again they walked through the streets, with black, smoke-covered faces, radiating the sticky odor of machine oil, and showing the gleam of hungry teeth. But now there was animation in their voices, and even gladness. The servitude of hard toil was over for the day. Supper awaited them at home, and respite.

The day was swallowed up by the factory; the machine sucked out of men's muscles as much vigor as it needed. The day was blotted out from life, not a trace of it left. Man made another imperceptible step toward his grave; but he saw close before him the delights of rest, the joys of the odorous tavern, and he was satisfied.

On holidays the workers slept until about ten o'clock. Then the staid and married people dressed themselves in their best clothes and, after duly scolding the young folks for their indifference to church, went to hear mass. When they returned from church, they ate pirogs, the Russian national pastry, and again lay down to sleep until the evening. The accumulated exhaustion of years had robbed them of their appetites, and to be able to eat they drank, long and deep, goading on their feeble stomachs with the biting, burning lash of vodka.

In the evening they amused themselves idly on the street; and those who had overshoes put them on, even if it was dry, and those who had umbrellas carried them, even if the sun was shining. Not everybody has overshoes and an umbrella, but everybody desires in some way, however small, to appear more important than his neighbor.

Meeting one another they spoke about the factory and the machines, had their fling against their foreman, conversed and thought only of matters closely and manifestly connected with their work. Only rarely, and then but faintly, did solitary sparks of impotent thought glimmer in the wearisome monotony of their talk. Returning home they quarreled with their wives, and often beat them, unsparing of their fists. The young people sat in the taverns, or enjoyed evening parties at one another's houses, played the accordion, sang vulgar songs devoid of beauty, danced, talked ribaldry, and drank.

Exhausted with toil, men drank swiftly, and in every heart there awoke and grew an incomprehensible, sickly irritation. It demanded an outlet. Clutching tenaciously at every pretext for unloading themselves of this disquieting sensation, they fell on one another for mere trifles, with the spiteful ferocity of beasts, breaking into bloody quarrels which sometimes ended in serious injury and on rare occasions even in murder.

This lurking malice steadily increased, inveterate as the incurable weariness in their muscles. They were born with this disease of the soul inherited from their fathers. Like a black shadow it accompanied them to their graves, spurring on their lives to crime, hideous in its aimless cruelty and brutality.

On holidays the young people came home late at night, dirty and dusty, their clothes torn, their faces bruised, boasting maliciously of the blows they had struck their companions, or the insults they had inflicted upon them; enraged or in tears over the indignities they themselves had suffered; drunken and piteous, unfortunate and repulsive. Sometimes the boys would be brought home by the mother or the father, who had picked them up in the street or in a tavern, drunk to insensibility. The parents scolded and swore at them peevishly, and beat their spongelike bodies, soaked with liquor; then more or less systematically put them to bed, in order to rouse them to work early next morning, when the bellow of the whistle should sullenly course through the air.

They scolded and beat the children soundly, notwithstanding the fact that drunkenness and brawls among young folk appeared perfectly legitimate to the old people. When they were young they, too, had drunk and fought; they, too, had been beaten by their mothers and fathers. Life had always been like that. It flowed on monotonously and slowly somewhere down the muddy, turbid stream, year after year; and it was all bound up in strong ancient customs and habits that led them to do one and the same thing day in and day out. None of them, it seemed, had either the time or the desire to attempt to change this state of life.

Once in a long while a stranger would come to the village. At first he attracted attention merely because he was a stranger. Then he aroused a light, superficial interest by the stories of the places where he had worked. Afterwards the novelty wore off, the people got used to him, and he remained unnoticed. From his stories it was clear that the life of the workingmen was the same everywhere. And if so, then what was there to talk about?

Occasionally, however, some stranger spoke curious things never heard of in the suburb. The men did not argue with him, but listened to his odd speeches with incredulity. His words aroused blind irritation in some, perplexed alarm in others, while still others were disturbed by a feeble, shadowy glimmer of the hope of something, they knew not what. And they all began to drink more in order to drive away the unnecessary, meddlesome excitement.

Noticing in the stranger something unusual, the villagers cherished it long against him and treated the man who was not like them with unaccountable apprehension. It was as if they feared he would throw something into their life which would disturb its straight, dismal course. Sad and difficult, it was yet even in its tenor. People were accustomed to the fact that life always oppressed them with the same power. Unhopeful of any turn for the better, they regarded every change as capable only of increasing their burden.

And the workingmen of the suburb tacitly avoided people who spoke unusual things to them. Then these people disappeared again, going off elsewhere, and those who remained in the factory lived apart, if they could not blend and make one whole with the monotonous mass in the village.

Living a life like that for some fifty years, a workman died.

◆

Thus also lived Michael Vlasov, a gloomy, sullen man, with little eyes which looked at everybody from under his thick eyebrows suspiciously, with a mistrustful, evil smile. He was the best locksmith in the factory, and the strongest man in the village. But he was insolent and disrespectful toward the foreman and the superintendent, and therefore earned little; every holiday he beat somebody, and everyone disliked and feared him.

More than one attempt was made to beat him in turn, but without success. When Vlasov found himself threatened with attack, he caught a stone in his hand, or a piece of wood or iron, and spreading out his legs stood waiting in silence for the enemy. His face overgrown with a dark beard from his eyes to his neck, and his hands thickly covered with woolly hair, inspired everybody with fear. People were especially afraid of his eyes. Small and keen, they seemed to bore through a man like steel gimlets, and everyone who met their gaze felt he was confronting a beast, a savage power, inaccessible to fear, ready to strike unmercifully.

"Well, pack off, dirty vermin!" he said gruffly. His coarse, yellow teeth glistened terribly through the thick hair on his face. The men walked off uttering coward abuse.

"Dirty vermin!" he snapped at them, and his eyes gleamed

with a smile sharp as an awl. Then holding his head in an attitude of direct challenge, with a short, thick pipe between his teeth, he walked behind them, and now and then called out: "Well, who wants death?"

No one wanted it.

He spoke little, and "dirty vermin" was his favorite expression. It was the name he used for the authorities of the factory, and the police, and it was the epithet with which he addressed his wife: "Look, you dirty vermin, don't you see my clothes are torn?"

When Pavel, his son, was a boy of fourteen, Vlasov was one day seized with the desire to pull him by the hair once more. But Pavel grasped a heavy hammer, and said curtly:

"Don't touch me!"

"What!" demanded his father, bending over the tall, slender figure of his son like a shadow on a birch tree.

"Enough!" said Pavel. "I am not going to give myself up any more."

And opening his dark eyes wide, he waved the hammer in the air.

His father looked at him, folded his shaggy hands on his back, and, smiling, said:

"All right." Then he drew a heavy breath and added: "Ah, you dirty vermin!"

Shortly after this he said to his wife:

"Don't ask me for money any more. Pasha will feed you now."

"And you will drink up everything?" she ventured to ask.

"None of your business, dirty vermin!" From that time, for three years, until his death, he did not notice, and did not speak to his son.

Vlasov had a dog as big and shaggy as himself. She accompanied him to the factory every morning, and every evening she waited for him at the gate. On holidays Vlasov started off on his round of the taverns. He walked in silence, and stared into people's faces as if looking for somebody. His dog trotted after him the whole day long. Returning home drunk he sat down to supper, and gave his dog to eat from his own bowl. He never beat her, never scolded, and never petted her. After supper he flung the dishes from the table—if his wife was not quick enough to remove them in time—put a bottle of whisky before him, and leaning his back against the wall, began in a hoarse voice that spread anguish about him to bawl a song, his mouth wide open and his eyes closed. The doleful sounds got entangled in his mustache, knocking off the crumbs of bread. He smoothed down the hair of his beard and mustache with his thick fingers and sang—sang unintelligible words, long drawn out. The melody recalled the wintry howl of wolves. He sang as long as there was whisky in the bottle, then he dropped on his side upon the bench, or let his head sink on the table, and slept in this way until the whistle began to blow. The dog lay at his side.

When he died, he died hard. For five days, turned all black, he rolled in his bed, gnashing his teeth, his eyes tightly closed. Sometimes he would say to his wife: "Give me arsenic. Poison me."

She called a physician. He ordered hot poultices, but said an operation was necessary and the patient must be taken at once to the hospital.

"Go to the devil! I will die by myself, dirty vermin!" said Michael.

And when the physician had left, and his wife with tears in her eyes began to insist on an operation, he clenched his fists and announced threateningly:

"Don't you dare! It will be worse for you if I get well."

He died in the morning at the moment when the whistle called the men to work. He lay in the coffin with open mouth, his eyebrows knit as if in a scowl. He was buried by his wife, his son, the dog, an old drunkard and thief, Daniel Vyesovshchikov, a discharged smelter, and a few beggars of the suburb. His wife wept a little and quietly; Pavel did not weep at all. The villagers who met the funeral in the street stopped, crossed themselves, and said to one another: "Guess Pelagueya is glad he died!" And some corrected: "He didn't die; he rotted away like a beast."

When the body was put in the ground, the people went away, but the dog remained for a long time, and sitting silently on the fresh soil, she sniffed at the grave.

CHAPTER II

Two weeks after the death of his father, on a Sunday, Pavel came home very drunk. Staggering he crawled to a corner in the front of the room, and striking his fist on the table as his father used to do, shouted to his mother:

"Supper!"

The mother walked up to him, sat down at his side, and with her arm around her son, drew his head upon her breast. With his hand on her shoulder he pushed her away and shouted:

"Mother, quick!"

"You foolish boy!" said the mother in a sad and affectionate voice, trying to overcome his resistance.

"I am going to smoke, too. Give me father's pipe," mumbled Pavel indistinctly, wagging his tongue heavily.

It was the first time he had been drunk. The alcohol weakened his body, but it did not quench his consciousness, and the question knocked at his brain: "Drunk? Drunk?"

The fondling of his mother troubled him, and he was touched by the sadness in her eyes. He wanted to weep, and in order to overcome this desire he endeavored to appear more drunk than he actually was.

The mother stroked his tangled hair, and said in a low voice:

"Why did you do it? You oughtn't to have done it."

He began to feel sick, and after a violent attack of nausea the mother put him to bed, and laid a wet towel over his pale forehead. He sobered a little, but under and around him everything seemed to be rocking; his eyelids grew heavy; he felt a bad, sour taste in his mouth; he looked through his eyelashes on his mother's large face, and thought disjointedly:

"It seems it's too early for me. Others drink and nothing happens—and I feel sick."

Somewhere from a distance came the mother's soft voice:

"What sort of a breadgiver will you be to me if you begin to drink?"

He shut his eyes tightly and answered:

"Everybody drinks."

The mother sighed. He was right. She herself knew that besides the tavern there was no place where people could enjoy themselves; besides the taste of whisky there was no other gratification. Nevertheless she said:

"But don't you drink. Your father drank for both of you. And he made enough misery for me. Take pity on your mother, then, will you not?"

Listening to the soft, pitiful words of his mother, Pavel remembered that in his father's lifetime she had remained unnoticed in the house. She had been silent and had always lived in anxious expectation of blows. Desiring to avoid his father, he had been home very little of late; he had become almost unaccustomed to his mother, and now, as he gradually sobered up, he looked at her fixedly.

She was tall and somewhat stooping. Her heavy body, broken down with long years of toil and the beatings of her husband, moved about noiselessly and inclined to one side, as if she were in constant fear of knocking up against something. Her broad oval face, wrinkled and puffy, was lighted up with a pair of dark eyes, troubled and melancholy as those of most of the women in the village. On her right eyebrow was a deep scar, which turned the eyebrow upward a little; her right ear, too, seemed to be higher than the left, which gave her face the appearance of alarmed listening. Gray locks glistened in her thick, dark hair, like the imprints of heavy blows. Altogether she was soft, melancholy, and submissive.

Tears slowly trickled down her cheeks.

"Wait, don't cry!" begged the son in a soft voice. "Give me a drink."

She rose and said:

"I'll give you some ice water."

But when she returned he was already asleep. She stood over him for a minute, trying to breathe lightly. The cup in her hand trembled, and the ice knocked against the tin. Then, setting the cup on the table, she knelt before the sacred image upon the wall, and began to pray in silence. The sounds of dark, drunken life beat against the window panes; an accordion screeched in the misty darkness of the autumn night; some one sang a loud song; some one was swearing with ugly, vile oaths, and the excited sounds of women's irritated, weary voices cut the air.

◆

Life in the little house of the Vlasovs flowed on monotonously, but more calmly and undisturbed than before, and somewhat different from everywhere else in the suburb.

The house stood at the edge of the village, by a low but steep and muddy declivity. A third of the house was occupied by the kitchen and a small room used for the mother's bedroom, separated from the kitchen by a partition reaching partially to the ceiling. The other two thirds formed a square room with two windows. In one corner stood Pavel's bed, in front a table and two benches. Some chairs, a washstand with a small looking-glass over it, a trunk with clothes, a clock on the wall, and two ikons—this was the entire outfit of the household.

Pavel tried to live like the rest. He did all a young lad should do—bought himself an accordion, a shirt with a starched front, a loud-colored necktie, overshoes, and a cane. Externally he became like all the other youths of his age. He went to evening parties and learned to dance a quadrille and a polka. On holidays he came home drunk, and always suffered greatly from the effects of liquor. In the morning his head ached, he was tormented by heartburns, his face was pale and dull.

Once his mother asked him:

"Well, did you have a good time yesterday?"

He answered dismally and with irritation:

"Oh, dreary as a graveyard! Everybody is like a machine. I'd better go fishing or buy myself a gun."

He worked faithfully, without intermission and without incurring fines. He was taciturn, and his eyes, blue and large like his mother's, looked out discontentedly. He did not buy a gun, nor did he go a-fishing; but he gradually began to avoid the beaten path trodden by all. His attendance at parties became less and less frequent, and although he went out somewhere on holidays, he always returned home sober. His mother watched him unobtrusively but closely, and saw the tawny face of her son grow keener and keener, and his eyes more serious. She noticed that his lips were compressed in a peculiar manner, imparting an odd expression of austerity to his face. It seemed as if he were always angry at something, or as if a canker gnawed at him. At first his friends came to visit him, but never finding him at home, they remained away.

The mother was glad to see her son turning out different from all the other factory youth; but a feeling of anxiety and apprehension stirred in her heart when she observed that he was obstinately and resolutely directing his life into obscure paths leading away from the routine existence about him—that he turned in his career neither to the right nor the left.

He began to bring books home with him. At first he tried to escape attention when reading them; and after he had finished a book, he hid it. Sometimes he copied a passage on a piece of paper, and hid that also.

"Aren't you well, Pavlusha?" the mother asked once.

"I'm all right," he answered.

"You are so thin," said the mother with a sigh.

He was silent.

They spoke infrequently, and saw each other very little. In the morning he drank tea in silence, and went off to work; at noon he came for dinner, a few insignificant remarks were passed at the table, and he again disappeared until the evening. And in the evening, the day's work ended, he washed himself, took supper, and then fell to his books, and read for a long time. On holidays he left home in the morning and returned late at night. She knew he went to the city and the theater; but nobody from the city ever came to visit him. It seemed to her that with the lapse of time her son spoke less and less; and at the same time she noticed that occasionally and with increasing frequency he used new words unintelligible to her, and that the coarse, rude, and hard expressions dropped from his speech. In his general conduct, also, certain traits appeared, forcing themselves upon his mother's attention. He ceased to affect the dandy, but became more attentive to the cleanliness of his body and dress, and moved more freely and alertly. The increasing softness and simplicity of his manner aroused a disquieting interest in his mother.

Once he brought a picture and hung it on the wall. It represented three persons walking lightly and boldly, and conversing.

"This is Christ risen from the dead, and going to Emmaus," explained Pavel.

The mother liked the picture, but she thought:

"You respect Christ, and yet you do not go to church."

Then more pictures appeared on the walls, and the number of books increased on the shelves neatly made for him by one of his carpenter friends. The room began to look like a home.

He addressed his mother with the reverential plural "you," and called her "mother" instead of "mamma." But sometimes he turned to her suddenly, and briefly used the simple and familiar form of the singular: "Mamma, please be not thou disturbed if I come home late to-night."

This pleased her; in such words she felt something serious and strong.

But her uneasiness increased. Since her son's strangeness was not clarified with time, her heart became more and more sharply troubled with a foreboding of something unusual. Every now and then she felt a certain dissatisfaction with him, and she thought: "All people are like people, and he is like a monk. He is so stern. It's not according to his years." At other times she thought: "Maybe he has become interested in some sort of a girl down there."

But to go about with girls, money is needed, and he gave almost all his earnings to her.

Thus weeks and months elapsed; and imperceptibly two years slipped by, two years of a strange, silent life, full of disquieting thoughts and anxieties that kept continually increasing.

Once, when after supper Pavel drew the curtain over the window, sat down in a corner, and began to read, his tin lamp hanging on the wall over his head, the mother, after removing the dishes, came out from the kitchen and carefully walked up to him. He raised his head, and without speaking looked at her with a questioning expression.

"Nothing, Pasha, just so!" she said hastily, and walked away, moving her eyebrows agitatedly. But after standing in the kitchen for a moment, motionless, thoughtful, deeply preoccupied, she washed her hands and approached her son again.

"I want to ask you," she said in a low, soft voice, "what you read all the time."

He put his book aside and said to her:

"Sit down, mother."

The mother sat down heavily at his side, and straightening herself into an attitude of intense, painful expectation waited for something momentous.

Without looking at her, Pavel spoke, not loudly, but for some reason very sternly:

"I am reading forbidden books. They are forbidden to be read because they tell the truth about our—about the workingmen's life. They are printed in secret, and if I am found with them I will be put in prison—I will be put in prison because I want to know the truth."

Breathing suddenly became difficult for her. Opening her eyes wide she looked at her son, and he seemed to her new, as if a stranger. His voice was different, lower, deeper, more sonorous. He pinched his thin, downy mustache, and looked oddly askance into the corner. She grew anxious for her son and pitied him.

"Why do you do this, Pasha?"

He raised his head, looked at her, and said in a low, calm voice:

"I want to know the truth."

His voice sounded placid, but firm; and his eyes flashed resolution. She understood with her heart that her son had consecrated himself forever to something mysterious and awful. Everything in life had always appeared to her inevitable; she was accustomed to submit without thought, and now, too, she only wept softly, finding no words, but in her heart she was oppressed with sorrow and distress.

"Don't cry," said Pavel, kindly and softly; and it seemed to her that he was bidding her farewell.

"Think what kind of a life you are leading. You are forty years old, and have you lived? Father beat you. I understand now that he avenged his wretchedness on your body, the wretchedness of his life. It pressed upon him, and he did not know whence it came. He worked for thirty years; he began to work when the whole factory occupied but two buildings; now there are seven of them. The mills grow, and people die, working for them."

She listened to him eagerly and awestruck. His eyes burned with a beautiful radiance. Leaning forward on the table he moved nearer to his mother, and looking straight into her face, wet with tears, he delivered his first speech to her about the truth which he had now come to understand. With the *naïveté* of youth, and the ardor of a young student proud of his knowledge, religiously confiding in its truth, he spoke about everything that was clear to him, and spoke not so much for his mother as to verify and strengthen his own opinions. At times he halted, finding no words, and then he saw before him a disturbed face, in which dimly shone a pair of kind eyes clouded with tears. They looked on with awe and perplexity. He was sorry for his mother, and began to speak again, about herself and her life.

"What joys did you know?" he asked. "What sort of a past can you recall?"

She listened and shook her head dolefully, feeling something new, unknown to her, both sorrowful and gladsome, like a caress to her troubled and aching heart. It was the first time she had heard such language about herself, her own life. It awakened in her misty, dim thoughts, long dormant; gently roused an almost extinct feeling of rebellion, perplexed dissatisfaction—thoughts and feelings of a remote youth. She often discussed life with her neighbors, spoke a great deal about everything; but all, herself included, only complained; no one explained why life was so hard and burdensome.

And now her son sat before her; and what he said about her— his eyes, his face, his words—it all clutched at her heart, filling her with a sense of pride for her son, who truly understood the life of his mother, and spoke the truth about her and her sufferings, and pitied her.

Mothers are not pitied. She knew it. She did not understand Pavel when speaking about matters not pertaining to herself, but all he said about her own woman's existence was bitterly familiar and true. Hence it seemed to her that every word of his was perfectly true, and her bosom throbbed with a gentle sensation which warmed it more and more with an unknown, kindly caress.

"What do you want to do, then?" she asked, interrupting his speech.

"Study and then teach others. We workingmen must study. We must learn, we must understand why life is so hard for us."

It was sweet to her to see that his blue eyes, always so serious and stern, now glowed with warmth, softly illuminating something new within him. A soft, contented smile played around her lips, although the tears still trembled in the wrinkles of her face. She wavered between two feelings: pride in her son who desired the good of all people, had pity for all, and understood the sorrow and affliction of life; and the involuntary regret for his youth, because he did not speak like everybody else, because he resolved to enter alone into a fight against the life to which all, including herself, were accustomed.

She wanted to say to him: "My dear, what can you do? People will crush you. You will perish."

But it was pleasant to her to listen to his speeches, and she feared to disturb her delight in her son, who suddenly revealed himself so new and wise, even if somewhat strange.

Pavel saw the smile around his mother's lips, the attention in her face, the love in her eyes; and it seemed to him that he compelled her to understand his truth; and youthful pride in the power of his word heightened his faith in himself. Seized with enthusiasm, he continued to talk, now smiling, now frowning. Occasionally hatred sounded in his words; and when his mother heard its bitter, harsh accents she shook her head, frightened, and asked in a low voice:

"Is it so, Pasha?"

"It is so!" he answered firmly. And he told her about people who wanted the good of men, and who sowed truth among them; and because of this the enemies of life hunted them down like beasts, thrust them into prisons, and exiled them, and set them to hard labor.

"I have seen such people!" he exclaimed passionately. "They are the best people on earth!"

These people filled the mother with terror, and she wanted to ask her son: "Is it so, Pasha?"

But she hesitated, and leaning back she listened to the stories of people incomprehensible to her, who taught her son to speak and think words and thoughts so dangerous to him. Finally she said:

"It will soon be daylight. You ought to go to bed. You've got to go to work."

"Yes, I'll go to bed at once," he assented. "Did you understand me?"

"I did," she said, drawing a deep breath. Tears rolled down from her eyes again, and breaking into sobs she added: "You will perish, my son!"

Pavel walked up and down the room.

"Well, now you know what I am doing and where I am going. I told you all. I beg of you, mother, if you love me, do not hinder me!"

"My darling, my beloved!" she cried, "maybe it would be better for me not to have known anything!"

He took her hand and pressed it firmly in his. The word "mother," pronounced by him with feverish emphasis, and that clasp of the hand so new and strange, moved her.

"I will do nothing!" she said in a broken voice. "Only be on your guard! Be on your guard!" Not knowing what he should be on his guard against, nor how to warn him, she added mournfully: "You are getting so thin."

And with a look of affectionate warmth, which seemed to embrace his firm, well-shaped body, she said hastily, and in a low voice:

"God be with you! Live as you want to. I will not hinder you. One thing only I beg of you—do not speak to people unguardedly! You must be on the watch with people; they all hate one another. They live in greed and envy; all are glad to do injury; people persecute out of sheer amusement. When you begin to accuse them and to judge them, they will hate you, and will hound you to destruction!"

Pavel stood in the doorway listening to the melancholy speech, and when the mother had finished he said with a smile:

"Yes, people are sorry creatures; but when I came to recognize that there is truth in the world, people became better." He smiled again and added: "I do not know how it happened myself! From childhood I feared everybody; as I grew up I began to hate everybody, some for their meanness, others—well, I do not know why—just so! And now I see all the people in a different way. I am grieved for them all! I cannot understand it; but my heart turned softer when I recognized that there is truth in men, and that not all are to blame for their foulness and filth."

He was silent as if listening to something within himself. Then he said in a low voice and thoughtfully:

"That's how truth lives."

She looked at him tenderly.

"May God protect you!" she sighed. "It is a dangerous change that has come upon you."

When he had fallen asleep, the mother rose carefully from her bed and came gently into her son's room. Pavel's swarthy, resolute, stern face was clearly outlined against the white pillow. Pressing her hand to her bosom, the mother stood at his bedside. Her lips moved mutely, and great tears rolled down her cheeks.

CHAPTER III

Again they lived in silence, distant and yet near to each other. Once, in the middle of the week, on a holiday, as he was preparing to leave the house he said to his mother:

"I expect some people here on Saturday."

"What people?" she asked.

"Some people from our village, and others from the city."

"From the city?" repeated the mother, shaking her head. And suddenly she broke into sobs.

"Now, mother, why this?" cried Pavel resentfully. "What for?"

Drying her face with her apron, she answered quietly:

"I don't know, but it is the way I feel."

He paced up and down the room, then halting before her, said:

"Are you afraid?"

"I am afraid," she acknowledged. "Those people from the city—who knows them?"

He bent down to look in her face, and said in an offended tone, and, it seemed to her, angrily, like his father:

"This fear is what is the ruin of us all. And some dominate us; they take advantage of our fear and frighten us still more. Mark this: as long as people are afraid, they will rot like the birches in the marsh. We must grow bold; it is time!"

"It's all the same," he said, as he turned from her; "they'll meet in my house, anyway."

"Don't be angry with me!" the mother begged sadly. "How can I help being afraid? All my life I have lived in fear!"

"Forgive me!" was his gentler reply, "but I cannot do otherwise," and he walked away.

For three days her heart was in a tremble, sinking in fright each time she remembered that strange people were soon to come to her house. She could not picture them to herself, but it seemed to her they were terrible people. It was they who had shown her son the road he was going.

On Saturday night Pavel came from the factory, washed himself, put on clean clothes, and when walking out of the house said to his mother without looking at her:

"When they come, tell them I'll be back soon. Let them wait a while. And please don't be afraid. They are people like all other people."

She sank into her seat almost fainting.

Her son looked at her soberly. "Maybe you'd better go away somewhere," he suggested.

The thought offended her. Shaking her head in dissent, she said:

"No, it's all the same. What for?"

It was the end of November. During the day a dry, fine snow had fallen upon the frozen earth, and now she heard it crunching outside the window under her son's feet as he walked away. A dense crust of darkness settled immovably upon the window panes, and seemed to lie in hostile watch for something. Supporting herself on the bench, the mother sat and waited, looking at the door.

It seemed to her that people were stealthily and watchfully walking about the house in the darkness, stooping and looking about on all sides, strangely attired and silent. There around the house some one was already coming, fumbling with his hands along the wall.

A whistle was heard. It circled around like the notes of a fine chord, sad and melodious, wandered musingly into the wilderness of darkness, and seemed to be searching for something. It came nearer. Suddenly it died away under the window, as if it had entered into the wood of the wall. The noise of feet was heard on the porch. The mother started, and rose with a strained, frightened look in her eyes.

The door opened. At first a head with a big, shaggy hat thrust itself into the room; then a slender, bending body crawled in, straightened itself out, and deliberately raised its right hand.

"Good evening!" said the man, in a thick, bass voice, breathing heavily.

The mother bowed in silence.

"Pavel is not at home yet?"

The stranger leisurely removed his short fur jacket, raised one foot, whipped the snow from his boot with his hat, then did the same with the other foot, flung his hat into a corner, and rocking on his thin legs walked into the room, looking back at the imprints he left on the floor. He approached the table, examined it as if to satisfy himself of its solidity, and finally sat down and, covering his mouth with his hand, yawned. His head was perfectly round and close-cropped, his face shaven except for a thin mustache, the ends of which pointed downward.

After carefully scrutinizing the room with his large, gray, protuberant eyes, he crossed his legs, and, leaning his head over the table, inquired:

"Is this your own house, or do you rent it?"

The mother, sitting opposite him, answered:

"We rent it."

"Not a very fine house," he remarked.

"Pasha will soon be here; wait," said the mother quietly.

"Why, yes, I am waiting," said the man.

His calmness, his deep, sympathetic voice, and the candor and simplicity of his face encouraged the mother. He looked at her openly and kindly, and a merry sparkle played in the depths of his transparent eyes. In the entire angular, stooping figure, with its thin legs, there was something comical, yet winning. He was dressed in a blue shirt, and dark, loose trousers thrust into his boots. She was seized with the desire to ask him who he was, whence he came, and whether he had known her son long. But suddenly he himself put a question, leaning forward with a swing of his whole body.

"Who made that hole in your forehead, mother?"

His question was uttered in a kind voice and with a noticeable smile in his eyes; but the woman was offended by the sally. She pressed her lips together tightly, and after a pause rejoined with cold civility:

"And what business is it of yours, sir?"

With the same swing of his whole body toward her, he said:

"Now, don't get angry! I ask because my foster mother had her head smashed just exactly like yours. It was her man who did it for her once, with a last—he was a shoemaker, you see. She was a washerwoman and he was a shoemaker. It was after she had taken me as her son that she found him somewhere, a drunkard, and married him, to her great misfortune. He beat her—I tell you, my skin almost burst with terror."

The mother felt herself disarmed by his openness. Moreover, it occurred to her that perhaps her son would be displeased with her harsh reply to this odd personage. Smiling guiltily she said:

"I am not angry, but—you see—you asked so very soon. It was my good man, God rest his soul! who treated me to the cut. Are you a Tartar?"

The stranger stretched out his feet, and smiled so broad a smile that the ends of his mustache traveled to the nape of his neck. Then he said seriously:

"Not yet. I'm not a Tartar yet."

"I asked because I rather thought the way you spoke was not exactly Russian," she explained, catching his joke.

"I am better than a Russian, I am!" said the guest laughingly. "I am a Little Russian from the city of Kanyev."

"And have you been here long?"

"I lived in the city about a month, and I came to your factory about a month ago. I found some good people, your son and a few others. I will live here for a while," he said, twirling his mustache.

The man pleased the mother, and, yielding to the impulse to repay him in some way for his kind words about her son, she questioned again:

"Maybe you'd like to have a glass of tea?"

"What! An entertainment all to myself!" he answered, raising his shoulders. "I'll wait for the honor until we are all here."

This allusion to the coming of others recalled her fear to her.

"If they all are only like this one!" was her ardent wish.

Again steps were heard on the porch. The door opened quickly, and the mother rose. This time she was taken completely aback by the newcomer in her kitchen—a poorly and lightly dressed girl of medium height, with the simple face of a peasant woman, and a head of thick, dark hair. Smiling she said in a low voice:

"Am I late?"

"Why, no!" answered the Little Russian, looking out of the living room. "Come on foot?"

"Of course! Are you the mother of Pavel Vlasov? Good evening! My name is Natasha."

"And your other name?" inquired the mother.

"Vasilyevna. And yours?"

"Pelagueya Nilovna."

"So here we are all acquainted."

"Yes," said the mother, breathing more easily, as if relieved, and looking at the girl with a smile.

The Little Russian helped her off with her cloak, and inquired:

"Is it cold?"

"Out in the open, very! The wind—goodness!"

Her voice was musical and clear, her mouth small and smiling, her body round and vigorous. Removing her wraps, she rubbed her ruddy cheeks briskly with her little hands, red with the cold, and walking lightly and quickly she passed into the room, the heels of her shoes rapping sharply on the floor.

"She goes without overshoes," the mother noted silently.

"Indeed it is cold," repeated the girl. "I'm frozen through—ooh!"

"I'll warm up the samovar for you!" the mother said, bustling and solicitous. "Ready in a moment," she called from the kitchen.

Somehow it seemed to her she had known the girl long, and even loved her with the tender, compassionate love of a mother. She was glad to see her; and recalling her guest's bright blue eyes, she smiled contentedly, as she prepared the samovar and listened to the conversation in the room.

"Why so gloomy, Nakhodka?" asked the girl.

"The widow has good eyes," answered the Little Russian. "I

was thinking maybe my mother has such eyes. You know, I keep thinking of her as alive."

"You said she was dead?"

"That's my adopted mother. I am speaking now of my real mother. It seems to me that perhaps she may be somewhere in Kiev begging alms and drinking whisky."

"Why do you think such awful things?"

"I don't know. And the policemen pick her up on the street drunk and beat her."

"Oh, you poor soul," thought the mother, and sighed.

Natasha muttered something hotly and rapidly; and again the sonorous voice of the Little Russian was heard.

"Ah, you are young yet, comrade," he said. "You haven't eaten enough onions yet. Everyone has a mother, none the less people are bad. For although it is hard to rear children, it is still harder to teach a man to be good."

"What strange ideas he has," the mother thought, and for a moment she felt like contradicting the Little Russian and telling him that here was she who would have been glad to teach her son good, but knew nothing herself. The door, however, opened and in came Nikolay Vyesovshchikov, the son of the old thief Daniel, known in the village as a misanthrope. He always kept at a sullen distance from people, who retaliated by making sport of him.

"You, Nikolay! How's that?" she asked in surprise.

Without replying he merely looked at the mother with his little gray eyes, and wiped his pockmarked, high-cheeked face with the broad palm of his hand.

"Is Pavel at home?" he asked hoarsely.

"No."

He looked into the room and said:

"Good evening, comrades."

"He, too. Is it possible?" wondered the mother resentfully, and was greatly surprised to see Natasha put her hand out to him in a kind, glad welcome.

The next to come were two young men, scarcely more than boys. One of them the mother knew. He was Yakob, the son of the factory watchman, Somov. The other, with a sharp-featured face, high forehead, and curly hair, was unknown to her; but he, too, was not terrible.

Finally Pavel appeared, and with him two men, both of whose faces she recognized as those of workmen in the factory.

"You've prepared the samovar! That's fine. Thank you!" said Pavel as he saw what his mother had done.

"Perhaps I should get some vodka," she suggested, not knowing how to express her gratitude to him for something which as yet she did not understand.

"No, we don't need it!" he responded, removing his coat and smiling affectionately at her.

It suddenly occurred to her that her son, by way of jest, had purposely exaggerated the danger of the gathering.

"Are these the ones they call illegal people?" she whispered.

"The very ones!" answered Pavel, and passed into the room.

She looked lovingly after him and thought to herself condescendingly:

"Mere children!"

When the samovar boiled, and she brought it into the room, she found the guests sitting in a close circle around the table, and Natasha installed in the corner under the lamp with a book in her hands.

"In order to understand why people live so badly," said Natasha.

"And why they are themselves so bad," put in the Little Russian.

"It is necessary to see how they began to live—"

"See, my dears, see!" mumbled the mother, making the tea.

They all stopped talking.

"What is the matter, mother?" asked Pavel, knitting his brows.

"What?" She looked around, and seeing the eyes of all upon her she explained with embarrassment, "I was just speaking to myself."

Natasha laughed and Pavel smiled, but the Little Russian said: "Thank you for the tea, mother."

"Hasn't drunk it yet and thanks me already," she commented inwardly. Looking at her son, she asked: "I am not in your way?"

"How can the hostess in her own home be in the way of her guests?" replied Natasha, and then continuing with childish plaintiveness: "Mother dear, give me tea quick! I am shivering with cold; my feet are all frozen."

"In a moment, in a moment!" exclaimed the mother, hurrying.

Having drunk a cup of tea, Natasha drew a long breath, brushed her hair back from her forehead, and began to read from a large yellow-covered book with pictures. The mother, careful not to make a noise with the dishes, poured tea into the glasses, and strained her untrained mind to listen to the girl's fluent reading. The melodious voice blended with the thin, musical hum of the samovar. The clear, simple narrative of savage people who lived in caves and killed the beasts with stones floated and quivered like a dainty ribbon in the room. It sounded like a tale, and the mother looked up to her son occasionally, wishing to ask him what was illegal in the story about wild men. But she soon ceased to follow the narrative and began to scrutinize the guests, unnoticed by them or her son.

Pavel sat at Natasha's side. He was the handsomest of them all. Natasha bent down very low over the book. At times she tossed back the thin curls that kept running down over her forehead, and lowered her voice to say something not in the book, with a kind look at the faces of her auditors. The Little Russian bent his broad chest over a corner of the table, and squinted his eyes in the effort to see the worn ends of his mustache, which he constantly twirled. Vyesovshchikov sat on his chair straight as a pole, his palms resting on his knees, and his pockmarked face, browless and thin-lipped, immobile as a mask. He kept his narrow-eyed gaze stubbornly fixed upon the reflection of his face in the glittering brass of the samovar. He seemed not even to breathe. Little Somov moved his lips mutely, as if repeating to himself the words in the book; and his curly-haired companion, with bent body, elbows on knees, his face supported on his hands, smiled abstractedly. One of the men who had entered at the same time as Pavel, a slender young chap with red, curly hair and merry green eyes, apparently wanted to say something; for he kept turning around impatiently. The other, light-haired and closely cropped, stroked his head with his hand and looked down on the floor so that his face remained invisible.

It was warm in the room, and the atmosphere was genial. The mother responded to this peculiar charm, which she had never before felt. She was affected by the purling of Natasha's voice, mingled with the quavering hum of the samovar, and recalled the noisy evening parties of her youth—the coarseness of the young men, whose breath always smelled of vodka—their cynical jokes. She remembered all this, and an oppressive sense of pity for her own self gently stirred her worn, outraged heart.

Before her rose the scene of the wooing of her husband. At one of the parties he had seized her in a dark porch, and pressing her with his whole body to the wall asked in a gruff, vexed voice:

"Will you marry me?"

She had been pained and had felt offended; but he rudely dug his fingers into her flesh, snorted heavily, and breathed his hot, humid breath into her face. She struggled to tear herself out of his grasp.

"Hold on!" he roared. "Answer me! Well?"

Out of breath, shamed and insulted, she remained silent.

"Don't put on airs now, you fool! I know your kind. You are mighty pleased."

Some one opened the door. He let her go leisurely, saying:

"I will send a matchmaker to you next Sunday."

And he did.

The mother covered her eyes and heaved a deep sigh.

◆

"I do not want to know how people used to live, but how they ought to live!" The dull, dissatisfied voice of Vyesovshchikov was heard in the room.

"That's it!" corroborated the red-headed man, rising.

"And I disagree!" cried Somov. "If we are to go forward, we must know everything."

"True, true!" said the curly-headed youth in a low tone.

A heated discussion ensued; and the words flashed like tongues of fire in a wood pile. The mother did not understand what they were shouting about. All faces glowed in an aureole of animation, but none grew angry, no one spoke the harsh, offensive words so familiar to her.

"They restrain themselves on account of a woman's presence," she concluded.

The serious face of Natasha pleased her. The young woman looked at all these young men so considerately, with the air of an elder person toward children.

"Wait, comrades," she broke out suddenly. And they all grew silent and turned their eyes upon her.

"Those who say that we ought to know everything are right. We ought to illumine ourselves with the light of reason, so that the people in the dark may see us; we ought to be able to answer every question honestly and truly. We must know all the truth, all the falsehood."

The Little Russian listened and nodded his head in accompaniment to her words. Vyesovshchikov, the red-haired fellow, and the other factory worker, who had come with Pavel, stood in a close circle of three. For some reason the mother did not like them.

When Natasha ceased talking, Pavel arose and asked calmly:

"Is filling our stomachs the only thing we want?"

"No!" he answered himself, looking hard in the direction of the three. "We want to be people. We must show those who sit on our necks, and cover up our eyes, that we see everything, that we are not foolish, we are not animals, and that we do not want merely to eat, but also to live like decent human beings. We must show our enemies that our life of servitude, of hard toil which they impose upon us, does not hinder us from measuring up to them in intellect, and as to spirit, that we rise far above them!"

The mother listened to his words, and a feeling of pride in her son stirred her bosom—how eloquently he spoke!

"People with well-filled stomachs are, after all, not a few, but honest people there are none," said the Little Russian. "We ought to build a bridge across the bog of this rotten life to a future of soulful goodness. That's our task, that's what we have to do, comrades!"

"When the time is come to fight, it's not the time to cure the finger," said Vyesovshchikov dully.

"There will be enough breaking of our bones before we get to fighting!" the Little Russian put in merrily.

It was already past midnight when the group began to break up. The first to go were Vyesovshchikov and the red-haired man—which again displeased the mother.

"Hm! How they hurry!" she thought, nodding them a not very friendly farewell.

"Will you see me home, Nakhodka?" asked Natasha.

"Why, of course," answered the Little Russian.

When Natasha put on her wraps in the kitchen, the mother said to her: "Your stockings are too thin for this time of the year. Let me knit some woolen ones for you, will you, please?"

"Thank you, Pelagueya Nilovna. Woolen stockings scratch," Natasha answered, smiling.

"I'll make them so they won't scratch."

Natasha looked at her rather perplexedly, and her fixed serious glance hurt the mother.

"Pardon me my stupidity; like my good will, it's from my heart, you know," she added in a low voice.

"How kind you are!" Natasha answered in the same voice, giving her a hasty pressure of the hand and walking out.

"Good night, mother!" said the Little Russian, looking into her eyes. His bending body followed Natasha out to the porch.

The mother looked at her son. He stood in the room at the door and smiled.

"The evening was fine," he declared, nodding his head energetically. "It was fine! But now I think you'd better go to bed; it's time."

"And it's time for you, too. I'm going in a minute."

She busied herself about the table gathering the dishes together, satisfied and even glowing with a pleasurable agitation. She was glad that everything had gone so well and had ended peaceably.

"You arranged it nicely, Pavlusha. They certainly are good people. The Little Russian is such a hearty fellow. And the young lady, what a bright, wise girl she is! Who is she?"

"A teacher," answered Pavel, pacing up and down the room.

"Ah! Such a poor thing! Dressed so poorly! Ah, so poorly! It doesn't take long to catch a cold. And where are her relatives?"

"In Moscow," said Pavel, stopping before his mother. "Look! her father is a rich man; he is in the hardware business, and owns much property. He drove her out of the house because she got into this movement. She grew up in comfort and warmth, she was coddled and indulged in everything she desired—and now she walks four miles at night all by herself."

The mother was shocked. She stood in the middle of the room, and looked mutely at her son. Then she asked quietly:

"Is she going to the city?"

"Yes."

"And is she not afraid?"

"No," said Pavel smiling.

"Why did she go? She could have stayed here overnight, and slept with me."

"That wouldn't do. She might have been seen here to-morrow morning, and we don't want that; nor does she."

The mother recollected her previous anxieties, looked thoughtfully through the window, and asked:

"I cannot understand, Pasha, what there is dangerous in all this, or illegal. Why, you are not doing anything bad, are you?"

She was not quite assured of the safety and propriety of his conduct, and was eager for a confirmation from her son. But he looked calmly into her eyes, and declared in a firm voice:

"There is nothing bad in what we're doing, and there's not going to be. And yet the prison is awaiting us all. You may as well know it."

Her hands trembled. "Maybe God will grant you escape somehow," she said with sunken voice.

"No," said the son kindly, but decidedly. "I cannot lie to you. We will not escape." He smiled. "Now go to bed. You are tired. Good night."

Left alone, she walked up to the window, and stood there looking into the street. Outside it was cold and cheerless. The wind howled, blowing the snow from the roofs of the little sleeping houses. Striking against the walls and whispering something, quickly it fell upon the ground and drifted the white clouds of dry snowflakes across the street.

"O Christ in heaven, have mercy upon us!" prayed the mother.

The tears began to gather in her eyes, as fear returned persistently to her heart, and like a moth in the night she seemed to see fluttering the woe of which her son spoke with such composure and assurance.

Before her eyes as she gazed a smooth plain of snow spread

out in the distance. The wind, carrying white, shaggy masses, raced over the plain, piping cold, shrill whistles. Across the snowy expanse moved a girl's figure, dark and solitary, rocking to and fro. The wind fluttered her dress, clogged her footsteps, and drove pricking snowflakes into her face. Walking was difficult; the little feet sank into the snow. Cold and fearful the girl bent forward, like a blade of grass, the sport of the wanton wind. To the right of her on the marsh stood the dark wall of the forest; the bare birches and aspens quivered and rustled with a mournful cry. Yonder in the distance, before her, the lights of the city glimmered dimly.

"Lord in heaven, have mercy!" the mother muttered again, shuddering with the cold and horror of an unformed fear.

CHAPTER IV

The days glided by one after the other, like the beads of a rosary, and grew into weeks and months. Every Saturday Pavel's friends gathered in his house; and each meeting formed a step up a long stairway, which led somewhere into the distance, gradually lifting the people higher and higher. But its top remained invisible.

New people kept coming. The small room of the Vlasovs became crowded and close. Natasha arrived every Saturday night, cold and tired, but always fresh and lively, in inexhaustible good spirits. The mother made stockings, and herself put them on the little feet. Natasha laughed at first; but suddenly grew silent and thoughtful, and said in a low voice to the mother:

"I had a nurse who was also ever so kind. How strange, Pelagueya Nilovna! The workingmen live such a hard, outraged life, and yet there is more heart, more goodness in them than in—those!" And she waved her hand, pointing somewhere far, very far from herself.

"See what sort of a person you are," the older woman answered. "You have left your own family and everything—" She was unable to finish her thought, and heaving a sigh looked silently into Natasha's face with a feeling of gratitude to the girl for she knew not what. She sat on the floor before Natasha, who smiled and fell to musing.

"I have abandoned my family?" she repeated, bending her head down. "That's nothing. My father is a stupid, coarse man—my brother also—and a drunkard, besides. My oldest sister—unhappy, wretched thing—married a man much older than herself, very rich, a bore and greedy. But my mother I am sorry for! She's a simple woman like you, a beaten-down, frightened creature, so tiny, like a little mouse—she runs so quickly and is afraid of everybody. And sometimes I want to see her so—my mother!"

"My poor thing!" said the mother sadly, shaking her head.

The girl quickly threw up her head and cried out:

"Oh, no! At times I feel such joy, such happiness!"

Her face paled and her blue eyes gleamed. Placing her hands on the mother's shoulders she said with a deep voice issuing from her very heart, quietly as if in an ecstasy:

"If you knew—if you but understood what a great, joyous work we are doing! You will come to feel it!" she exclaimed with conviction.

A feeling akin to envy touched the heart of the mother. Rising from the floor she said plaintively:

"I am too old for that—ignorant and old."

Pavel spoke more and more often and at greater length, discussed more and more hotly, and—grew thinner and thinner. It seemed to his mother that when he spoke to Natasha or looked at her his eyes turned softer, his voice sounded fonder, and his entire bearing became simpler.

"Heaven grant!" she thought; and imagining Natasha as her daughter-in-law, she smiled inwardly.

Whenever at the meetings the disputes waxed too hot and stormy, the Little Russian stood up, and rocking himself to and fro like the tongue of a bell, he spoke in his sonorous, resonant voice simple and good words which allayed their excitement and recalled them to their purpose. Vyesovshchikov always kept hurrying everybody on somewhere. He and the red-haired youth called Samoylov were the first to begin all disputes. On their side were always Ivan Bukin, with the round head and the white eyebrows and lashes, who looked as if he had been hung out to dry, or washed out with lye; and the curly-headed, lofty-browed Fedya Mazin. Modest

Yakob Somov, always smoothly combed and clean, spoke little and briefly, with a quiet, serious voice, and always took sides with Pavel and the Little Russian.

Sometimes, instead of Natasha, Alexey Ivanovich, a native of some remote government, came from the city. He wore eyeglasses, his beard was shiny, and he spoke with a peculiar singing voice. He produced the impression of a stranger from a far-distant land. He spoke about simple matters—about family life, about children, about commerce, the police, the price of bread and meat—about everything by which people live from day to day; and in everything he discovered fraud, confusion, and stupidity, sometimes setting these matters in a humorous light, but always showing their decided disadvantage to the people.

To the mother, too, it seemed that he had come from far away, from another country, where all the people lived a simple, honest, easy life, and that here everything was strange to him, that he could not get accustomed to this life and accept it as inevitable, that it displeased him, and that it aroused in him a calm determination to rearrange it after his own model. His face was yellowish, with thin, radiate wrinkles around his eyes, his voice low, and his hands always warm. In greeting the mother he would enfold her entire hand in his long, powerful fingers, and after such a vigorous hand clasp she felt more at ease and lighter of heart.

Other people came from the city, oftenest among them a tall, well-built young girl with large eyes set in a thin, pale face. She was called Sashenka. There was something manly in her walk and movements; she knit her thick, dark eyebrows in a frown, and when she spoke the thin nostrils of her straight nose quivered.

She was the first to say, "We are socialists!" Her voice when she said it was loud and strident.

When the mother heard this word, she stared in dumb fright into the girl's face. But Sashenka, half closing her eyes, said sternly and resolutely: "We must give up all our forces to the cause of the regeneration of life; we must realize that we will receive no recompense."

The mother understood that the socialists had killed the Czar. It had happened in the days of her youth; and people had then said that the landlords, wishing to revenge themselves on the Czar for liberating the peasant serfs, had vowed not to cut their hair until the Czar should be killed. These were the persons who had been called socialists. And now she could not understand why it was that her son and his friends were socialists.

When they had all departed, she asked Pavel:

"Pavlusha, are you a socialist?"

"Yes," he said, standing before her, straight and stalwart as always. "Why?"

The mother heaved a heavy sigh, and lowering her eyes, said:

"So, Pavlusha? Why, they are against the Czar; they killed one."

Pavel walked up and down the room, ran his hand across his face, and, smiling, said:

"We don't need to do that!"

He spoke to her for a long while in a low, serious voice. She looked into his face and thought:

"He will do nothing bad; he is incapable of doing bad!"

And thereafter the terrible word was repeated with increasing frequency; its sharpness wore off, and it became as familiar to her ear as scores of other words unintelligible to her. But Sashenka did not please her, and when she came the mother felt troubled and ill at ease.

Once she said to the Little Russian, with an expression of dissatisfaction about the mouth:

"What a stern person this Sashenka is! Flings her commands around!—You must do this and you must do that!"

The Little Russian laughed aloud.

"Well said, mother! You struck the nail right on the head! Hey, Pavel?"

And with a wink to the mother, he said with a jovial gleam in his eyes:

"You can't drain the blue blood out of a person even with a pump!"

Pavel remarked dryly:

"She is a good woman!" His face glowered.

"And that's true, too!" the Little Russian corroborated. "Only she does not understand that she ought to—"

They started up an argument about something the mother did not understand. The mother noticed, also, that Sashenka was most stern with Pavel, and that sometimes she even scolded him. Pavel smiled, was silent, and looked in the girl's face with that soft look he had formerly given Natasha. This likewise displeased the mother.

The gatherings increased in number, and began to be held twice a week; and when the mother observed with what avidity the young people listened to the speeches of her son and the Little Russian, to the interesting stories of Sashenka, Natasha, Alexey Ivanovich, and the other people from the city, she forgot her fears and shook her head sadly as she recalled the days of her youth.

Sometimes they sang songs, the simple, familiar melodies, aloud and merrily. But often they sang new songs, the words and music in perfect accord, sad and quaint in tune. These they sang in an undertone, pensively and seriously as church hymns are chanted. Their faces grew pale, yet hot, and a mighty force made itself felt in their ringing words.

"It is time for us to sing these songs in the street," said Vyesovshchikov somberly.

And sometimes the mother was struck by the spirit of lively, boisterous hilarity that took sudden possession of them. It was incomprehensible to her. It usually happened on the evenings when they read in the papers about the working people in other countries. Then their eyes sparkled with bold, animated joy; they became strangely, childishly happy; the room rang with merry peals of laughter, and they struck one another on the shoulder affectionately.

"Capital fellows, our comrades the French!" cried some one, as if intoxicated with his own mirth.

"Long live our comrades, the workingmen of Italy!" they shouted another time.

And sending these calls into the remote distance to friends who did not know them, who could not have understood their language, they seemed to feel confident that these people unknown to them heard and comprehended their enthusiasm and their ecstasy.

The Little Russian spoke, his eyes beaming, his love larger than the love of the others:

"Comrades, it would be well to write to them over there!

Let them know that they have friends living in far-away Russia, workingmen who confess and believe in the same religion as they, comrades who pursue the same aims as they, and who rejoice in their victories!"

And all, with smiles on their faces dreamily spoke at length of the Germans, the Italians, the Englishmen, and the Swedes, of the working people of all countries, as of their friends, as of people near to their hearts, whom without seeing they loved and respected, whose joys they shared, whose pain they felt.

In the small room a vast feeling was born of the universal kinship of the workers of the world, at the same time its masters and its slaves, who had already been freed from the bondage of prejudice and who felt themselves the new masters of life. This feeling blended all into a single soul; it moved the mother, and, although inaccessible to her, it straightened and emboldened her, as it were, with its force, with its joys, with its triumphant, youthful vigor, intoxicating, caressing, full of hope.

"What queer people you are!" said the mother to the Little Russian one day. "All are your comrades—the Armenians and the Jews and the Austrians. You speak about all as of your friends; you grieve for all, and you rejoice for all!"

"For all, mother dear, for all! The world is ours! The world is for the workers! For us there is no nation, no race. For us there are only comrades and foes. All the workingmen are our comrades; all the rich, all the authorities are our foes. When you see how numerous we workingmen are, how tremendous the power of the spirit in us, then your heart is seized with such joy, such happiness, such a great holiday sings in your bosom! And, mother, the Frenchman and the German feel the same way when they look upon life, and the Italian also. We are all children of one mother—the great, invincible idea of the brotherhood of the workers of all countries over all the earth. This idea grows, it warms us like the sun; it is a second sun in the heaven of justice, and this heaven resides in the workingman's heart. Whoever he be, whatever his name, a socialist is our brother in spirit now and always, and through all the ages forever and ever!"

This intoxicated and childish joy, this bright and firm faith came over the company more and more frequently; and it grew ever stronger, ever mightier.

And when the mother saw this, she felt that in very truth a great dazzling light had been born into the world like the sun in the sky and visible to her eyes.

On occasions when his father had stolen something again and was in prison, Nikolay would announce to his comrades: "Now we can hold our meetings at our house. The police will think us thieves, and they love thieves!"

Almost every evening after work one of Pavel's comrades came to his house, read with him, and copied something from the books. So greatly occupied were they that they hardly even took the time to wash. They ate their supper and drank tea with the books in their hands; and their talks became less and less intelligible to the mother.

"We must have a newspaper!" Pavel said frequently.

Life grew ever more hurried and feverish; there was a constant rushing from house to house, a passing from one book to another, like the flirting of bees from flower to flower.

"They are talking about us!" said Vyesovshchikov once. "We must get away soon."

"What's a quail for but to be caught in the snare?" retorted the Little Russian.

Vlasova liked the Little Russian more and more. When he called her "mother," it was like a child's hand patting her on the cheek. On Sunday, if Pavel had no time, he chopped wood for her; once he came with a board on his shoulder, and quickly and skillfully replaced the rotten step on the porch. Another time he repaired the tottering fence with just as little ado. He whistled as he worked. It was a beautifully sad and wistful whistle.

Once the mother said to the son:

"Suppose we take the Little Russian in as a boarder. It will be better for both of you. You won't have to run to each other so much!"

"Why need you trouble and crowd yourself?" asked Pavel, shrugging his shoulders.

"There you have it! All my life I've had trouble for I don't know what. For a good person it's worth the while."

"Do as you please. If he comes I'll be glad."

And the Little Russian moved into their home.

CHAPTER V

The little house at the edge of the village aroused attention. Its walls already felt the regard of scores of suspecting eyes. The motley wings of rumor hovered restlessly above them.

People tried to surprise the secret hidden within the house by the ravine. They peeped into the windows at night. Now and then somebody would rap on the pane, and quickly take to his heels in fright.

Once the tavern keeper stopped Vlasova on the street. He was a dapper old man, who always wore a black silk neckerchief around his red, flabby neck, and a thick, lilac-colored waistcoat of velvet around his body. On his sharp, glistening nose there always sat a pair of glasses with tortoise-shell rims, which secured him the sobriquet of "bony eyes."

In a single breath and without awaiting an answer, he plied Vlasova with dry, crackling words:

"How are you, Pelagueya Nilovna, how are you? How is your son? Thinking of marrying him off, hey? He's a youth full ripe for matrimony. The sooner a son is married off, the safer it is for his folks. A man with a family preserves himself better both in the spirit and the flesh. With a family he is like mushrooms in vinegar. If I were in your place I would marry him off. Our times require a strict watch over the animal called man; people are beginning to live in their brains. Men have run amuck with their thoughts, and they do things that are positively criminal. The church of God is avoided by the young folk; they shun the public places, and assemble in secret in out-of-the-way corners. They speak in whispers. Why speak in whispers, pray? All this they don't dare say before people in the tavern, for example. What is it, I ask? A secret? The secret place is our holy church, as old as the apostles. All the other secrets hatched in the corners are the offspring of delusions. I wish you good health."

Raising his hand in an affected manner, he lifted his cap, and waving it in the air, walked away, leaving the mother to her perplexity.

Vlasova's neighbor, Marya Korsunova, the blacksmith's widow, who sold food at the factory, on meeting the mother in the market place also said to her:

"Look out for your son, Pelagueya!"

"What's the matter?"

"They're talking!" Marya tendered the information in a hushed voice. "And they don't say any good, mother of mine! They speak as if he's getting up a sort of union, something like those Flagellants—sects, that's the name! They'll whip one another like the Flagellants——"

"Stop babbling nonsense, Marya! Enough!"

"I'm not babbling nonsense! I talk because I know."

The mother communicated all these conversations to her son. He shrugged his shoulders in silence, and the Little Russian laughed with his thick, soft laugh.

"The girls also have a crow to pick with you!" she said. "You'd make enviable bridegrooms for any of them; you're all good workers, and you don't drink—but you don't pay any attention to them. Besides, people are saying that girls of questionable character come to you."

"Well, of course!" exclaimed Pavel, his brow contracting in a frown of disgust.

"In the bog everything smells of rottenness!" said the Little Russian with a sigh. "Why don't you, mother, explain to the foolish girls what it is to be married, so that they shouldn't be in such a hurry to get their bones broken?"

"Oh, well," said the mother, "they see the misery in store for them, they understand, but what can they do? They have no other choice!"

"It's a queer way they have of understanding, else they'd find a choice," observed Pavel.

The mother looked into his austere face.

"Why don't you teach them? Why don't you invite some of the cleverer ones?"

"That won't do!" the son replied dryly.

"Suppose we try?" said the Little Russian.

After a short silence Pavel said:

"Couples will be formed; couples will walk together; then some will get married, and that's all."

The mother became thoughtful. Pavel's austerity worried her. She saw that his advice was taken even by his older comrades, such as the Little Russian; but it seemed to her that all were afraid of him, and no one loved him because he was so stern.

Once when she had lain down to sleep, and her son and the Little Russian were still reading, she overheard their low conversation through the thin partition.

"You know I like Natasha," suddenly ejaculated the Little Russian in an undertone.

"I know," answered Pavel after a pause.

"Yes!"

The mother heard the Little Russian rise and begin to walk. The tread of his bare feet sounded on the floor, and a low, mournful whistle was heard. Then he spoke again:

"And does she notice it?"

Pavel was silent.

"What do you think?" the Little Russian asked, lowering his voice.

"She does," replied Pavel. "That's why she has refused to attend our meetings."

The Little Russian dragged his feet heavily over the floor, and again his low whistle quivered in the room. Then he asked:

"And if I tell her?"

"What?" The brief question shot from Pavel like the discharge of a gun.

"That I am—" began the Little Russian in a subdued voice.

"Why?" Pavel interrupted.

The mother heard the Little Russian stop, and she felt that he smiled.

"Yes, you see, I consider that if you love a girl you must tell her about it; else there'll be no sense to it!"

Pavel clapped the book shut with a bang.

"And what sense do you expect?"

Both were silent for a long while.

"Well?" asked the Little Russian.

"You must be clear in your mind, Andrey, as to what you want to do," said Pavel slowly. "Let us assume that she loves you, too—I do not think so, but let us assume it. Well, you get married. An interesting union—the intellectual with the workingman! Children come along; you will have to work all by yourself and very hard. Your life will become the ordinary life of a struggle for a piece of bread and a shelter for yourself and children. For the cause, you will become nonexistent, both of you!"

Silence ensued. Then Pavel began to speak again in a voice that sounded softer:

"You had better drop all this, Andrey. Keep quiet, and don't worry her. That's the more honest way."

"And do you remember what Alexey Ivanovich said about the necessity for a man to live a complete life—with all the power of his soul and body—do you remember?"

"That's not for us! How can you attain completion? It does not exist for you. If you love the future you must renounce everything in the present—everything, brother!"

"That's hard for a man!" said the Little Russian in a lowered voice.

"What else can be done? Think!"

The indifferent pendulum of the clock kept chopping off the seconds of life, calmly and precisely. At last the Little Russian said:

"Half the heart loves, and the other half hates! Is that a heart?"

"I ask you, what else can we do?"

The pages of a book rustled. Apparently Pavel had begun to read again. The mother lay with closed eyes, and was afraid to stir. She was ready to weep with pity for the Little Russian; but she was grieved still more for her son.

"My dear son! My consecrated one!" she thought.

Suddenly the Little Russian asked:

"So I am to keep quiet?"

"That's more honest, Andrey," answered Pavel softly.

"All right! That's the road we will travel." And in a few seconds he added, in a sad and subdued voice: "It will be hard for you, Pasha, when you get to that yourself."

"It is hard for me already."

"Yes?"

"Yes."

The wind brushed along the walls of the house, and the pendulum marked the passing time.

"Um," said the Little Russian leisurely, at last. "That's too bad."

The mother buried her head in the pillow and wept inaudibly.

In the morning Andrey seemed to her to be lower in stature and all the more winning. But her son towered thin, straight, and taciturn as ever. She had always called the Little Russian Andrey Stepanovich, in formal address, but now, all at once, involuntarily and unconsciously she said to him:

"Say, Andriusha, you had better get your boots mended. You are apt to catch cold."

"On pay day, mother, I'll buy myself a new pair," he answered, smiling. Then suddenly placing his long hand on her shoulder, he added: "You know, you are my real mother. Only you don't want to acknowledge it to people because I am so ugly."

She patted him on the hand without speaking. She would have liked to say many endearing things, but her heart was wrung with pity, and the words would not leave her tongue.

◆

They spoke in the village about the socialists who distributed broadcast leaflets in blue ink. In these leaflets the conditions prevailing in the factory were trenchantly and pointedly depicted, as well as the strikes in St. Petersburg and southern Russia; and the workingmen were called upon to unite and fight for their interests.

The staid people who earned good pay waxed wroth as they read the literature, and said abusively: "Breeders of rebellion! For such business they ought to get their eyes blacked." And they carried the pamphlets to the office.

The young people read the proclamations eagerly, and said excitedly: "It's all true!"

The majority, broken down with their work, and indifferent to everything, said lazily: "Nothing will come of it. It is impossible!"

But the leaflets made a stir among the people, and when a week passed without their getting any, they said to one another:

"None again to-day! It seems the printing must have stopped."

Then on Monday the leaflets appeared again; and again there was a dull buzz of talk among the workingmen.

In the taverns and the factory strangers were noticed, men whom no one knew. They asked questions, scrutinized everything and everybody; looked around, ferreted about, and at once attracted universal attention, some by their suspicious watchfulness, others by their excessive obtrusiveness.

The mother knew that all this commotion was due to the work of her son Pavel. She saw how all the people were drawn together about him. He was not alone, and therefore it was not so dangerous. But pride in her son mingled with her apprehension for his fate; it was his secret labors that discharged themselves in fresh currents into the narrow, turbid stream of life.

One evening Marya Korsunova rapped at the window from the street, and when the mother opened it, she said in a loud whisper:

"Now, take care, Pelagueya; the boys have gotten themselves into a nice mess! It's been decided to make a search to-night in your house, and Mazin's and Vyesovshchikov's———"

The mother heard only the beginning of the woman's talk; all the rest of the words flowed together in one stream of ill-boding, hoarse sounds.

Marya's thick lips flapped hastily one against the other. Snorts issued from her fleshy nose, her eyes blinked and turned from side to side as if on the lookout for somebody in the street.

"And, mark you, I do not know anything, and I did not say anything to you, mother dear, and did not even see you to-day, you understand?"

Then she disappeared.

The mother closed the window and slowly dropped on a chair, her strength gone from her, her brain a desolate void. But the consciousness of the danger threatening her son quickly brought her to her feet again. She dressed hastily, for some reason wrapped her shawl tightly around her head, and ran to Fedya Mazin, who, she knew, was sick and not working. She found him sitting at the window reading a book, and moving his right hand to and fro with his left, his thumb spread out. On learning the news he jumped up nervously, his lips trembled, and his face paled.

"There you are! And I have an abscess on my finger!" he mumbled.

"What are we to do?" asked Vlasova, wiping the perspiration from her face with a hand that trembled nervously.

"Wait a while! Don't be afraid," answered Fedya, running his sound hand through his curly hair.

"But you are afraid yourself!"

"I?" He reddened and smiled in embarrassment. "Yes—h-m— I had a fit of cowardice, the devil take it! We must let Pavel know. I'll send my little sister to him. You go home. Never mind! They're not going to beat us."

On returning home she gathered together all the books, and pressing them to her bosom walked about the house for a long time, looking into the oven, under the oven, into the pipe of the samovar, and even into the water vat. She thought Pavel would at once drop work and come home; but he did not come. Finally she sat down exhausted on the bench in the kitchen, putting the books under her; and she remained in that position, afraid to rise, until Pavel and the Little Russian returned from the factory.

"Do you know?" she exclaimed without rising.

"We know!" said Pavel with a composed smile. "Are you afraid?"

"Oh, I'm so afraid, so afraid!"

"You needn't be afraid," said the Little Russian. "That won't help anybody."

"Didn't even prepare the samovar," remarked Pavel.

The mother rose, and pointed to the books with a guilty air.

"You see, it was on account of them—all the time—I was——"

The son and the Little Russian burst into laughter; and this relieved her. Then Pavel picked out some books and carried them out into the yard to hide them, while the Little Russian remained to prepare the samovar.

"There's nothing terrible at all in this, mother. It's only a shame for people to occupy themselves with such nonsense. Grown-up men in gray come in with sabers at their sides, with spurs on their feet, and rummage around, and dig up and search everything. They look under the bed, and climb up to the garret; if there is a cellar they crawl down into it. The cobwebs get on their faces, and they puff and snort. They are bored and ashamed. That's why they put on the appearance of being very wicked and very mad with us. It's dirty work, and they understand it, of course they do! Once they turned everything topsy-turvy in my place, and went away abashed, that's all. Another time they took me along with them. Well, they put me in prison, and I stayed there with them for about four months. You sit and sit, then you're called out, taken to the street under an escort of soldiers, and you're asked certain questions. They're stupid people, they talk such incoherent stuff. When they're done with you, they tell the soldiers to take you back to prison. So they lead you here, and they lead you there—they've got to justify their salaries somehow. And then they let you go free. That's all."

"How you always do speak, Andriusha!" exclaimed the mother involuntarily.

Kneeling before the samovar he diligently blew into the pipe; but presently he turned his face, red with exertion, toward her, and smoothing his mustache with both hands inquired:

"And how do I speak, pray?"

"As if nobody had ever done you any wrong."

He rose, approached her, and shaking his head, said:

"Is there an unwronged soul anywhere in the wide world? But I have been wronged so much that I have ceased to feel wronged. What's to be done if people cannot help acting as they do? The wrongs I undergo hinder me greatly in my work. It is impossible to avoid them. But to stop and pay attention to them is useless waste of time. Such a life! Formerly I would occasionally get angry—but I thought to myself: all around me I see people broken in heart. It seemed as if each one were afraid that his neighbor would strike him, and so he tried to get ahead and strike the other first. Such a life it is, mother dear."

His speech flowed on serenely. He resolutely distracted her mind from alarm at the expected police search. His luminous, protuberant eyes smiled sadly. Though ungainly, he seemed made of stuff that bends but never breaks.

The mother sighed and uttered the warm wish:

"May God grant you happiness, Andriusha!"

The Little Russian stalked to the samovar with long strides, sat in front of it again on his heels, and mumbled:

"If he gives me happiness, I will not decline it; ask for it I won't, to seek it I have no time."

And he began to whistle.

Pavel came in from the yard and said confidently:

"They won't find them!" He started to wash himself. Then carefully rubbing his hands dry, he added: "If you show them, mother, that you are frightened, they will think there must be something in this house because you tremble. And we have done nothing as yet, nothing! You know that we don't want anything bad; on our side is truth, and we will work for it all our lives. This is our entire guilt. Why, then, need we fear?"

"I will pull myself together, Pasha!" she assured him. And the next moment, unable to repress her anxiety, she exclaimed: "I wish they'd come soon, and it would all be over!"

But they did not come that night, and in the morning, in anticipation of the fun that would probably be poked at her for her alarm, the mother began to joke at herself.

CHAPTER VI

The searchers appeared at the very time they were not expected, nearly a month after this anxious night. Nikolay Vyesovshchikov was at Pavel's house talking with him and Andrey about their newspaper. It was late, about midnight. The mother was already in bed. Half awake, half asleep, she listened to the low, busy voices. Presently Andrey got up and carefully picked his way through and out of the kitchen, quietly shutting the door after him. The noise of the iron bucket was heard on the porch. Suddenly the door was flung wide open; the Little Russian entered the kitchen, and announced in a loud whisper:

"I hear the jingling of spurs in the street!"

The mother jumped out of bed, catching at her dress with a trembling hand; but Pavel came to the door and said calmly:

"You stay in bed; you're not feeling well."

A cautious, stealthy sound was heard on the porch. Pavel went to the door and knocking at it with his hand asked:

"Who's there?"

A tall, gray figure tumultuously precipitated itself through the doorway; after it another; two gendarmes pushed Pavel back, and stationed themselves on either side of him, and a loud mocking voice called out:

"No one you expect, eh?"

The words came from a tall, lank officer, with a thin, black mustache. The village policeman, Fedyakin, appeared at the bedside of the mother, and, raising one hand to his cap, pointed the other at her face and, making terrible eyes, said:

"This is his mother, your honor!" Then, waving his hand toward Pavel: "And this is he himself."

"Pavel Vlasov?" inquired the officer, screwing up his eyes; and when Pavel silently nodded his head, he announced, twirling his mustache:

"I have to make a search in your house. Get up, old woman!"

"Who is there?" he asked, turning suddenly and making a dash for the door.

"Your name?" His voice was heard from the other room.

Two other men came in from the porch: the old smelter Tveryakov and his lodger, the stoker Rybin, a staid, dark-colored peasant. He said in a thick, loud voice:

"Good evening, Nilovna."

She dressed herself, all the while speaking to herself in a low voice, so as to give herself courage:

"What sort of a thing is this? They come at night. People are asleep and they come——"

The room was close, and for some reason smelled strongly of shoe blacking. Two gendarmes and the village police commissioner, Ryskin, their heavy tread resounding on the floor, removed the books from the shelves and put them on the table before the officer. Two others rapped on the walls with their fists, and looked under the chairs. One man clumsily clambered up on the stove in the corner. Nikolay's pockmarked face became covered with red patches, and his little gray eyes were steadfastly fixed upon the officer. The Little

Russian curled his mustache, and when the mother entered the room, he smiled and gave her an affectionate nod of the head.

Striving to suppress her fear, she walked, not sideways as always, but erect, her chest thrown out, which gave her figure a droll, stilted air of importance. Her shoes made a knocking sound on the floor, and her brows trembled.

The officer quickly seized the books with the long fingers of his white hand, turned over the pages, shook them, and with a dexterous movement of the wrist flung them aside. Sometimes a book fell to the floor with a light thud. All were silent. The heavy breathing of the perspiring gendarmes was audible; the spurs clanked, and sometimes the low question was heard: "Did you look here?"

The mother stood by Pavel's side against the wall. She folded her arms over her bosom, like her son, and both regarded the officer. The mother felt her knees trembling, and her eyes became covered with a dry mist.

Suddenly the piercing voice of Nikolay cut into the silence:

"Why is it necessary to throw the books on the floor?"

The mother trembled. Tveryakov rocked his head as if he had been struck on the back. Rybin uttered a peculiar cluck, and regarded Nikolay attentively.

The officer threw up his head, screwed up his eyes, and fixed them for a second upon the pockmarked, mottled, immobile face. His fingers began to turn the leaves of the books still more rapidly. His face was yellow and pale; he twisted his lips continually. At times he opened his large gray eyes wide, as if he suffered from an intolerable pain, and was ready to scream out in impotent anguish.

"Soldier!" Vyesovshchikov called out again. "Pick the books up!"

All the gendarmes turned their eyes on him, then looked at the officer. He again raised his head, and taking in the broad figure of Nikolay with a searching stare, he drawled:

"Well, well, pick up the books."

One gendarme bent down, and, looking slantwise at Vyesovshchikov, began to collect the books scattered on the floor.

"Why doesn't Nikolay keep quiet?" the mother whispered to Pavel. He shrugged his shoulders. The Little Russian drooped his head.

"What's the whispering there? Silence, please! Who reads the Bible?"

"I!" said Pavel.

"Aha! And whose books are all these?"

"Mine!" answered Pavel.

"So!" exclaimed the officer, throwing himself on the back of the chair. He made the bones of his slender hand crack, stretched his legs under the table, and adjusting his mustache, asked Nikolay: "Are you Andrey Nakhodka?"

"Yes!" answered Nikolay, moving forward. The Little Russian put out his hand, took him by the shoulder, and pulled him back.

"He made a mistake; I am Andrey!"

The officer raised his hand, and threatening Vyesovshchikov with his little finger, said:

"Take care!"

He began to search among his papers. From the street the bright, moonlit night looked on through the window with soulless eyes. Some one was loafing about outside the window, and the snow crunched under his tread.

"You, Nakhodka, you have been searched for political offenses before?" asked the officer.

"Yes, I was searched in Rostov and Saratov. Only there the gendarmes addressed me as 'Mr.'"

The officer winked his right eye, rubbed it, and showing his fine teeth, said:

"And do you happen to know, *Mr.* Nakhodka—yes, you, *Mr.* Nakhodka—who those scoundrels are who distribute criminal proclamations and books in the factory, eh?"

The Little Russian swayed his body, and with a broad smile on his face was about to say something, when the irritating voice of Nikolay again rang out:

"This is the first time we have seen scoundrels here!"

Silence ensued. There was a moment of breathless suspense. The scar on the mother's face whitened, and her right eyebrow traveled upward. Rybin's black beard quivered strangely. He dropped his eyes, and slowly scratched one hand with the other.

"Take this dog out of here!" said the officer.

Two gendarmes seized Nikolay under the arm and rudely pulled him into the kitchen. There he planted his feet firmly on the floor and shouted:

"Stop! I am going to put my coat on."

The police commissioner came in from the yard and said:

"There is nothing out there. We searched everywhere!"

"Well, of course!" exclaimed the officer, laughing. "I knew it! There's an experienced man here, it goes without saying."

The mother listened to his thin, dry voice, and looking with terror into the yellow face, felt an enemy in this man, an enemy without pity, with a heart full of aristocratic disdain of the people. Formerly she had but rarely seen such persons, and now she had almost forgotten they existed.

"Then this is the man whom Pavel and his friends have provoked," she thought.

"I place you, *Mr.* Andrey Onisimov Nakhodka, under arrest."

"What for?" asked the Little Russian composedly.

"I will tell you later!" answered the officer with spiteful civility, and turning to Vlasova, he shouted:

"Say, can you read or write?"

"No!" answered Pavel.

"I didn't ask you!" said the officer sternly, and repeated: "Say, old woman, can you read or write?"

The mother involuntarily gave way to a feeling of hatred for the man. She was seized with a sudden fit of trembling, as if she had jumped into cold water. She straightened herself, her scar turned purple, and her brow drooped low.

"Don't shout!" she said, flinging out her hand toward him. "You are a young man still; you don't know misery or sorrow——"

"Calm yourself, mother!" Pavel intervened.

"In this business, mother, you've got to take your heart between your teeth and hold it there tight," said the Little Russian.

"Wait a moment, Pasha!" cried the mother, rushing to the table and then addressing the officer: "Why do you snatch people away thus?"

"That does not concern you. Silence!" shouted the officer, rising.

"Bring in the prisoner Vyesovshchikov!" he commanded, and

began to read aloud a document which he raised to his face.

Nikolay was brought into the room.

"Hats off!" shouted the officer, interrupting his reading.

Rybin went up to Vlasova, and patting her on the back, said in an undertone:

"Don't get excited, mother!"

"How can I take my hat off if they hold my hands?" asked Nikolay, drowning the reading.

The officer flung the paper on the table.

"Sign!" he said curtly.

The mother saw how everyone signed the document, and her excitement died down, a softer feeling taking possession of her heart. Her eyes filled with tears—burning tears of insult and impotence—such tears she had wept for twenty years of her married life, but lately she had almost forgotten their acid, heart-corroding taste.

The officer regarded her contemptuously. He scowled and remarked:

"You bawl ahead of time, my lady! Look out, or you won't have tears left for the future!"

"A mother has enough tears for everything, everything! If you have a mother, she knows it!"

The officer hastily put the papers into his new portfolio with its shining lock.

"How independent they all are in your place!" He turned to the police commissioner.

"An impudent pack!" mumbled the commissioner.

"March!" commanded the officer.

"Good-by, Andrey! Good-by, Nikolay!" said Pavel warmly and softly, pressing his comrades' hands.

"That's it! Until we meet again!" the officer scoffed.

Vyesovshchikov silently pressed Pavel's hands with his short fingers and breathed heavily. The blood mounted to his thick neck; his eyes flashed with rancor. The Little Russian's face beamed with a sunny smile. He nodded his head, and said something to the mother; she made the sign of the cross over him.

"God sees the righteous," she murmured.

At length the throng of people in the gray coats tumbled out on the porch, and their spurs jingled as they disappeared. Rybin went last. He regarded Pavel with an attentive look of his dark eyes and said thoughtfully: "Well, well—good-by!" and coughing in his beard he leisurely walked out on the porch.

Folding his hands behind his back, Pavel slowly paced up and down the room, stepping over the books and clothes tumbled about on the floor. At last he said somberly:

"You see how it's done! With insult—disgustingly—yes! They left me behind."

Looking perplexedly at the disorder in the room, the mother whispered sadly:

"They will take you, too, be sure they will. Why did Nikolay speak to them the way he did?"

"He got frightened, I suppose," said Pavel quietly. "Yes—It's impossible to speak to them, absolutely impossible! They cannot understand!"

"They came, snatched, and carried off!" mumbled the mother, waving her hands. As her son remained at home, her heart began to beat more lightly. Her mind stubbornly halted before one fact and refused to be moved. "How he scoffs at us, that yellow ruffian! How he threatens us!"

"All right, mamma!" Pavel suddenly said with resolution. "Let us pick all this up!"

He called her "mamma," the word he used only when he came nearer to her. She approached him, looked into his face, and asked softly:

"Did they insult you?"

"Yes," he answered. "That's—hard! I would rather have gone with them."

It seemed to her that she saw tears in his eyes, and wishing to soothe him, with an indistinct sense of his pain, she said with a sigh:

"Wait a while—they'll take you, too!"

"They will!" he replied.

After a pause the mother remarked sorrowfully:

"How hard you are, Pasha! If you'd only reassure me once in a while! But you don't. When I say something horrible, you say something worse."

He looked at her, moved closer to her, and said gently:

"I cannot, mamma! I cannot lie! You have to get used to it."

CHAPTER VII

The next day they knew that Bukin, Samoylov, Somov, and five more had been arrested. In the evening Fedya Mazin came running in upon them. A search had been made in his house also. He felt himself a hero.

"Were you afraid, Fedya?" asked the mother.

He turned pale, his face sharpened, and his nostrils quivered.

"I was afraid the officer might strike me. He has a black beard, he's stout, his fingers are hairy, and he wears dark glasses, so that he looks as if he were without eyes. He shouted and stamped his feet. He said I'd rot in prison. And I've never been beaten either by my father or mother; they love me because I'm their only son. Everyone gets beaten everywhere, but I never!"

He closed his eyes for a moment, compressed his lips, tossed his hair back with a quick gesture of both hands, and looking at Pavel with reddening eyes, said:

"If anybody ever strikes me, I will thrust my whole body into him like a knife—I will bite my teeth into him—I'd rather he'd kill me at once and be done!"

"To defend yourself is your right," said Pavel. "But take care not to attack!"

"You are delicate and thin," observed the mother. "What do you want with fighting?"

"I *will* fight!" answered Fedya in a low voice.

When he left, the mother said to Pavel:

"This young man will go down sooner than all the rest."

Pavel was silent.

A few minutes later the kitchen door opened slowly and Rybin entered.

"Good evening!" he said, smiling. "Here I am again. Yesterday they brought me here; to-day I come of my own accord. Yes, yes!"

He gave Pavel a vigorous handshake, then put his hand on the mother's shoulder, and asked: "Will you give me tea?"

Pavel silently regarded his swarthy, broad countenance, his thick, black beard, and dark, intelligent eyes. A certain gravity spoke out of their calm gaze; his stalwart figure inspired confidence.

The mother went into the kitchen to prepare the samovar. Rybin sat down, stroked his beard, and placing his elbows on the table, scanned Pavel with his dark look.

"That's the way it is," he said, as if continuing an interrupted conversation. "I must have a frank talk with you. I observed you long before I came. We live almost next door to each other. I see many people come to you, and no drunkenness, no carrying on. That's the main thing. If people don't raise the devil, they immediately attract attention. What's that? There you are! That's why all eyes are on me, because I live apart and give no offense."

His speech flowed along evenly and freely. It had a ring that won him confidence.

"So. Everybody prates about you. My masters call you a heretic; you don't go to church. I don't, either. Then the papers appeared, those leaflets. Was it you that thought them out?"

"Yes, I!" answered Pavel, without taking his eyes off Rybin's face. Rybin also looked steadily into Pavel's eyes.

"You alone!" exclaimed the mother, coming into the room. "It wasn't you alone."

Pavel smiled; Rybin also.

The mother sniffed, and walked away, somewhat offended because they did not pay attention to her words.

"Those leaflets are well thought out. They stir the people up. There were twelve of them, weren't there?"

"Yes."

"I have read them all! Yes, yes. Sometimes they are not clear, and some things are superfluous. But when a man speaks a great deal, it's natural he should occasionally say things out of the way."

Rybin smiled. His teeth were white and strong.

"Then the search. That won me over to you more than anything else. You and the Little Russian and Nikolay, you all got caught!" He paused for the right word and looked at the window, rapping the table with his fingers. "They discovered your resolve. You attend to your business, your honor, you say, and we'll attend to ours. The Little Russian's a fine fellow, too. The other day I heard how he speaks in the factory, and thinks I to myself: that man isn't going to be vanquished; it's only one thing will knock him out, and that's death! A sturdy chap! Do you trust me, Pavel?"

"Yes, I trust you!" said Pavel, nodding.

"That's right. Look! I am forty years old; I am twice as old as you, and I've seen twenty times as much as you. For three years long I wore my feet to the bone marching in the army. I have been married twice. I've been in the Caucasus, I know the Dukhobors. They're not masters of life, no, they aren't!"

The mother listened eagerly to his direct speech. It pleased her to have an older man come to her son and speak to him just as if he were confessing to him. But Pavel seemed to treat the guest too curtly, and the mother, to introduce a softer element, asked Rybin:

"Maybe you'll have something to eat."

"Thank you, mother! I've had my supper already. So then, Pavel, you think that life does not go as it should?"

Pavel arose and began to pace the room, folding his hands behind his back.

"It goes all right," he said. "Just now, for instance, it has brought you here to me with an open heart. We who work our whole life long—it unites us gradually and more and more every day. The time will come when we shall all be united. Life is arranged unjustly for us and is made a burden. At the same time, however, life itself is opening our eyes to its bitter meaning and is itself showing man the way to accelerate its pace. We all of us think just as we live."

"True. But wait!" Rybin stopped him. "Man ought to be renovated—that's what I think! When a man grows scabby, take him to the bath, give him a thorough cleaning, put clean clothes on him—and he will get well. Isn't it so? And if the heart grows scabby, take its skin off, even if it bleeds, wash it, and dress it up all afresh. Isn't it so? How else can you clean the inner man? There now!"

Pavel began to speak hotly and bitterly about God, about the Czar, about the government authorities, about the factory, and how in foreign countries the workingmen stand up for their rights. Rybin smiled occasionally; sometimes he struck a finger on the table as if punctuating a period. Now and then he cried out briefly: "So!" And once, laughing out, he said quietly: "You're young. You know people but little!"

Pavel stopping before him said seriously:

"Let's not talk of being old or being young. Let us rather see whose thoughts are truer."

"That is, according to you, we've been fooled about God also. So! I, too, think that our religion is false and injurious to us."

Here the mother intervened. When her son spoke about God and about everything that she connected with her faith in him, which was dear and sacred to her, she sought to meet his eyes, she wanted to ask her son mutely not to chafe her heart with the sharp, bitter words of his unbelief. And she felt that Rybin, an older man, would also be displeased and offended. But when Rybin calmly put his question to Pavel, she could no longer contain herself, and said firmly: "When you speak of God, I wish you were more careful. You can do whatever you like. You have your compensation in your work." Catching her breath she continued with still greater vehemence: "But I, an old woman, I will have nothing to lean upon in my distress if you take my God away from me."

Her eyes filled with tears. She was washing the dishes, and her fingers trembled.

"You did not understand us, mother!" Pavel said softly and kindly.

"Beg your pardon, mother!" Rybin added in a slow, thick voice. He looked at Pavel and smiled. "I forgot that you're too old to cut out your warts."

"I did not speak," continued Pavel, "about that good and gracious God in whom you believe, but about the God with whom the priests threaten us as with a stick, about the God in whose name they want to force all of us to the evil will of the few."

"That's it, right you are!" exclaimed Rybin, striking his fingers upon the table. "They have mutilated even our God for us, they have turned everything in their hands against us. Mark you, mother, God created man in his own image and after his own likeness. Therefore he is like man if man is like him. But we have become, not like

God, but like wild beasts! In the churches they set up a scarecrow before us. We have got to change our God, mother; we must cleanse him! They have dressed him up in falsehood and calumny; they have distorted his face in order to destroy our souls!"

He talked composedly and very distinctly and intelligibly. Every word of his speech fell upon the mother's ears like a blow. And his face set in the frame of his black beard, his broad face attired, as it were, in mourning, frightened her. The dark gleam of his eyes was insupportable to her. He aroused in her a sense of anguish, and filled her heart with terror.

"No, I'd better go away," she said, shaking her head in negation. "It's not in my power to listen to this. I cannot!"

And she quickly walked into the kitchen followed by the words of Rybin:

"There you have it, Pavel! It begins not in the head, but in the heart. The heart is such a place that nothing else will grow in it."

"Only reason," said Pavel firmly, "only reason will free mankind."

"Reason does not give strength!" retorted Rybin emphatically. "The heart gives strength, and not the head, I tell you."

The mother undressed and lay down in bed without saying her prayer. She felt cold and miserable. And Rybin, who at first seemed such a staid, wise man, now aroused in her a blind hostility.

"Heretic! Sedition-maker!" she thought, listening to his even voice flowing resonantly from his deep chest. He, too, had come—he was indispensable.

He spoke confidently and composedly:

"The holy place must not be empty. The spot where God dwells is a place of pain; and if he drops out from the heart, there will be a wound in it, mark my word! It is necessary, Pavel, to invent a new faith; it is necessary to create a God for all. Not a judge, not a warrior, but a God who shall be the friend of the people."

"You had one! There was Christ!"

"Wait a moment! Christ was not strong in spirit. 'Let the cup pass from me,' he said. And he recognized Cæsar. God cannot recognize human powers. He himself is the whole of power. He does not divide his soul saying: so much for the godly, so much for the human. If Christ came to affirm the divine he had no need for anything human. But he recognized trade, and he recognized marriage. And it was unjust of him to condemn the fig tree. Was it of its own will that it was barren of fruit? Neither is the soul barren of good of its own accord. Have I sown the evil in it myself? Of course not!"

The two voices hummed continuously in the room, as if clutching at each other and wrestling in exciting play. Pavel walked hurriedly up and down the room; the floor cracked under his feet. When he spoke all other sounds were drowned by his voice; but above the slow, calm flow of Rybin's dull utterance were heard the strokes of the pendulum and the low creaking of the frost, as of sharp claws scratching the walls of the house.

"I will speak to you in my own way, in the words of a stoker. God is like fire. He does not strengthen anything. He cannot. He merely burns and fuses when he gives light. He burns down churches, he does not raise them. He lives in the heart."

"And in the mind!" insisted Pavel.

"That's it! In the heart and in the mind. There's the rub. It's this that makes all the trouble and misery and misfortune. We have severed ourselves from our own selves. The heart was severed from the mind, and the mind has disappeared. Man is not a unit. It is God that makes him a unit, that makes him a round, circular thing. God always makes things round. Such is the earth and all the stars and everything visible to the eye. The sharp, angular things are the work of men."

The mother fell asleep and did not hear Rybin depart.

But he began to come often, and if any of Pavel's comrades were present, Rybin sat in a corner and was silent, only occasionally interjecting: "That's so!"

And once looking at everybody from his corner with his dark glance he said somberly:

"We must speak about that which is; that which will be is unknown to us. When the people have freed themselves, they will see for themselves what is best. Enough, quite enough of what they do not want at all has been knocked into their heads. Let there be an end of this! Let them contrive for themselves. Maybe they will want to reject everything, all life, and all knowledge; maybe they will see that everything is arranged against them. You just deliver all the books into their hands, and they will find an answer for themselves, depend upon it! Only let them remember that the tighter the collar round the horse's neck, the worse the work."

But when Pavel was alone with Rybin they at once began an endless but always calm disputation, to which the mother listened anxiously, following their words in silence, and endeavoring to understand. Sometimes it seemed to her as if the broad-shouldered, black-bearded peasant and her well-built, sturdy son had both gone blind. In that little room, in the darkness, they seemed to be knocking about from side to side in search of light and an outlet, to be grasping out with powerful but blind hands; they seemed to fall upon the floor, and having fallen, to scrape and fumble with their feet. They hit against everything, groped about for everything, and flung it away, calm and composed, losing neither faith nor hope.

They got her accustomed to listen to a great many words, terrible in their directness and boldness; and these words had now ceased to weigh down on her so heavily as at first. She learned to push them away from her ears. And although Rybin still displeased her as before, he no longer inspired her with hostility.

Once a week she carried underwear and books to the Little Russian in prison. On one occasion they allowed her to see him and talk to him; and on returning home she related enthusiastically:

"He is as if he were at home there, too! He is good and kind to everybody; everybody jokes with him; just as if there were a holiday in his heart all the time. His lot is hard and heavy, but he does not want to show it."

"That's right! That's the way one should act," observed Rybin. "We are all enveloped in misery as in our skins. We breathe misery, we wear misery. But that's nothing to brag about. Not all people are blind; some close their eyes of their own accord, indeed! And if you are stupid you have to suffer for it."

CHAPTER VIII

The little old gray house of the Vlasovs attracted the attention of the village more and more; and although there was much suspicious chariness and unconscious hostility in this notice, yet at the same time a confiding curiosity grew up also. Now and then some one would come over, and looking carefully about him would say to Pavel: "Well, brother, you are reading books here, and you know the laws. Explain to me, then——"

And he would tell Pavel about some injustice of the police or the factory administration. In complicated cases Pavel would give the man a note to a lawyer friend in the city, and when he could, he would explain the case himself.

Gradually people began to look with respect upon this young, serious man, who spoke about everything simply and boldly, and almost never laughed, who looked at everybody and listened to everybody with an attention which searched stubbornly into every circumstance, and always found a certain general and endless thread binding people together by a thousand tightly drawn knots.

Vlasova saw how her son had grown up; she strove to understand his work, and when she succeeded, she rejoiced with a childlike joy.

Pavel rose particularly in the esteem of the people after the appearance of his story about the "Muddy Penny."

Back of the factory, almost encircling it with a ring of putrescence, stretched a vast marsh grown over with fir trees and birches. In the summer it was covered with thick yellow and green scum, and swarms of mosquitoes flew from it over the village, spreading fever in their course. The marsh belonged to the factory, and the new manager, wishing to extract profit from it, conceived the plan of draining it and incidentally gathering in a fine harvest of peat. Representing to the workingmen how much this measure would contribute to the sanitation of the locality and the improvement of the general condition of all, the manager gave orders to deduct a kopeck from every ruble of their earnings, in order to cover the expense of draining the marsh. The workingmen rebelled; they especially resented the fact that the office clerks were exempted from paying the new tax.

Pavel was ill on the Saturday when posters were hung up announcing the manager's order in regard to the toll. He had not gone to work and he knew nothing about it. The next day, after mass, a dapper old man, the smelter Sizov, and the tall, vicious-looking locksmith Makhotin, came to him and told him of the manager's decision.

"A few of us older ones got together," said Sizov, speaking sedately, "talked the matter over, and our comrades, you see, sent us over to you, as you are a knowing man among us. Is there such a law as gives our manager the right to make war upon mosquitoes with our kopecks?"

"Think!" said Makhotin, with a glimmer in his narrow eyes. "Three years ago these sharpers collected a tax to build a bath house. Three thousand eight hundred rubles is what they gathered in. Where are those rubles? And where is the bath house?"

Pavel explained the injustice of the tax, and the obvious advantage of such a procedure to the factory owners; and both of his visitors went away in a surly mood.

The mother, who had gone with them to the door, said, laughing:

"Now, Pasha, the old people have also begun to come to seek wisdom from you."

Without replying, Pavel sat down at the table with a busy air and began to write. In a few minutes he said to her: "Please go to the city immediately and deliver this note."

"Is it dangerous?" she asked.

"Yes! A newspaper is being published for us down there! That 'Muddy Penny' story must go into the next issue."

"I'll go at once," she replied, beginning hurriedly to put on her wraps.

This was the first commission her son had given her. She was happy that he spoke to her so openly about the matter, and that she might be useful to him in his work.

"I understand all about it, Pasha," she said. "It's a piece of robbery. What's the name of the man? Yegor Ivanovich?"

"Yes," said Pavel, smiling kindly.

She returned late in the evening, exhausted but contented.

"I saw Sashenka," she told her son. "She sends you her regards.

And this Yegor Ivanovich is such a simple fellow, such a joker! He speaks so comically."

"I'm glad you like them," said Pavel softly.

"They are simple people, Pasha. It's good when people are simple. And they all respect you."

Again, Monday, Pavel did not go to work. His head ached. But at dinner time Fedya Mazin came running in, excited, out of breath, happy, and tired.

"Come! The whole factory has arisen! They've sent for you. Sizov and Makhotin say you can explain better than anybody else. My! What a hullabaloo!"

Pavel began to dress himself silently.

"A crowd of women are gathered there; they are screaming!"

"I'll go, too," declared the mother. "You're not well, and—what are they doing? I'm going, too."

"Come," Pavel said briefly.

They walked along the street quickly and silently. The mother panted with the exertion of the rapid gait and her excitement. She felt that something big was happening. At the factory gates a throng of women were discussing the affair in shrill voices. When the three pushed into the yard, they found themselves in the thick of a crowd buzzing and humming in excitement. The mother saw that all heads were turned in the same direction, toward the blacksmith's wall, where Sizov, Makhotin, Vyalov, and five or six influential, solid workingmen were standing on a high pile of old iron heaped on the red brick paving of the court, and waving their hands.

"Vlasov is coming!" somebody shouted.

"Vlasov? Bring him along!"

Pavel was seized and pushed forward, and the mother was left alone.

"Silence!" came the shout from various directions. Near by the even voice of Rybin was heard:

"We must make a stand, not for the kopeck, but for justice. What is dear to us is not our kopeck, because it's no rounder than any other kopeck; it's only heavier; there's more human blood in it than in the manager's ruble. That's the truth!"

The words fell forcibly on the crowd and stirred the men to hot responses:

"That's right! Good, Rybin!"

"Silence! The devil take you!"

"Vlasov's come!"

The voices mingled in a confused uproar, drowning the ponderous whir of the machinery, the sharp snorts of the steam, and the flapping of the leather belts. From all sides people came running, waving their hands; they fell into arguments, and excited one another with burning, stinging words. The irritation that had found no vent, that had always lain dormant in tired breasts, had awakened, demanded an outlet, and burst from their mouths in a volley of words. It soared into the air like a great bird spreading its motley wings ever wider and wider, clutching people and dragging them after it, and striking them against one another. It lived anew, transformed into flaming wrath. A cloud of dust and soot hung over the crowd; their faces were all afire, and black drops of sweat trickled down their cheeks. Their eyes gleamed from darkened countenances; their teeth glistened.

Pavel appeared on the spot where Sizov and Makhotin were standing, and his voice rang out:

"Comrades!"

The mother saw that his face paled and his lips trembled; she involuntarily pushed forward, shoving her way through the crowd.

"Where are you going, old woman?"

She heard the angry question, and the people pushed her, but she would not stop, thrusting the crowd aside with her shoulders and elbows. She slowly forced her way nearer to her son, yielding to the desire to stand by his side. When Pavel had thrown out the word to which he was wont to attach a deep and significant meaning, his throat contracted in a sharp spasm of the joy of fight. He was seized with an invincible desire to give himself up to the strength of his faith; to throw his heart to the people. His heart kindled with the dream of truth.

"Comrades!" he repeated, extracting power and rapture from the word. "We are the people who build churches and factories, forge chains and coin money, make toys and machines. We are that living force which feeds and amuses the world from the cradle to the grave."

"There!" Rybin exclaimed.

"Always and everywhere we are first in work but last in life. Who cares for us? Who wishes us good? Who regards us as human beings? No one!"

"No one!" echoed from the crowd.

Pavel, mastering himself, began to talk more simply and calmly; the crowd slowly drew about him, blending into one dark, thick, thousand-headed body. It looked into his face with hundreds of attentive eyes; it sucked in his words in silent, strained attention.

"We will not attain to a better life until we feel ourselves as comrades, as one family of friends firmly bound together by one desire—the desire to fight for our rights."

"Get down to business!" somebody standing near the mother shouted rudely.

"Don't interrupt!" "Shut up!" The two muffled exclamations were heard in different places. The soot-covered faces frowned in sulky incredulity; scores of eyes looked into Pavel's face thoughtfully and seriously.

"A socialist, but no fool!" somebody observed.

"I say, he does speak boldly!" said a tall, crippled workingman, tapping the mother on the shoulder.

"It is time, comrades, to take a stand against the greedy power that lives by our labor. It is time to defend ourselves; we must all understand that no one except ourselves will help us. One for all and all for one—this is our law, if we want to crush the foe!"

"He's right, boys!" Makhotin shouted. "Listen to the truth!" And, with a broad sweep of his arm, he shook his fist in the air.

"We must call out the manager at once," said Pavel. "We must ask him."

As if struck by a tornado, the crowd rocked to and fro; scores of voices shouted:

"The manager! The manager! Let him come! Let him explain!"

"Send delegates for him! Bring him here!"

"No, don't; it's not necessary!"

The mother pushed her way to the front and looked up at

her son. She was filled with pride. Her son stood among the old, respected workingmen; all listened to him and agreed with him! She was pleased that he was so calm and talked so simply; not angrily, not swearing, like the others. Broken exclamations, wrathful words and oaths descended like hail on iron. Pavel looked down on the people from his elevation, and with wide-open eyes seemed to be seeking something among them.

"Delegates!"

"Let Sizov speak!"

"Vlasov!"

"Rybin! He has a terrible tongue!"

Finally Sizov, Rybin, and Pavel were chosen for the interview with the manager. When just about to send for the manager, suddenly low exclamations were heard in the crowd:

"Here he comes himself!"

"The manager?"

"Ah!"

The crowd opened to make way for a tall, spare man with a pointed beard, an elongated face and blinking eyes.

"Permit me," he said, as he pushed the people aside with a short motion of his hand, without touching them. With the experienced look of a ruler of people, he scanned the workingmen's faces with a searching gaze. They took their hats off and bowed to him. He walked past them without acknowledging their greetings. His presence silenced and confused the crowd, and evoked embarrassed smiles and low exclamations, as of repentant children who had already come to regret their prank.

Now he passed by the mother, casting a stern glance at her face, and stopped before the pile of iron. Somebody from above extended a hand to him; he did not take it, but with an easy, powerful movement of his body he clambered up and stationed himself in front of Pavel and Sizov. Looking around the silent crowd, he asked:

"What's the meaning of this crowd? Why have you dropped your work?"

For a few seconds silence reigned. Sizov waved his cap in the air, shrugged his shoulders, and dropped his head.

"I am asking you a question!" continued the manager.

Pavel moved alongside of him and said in a low voice, pointing to Sizov and Rybin:

"We three are authorized by all the comrades to ask you to revoke your order about the kopeck discount."

"Why?" asked the manager, without looking at Pavel.

"We do not consider such a tax just!" Pavel replied loudly.

"So, in my plan to drain the marsh you see only a desire to exploit the workingmen and not a desire to better their conditions; is that it?"

"Yes!" Pavel replied.

"And you, also?" the manager asked Rybin.

"The very same!"

"How about you, my worthy friend?" The manager turned to Sizov.

"I, too, want to ask you to let us keep our kopecks." And drooping his head again, Sizov smiled guiltily. The manager slowly bent his look upon the crowd again, shrugged his shoulders, and then, regarding Pavel searchingly, observed:

"You appear to be a fairly intelligent man. Do you not understand the usefulness of this measure?"

Pavel replied loudly:

"If the factory should drain the marsh at its own expense, we would all understand it!"

"This factory is not in the philanthropy business!" remarked the manager dryly. "I order you all to start work at once!"

And he began to descend, cautiously feeling the iron with his feet, and without looking at anyone.

A dissatisfied hum was heard in the crowd.

"What!" asked the manager, halting.

All were silent; then from the distance came a solitary voice:

"You go to work yourself!"

"If in fifteen minutes you do not start work, I'll order every single one of you to be discharged!" the manager announced dryly and distinctly.

He again proceeded through the crowd, but now an indistinct murmur followed him, and the shouting grew louder as his figure receded.

"Speak to him!"

"That's what you call justice! Worse luck!"

Some turned to Pavel and shouted:

"Say, you great lawyer, you, what's to be done now? You talked and talked, but the moment he came it all went up in the air!"

"Well, Vlasov, what now?"

When the shouts became more insistent, Pavel raised his hand and said:

"Comrades, I propose that we quit work until he gives up that kopeck!"

Excited voices burst out:

"He thinks we're fools!"

"We ought to do it!"

"A strike?"

"For one kopeck?"

"Why not? Why not strike?"

"We'll all be discharged!"

"And who is going to do the work?"

"There are others!"

"Who? Judases?"

"Every year I would have to give three rubles and sixty kopecks to the mosquitoes!"

"All of us would have to give it!"

Pavel walked down and stood at the side of his mother. No one paid any attention to him now. They were all yelling and debating hotly with one another.

"You cannot get them to strike!" said Rybin, coming up to Pavel. "Greedy as these people are for a penny, they are too cowardly. You may, perhaps, induce about three hundred of them to follow you, no more. It's a heap of dung you won't lift with one toss of the pitchfork, I tell you!"

Pavel was silent. In front of him the huge black face of the crowd was rocking wildly, and fixed on him an importunate stare. His heart beat in alarm. It seemed to him as if all the words he had spoken vanished in the crowd without leaving any trace, like scattered drops of rain falling on parched soil. One after the other, workmen approached him praising his speech, but doubting the success of a strike, and complaining how little the people understood their own interests and realized their own strength.

Pavel had a sense of injury and disappointment as to his own power. His head ached; he felt desolate. Hitherto, whenever he pictured the triumph of his truth, he wanted to cry with the delight that seized his heart. But here he had spoken his truth to the people, and behold! when clothed in words it appeared so pale, so powerless, so incapable of affecting anyone. He blamed himself; it seemed to him that he had concealed his dream in a poor, disfiguring garment and no one could, therefore, detect its beauty.

He went home, tired and moody. He was followed by his mother and Sizov, while Rybin walked alongside, buzzing into his ear:

"You speak well, but you don't speak to the heart! That's the trouble! The spark must be thrown into the heart, into its very depths!"

"It's time we lived and were guided by reason," Pavel said in a low voice.

"The boot does not fit the foot; it's too thin and narrow! The foot won't get in! And if it does, it will wear the boot out mighty quick. That is the trouble."

Sizov, meanwhile, talked to the mother.

"It's time for us old folks to get into our graves. Nilovna! A new people is coming. What sort of a life have we lived? We crawled on our knees, and always crouched on the ground! But here are the new people. They have either come to their senses, or else are blundering worse than we; but they are not like us, anyway. Just look at those youngsters talking to the manager as to their equal! Yes, ma'am! Oh, if only my son Matvey were alive! Good-by, Pavel Vlasov! You stand up for the people all right, brother. God grant you his favor! Perhaps you'll find a way out. God grant it!" And he walked away.

"Yes, you may as well die straight off!" murmured Rybin. "You are no men, now. You are only putty—good to fill cracks with, that's all! Did you see, Pavel, who it was that shouted to make you a delegate? It was those who call you socialist—agitator—yes!—

thinking you'd be discharged, and it would serve you right!"

"They are right, according to their lights!" said Pavel.

"So are wolves when they tear one another to pieces!" Rybin's face was sullen, his voice unusually tremulous.

The whole day Pavel felt ill at ease, as if he had lost something, he did not know what, and anticipated a further loss.

At night when the mother was asleep and he was reading in bed, gendarmes appeared and began to search everywhere—in the yard, in the attic. They were sullen; the yellow-faced officer conducted himself as on the first occasion, insultingly, derisively, delighting in abuse, endeavoring to cut down to the very heart. The mother, in a corner, maintained silence, never removing her eyes from her son's face. He made every effort not to betray his emotion; but whenever the officer laughed, his fingers twitched strangely, and the old woman felt how hard it was for him not to reply, and to bear the jesting. This time the affair was not so terrorizing to her as at the first search. She felt a greater hatred to these gray, spurred night callers, and her hatred swallowed up her alarm.

Pavel managed to whisper:

"They'll arrest me."

Inclining her head, she quietly replied:

"I understand."

She did understand—they would put him in jail for what he had said to the workingmen that day. But since all agreed with what he had said, and all ought to stand up for him, he would not be detained long.

She longed to embrace him and cry over him; but there stood the officer, watching her with a malevolent squint of his eyes. His lips trembled, his mustache twitched. It seemed to Vlasova that the officer was but waiting for her tears, complaints, and supplications. With a supreme effort endeavoring to say as little as possible, she pressed her son's hand, and holding her breath said slowly, in a low tone:

"Good-by, Pasha. Did you take everything you need?"

"Everything. Don't worry!"

"Christ be with you!"

CHAPTER IX

When the police had led Pavel away, the mother sat down on the bench, and closing her eyes began to weep quietly. She leaned her back against the wall, as her husband used to do, her head thrown backward. Bound up in her grief and the injured sense of her impotence, she cried long, gently, and monotonously, pouring out all the pain of her wounded heart in her sobs. And before her, like an irremovable stain, hung that yellow face with the scant mustache, and the squinting eyes staring at her with malicious pleasure. Resentment and bitterness were winding themselves about her breast like black threads on a spool; resentment and bitterness toward those who tear a son away from his mother because he is seeking truth.

It was cold; the rain pattered against the window panes; something seemed to be creeping along the walls. She thought she heard, walking watchfully around the house, gray, heavy figures, with broad, red faces, without eyes, and with long arms. It seemed to her that she almost heard the jingling of their spurs.

"I wish they had taken me, too!" she thought.

The whistle blew, calling the people to work. This time its sounds were low, indistinct, uncertain. The door opened and Rybin entered. He stood before her, wiping the raindrops from his beard.

"They snatched him away, did they?" he asked.

"Yes, they did, the dogs!" she replied, sighing.

"That's how it is," said Rybin, with a smile; "they searched me, too; went all through me—yes! Abused me to their heart's content, but did me no harm beyond that. So they carried off Pavel, did they? The manager tipped the wink, the gendarme said 'Amen!' and lo! a man has disappeared. They certainly are thick together. One goes through the people's pockets while the other holds the gun."

"You ought to stand up for Pavel!" cried the mother, rising to her feet. "It's for you all that he's gone!"

"Who ought to stand up for him?" asked Rybin.

"All of you!"

"You want too much! We'll do nothing of the kind! Our masters have been gathering strength for thousands of years; they have driven our hearts full of nails. We cannot unite at once. We must first extract from ourselves, each from the other, the iron spikes that prevent us from standing close to one another."

And thus he departed, with his heavy gait, leaving the mother to her grief, aggravated by the stern hopelessness of his words.

The day passed in a thick mist of empty, senseless longing. She made no fire, cooked no dinner, drank no tea, and only late in the evening ate a piece of bread. When she went to bed it occurred to her that her life had never yet been so humiliating, so lonely and void. During the last years she had become accustomed to live constantly in the expectation of something momentous, something good. Young people were circling around her, noisy, vigorous, full of life. Her son's thoughtful and earnest face was always before her, and he seemed to be the master and creator of this thrilling and noble life. Now he was gone, everything was gone. In the whole day, no one except the disagreeable Rybin had called.

Beyond the window, the dense, cold rain was sighing and knocking at the panes. The rain and the drippings from the roof filled the air with a doleful, wailing melody. The whole house appeared to be rocking gently to and fro, and everything around her seemed aimless and unnecessary.

A gentle rap was heard at the door. It came once, and then a second time. She had grown accustomed to these noises; they no longer frightened her. A soft, joyous sensation thrilled her heart, and a vague hope quickly brought her to her feet. Throwing a shawl over her shoulders, she hurried to the door and opened it.

Samoylov walked in, followed by another man with his face hidden behind the collar of his overcoat and under a hat thrust over his eyebrows.

"Did we wake you?" asked Samoylov, without greeting the mother, his face gloomy and thoughtful, contrary to his wont.

"I was not asleep," she said, looking at them with expectant eyes.

Samoylov's companion took off his hat, and breathing heavily and hoarsely said in a friendly basso, like an old acquaintance, giving her his broad, short-fingered hand:

"Good evening, granny! You don't recognize me?"

"Is it you?" exclaimed Nilovna, with a sudden access of delight. "Yegor Ivanovich?"

"The very same identical one!" replied he, bowing his large head with its long hair. There was a good-natured smile on his face, and a clear, caressing look in his small gray eyes. He was like a samovar—rotund, short, with thick neck and short arms. His face was shiny and glossy, with high cheek bones. He breathed noisily, and his chest kept up a continuous low wheeze.

"Step into the room. I'll be dressed in a minute," the mother said.

"We have come to you on business," said Samoylov thoughtfully, looking at her out of the corner of his eyes.

Yegor Ivanovich passed into the room, and from there said:

"Nikolay got out of jail this morning, granny. You know him?"

"How long was he there?" she asked.

"Five months and eleven days. He saw the Little Russian there, who sends you his regards, and Pavel, who also sends you his regards and begs you not to be alarmed. As a man travels on his way, he says, the jails constitute his resting places, established and maintained by the solicitous authorities! Now, granny, let us get to the point. Do you know how many people were arrested yesterday?"

"I do not. Why, were there any others arrested besides Pavel?" she exclaimed.

"He was the forty-ninth!" calmly interjected Yegor Ivanovich. "And we may expect about ten more to be taken! This gentleman here, for example."

"Yes; me, too!" said Samoylov with a frown.

Nilovna somehow felt relieved.

"He isn't there alone," she thought.

When she had dressed herself, she entered the room and, smiling bravely, said:

"I guess they won't detain them long, if they arrested so many."

"You are right," assented Yegor Ivanovich; "and if we can manage to spoil this mess for them, we can make them look altogether like fools. This is the way it is, granny. If we were now to cease smuggling our literature into the factory, the gendarmes would take advantage of such a regrettable circumstance, and would use it against Pavel and his comrades in jail."

"How is that? Why should they?" the mother cried in alarm.

"It's very plain, granny," said Yegor Ivanovich softly. "Sometimes even gendarmes reason correctly. Just think! Pavel was, and there were books and there were papers; Pavel is not, and no books and no papers! Ergo, it was Pavel who distributed these books! Aha! Then they'll begin to eat them all alive. Those gendarmes dearly love so to unman a man that what remains of him is only a shred of himself, and a touching memory."

"I see, I see," said the mother dejectedly. "O God! What's to be done, then?"

"They have trapped them all, the devil take them!" came Samoylov's voice from the kitchen. "Now we must continue our work the same as before, and not only for the cause itself, but also to save our comrades!"

"And there is no one to do the work," added Yegor, smiling. "We have first-rate literature. I saw to that myself. But how to get it into the factory, that's the question!"

"They search everybody at the gates now," said Samoylov.

The mother divined that something was expected of her. She understood that she could be useful to her son, and she hastened to ask:

"Well, now? What are we to do?"

Samoylov stood in the doorway to answer.

"Pelagueya Nilovna, you know Marya Korsunova, the peddler."

"I do. Well?"

"Speak to her; see if you can't get her to smuggle in our wares."

"We could pay her, you know," interjected Yegor.

The mother waved her hands in negation.

"Oh, no! The woman is a chatterbox. No! If they find out it comes from me, from this house—oh, no!"

Then, inspired by a sudden idea, she began gladly and in a low voice:

"Give it to me, give it to me. I'll manage it myself. I'll find a way. I will ask Marya to make me her assistant. I have to earn my living, I have to work. Don't I? Well, then, I'll carry dinners to the factory. Yes, I'll manage it!"

Pressing her hands to her bosom, she gave hurried assurances that she would carry out her mission well and escape detection. Finally she exclaimed in triumph: "They'll find out—Pavel Vlasov is away, but his arm reaches out even from jail. They'll find out!"

All three became animated. Briskly rubbing his hands, Yegor smiled and said:

"It's wonderful, stupendous! I say, granny, it's superb—simply magnificent!"

"I'll sit in jail as in an armchair, if this succeeds," said Samoylov, laughing and rubbing his hands.

"You are fine, granny!" Yegor hoarsely cried.

The mother smiled. It was evident to her that if the leaflets should continue to appear in the factory, the authorities would be forced to recognize that it was not her son who distributed them. And feeling assured of success, she began to quiver all over with joy.

"When you go to see Pavel," said Yegor, "tell him he has a good mother."

"I'll see him very soon, I assure you," said Samoylov, smiling.

The mother grasped his hand and said earnestly:

"Tell him that I'll do everything, everything necessary. I want him to know it."

"And suppose they don't put him in prison?" asked Yegor, pointing at Samoylov.

The mother sighed and said sadly:

"Well, then, it can't be helped!"

Both of them burst out laughing. And when she realized her ridiculous blunder, she also began to laugh in embarrassment, and lowering her eyes said somewhat slyly:

"Bothering about your own folk keeps you from seeing other people straight."

"That's natural!" exclaimed Yegor. "And as to Pavel, you need not worry about him. He'll come out of prison a still better man. The prison is our place of rest and study—things we have no time for when we are at large. I was in prison three times, and each time, although I got scant pleasure, I certainly derived benefit for my heart and mind."

"You breathe with difficulty," she said, looking affectionately at his open face.

"There are special reasons for that," he replied, raising his finger. "So the matter's settled, granny? Yes? To-morrow we'll deliver the matter to you—and the wheels that grind the centuried darkness to destruction will again start a-rolling. Long live free speech! And long live a mother's heart! And in the meantime, good-by."

"Good-by," said Samoylov, giving her a vigorous handshake. "To my mother, I don't dare even hint about such matters. Oh, no!"

"Everybody will understand in time," said Nilovna, wishing to please him. "Everybody will understand."

When they left, she locked the door, and kneeling in the middle of the room began to pray, to the accompaniment of the patter of the rain. It was a prayer without words, one great thought of men, of all those people whom Pavel introduced into her life. It was as if they passed between her and the ikons upon which she held her eyes riveted. And they all looked so simple, so strangely near to one another, yet so lone in life.

Early next morning the mother went to Marya Korsunova. The peddler, noisy and greasy as usual, greeted her with friendly sympathy.

"You are grieving?" Marya asked, patting the mother on the back. "Now, don't. They just took him, carried him off. Where is the calamity? There is no harm in it. It used to be that men were thrown into dungeons for stealing, now they are there for telling the truth. Pavel may have said something wrong, but he stood up for all, and they all know it. Don't worry! They don't all say so, but they all know a good man when they see him. I was going to call on you right along, but had no time. I am always cooking and selling, but will end my days a beggar, I guess, all the same. My needs get the best of me, confound them! They keep nibbling and nibbling like mice at a piece of cheese. No sooner do I manage to scrape together ten rubles or so, when along comes some heathen, and makes away with all my money. Yes. It's hard to be a woman! It's a wretched business! To live alone is hard, to live with anyone, still harder!"

"And I came to ask you to take me as your assistant," Vlasova broke in, interrupting her prattle.

"How is that?" asked Marya. And after hearing her friend's explanation, she nodded her head assentingly.

"That's possible! You remember how you used to hide me from my husband? Well, now I am going to hide you from want. Everyone ought to help you, for your son is perishing for the public cause. He is a fine chap, your son is! They all say so, every blessed soul of them. And they all pity him. I'll tell you something. No good is going to come to the authorities from these arrests, mark my word! Look what's going on in the factory! Hear them talk! They are in an ugly mood, my dear! The officials imagine that when they've bitten at a man's heel, he won't be able to go far. But it turns out that when ten men are hit, a hundred men get angry. A workman must be handled with care! He may go on patiently enduring and suffering everything that's heaped upon him for a long, long time, but then he can also explode all of a sudden!"

CHAPTER X

The upshot of the conversation was that the next day at noon the mother was seen in the factory yard with two pots of eatables from Marya's culinary establishment, while Marya herself transferred her base of operations to the market place.

The workmen immediately noticed their new caterer. Some of them approached her and said approvingly:

"Gone into business, Nilovna?"

They comforted her, arguing that Pavel would certainly be released soon because his cause was a good one. Others filled her sad heart with alarm by their cautious condolence, while still others awoke a responsive echo in her by openly and bitterly abusing the manager and the gendarmes. Some there were who looked at her with a vindictive expression, among them Isay Gorbov, who, speaking through his teeth, said:

"If I were the governor, I would have your son hanged! Let him not mislead the people!"

This vicious threat went through her like the chill blast of death. She made no reply, glanced at his small, freckled face, and with a sigh cast down her eyes.

She observed considerable agitation in the factory; the workmen gathered in small groups and talked in an undertone, with great animation; the foremen walked about with careworn faces, poking their noses into everything; here and there were heard angry oaths and irritated laughter.

Two policemen escorted Samoylov past her. He walked with one hand in his pocket, the other smoothing his red hair.

A crowd of about a hundred workmen followed him, and plied the policemen with oaths and banter.

"Going to take a promenade, Grisha?" shouted one.

"They do honor to us fellows!" chimed in another.

"When we go to promenading, we have a bodyguard to escort us," said a third, and uttered a harsh oath.

"It does not seem to pay any longer to catch thieves!" exclaimed a tall, one-eyed workingman in a loud, bitter voice. "So they take to arresting honest people."

"They don't even do it at night!" broke in another. "They come and drag them away in broad daylight, without shame, the impudent scoundrels!"

The policemen walked on rapidly and sullenly, trying to avoid the sight of the crowd, and feigning not to hear the angry exclamations showered upon them from all sides. Three workmen carrying a big iron bar happened to come in front of them, and thrusting the bar against them, shouted:

"Look out there, fishermen!"

As he passed Nilovna, Samoylov nodded to her, and smiling, said:

"Behold, this is Gregory, the servant of God, being arrested."

She made a low bow to him in silence. These men, so young, sober, and clever, who went to jail with a smile, moved her, and she unconsciously felt for them the pitying affection of a mother. It pleased her to hear the sharp comments leveled against the authorities. She saw therein her son's influence.

Leaving the factory, she passed the remainder of the day at

Marya's house, assisting her in her work, and listening to her chatter. Late in the evening she returned home and found it bare, chilly and disagreeable. She moved about from corner to corner, unable to find a resting place, and not knowing what to do with herself. Night was fast approaching, and she grew worried, because Yegor Ivanovich had not yet come and brought her the literature which he had promised.

Behind the window, gray, heavy flakes of spring snow fluttered and settled softly and noiselessly upon the pane. Sliding down and melting, they left a watery track in their course. The mother thought of her son.

A cautious rap was heard. She rushed to the door, lifted the latch, and admitted Sashenka. She had not seen her for a long while, and the first thing that caught her eye was the girl's unnatural stoutness.

"Good evening!" she said, happy to have a visitor at such a time, to relieve her solitude for a part of the night. "You haven't been around for a long while! Were you away?"

"No, I was in prison," replied the girl, smiling, "with Nikolay Ivanovich. Do you remember him?"

"I should think I do!" exclaimed the mother. "Yegor Ivanovich told me yesterday that he had been released, but I knew nothing about you. Nobody told me that you were there."

"What's the good of telling? I should like to change my dress before Yegor Ivanovich comes!" said the girl, looking around.

"You are all wet."

"I've brought the booklets."

"Give them here, give them to me!" cried the mother impatiently.

"Directly," replied the girl. She untied her skirt and shook it, and like leaves from a tree, down fluttered a lot of thin paper parcels on the floor around her. The mother picked them up, laughing, and said:

"I was wondering what made you so stout. Oh, what a heap of them you have brought! Did you come on foot?"

"Yes," said Sashenka. She was again her graceful, slender self. The mother noticed that her cheeks were shrunken, and that dark rings were under her unnaturally large eyes.

"You are just out of prison. You ought to rest, and there you are carrying a load like that for seven versts!" said the mother, sighing and shaking her head.

"It's got to be done!" said the girl. "Tell me, how is Pavel? Did he stand it all right? He wasn't very much worried, was he?" Sashenka asked the question without looking at the mother. She bent her head and her fingers trembled as she arranged her hair.

"All right," replied the mother. "You can rest assured he won't betray himself."

"How strong he is!" murmured the girl quietly.

"He has never been sick," replied the mother. "Why, you are all in a shiver! I'll get you some tea, and some raspberry jam."

"That's fine!" exclaimed the girl with a faint smile. "But don't you trouble! It's too late. Let me do it myself."

"What! Tired as you are?" the mother reproached her, hurrying into the kitchen, where she busied herself with the samovar. The girl followed into the kitchen, sat down on the bench, and folded her hands behind her head before she replied:

"Yes, I'm very tired! After all, the prison makes one weak. The awful thing about it is the enforced inactivity. There is nothing more tormenting. We stay a week, five weeks. We know how much there is to be done. The people are waiting for knowledge. We're in a position to satisfy their wants, and there we are locked up in a cage like animals! That's what is so trying, that's what dries up the heart!"

"Who will reward you for all this?" asked the mother; and with a sigh she answered the question herself. "No one but God! Of course you don't believe in Him either?"

"No!" said the girl briefly, shaking her head.

"And I don't believe you!" the mother ejaculated in a sudden burst of excitement. Quickly wiping her charcoal-blackened hands on her apron she continued, with deep conviction in her voice:

"You don't understand your own faith! How could you live the kind of life you are living, without faith in God?"

A loud stamping of feet and a murmur of voices were heard on the porch. The mother started; the girl quickly rose to her feet, and whispered hurriedly:

"Don't open the door! If it's the gendarmes, you don't know me.

I walked into the wrong house, came here by accident, fainted away, you undressed me, and found the books around me. You understand?"

"Why, my dear, what for?" asked the mother tenderly.

"Wait a while!" said Sashenka listening. "I think it's Yegor."

It was Yegor, wet and out of breath.

"Aha! The samovar!" he cried. "That's the best thing in life, granny! You here already, Sashenka?"

His hoarse voice filled the little kitchen. He slowly removed his heavy ulster, talking all the time.

"Here, granny, is a girl who is a thorn in the flesh of the police! Insulted by the overseer of the prison, she declared that she would starve herself to death if he did not ask her pardon. And for eight days she went without eating, and came within a hair's breadth of dying. It's not bad! She must have a mighty strong little stomach."

"Is it possible you took no food for eight days in succession?" asked the mother in amazement.

"I had to get him to beg my pardon," answered the girl with a stoical shrug of her shoulders. Her composure and her stern persistence seemed almost like a reproach to the mother.

"And suppose you had died?" she asked again.

"Well, what can one do?" the girl said quietly. "He did beg my pardon after all. One ought never to forgive an insult, never!"

"Ye-es!" responded the mother slowly. "Here are we women who are insulted all our lives long."

"I have unloaded myself!" announced Yegor from the other room. "Is the samovar ready? Let me take it in!"

He lifted the samovar and talked as he carried it.

"My own father used to drink not less than twenty glasses of tea a day, wherefor his days upon earth were long, peaceful, and strong; for he lived to be seventy-three years old, never having suffered from any ailment whatsoever. In weight he reached the respectable figure of three hundred and twenty pounds, and by profession he was a sexton in the village of Voskresensk."

"Are you Ivan's son?" exclaimed the mother.

"I am that very mortal. How did you know his name?"

"Why, I am a Voskresenskian myself!"

"A fellow countrywoman! Who were your people?"

"Your neighbors. I am a Sereguin."

"Are you a daughter of Nil the Lame? I thought your face was familiar! Why, I had my ears pulled by him many and many a time!"

They stood face to face plying each other with questions and laughing. Sashenka looked at them and smiled, and began to prepare the tea. The clatter of the dishes recalled the mother to the realities of the present.

"Oh, excuse me! I quite forgot myself, talking about old times. It is so sweet to recall your youth."

"It's I who ought to beg your pardon for carrying on like this in your house!" said Sashenka. "But it is eleven o'clock already, and I have so far to go."

"Go where? To the city?" the mother asked in surprise.

"Yes."

"What are you talking about! It's dark and wet, and you are so tired. Stay here overnight. Yegor Ivanovich will sleep in the kitchen, and you and I here."

"No, I must go," said the girl simply.

"Yes, countrywoman, she must go. The young lady must disappear. It would be bad if she were to be seen on the street to-morrow."

"But how can she go? By herself?"

"By herself," said Yegor, laughing.

The girl poured tea for herself, took a piece of rye bread, salted it, and started to eat, looking at the mother contemplatively.

"How can you go that way? Both you and Natasha. I wouldn't. I'm afraid!"

"She's afraid, too," said Yegor. "Aren't you afraid, Sasha?"

"Of course!"

The mother looked at her, then at Yegor, and said in a low voice, "What strange—"

"Give me a glass of tea, granny," Yegor interrupted her.

When Sashenka had drunk her glass of tea, she pressed Yegor's hand in silence, and walked out into the kitchen. The mother followed her. In the kitchen Sashenka said:

"When you see Pavel, give him my regards, please." And taking hold of the latch, she suddenly turned around, and asked in a low voice: "May I kiss you?"

The mother embraced her in silence, and kissed her warmly.

"Thank you!" said the girl, and nodding her head, walked out.

Returning to the room, the mother peered anxiously through the window. Wet flakes of snow fluttered through the dense, moist darkness.

"And do you remember Prozorov, the storekeeper?" asked Yegor. "He used to sit with his feet sprawling, and blow noisily into his glass of tea. He had a red, satisfied, sweet-covered face."

"I remember, I remember," said the mother, coming back to the table. She sat down, and looking at Yegor with a mournful expression in her eyes, she spoke pityingly: "Poor Sashenka! How will she ever get to the city?"

"She will be very much worn out," Yegor agreed. "The prison has shaken her health badly. She was stronger before. Besides, she has had a delicate bringing up. It seems to me she has already ruined her lungs. There is something in her face that reminds one of consumption."

"Who is she?"

"The daughter of a landlord. Her father is a rich man and a big scoundrel, according to what she says. I suppose you know, granny, that they want to marry?"

"Who?"

"She and Pavel. Yes, indeed! But so far they have not yet been able. When he is free, she is in prison, and *vice versa*." Yegor laughed.

"I didn't know it!" the mother replied after a pause. "Pasha never speaks about himself."

Now she felt a still greater pity for the girl, and looking at her guest with involuntary hostility, she said:

"You ought to have seen her home."

"Impossible!" Yegor answered calmly. "I have a heap of work to do here, and the whole day to-morrow, from early morning, I shall have to walk and walk and walk. No easy job, considering my asthma."

"She's a fine girl!" said the mother, vaguely thinking of what Yegor had told her. She felt hurt that the news should have come to her, not from her son, but from a stranger, and she pressed her lips together tightly, and lowered her eyebrows.

"Yes, a fine girl!" Yegor nodded assent. "There's a bit of the noblewoman in her yet, but it's growing less and less all the time. You are sorry for her, I see. What's the use? You won't find heart enough, if you start to grieve for all of us rebels, granny dear. Life is not made very easy for us, I admit. There, for instance, is the case of a friend of mine who returned a short while ago from exile. When he went through Novgorod, his wife and child awaited him in Smolensk, and when he arrived in Smolensk, they were already in prison in Moscow. Now it's the wife's turn to go to Siberia. To be a revolutionary and to be married is a very inconvenient arrangement—inconvenient for the husband, inconvenient for the wife and in the end for the cause also! I, too, had a wife, an excellent woman, but five years of this kind of life landed her in the grave."

He emptied the glass of tea at one gulp, and continued his narrative. He enumerated the years and months he had passed in prison and in exile, told of various accidents and misfortunes, of the slaughters in prisons, and of hunger in Siberia. The mother looked at him, listened with wonderment to the simple way in which he spoke of this life, so full of suffering, of persecution, of wrong, and abuse of men.

"Well, let's get down to business!"

His voice changed, and his face grew more serious. He asked questions about the way in which the mother intended to smuggle the literature into the factory, and she marveled at his clear knowledge of all the details.

Then they returned to reminiscences of their native village. He joked, and her mind roved thoughtfully through her past. It seemed to her strangely like a quagmire uniformly strewn with hillocks, which were covered with poplars trembling in constant fear; with low firs, and with white birches straying between the hillocks. The birches grew slowly, and after standing for five years on the unstable, putrescent soil, they dried up, fell down, and rotted away. She looked at this picture, and a vague feeling of insufferable sadness overcame her. The figure of a girl with a sharp, determined face stood before her. Now the figure walks somewhere in the darkness amid the snowflakes, solitary, weary. And her son sits in a little cell, with iron gratings over the window. Perhaps he is not yet asleep, and is thinking. But he is thinking not of his mother. He has one nearer to him than herself. Heavy, chaotic thoughts, like a tangled mass of clouds, crept over her, and encompassed her and oppressed her bosom.

"You are tired, granny! Let's go to bed!" said Yegor, smiling.

She bade him good night, and sidled carefully into the kitchen, carrying away a bitter, caustic feeling in her heart.

In the morning, after breakfast, Yegor asked her:

"Suppose they catch you and ask you where you got all these heretical books from. What will you say?"

"I'll say, 'It's none of your business!'" she answered, smiling.

"You'll never convince them of that!" Yegor replied confidently. "On the contrary, they are profoundly convinced that this is precisely their business. They will question you very, very diligently, and very, very long!"

"I won't tell, though!"

"They'll put you in prison!"

"Well, what of it? Thank God that I am good at least for that," she said with a sigh. "Thank God! Who needs me? Nobody!"

"H'm!" said Yegor, fixing his look upon her. "A good person ought to take care of himself."

"I couldn't learn that from you, even if I were good," the mother replied, laughing.

Yegor was silent, and paced up and down the room; then he walked up to her and said: "This is hard, countrywoman! I feel it, it's very hard for you!"

"It's hard for everybody," she answered, with a wave of her hand. "Maybe only for those who understand, it's easier. But I understand a little, too. I understand what it is the good people want."

"If you do understand, granny, then it means that everybody needs you, everybody!" said Yegor earnestly and solemnly.

She looked at him and laughed without saying anything.

CHAPTER XI

At noon, calmly and in a businesslike way she put the books around her bosom, and so skillfully and snugly that Yegor announced, smacking his lips with satisfaction:

"*Sehr gut!* as the German says when he has drunk a keg of beer. Literature has not changed you, granny. You still remain the good, tall, portly, elderly woman. May all the numberless gods grant you their blessings on your enterprise!"

Within half an hour she stood at the factory gate, bent with the weight of her burden, calm and assured. Two guards, irritated by the oaths and railery of the workingmen, examined all who entered the gate, handling them roughly and swearing at them. A policeman and a thin-legged man with a red face and alert eyes stood at one side. The mother, shifting the rod resting on her shoulders, with a pail suspended from either end of it, watched the man from the corner of her eye. She divined that he was a spy.

A tall, curly-headed fellow with his hat thrown back over his neck, cried to the guardsmen who searched him:

"Search the head and not the pockets, you devils!"

"There is nothing but lice on your head," retorted one of the guardsmen.

"Catching lice is an occupation more suited to you than hunting human game!" rejoined the workman. The spy scanned him with a rapid glance.

"Will you let me in?" asked the mother. "See, I'm bent double with my heavy load. My back is almost breaking."

"Go in! Go in!" cried the guard sullenly. "She comes with arguments, too."

The mother walked to her place, set her pails on the ground, and wiping the perspiration from her face looked around her.

The Gusev brothers, the locksmiths, instantly came up to her, and the older of them, Vasily, asked aloud, knitting his eyebrows:

"Got any pirogs?"

"I'll bring them to-morrow," she answered.

This was the password agreed upon. The faces of the brothers brightened. Ivan, unable to restrain himself, exclaimed:

"Oh, you jewel of a mother!"

Vasily squatted down on his heels, looked into the pot, and a bundle of books disappeared into his bosom.

"Ivan!" he said aloud. "Let's not go home, let's get our dinner here from her!" And he quickly shoved the books into the legs of his boots. "We must give our new peddler a lift, don't you think so?"

"Yes, indeed!" Ivan assented, and laughed aloud.

The mother looked carefully about her, and called out:

"Sour cabbage soup! Hot vermicelli soup! Roast meat!"

Then deftly and secretly taking out one package of books after the other, she shoved them into the hands of the brothers. Each time a bundle disappeared from her hands, the sickly, sneering face of the officer of gendarmes flashed up before her like a yellow stain, like the flame of a match in a dark room, and she said to him in her mind, with a feeling of malicious pleasure:

"Take this, sir!" And when she handed over the last package she added with an air of satisfaction: "And here is some more, take it!"

Workmen came up to her with cups in their hands, and when they were near Ivan and Vasily, they began to laugh aloud. The mother calmly suspended the transfer of the books, and poured sour soup and vermicelli soup, while the Gusevs joked her.

"How cleverly Nilovna does her work!"

"Necessity drives one even to catching mice," remarked a stoker somberly. "They have snatched away your breadgiver, the scoundrels! Well, give us three cents' worth of vermicelli. Never mind, mother! You'll pull through!"

"Thanks for the good word!" she returned, smiling.

He walked off to one side and mumbled, "It doesn't cost me much to say a good word!"

"But there's no one to say it to!" observed a blacksmith, with a smile, and shrugging his shoulders in surprise added: "There's a life for you, fellows! There's no one to say a good word to; no one is worth it. Yes, sir!"

Vasily Gusev rose, wrapped his coat tightly around him, and exclaimed:

"What I ate was hot, and yet I feel cold."

Then he walked away. Ivan also rose, and ran off whistling merrily.

Cheerful and smiling, Nilovna kept on calling her wares:

"Hot! Hot! Sour soup! Vermicelli soup! Porridge!"

She thought of how she would tell her son about her first experience; and the yellow face of the officer was still standing before her, perplexed and spiteful. His black mustache twitched uneasily, and his upper lip turned up nervously, showing the gleaming white enamel of his clenched teeth. A keen joy beat and sang in her heart like a bird, her eyebrows quivered, and continuing deftly to serve her customers she muttered to herself:

"There's more! There's more!"

Through the whole day she felt a sensation of delightful newness which embraced her heart as with a fondling caress. And in the evening, when she had concluded her work at Marya's house, and was drinking tea, the splash of horses' hoofs in the mud was heard, and the call of a familiar voice. She jumped up, hurried into the kitchen, and made straight for the door. Somebody walked quickly through the porch; her eyes grew dim, and leaning against the doorpost, she pushed the door open with her foot.

"Good evening, mother!" a familiar, melodious voice rang out, and a pair of dry, long hands were laid on her shoulders.

The joy of seeing Andrey was mingled in her bosom with the sadness of disappointment; and the two contrary feelings blended into one burning sensation which embraced her like a hot wave. She buried her face in Andrey's bosom. He pressed her tightly to himself, his hands trembled. The mother wept quietly without speaking, while he stroked her hair, and spoke in his musical voice:

"Don't cry, mother. Don't wring my heart. Upon my honest word, they will let him out soon! They haven't a thing against him; all the boys will keep quiet as cooked fish."

Putting his long arm around the mother's shoulders he led her into the room, and nestling up against him with the quick gesture of a squirrel, she wiped the tears from her face, while her heart greedily drank in his tender words.

"Pavel sends you his love. He is as well and cheerful as can be.

It's very crowded in the prison. They have thrown in more than a hundred of our people, both from here and from the city. Three and four persons have been put into one cell. The prison officials are rather a good set. They are exhausted with the quantity of work the gendarmes have been giving them. The prison authorities are not extremely rigorous, they don't order you about roughly. They simply say: 'Be quiet as you can, gentlemen. Don't put us in an awkward position!' So everything goes well. We talk with one another, we give books to one another, and we share our food. It's a good prison! Old and dirty, but so soft and so light. The criminals are also nice people; they help us a good deal. Bukin, four others, and myself were released. It got too crowded. They'll let Pavel go soon, too. I'm telling you the truth, believe me. Vyesovshchikov will be detained the longest. They are very angry at him. He scolds and swears at everybody all the time. The gendarmes can't bear to look at him. I guess he'll get himself into court, or receive a sound thrashing some day. Pavel tries to dissuade him. 'Stop, Nikolay!' he says to him. 'Your swearing won't reform them.' But he bawls: 'Wipe them off the face of the earth like a pest!' Pavel conducts himself finely out there; he treats all alike, and is as firm as a rock! They'll soon let him go."

"Soon?" said the mother, relieved now and smiling. "I know he'll be let out soon!"

"Well, if you know, it's all right! Give me tea, mother. Tell me how you've been, how you've passed your time."

He looked at her, smiling all over, and seemed so near to her, such a splendid fellow. A loving, somewhat melancholy gleam flashed from the depths of his round, blue eyes.

"I love you dearly, Andriusha!" the mother said, heaving a deep sigh, as she looked at his thin face grotesquely covered with tufts of hair.

"People are satisfied with little from me! I know you love me; you are capable of loving everybody; you have a great heart," said the Little Russian, rocking in his chair, his eyes straying about the room.

"No, I love you very differently!" insisted the mother. "If you had a mother, people would envy her because she had such a son."

The Little Russian swayed his head, and rubbed it vigorously with both hands.

"I have a mother, somewhere!" he said in a low voice.

"Do you know what I did to-day?" she exclaimed, and reddening a little, her voice choking with satisfaction, she quickly recounted how she had smuggled literature into the factory.

For a moment he looked at her in amazement with his eyes wide open; then he burst out into a loud guffaw, stamped his feet, thumped his head with his fingers, and cried joyously:

"Oho! That's no joke any more! That's business! Won't Pavel be glad, though! Oh, you're a trump. That's good, mother! You have no idea *how* good it is! Both for Pavel and all who were arrested with him!"

He snapped his fingers in ecstasy, whistled, and fairly doubled over, all radiant with joy. His delight evoked a vigorous response from the mother.

"My dear, my Andriusha!" she began, as if her heart had burst open, and gushed over merrily with a limpid stream of living words full of serene joy. "I've thought all my life, 'Lord Christ in heaven! what did I live for?' Beatings, work! I saw nothing except my husband. I knew nothing but fear! And how Pasha grew I did not see, and I hardly know whether I loved him when my husband was alive. All my concerns, all my thoughts were centered upon one thing—to feed my beast, to propitiate the master of my life with enough food, pleasing to his palate, and served on time, so as not to incur his displeasure, so as to escape the terrors of a beating, to get him to spare me but once! But I do not remember that he ever did spare me. He beat me so—not as a wife is beaten, but as one whom you hate and detest. Twenty years I lived like that, and what was up to the time of my marriage I do not recall. I remember certain things, but I see nothing! I am as a blind person. Yegor Ivanovich was here—we are from the same village—and he spoke about this and about that. I remember the houses, the people, but how they lived, what they spoke about, what happened to this one and what to that one—I forget, I do not see! I remember fires—two fires. It seems that everything has been beaten out of me, that my soul has been locked up and sealed tight. It's grown blind, it does not hear!"

Her quick-drawn breath was almost a sob. She bent forward, and continued in a lowered voice: "When my husband died I turned to my son; but he went into this business, and I was seized with a pity for him, such a yearning pity—for if he should perish, how was I to live alone? What dread, what fright I have undergone! My heart was rent when I thought of his fate.

"Our woman's love is not a pure love! We love that which we need. And here are you! You are grieving about your mother. What do you want her for? And all the others go and suffer for the people, they go to prison, to Siberia, they die for them, many are hung. Young girls walk alone at night, in the snow, in the mud, in the rain. They walk seven versts from the city to our place. Who drives them? Who pursues them? They love! You see, theirs is pure love! They believe! Yes, indeed, they believe, Andriusha! But here am I—I can't love like that! I love my own, the near ones!"

"Yes, you can!" said the Little Russian, and turning away his face from her, he rubbed his head, face, and eyes vigorously as was his wont. "Everybody loves those who are near," he continued. "To a large heart, what is far is also near. You, mother, are capable of a great deal. You have a large capacity of motherliness!"

"God grant it!" she said quietly. "I feel that it is good to live like that! Here are you, for instance, whom I love. Maybe I love you better than I do Pasha. He is always so silent. Here he wants to get married to Sashenka, for example, and he never told me, his mother, a thing about it."

"That's not true," the Little Russian retorted abruptly. "I know it isn't true. It's true he loves her, and she loves him. But marry? No, they are not going to marry! She'd want to, but Pavel—he can't! He doesn't want to!"

"See how you are!" said the mother quietly, and she fixed her eyes sadly and musingly on the Little Russian's face. "You see how you are! You offer up your own selves!"

"Pavel is a rare man!" the Little Russian uttered in a low voice. "He is a man of iron!"

"Now he sits in prison," continued the mother reflectively. "It's awful, it's terrible! It's not as it used to be before! Life altogether is not as it used to be, and the terror is different from the old terror.

You feel a pity for everybody, and you are alarmed for everybody! And the heart is different. The soul has opened its eyes, it looks on, and is sad and glad at the same time. There's much I do not understand, and I feel so bitter and hurt that you do not believe in the Lord God. Well, I guess I can't help that! But I see and know that you are good people. And you have consecrated yourselves to a stern life for the sake of the people, to a life of hardship for the sake of truth. The truth you stand for, I comprehend: as long as there will be the rich, the people will get nothing, neither truth nor happiness, nothing! Indeed, that's so, Andriusha! Here am I living among you, while all this is going on. Sometimes at night my thoughts wander off to my past. I think of my youthful strength trampled under foot, of my young heart torn and beaten, and I feel sorry for myself and embittered. But for all that I live better now, I see myself more and more, I feel myself more."

The Little Russian arose, and trying not to scrape with his feet, began to walk carefully up and down the room, tall, lean, absorbed in thought.

"Well said!" he exclaimed in a low voice. "Very well! There was a young Jew in Kerch who wrote verses, and once he wrote:

"And the innocently slain, Truth will raise to life again.

"He himself was killed by the police in Kerch, but that's not the point. He knew the truth and did a great deal to spread it among the people. So here you are one of the innocently slain. He spoke the truth!"

"There, I am talking now," the mother continued. "I talk and do not hear myself, don't believe my own ears! All my life I was silent, I always thought of one thing—how to live through the day apart, how to pass it without being noticed, so that nobody should touch me! And now I think about everything. Maybe I don't understand your affairs so very well; but all are near me, I feel sorry for all, and I wish well to all. And to you, Andriusha, more than all the rest."

He took her hand in his, pressed it tightly, and quickly turned aside. Fatigued with emotion and agitation, the mother leisurely and silently washed the cups; and her breast gently glowed with a bold feeling that warmed her heart.

Walking up and down the room the Little Russian said:

"Mother, why don't you sometimes try to befriend Vyesovshchikov and be kind to him? He is a fellow that needs it. His father sits in prison—a nasty little old man. Nikolay sometimes catches sight of him through the window and he begins to swear at him. That's bad, you know. He is a good fellow, Nikolay is. He is fond of dogs, mice, and all sorts of animals, but he does not like people. That's the pass to which a man can be brought."

"His mother disappeared without a trace, his father is a thief and a drunkard," said Nilovna pensively.

When Andrey left to go to bed, the mother, without being noticed, made the sign of the cross over him, and after about half an hour, she asked quietly, "Are you asleep, Andriusha?"

"No. Why?"

"Nothing! Good night!"

"Thank you, mother, thank you!" he answered gently.

CHAPTER XII

The next day when Nilovna came up to the gates of the factory with her load, the guides stopped her roughly, and ordering her to put the pails down on the ground, made a careful examination.

"My eatables will get cold," she observed calmly, as they felt around her dress.

"Shut up!" said a guard sullenly.

Another one, tapping her lightly on the shoulder, said with assurance:

"Those books are thrown across the fence, I say!"

Old man Sizov came up to her and looking around said in an undertone:

"Did you hear, mother?"

"What?"

"About the pamphlets. They've appeared again. They've just scattered them all over like salt over bread. Much good those arrests and searches have done! My nephew Mazin has been hauled away to prison, your son's been taken. Now it's plain it isn't he!" And stroking his beard Sizov concluded, "It's not people, but thoughts, and thoughts are not fleas; you can't catch them!"

He gathered his beard in his hand, looked at her, and said as he walked away:

"Why don't you come to see me some time? I guess you are lonely all by yourself."

She thanked him, and calling her wares, she sharply observed the unusual animation in the factory. The workmen were all elated, they formed little circles, then parted, and ran from one group to another. Animated voices and happy, satisfied faces all around! The soot-filled atmosphere was astir and palpitating with something bold and daring. Now here, now there, approving ejaculations were heard, mockery, and sometimes threats.

"Aha! It seems truth doesn't agree with them," she heard one say.

The younger men were in especially good spirits, while the elder workmen had cautious smiles on their faces. The authorities walked about with a troubled expression, and the police ran from place to place. When the workingmen saw them, they dispersed, and walked away slowly, or if they remained standing, they stopped their conversation, looking silently at the agitated, angry faces.

The workingmen seemed for some reason to be all washed and clean. The figure of Gusev loomed high, and his brother stalked about like a drake, and roared with laughter. The joiner's foreman, Vavilov, and the record clerk, Isay, walked slowly past the mother. The little, wizened clerk, throwing up his head and turning his neck to the left, looked at the frowning face of the foreman, and said quickly, shaking his reddish beard:

"They laugh, Ivan Ivanovich. It's fun to them. They are pleased, although it's no less a matter than the destruction of the government, as the manager said. What must be done here, Ivan Ivanovich, is not merely to weed but to plow!"

Vavilov walked with his hands folded behind his back, and his fingers tightly clasped.

"You print there what you please, you blackguards!" he cried aloud. "But don't you dare say a word about me!"

Vasily Gusev came up to Nilovna and declared:

"I am going to eat with you again. Is it good to-day?"

And lowering his head and screwing up his eyes, he added in an undertone: "You see? It hit exactly! Good! Oh, mother, very good!"

She nodded her head affably to him, flattered that Gusev, the sauciest fellow in the village, addressed her with a respectful plural "you," as he talked to her in secret. The general stir and animation in the factory also pleased her, and she thought to herself: "What would they do without me?"

Three common laborers stopped at a short distance from her, and one of them said with disappointment in his voice: "I couldn't find any anywhere!"

Another remarked: "I'd like to hear it, though. I can't read myself, but I understand it hits them just in the right place."

The third man looked around him, and said: "Let's go into the boiler room. I'll read it for you there!"

"It works!" Gusev whispered, a wink lurking in his eye.

Nilovna came home in gay spirits. She had now seen for herself how people are moved by books.

"The people down there are sorry they can't read," she said to Andrey, "and here am I who could when I was young, but have forgotten."

"Learn over again, then," suggested the Little Russian.

"At my age? What do you want to make fun of me for?"

Andrey, however, took a book from the shelf and pointing with the tip of a knife at a letter on the cover, asked: "What's this?"

"R," she answered, laughing.

"And this?"

"A."

She felt awkward, hurt, and offended. It seemed to her that Andrey's eyes were laughing at her, and she avoided their look. But his voice sounded soft and calm in her ears. She looked askance at his face, once, and a second time. It was earnest and serious.

"Do you really wish to teach me to read?" she asked with an involuntary smile.

"Why not?" he responded. "Try! If you once knew how to read, it will come back to you easily. 'If no miracle it's no ill, and if a miracle better still!'"

"But they say that one does not become a saint by looking at a sacred image!"

"Eh," said the Little Russian, nodding his head. "There are proverbs galore! For example: 'The less you know, the better you sleep'—isn't that it? Proverbs are the material the stomach thinks with; it makes bridles for the soul, to be able to control it better. What the stomach needs is a rest, and the soul needs freedom. What letter is this?"

"M."

"Yes, see how it sprawls. And this?"

Straining her eyes and moving her eyebrows heavily, she recalled with an effort the forgotten letters, and unconsciously yielding to the force of her exertions, she was carried away by them, and forgot herself. But soon her eyes grew tired. At first they became moist with tears of fatigue; and then tears of sorrow rapidly dropped down on the page.

"I'm learning to read," she said, sobbing. "It's time for me to die, and I'm just learning to read!"

"You mustn't cry," said the Little Russian gently. "It wasn't your fault you lived the way you did; and yet you understand that you lived badly. There are thousands of people who could live better than you, but who live like cattle and then boast of how well they live. But what is good in their lives? To-day, their day's work over, they eat, and to-morrow, their day's work over, they eat, and so on through all their years—work and eat, work and eat! Along with this they bring forth children, and at first amuse themselves with them, but when they, too, begin to eat much, they grow surly and scold: 'Come on, you gluttons! Hurry along! Grow up quick! It's time you get to work!' and they would like to make beasts of burden of their children. But the children begin to work for their own stomachs, and drag their lives along as a thief drags a worthless stolen mop. Their souls are never stirred with joy, never quickened with a thought that melts the heart. Some live like mendicants—always begging; some like thieves—always snatching out of the hands of others. They've made thieves' laws, placed men with sticks over the people, and said to them: 'Guard our laws; they are very convenient laws; they permit us to suck the blood out of the people!' They try to squeeze the people from the outside, but the people resist, and so they drive the rules inside so as to crush the reason, too."

Leaning his elbows on the table and looking into the mother's face with pensive eyes, he continued in an even, flowing voice:

"Only those are men who strike the chains from off man's body and from off his reason. And now you, too, are going into this work according to the best of your ability."

"I? Now, now! How can I?"

"Why not? It's just like rain. Every drop goes to nourish the seed! And when you are able to read, then—" He stopped and began to laugh; then rose and paced up and down the room.

"Yes, you must learn to read! And when Pavel gets back, won't you surprise him, eh?"

"Oh, Andriusha! For a young man everything is simple and easy! But when you have lived to my age, you have lots of trouble, little strength, and no mind at all left."

In the evening the Little Russian went out. The mother lit a lamp and sat down at a table to knit stockings. But soon she rose again, walked irresolutely into the kitchen, bolted the outer door, and straining her eyebrows walked back into the living room. She pulled down the window curtains, and taking a book from the shelf, sat down at the table again, looked around, bent down over the book, and began to move her lips. When she heard a noise on the street, she started, clapped the book shut with the palm of her hand, and listened intently. And again, now closing, now opening her eyes, she whispered:

"E—z—a."

With even precision and stern regularity the dull tick of the pendulum marked the dying seconds.

A knock at the door was heard; the mother jumped quickly to her feet, thrust the book on the shelf, and walking up to the door asked anxiously:

"Who's there?"

CHAPTER XIII

Rybin came in, greeted her, and stroking his beard in a dignified manner and peeping into the room with his dark eyes, remarked:

"You used to let people into your house before, without inquiring who they were. Are you alone?"

"Yes."

"You are? I thought the Little Russian was here. I saw him to-day. The prison doesn't spoil a man. Stupidity, that's what spoils most of all."

He walked into the room, sat down and said to the mother:

"Let's have a talk together. I have something to tell you. I have a theory!" There was a significant and mysterious expression in his face as he said this. It filled the mother with a sense of foreboding. She sat down opposite him and waited in mute anxiety for him to speak.

"Everything costs money!" he began in his gruff, heavy voice. "It takes money to be born; it takes money to die. Books and leaflets cost money, too. Now, then, do you know where all this money for the books comes from?"

"No, I don't know," replied the mother in a low voice, anticipating danger.

"Nor do I! Another question I've got to ask is: Who writes those books? The educated folks. The masters!" Rybin spoke curtly and decisively, his voice grew gruffer and gruffer, and his bearded face reddened as with the strain of exertion. "Now, then, the masters write the books and distribute them. But the writings in the books are against these very masters. Now, tell me, why do they spend their money and their time to stir up the people against themselves? Eh?"

Nilovna blinked, then opened her eyes wide and exclaimed in fright:

"What do you think? Tell me."

"Aha!" exclaimed Rybin, turning in his chair like a bear. "There you are! When I reached that thought I was seized with a cold shiver, too."

"Now what is it? Tell me! Did you find out anything?"

"Deception! Fraud! I feel it. It's deception. I know nothing, but I feel sure there's deception in it. Yes! The masters are up to some clever trick, and I want nothing of it. I want the truth. I understand what it is; I understand it. But I will not go hand in hand with the masters. They'll push me to the front when it suits them, and then walk over my bones as over a bridge to get where they want to."

At the sound of his morose words, uttered in a stubborn, thick, and forceful voice, the mother's heart contracted in pain.

"Good Lord!" she exclaimed in anguish. "Where is the truth? Can it be that Pavel does not understand? And all those who come here from the city—is it possible that they don't understand?" The serious, honest faces of Yegor, Nikolay Ivanovich, and Sashenka passed before her mind, and her heart fluttered.

"No, no!" she said, shaking her head as if to dismiss the thought. "I can't believe it. They are for truth and honor and conscience; they have no evil designs; oh, no!"

"Whom are you talking about?" asked Rybin thoughtfully.

"About all of them! Every single one I met. They are not the people who will traffic in human blood, oh, no!" Perspiration burst out on her face, and her fingers trembled.

"You are not looking in the right place, mother; look farther back," said Rybin, drooping his head. "Those who are directly working in the movement may not know anything about it themselves. They think it must be so; they have the truth at heart. But there may be people behind them who are looking out only for their own selfish interests. Men won't go against themselves." And with the firm conviction of a peasant fed on centuries of distrust, he added: "No good will ever come from the masters! Take my word for it!"

"What concoction has your brain put together?" the mother asked, again seized with anxious misgiving.

"I?" Rybin looked at her, was silent for a while, then repeated: "Keep away from the masters! That's what!" He grew morosely silent again, and seemed to shrink within himself.

"I'll go away, mother," he said after a pause. "I wanted to join the fellows, to work along with them. I'm fit for the work. I can read and write. I'm persevering and not a fool. And the main thing is, I know what to say to people. But now I will go. I can't believe, and therefore I must go. I know, mother, that the people's souls are foul and besmirched. All live on envy, all want to gorge themselves; and since there's little to eat, each seeks to eat the other up."

He let his head droop, and remained absorbed in thought for a while. Finally he said:

"I'll go all by myself through village and hamlet and stir the people up. It's necessary that the people should take the matter in their own hands and get to work themselves. Let them but understand—they'll find a way themselves. And so, I'm going to try to make them understand. There is no hope for them except in themselves; there's no understanding for them except in their own understanding! And that's the truth!"

"They will seize you!" said the mother in a low voice.

"They will seize me, and let me out again. And then I'll go ahead again!"

"The peasants themselves will bind you, and you will be thrown into jail."

"Well, I'll stay in jail for a time, then be released, and I'll go on again. As for the peasants, they'll bind me once, twice, and then they will understand that they ought not to bind me, but listen to me. I'll tell them: "I don't ask you to believe me; I want you just to listen to me!" And if they listen, they will believe."

Both the mother and Rybin spoke slowly, as if testing every word before uttering it.

"There's little joy for me in this, mother," said Rybin. "I have lived here of late, and gobbled up a deal of stuff. Yes; I understand some, too! And now I feel as if I were burying a child."

"You'll perish, Mikhaïl Ivanych!" said the mother, shaking her head sadly.

His dark, deep eyes looked at her with a questioning, expectant look. His powerful body bent forward, propped by his hands resting on the seat of the chair, and his swarthy face seemed pale in the black frame of his beard.

"Did you hear what Christ said about the seed? 'Thou shalt not die, but rise to life again in the new ear.' I don't regard myself as near death at all. I am shrewd. I follow a straighter course than the others. You can get further that way. Only, you see, I feel sorry—I don't know why." He fidgeted on his chair, then slowly rose. "I'll go to the tavern and be with the people a while. The Little Russian is not coming. Has he gotten busy already?"

"Yes!" The mother smiled. "No sooner out of prison than they rush to their work."

"That's the way it should be. Tell him about me."

They walked together slowly into the kitchen, and without looking at each other exchanged brief remarks:

"I'll tell him," she promised.

"Well, good-by!"

"Good-by! When do you quit your job?"

"I have already."

"When are you going?"

"To-morrow, early in the morning. Good-by!"

He bent his head and crawled off the porch reluctantly, it seemed, and clumsily. The mother stood for a moment at the door listening to the heavy departing footsteps and to the doubts that stirred in her heart. Then she noiselessly turned away into the room, and drawing the curtain peered through the window. Black darkness stood behind, motionless, waiting, gaping, with its flat, abysmal mouth.

"I live in the night!" she thought. "In the night forever!" She felt a pity for the black-bearded, sedate peasant. He was so broad and strong—and yet there was a certain helplessness about him, as about all the people.

Presently Andrey came in gay and vivacious. When the mother told him about Rybin, he exclaimed:

"Going, is he? Well, let him go through the villages. Let him ring forth the word of truth. Let him arouse the people. It's hard for him here with us."

"He was talking about the masters. Is there anything in it?" she inquired circumspectly. "Isn't it possible that they want to deceive you?"

"It bothers you, mother, doesn't it?" The Little Russian laughed. "Oh, mother dear—money! If we only had money! We are still living on charity. Take, for instance, Nikolay Ivanych. He earns seventy-five rubles a month, and gives us fifty! And others do the same. And the hungry students send us money sometimes, which they collect penny by penny. And as to the masters, of course there are different kinds among them. Some of them will deceive us, and some will leave us; but the best will stay with us and march with us up to our holiday." He clapped his hands, and rubbing them vigorously against each other continued: "But not even the flight of an eagle's wings will enable anyone to reach that holiday, so we'll make a little one for the first of May. It will be jolly."

His words and his vivacity dispelled the alarm excited in the mother's heart by Rybin. The Little Russian walked up and down the room, his feet sounding on the floor. He rubbed his head with one hand and his chest with the other, and spoke looking at the floor:

"You know, sometimes you have a wonderful feeling living in your heart. It seems to you that wherever you go, all men are comrades; all burn with one and the same fire; all are merry; all are good. Without words they all understand one another; and no one wants to hinder or insult the other. No one feels the need of it. All live in unison, but each heart sings its own song. And the songs flow like brooks into one stream, swelling into a huge river of bright joys, rolling free and wide down its course. And when you think that this will be—that it cannot help being if we so wish it—then the wonderstruck heart melts with joy. You feel like weeping—you feel so happy."

He spoke and looked as if he were searching something within himself. The mother listened and tried not to stir, so as not to disturb him and interrupt his speech. She always listened to him with more attention than to anybody else. He spoke more simply than all the rest, and his words gripped her heart more powerfully. Pavel, too, was probably looking to the future. How could it be otherwise, when one is following such a course of life? But when he looked into the remote future it was always by himself; he never spoke of what he saw. This Little Russian, however, it seemed to her, was always there with a part of his heart; the legend of the future holiday for all upon earth, always sounded in his speech. This legend rendered the meaning of her son's life, of his work, and that of all of his comrades, clear to the mother.

"And when you wake up," continued the Little Russian, tossing his head and letting his hands drop alongside his body, "and look around, you see it's all filthy and cold. All are tired and angry; human life is all churned up like mud on a busy highway, and trodden underfoot!"

He stopped in front of the mother, and with deep sorrow in his eyes, and shaking his head, added in a low, sad voice:

"Yes, it hurts, but you must—you must distrust man; you must fear him, and even hate him! Man is divided, he is cut in two by life. You'd like only to love him; but how is it possible? How can you forgive a man if he goes against you like a wild beast, does not recognize that there is a living soul in you, and kicks your face—a human face! You must not forgive. It's not for yourself that you mustn't. I'd stand all the insults as far as I myself am concerned; but I don't want to show indulgence for insults. I don't want to let them learn on my back how to beat others!"

His eyes now sparkled with a cold gleam; he inclined his head doggedly, and continued in a more resolute tone:

"I must not forgive anything that is noxious, even though it does not hurt! I'm not alone in the world. If I allow myself to be insulted to-day—maybe I can afford to laugh at the insult, maybe it doesn't sting me at all—but, having tested his strength on me, the offender will proceed to flay some one else the next day! That's why one is compelled to discriminate between people, to keep a firm grip on one's heart, and to classify mankind—these belong to me, those are strangers."

The mother thought of the officer and Sashenka, and said with a sigh:

"What sort of bread can you expect from unbolted meal?"

"That's it; that's the trouble!" the Little Russian exclaimed. "You must look with two kinds of eyes; two hearts throb in your bosom. The one loves all; the other says: 'Halt! You mustn't!'"

The figure of her husband, somber and ponderous, like a huge moss-covered stone, now rose in her memory. She made a mental image for herself of the Little Russian as married to Natasha, and her son as the husband of Sashenka.

"And why?" asked the Little Russian, warming up. "It's so plainly evident that it's downright ridiculous—simply because men don't stand on an equal footing. Then let's equalize them, put them all in one row! Let's divide equally all that's produced by the brains and all that's made by the hands. Let's not keep one another in the slavery of fear and envy, in the thraldom of greed and stupidity!"

The mother and the Little Russian now began to carry on such conversations with each other frequently. He was again taken into the factory. He turned over all his earnings to the mother, and she took the money from him with as little fuss as from Pavel. Sometimes Andrey would suggest with a twinkle in his eyes:

"Shall we read a little, mother, eh?"

She would invariably refuse, playfully but resolutely. The twinkle in his eyes discomfited her, and she thought to herself, with a slight feeling of offense: "If you laugh at me, then why do you ask me to read with you?"

He noticed that the mother began to ask him with increasing frequency for the meaning of this or that book word. She always looked aside when asking for such information, and spoke in a monotonous tone of indifference. He divined that she was studying by herself in secret, understood her bashfulness, and ceased to invite her to read with him. Shortly afterwards she said to him:

"My eyes are getting weak, Andriusha. I guess I need glasses."

"All right! Next Sunday I'll take you to a physician in the city, a friend of mine, and you shall have glasses!"

She had already been three times in the prison to ask for a meeting with Pavel, and each time the general of the gendarmes, a gray old man with purple cheeks and a huge nose, turned her gently away.

"In about a week, little mother, not before! A week from now we shall see, but at present it's impossible!"

He was a round, well-fed creature, and somehow reminded her of a ripe plum, somewhat spoiled by too long keeping, and already covered with a downy mold. He kept constantly picking his small, white teeth with a sharp yellow toothpick. There was a little smile in his small greenish eyes, and his voice had a friendly, caressing sound.

"Polite!" said the mother to the Little Russian with a thoughtful air. "Always with a smile on him. I don't think it's right. When a man is tending to affairs like these, I don't think he ought to grin."

"Yes, yes. They are so gentle, always smiling. If they should be told: 'Look here, this man is honest and wise, he is dangerous to us; hang him!' they would still smile and hang him, and keep on smiling."

"The one who made the search in our place is the better of the two; he is simpler. You can see at once that he is a dog."

"None of them are human beings; they are used to stun the people and render them insensible. They are tools, the means wherewith our kind is rendered more convenient to the state. They themselves have already been so fixed that they have become convenient instruments in the hand that governs us. They can do whatever they are told to do without thought, without asking why it is necessary to do it."

At last Vlasova got permission to see her son, and one Sunday she was sitting modestly in a corner of the prison office, a low, narrow, dingy apartment, where a few more people were sitting and waiting for permission to see their relatives and friends. Evidently it was not the first time they were here, for they knew one another and in a low voice kept up a lazy, languid conversation.

"Have you heard?" said a stout woman with a wizened face and a traveling bag on her lap. "At early mass to-day the church regent again ripped up the ear of one of the choir boys."

An elderly man in the uniform of a retired soldier coughed aloud and remarked:

"These choir boys are such loafers!"

A short, bald, little man with short legs, long arms, and protruding jaw, ran officiously up and down the room. Without stopping he said in a cracked, agitated voice:

"The cost of living is getting higher and higher. An inferior quality of beef, fourteen cents; bread has again risen to two and a half."

Now and then prisoners came into the room—gray, monotonous, with coarse, heavy, leather shoes. They blinked as they entered; iron chains rattled at the feet of one of them. The quiet and calm and simplicity all around produced a strange, uncouth impression. It seemed as if all had grown accustomed to their situation. Some sat there quietly, others looked on idly, while still others seemed to pay their regular visits with a sense of weariness. The mother's heart quivered with impatience, and she looked with a puzzled air at everything around her, amazed at the oppressive simplicity of life in this corner of the world.

Next to Vlasova sat a little old woman with a wrinkled face, but youthful eyes. She kept her thin neck turned to listen to the conversation, and looked about on all sides with a strange expression of eagerness in her face.

"Whom have you here?" Vlasova asked softly.

"A son, a student," answered the old woman in a loud, brusque voice. "And you?"

"A son, also. A workingman."

"What's the name?"

"Vlasov."

"Never heard of him. How long has he been in prison?"

"Seven weeks."

"And mine has been in for ten months," said the old woman, with a strange note of pride in her voice which did not escape the notice of the mother.

A tall lady dressed in black, with a thin, pale face, said lingeringly:

"They'll soon put all the decent people in prison. They can't endure them, they loathe them!"

"Yes, yes!" said the little old bald man, speaking rapidly. "All patience is disappearing. Everybody is excited; everybody is clamoring, and prices are mounting higher and higher. As a consequence the value of men is depreciating. And there is not a single, conciliatory voice heard, not one!"

"Perfectly true!" said the retired military man. "It's monstrous! What's wanted is a voice, a firm voice to cry, 'Silence!' Yes, that's what we want—a firm voice!"

The conversation became more general and animated. Everybody was in a hurry to give his opinion about life; but all spoke in a half-subdued voice, and the mother noticed a tone of hostility in all, which was new to her. At home they spoke differently, more intelligibly, more simply, and more loudly.

The fat warden with a square red beard called out her name, looked her over from head to foot, and telling her to follow him, walked off limping. She followed him, and felt like pushing him to make him go faster. Pavel stood in a small room, and on seeing his mother smiled and put out his hand to her. She grasped it, laughed, blinked swiftly, and at a loss for words merely asked softly:

"How are you? How are you?"

"Compose yourself, mother." Pavel pressed her hand.

"It's all right! It's all right!"

"Mother," said the warden, fetching a sigh, "suppose you move away from each other a bit. Let there be some distance between you." He yawned aloud.

Pavel asked the mother about her health and about home. She waited for some other questions, sought them in her son's eyes, but could not find them. He was calm as usual, although his face had grown paler, and his eyes seemed larger.

"Sasha sends you her regards," she said. Pavel's eyelids quivered and fell. His face became softer and brightened with a clear, open smile. A poignant bitterness smote the mother's heart.

"Will they let you out soon?" she inquired in a tone of sudden injury and agitation. "Why have they put you in prison? Those papers and pamphlets have appeared in the factory again, anyway."

Pavel's eyes flashed with delight.

"Have they? When? Many of them?"

"It is forbidden to talk about this subject!" the warden lazily announced. "You may talk only of family matters."

"And isn't this a family matter?" retorted the mother.

"I don't know. I only know it's forbidden. You may talk about his wash and underwear and food, but nothing else!" insisted the warden, his voice, however, expressing utter indifference.

"All right," said Pavel. "Keep to domestic affairs, mother. What are you doing?"

She answered boldly, seized with youthful ardor:

"I carry all this to the factory." She paused with a smile and continued: "Sour soup, gruel, all Marya's cookery, and other stuff."

Pavel understood. The muscles of his face quivered with restrained laughter. He ran his fingers through his hair and said in a tender tone, such as she had never heard him use:

"My own dear mother! That's good! It's good you've found something to do, so it isn't tedious for you. You don't feel lonesome, do you, mother?"

"When the leaflets appeared, they searched me, too," she said, not without a certain pride.

"Again on this subject!" said the warden in an offended tone. "I tell you it's forbidden, it's not allowed. They have deprived him of liberty so that he shouldn't know anything about it; and here you are with your news. You ought to know it's forbidden!"

"Well, leave it, mother," said Pavel. "Matvey Ivanovich is a good man. You mustn't do anything to provoke him. We get along together very well. It's by chance he's here to-day with us. Usually, it's the assistant superintendent who is present on such occasions. That's why Matvey Ivanovich is afraid you will say something you oughtn't to."

"Time's up!" announced the warden looking at his watch. "Take your leave!"

"Well, thank you," said Pavel. "Thank you, my darling mother! Don't worry now. They'll let me out soon."

He embraced her, pressed her warmly to his bosom, and kissed her. Touched by his endearments, and happy, she burst into tears.

"Now separate!" said the warden, and as he walked off with the mother he mumbled:

"Don't cry! They'll let him out; they'll let everybody out. It's too crowded here."

At home the mother told the Little Russian of her conversation with Pavel, and her face wore a broad smile.

"I told him! Yes, indeed! And cleverly, too. He understood!" and, heaving a melancholy sigh: "Oh, yes, he understood; otherwise he wouldn't have been so tender and affectionate. He has never been that way before."

"Oh, mother!" the Little Russian laughed. "No matter what other people may want, a mother always wants affection. You certainly have a heart plenty big enough for one man!"

"But those people! Just think, Andriusha!" she suddenly exclaimed, amazement in her tone. "How used they get to all this!

Their children are taken away from them, are thrown into dungeons, and, mind you, it's as nothing to them! They come, sit about, wait, and talk. What do you think of that? If intelligent people are that way, if they can so easily get accustomed to a thing like that, then what's to be said about the common people?"

"That's natural," said the Little Russian with his usual smile. "The law after all is not so harsh toward them as toward us. And they need the law more than we do. So that when the law hits them on the head, although they cry out they do not cry very loud. Your own stick does not fall upon you so heavily. For them the laws are to some extent a protection, but for us they are only chains to keep us bound so we can't kick."

Three days afterwards in the evening, when the mother sat at the table knitting stockings and the Little Russian was reading to her from a book about the revolt of the Roman slaves, a loud knock was heard at the door. The Little Russian went to open it and admitted Vyesovshchikov with a bundle under his arm, his hat pushed back on his head, and mud up to his knees.

"I was passing by, and seeing a light in your house, I dropped in to ask you how you are. I've come straight from the prison."

He spoke in a strange voice. He seized Vlasov's hand and wrung it violently as he added: "Pavel sends you his regards." Irresolutely seating himself in a chair he scanned the room with his gloomy, suspicious look.

The mother was not fond of him. There was something in his angular, close-cropped head and in his small eyes that always scared her; but now she was glad to see him, and with a broad smile lighting her face she said in a tender, animated voice:

"How thin you've become! Say, Andriusha, let's dose him with tea."

"I'm putting up the samovar already!" the Little Russian called from the kitchen.

"How is Pavel? Have they let anybody else out besides yourself?"

Nikolay bent his head and answered:

"I'm the only one they've let go." He raised his eyes to the mother's face and said slowly, speaking through his teeth with ponderous emphasis: "I told them: 'Enough! Let me go! Else I'll kill some one here, and myself, too!' So they let me go!"

"Hm, hm—ye-es," said the mother, recoiling from him and involuntarily blinking when her gaze met his sharp, narrow eyes.

"And how is Fedya Mazin?" shouted the Little Russian from the kitchen. "Writing poetry, is he?"

"Yes! I don't understand it," said Nikolay, shaking his head. "They've put him in a cage and he sings. There's only one thing I'm sure about, and that is I have no desire to go home."

"Why should you want to go home? What's there to attract you?" said the mother pensively. "It's empty, there's no fire burning, and it's chilly all over."

Vyesovshchikov sat silent, his eyes screwed up. Taking a box of cigarettes from his pocket he leisurely lit one of them, and looking at the gray curl of smoke dissolve before him he grinned like a big, surly dog.

"Yes, I guess it's cold. And the floor is filled with frozen cockroaches, and even the mice are frozen, too, I suppose. Pelagueya Nilovna, will you let me sleep here to-night, please?" he asked hoarsely without looking at her.

"Why, of course, Nikolay! You needn't even ask it!" the mother quickly replied. She felt embarrassed and ill at ease in Nikolay's presence, and did not know what to speak to him about. But he himself went on to talk in a strangely broken voice.

"We live in a time when children are ashamed of their own parents."

"What!" exclaimed the mother, starting.

He glanced up at her and closed his eyes. His pockmarked face looked like that of a blind man.

"I say that children have to be ashamed of their parents," he repeated, sighing aloud. "Now, don't you be afraid. It's not meant for you. Pavel will never be ashamed of you. But I am ashamed of my father, and shall never enter his house again. I have no father, no home! They have put me under the surveillance of the police, else I'd go to Siberia. I think a man who won't spare himself could do a great deal in Siberia. I would free convicts there and arrange for their escape."

The mother understood, with her ready feelings, what agony this man must be undergoing, but his pain awoke no sympathetic response in her.

"Well, of course, if that's the case, then it's better for you to go," she said, in order not to offend him by silence.

Andrey came in from the kitchen, and said, smiling:

"Well, are you sermonizing, eh?"

The mother rose and walked away, saying:

"I'm going to get something to eat."

Vyesovshchikov looked at the Little Russian fixedly and suddenly declared:

"I think that some people ought to be killed off!"

"Oho! And pray what for?" asked the Little Russian calmly.

"So they cease to be."

"Ahem! And have you the right to make corpses out of living people?"

"Yes, I have."

"Where did you get it from?"

"The people themselves gave it to me."

The Little Russian stood in the middle of the room, tall and spare, swaying on his legs, with his hands thrust in his pockets, and looked down on Nikolay. Nikolay sat firmly in his chair, enveloped in clouds of smoke, with red spots on his face showing through.

"The people gave it to me!" he repeated clenching his fist. "If they kick me I have the right to strike them and punch their eyes out! Don't touch me, and I won't touch you! Let me live as I please, and I'll live in peace and not touch anybody. Maybe I'd prefer to live in the woods. I'd build myself a cabin in the ravine by the brook and live there. At any rate, I'd live alone."

"Well, go and live that way, if it pleases you," said the Little Russian, shrugging his shoulders.

"Now?" asked Nikolay. He shook his head in negation and replied, striking his fist on his knee:

"Now it's impossible!"

"Who's in your way?"

"The people!" Vyesovshchikov retorted brusquely. "I'm hitched to them even unto death. They've hedged my heart around with hatred and tied me to themselves with evil. That's a strong tie! I hate them, and I will not go away; no, never! I'll be in their way. I'll harass their lives. They are in my way, I'll be in theirs. I'll answer only for myself, only for myself, and for no one else. And if my father is a thief—"

"Oh!" said the Little Russian in a low voice, moving up to Nikolay.

"And as for Isay Gorbov, I'll wring his head off! You shall see!"

"What for?" asked the Little Russian in a quiet, earnest voice.

"He shouldn't be a spy; he shouldn't go about denouncing people. It's through him my father's gone to the dogs, and it's owing to him that he now is aiming to become a spy," said Vyesovshchikov, looking at Andrey with a dark, hostile scowl.

"Oh, that's it!" exclaimed the Little Russian. "And pray, who'd blame you for that? Fools!"

"Both the fools and the wise are smeared with the same oil!" said Nikolay heavily. "Here are you a wise fellow, and Pavel, too. And do you mean to say that I am the same to you as Fedya Mazin or Samoylov, or as you two are to each other? Don't lie! I won't believe you, anyway. You all push me aside to a place apart, all by myself."

"Your heart is aching, Nikolay!" said the Little Russian softly and tenderly sitting down beside him.

"Yes, it's aching, and so is your heart. But your aches seem nobler to you than mine. We are all scoundrels toward one another, that's what I say. And what have you to say to that?"

He fixed his sharp gaze on Andrey, and waited with set teeth. His mottled face remained immobile, and a quiver passed over his thick lips, as if scorched by a flame.

"I have nothing to say!" said the Little Russian, meeting Vyesovshchikov's hostile glance with a bright, warm, yet melancholy look of his blue eyes. "I know that to argue with a man at a time when all the wounds of his heart are bleeding, is only to insult him. I know it, brother."

"It's impossible to argue with me; I can't," mumbled Nikolay, lowering his eyes.

"I think," continued the Little Russian, "that each of us has gone through that, each of us has walked with bare feet over broken glass, each of us in his dark hour has gasped for breath as you are now."

"You have nothing to tell me!" said Vyesovshchikov slowly. "Nothing! My heart is so—it seems to me as if wolves were howling there!"

"And I don't want to say anything to you. Only I know that you'll get over this, perhaps not entirely, but you'll get over it!" He smiled, and added, tapping Nikolay on the back: "Why, man, this is a children's disease, something like measles! We all suffer from it, the strong less, the weak more. It comes upon a man at the period when he has found himself, but does not yet understand life, and his own place in life. And when you do not see your place, and are unable to appraise your own value, it seems that you are the only, the inimitable cucumber on the face of the earth, and that no one can measure, no one can fathom your worth, and that all are eager only to eat you up. After a while you'll find out that the hearts in other people's breasts are no worse than a good part of your own heart, and you'll begin to feel better. And somewhat ashamed, too! Why should you climb up to the belfry tower, when your bell is so small that it can't be heard in the great peal of the holiday bells? Moreover, you'll see that in chorus the sound of your bell will be heard, too, but by itself the old church bells will drown it in their rumble as a fly is drowned in oil. Do you understand what I am saying?"

"Maybe I understand," Nikolay said, nodding his head. "Only I don't believe it."

The Little Russian broke into a laugh, jumped to his feet, and began to run noisily up and down the room.

"I didn't believe it either. Ah, you—wagonload!"

"Why a wagonload?" Nikolay asked with a sad smile, looking at the Little Russian.

"Because there's a resemblance!"

Suddenly Nikolay broke into a loud guffaw, his mouth opening wide.

"What is it?" the Little Russian asked in surprise, stopping in front of him.

"It struck me that he'd be a fool who'd want to insult you!" Nikolay declared, shaking his head.

"Why, how can you insult me?" asked the Little Russian, shrugging his shoulders.

"I don't know," said Vyesovshchikov, grinning good-naturedly or perhaps condescendingly. "I only wanted to say that a man must feel mighty ashamed of himself after he'd insulted you."

"There now! See where you got to!" laughed the Little Russian.

"Andriusha!" the mother called from the kitchen. "Come get the samovar. It's ready!"

Andrey walked out of the room, and Vyesovshchikov, left alone, looked about, stretched out his foot sheathed in a coarse, heavy boot, looked at it, bent down, and felt the stout calf of his legs. Then he raised one hand to his face, carefully examined the palm, and turned it around. His short-fingered hand was thick, and covered with yellowish hair. He waved it in the air, and arose.

When Andrey brought in the samovar, Vyesovshchikov was standing before the mirror, and greeted him with these words:

"It's a long time since I've seen my face." Then he laughed and added: "It's an ugly face I have!"

"What's that to you?" asked Andrey, turning a curious look upon him.

"Sashenka says the face is the mirror of the heart!" Nikolay replied, bringing out the words slowly.

"It's not true, though!" the little Russian ejaculated. "She has a nose like a mushroom, cheek bones like a pair of scissors; yet her heart is like a bright little star."

They sat down to drink tea.

Vyesovshchikov took a big potato, heavily salted a slice of bread, and began to chew slowly and deliberately, like an ox.

"And how are matters here?" he asked, with his mouth full.

When Andrey cheerfully recounted to him the growth of the socialist propaganda in the factory, he again grew morose and remarked dully:

"It takes too long! Too long, entirely! It ought to go faster!"

The mother regarded him, and was seized with a feeling of hostility toward this man.

"Life is not a horse; you can't set it galloping with a whip," said Andrey.

But Vyesovshchikov stubbornly shook his head, and proceeded:

"It's slow! I haven't the patience. What am I to do?" He opened his arms in a gesture of helplessness, and waited for a response.

"We all must learn and teach others. That's our business!" said Andrey, bending his head.

Vyesovshchikov asked:

"And when are we going to fight?"

"There'll be more than one butchery of us up to that time, that I know!" answered the Little Russian with a smile. "But when we shall be called on to fight, that I don't know! First, you see, we must equip the head, and then the hand. That's what I think."

"The heart!" said Nikolay laconically.

"And the heart, too."

Nikolay became silent, and began to eat again. From the corner of her eye the mother stealthily regarded his broad, pockmarked face, endeavoring to find something in it to reconcile her to the unwieldy, square figure of Vyesovshchikov. Her eyebrows fluttered whenever she encountered the shooting glance of his little eyes. Andrey held his head in his hands; he became restless—he suddenly laughed, and then abruptly stopped, and began to whistle.

It seemed to the mother that she understood his disquietude. Nikolay sat at the table without saying anything; and when the Little Russian addressed a question to him, he answered briefly, with evident reluctance.

The little room became too narrow and stifling for its two occupants, and they glanced, now the one, now the other, at their guest.

At length Nikolay rose and said: "I'd like to go to bed. I sat and sat in prison—suddenly they let me go; I'm off!—I'm tired!"

He went into the kitchen and stirred about for a while. Then a sudden stillness settled down. The mother listened for a sound, and whispered to Andrey: "He has something terrible in his mind!"

"Yes, he's hard to understand!" the Little Russian assented, shaking his head. "But you go to bed, mother, I am going to stay and read a while."

She went to the corner where the bed was hidden from view by chintz curtains. Andrey, sitting at the table, for a long while listened to the warm murmur of her prayers and sighs. Quickly turning the pages of the book Andrey nervously rubbed his lips, twitched his mustache with his long fingers, and scraped his feet on the floor. Ticktock, ticktock went the pendulum of the clock; and the wind moaned as it swept past the window.

Then the mother's low voice was heard:

"Oh, God! How many people there are in the world, and each one wails in his own way. Where, then, are those who feel rejoiced?"

"Soon there will be such, too, soon!" announced the Little Russian.

CHAPTER XIV

Life flowed on swiftly. The days were diversified and full of color. Each one brought with it something new, and the new ceased to alarm the mother. Strangers came to the house in the evening more and more frequently, and they talked with Andrey in subdued voices with an engrossed air. Late at night they went out into the darkness, their collars up, their hats thrust low over their faces, noiselessly, cautiously. All seemed to feel a feverish excitement, which they kept under restraint, and had the air of wanting to sing and laugh if they only had the time. They were all in a perpetual hurry. All of them—the mocking and the serious, the frank, jovial youth with effervescing strength, the thoughtful and quiet—all of them in the eyes of the mother were identical in the persistent faith that characterized them; and although each had his own peculiar cast of countenance, for her all their faces blended into one thin, composed, resolute face with a profound expression in its dark eyes, kind yet stern, like the look in Christ's eyes on his way to Emmaus.

The mother counted them, and mentally gathered them together into a group around Pavel. In that throng he became invisible to the eyes of the enemy.

One day a vivacious, curly-haired girl appeared from the city, bringing some parcel for Andrey; and on leaving she said to Vlasova, with a gleam in her merry eyes:

"Good-by, comrade!"

"Good-by!" the mother answered, restraining a smile. After seeing the girl to the door, she walked to the window and, smiling, looked out on the street to watch her comrade as she trotted away, nimbly raising and dropping her little feet, fresh as a spring flower and light as a butterfly.

"Comrade!" said the mother when her guest had disappeared from her view. "Oh, you dear! God grant you a comrade for all your life!"

She often noticed in all the people from the city a certain childishness, for which she had the indulgent smile of an elderly person; but at the same time she was touched and joyously surprised by their faith, the profundity of which she began to realize more and more clearly. Their visions of the triumph of justice captivated her and warmed her heart. As she listened to their recital of future victories, she involuntarily sighed with an unknown sorrow. But what touched her above all was their simplicity, their beautiful, grand, generous unconcern for themselves.

She had already come to understand a great deal of what was said about life. She felt they had in reality discovered the true source of the people's misfortune, and it became a habit with her to agree with their thoughts. But at the bottom of her heart she did not believe that they could remake the whole of life according to their idea, or that they would have strength enough to gather all the working people about their fire. Everyone, she knew, wants to fill his stomach to-day, and no one wants to put his dinner off even for a week, if he can eat it up at once. Not many would consent to travel the long and difficult road; and not all eyes could see at the end the promised kingdom where all men are brothers. That's why all these good people, despite their beards and worn faces, seemed to her mere children.

"My dear ones!" she thought, shaking her head.

But they all now lived a good, earnest, and sensible life; they all spoke of the common weal; and in their desire to teach other people what they knew, they did not spare themselves. She understood that it was possible to love such a life, despite its dangers; and with a sigh she looked back to bygone days in which her past dragged along flatly and monotonously, a thin, black thread. Imperceptibly she grew conscious of her usefulness in this new life—a consciousness that gave her poise and assurance. She had never before felt herself necessary to anybody. When she had lived with her husband, she knew that if she died he would marry another woman. It was all the same to him whether a dark-haired or a red-haired woman lived with him and prepared his meals. When Pavel grew up and began to run about in the street, she saw that she was not needed by him. But now she felt that she was helping a good work. It was new to her and pleasant. It set her head erect on her shoulders.

She considered it her duty to carry the books regularly to the factory. Indeed, she elaborated a number of devices for escaping detection. The spies, grown accustomed to her presence on the factory premises, ceased to pay attention to her. She was searched several times, but always the day after the appearance of the leaflets in the factory. When she had no literature about her, she knew how to arouse the suspicion of the guards and spies. They would halt her, and she would pretend to feel insulted, and would remonstrate with them, and then walk off blushing, proud of her clever ruse. She began to enjoy the fun of the game.

Vyesovshchikov was not taken back to the factory, and went to work for a lumberman. The whole day long he drove about the village with a pair of black horses pulling planks and beams after them. The mother saw him almost daily with the horses as they plodded along the road, their feet trembling under the strain and dropping heavily upon the ground. They were both old and bareboned, their heads shook wearily and sadly, and their dull, jaded eyes blinked heavily. Behind them jerkingly trailed a long beam, or a pile of boards clattering loudly. And by their side Nikolay trudged along, holding the slackened reins in his hand, ragged, dirty, with heavy boots, his hat thrust back, uncouth as a stump just turned up from the ground. He, too, shook his head and looked down at his feet, refusing to see anything. His horses blindly ran into the people and wagons going the opposite direction. Angry oaths buzzed about him like hornets, and sinister shouts rent the air. He did not raise his head, did not answer them, but went on, whistling a sharp, shrill whistle, mumbling dully to the horses.

Every time that Andrey's comrades gathered at the mother's house to read pamphlets or the new issue of the foreign papers, Nikolay came also, sat down in a corner, and listened in silence for an hour or two. When the reading was over the young people entered into long discussions; but Vyesovshchikov took no part in the arguments. He remained longer than the rest, and when alone, face to face with Andrey, he glumly put to him the question:

"And who is the most to blame? The Czar?"

"The one to blame is he who first said: 'This is mine.' That man has now been dead some several thousand years, and it's not worth the while to bear him a grudge," said the Little Russian, jesting. His eyes, however, had a perturbed expression.

"And how about the rich, and those who stand up for them? Are they right?"

The Little Russian clapped his hands to his head; then pulled his mustache, and spoke for a long time in simple language about life and about the people. But from his talk it always appeared as if all the people were to blame, and this did not satisfy Nikolay. Compressing his thick lips tightly, he shook his head in demur, and declared that he could not believe it was so, and that he did not understand it. He left dissatisfied and gloomy. Once he said:

"No, there must be people to blame! I'm sure there are! I tell you, we must plow over the whole of life like a weedy field, showing no mercy!"

"That's what Isay, the record clerk, once said about us!" the mother said. For a while the two were silent.

"Isay?"

"Yes, he's a bad man. He spies after everybody, fishes about everywhere for information. He has begun to frequent this street, and peers into our windows."

"Peers into your windows?"

The mother was already in bed and did not see his face. But she understood that she had said too much, because the Little Russian hastened to interpose in order to conciliate Nikolay.

"Let him peer! He has leisure. That's his way of killing time."

"No hold on!" said Nikolay. "*There!* He is to blame!"

"To blame for what?" the Little Russian asked brusquely. "Because he's a fool?"

But Vyesovshchikov did not stop to answer and walked away.

The Little Russian began to pace up and down the room, slowly and languidly. He had taken off his boots as he always did when the mother was in bed in order not to disturb her. But she was not asleep, and when Nikolay had left she said anxiously:

"I'm so afraid of that man. He's just like an overheated oven. He does not warm things, but scorches them."

"Yes, yes!" the Little Russian drawled. "He's an irascible boy. I wouldn't talk to him about Isay, mother. That fellow Isay is really spying and getting paid for it, too."

"What's so strange in that? His godfather is a gendarme," observed the mother.

"Well, Nikolay will give him a dressing. What of it?" the Little Russian continued uneasily. "See what hard feelings the rulers of our life have produced in the rank and file? When such people as Nikolay come to recognize their wrong and lose their patience, what will happen then? The sky will be sprinkled with blood, and the earth will froth and foam with it like the suds of soap water."

"It's terrible, Andriusha!" the mother exclaimed in a low voice.

"They have swallowed flies, and have to vomit them now!" said Andrey after a pause. "And after all, mother, every drop of their blood that may be shed will have been washed in seas of the people's tears."

Suddenly he broke into a low laugh and added:

"That's true; but it's no comfort!"

Once on a holiday the mother, on returning home from a store, opened the door of the porch, and remained fixed to the spot, suddenly bathed in the sunshine of joy. From the room she heard the sound of Pavel's voice.

"There she is!" cried the Little Russian.

The mother saw Pavel turn about quickly, and saw how his face lighted up with a feeling that held out the promise of something great to her.

"There you are—come home!" she mumbled, staggered by the unexpectedness of the event. She sat down.

He bent down to her with a pale face, little tears glistened brightly in the corners of his eyes, and his lips trembled. For a moment he was silent. The mother looked at him, and was silent also.

The Little Russian, whistling softly, passed by them with bent head and walked out into the yard.

"Thank you, mother," said Pavel in a deep, low voice, pressing her hand with his trembling fingers. "Thank you, my dear, my own mother!"

Rejoiced at the agitated expression of her son's face and the touching sound of his voice, she stroked his hair and tried to restrain the palpitation of her heart. She murmured softly:

"Christ be with you! What have I done for you? It isn't I who have made you what you are. It's you yourself—"

"Thank you for helping our great cause!" he said. "When a man can call his mother his own in spirit also—that's rare fortune!"

She said nothing, and greedily swallowed his words. She admired her son as he stood before her so radiant and so near.

"I was silent, mother dear. I saw that many things in my life hurt you. I was sorry for you, and yet I could not help it. I was powerless! I thought you could never get reconciled to us, that you could never adopt our ideas as yours, but that you would suffer in silence as you had suffered all your life long. It was hard."

"Andriusha made me understand many things!" she declared, in her desire to turn her son's attention to his comrade.

"Yes, he told me about you," said Pavel, laughing.

"And Yegor, too! He is a countryman of mine, you know. Andriusha wanted to teach me to read, also."

"And you got offended, and began to study by yourself in secret."

"Oh, so he found me out!" she exclaimed in embarrassment. Then troubled by this abundance of joy which filled her heart she again suggested to Pavel:

"Shan't we call him in? He went out on purpose, so as not to disturb us. He has no mother."

"Andrey!" shouted Pavel, opening the door to the porch. "Where are you?"

"Here. I want to chop some wood."

"Never mind! There's time enough! Come here!"

"All right! I'm coming!"

But he did not come at once; and on entering the kitchen he said in a housekeeper-like fashion:

"We must tell Nikolay to bring us wood. We have very little wood left. You see, mother, how well Pavel looks? Instead of punishing the rebels, the government only fattens them."

The mother laughed. Her heart was still leaping with joy. She was fairly intoxicated with happiness. But a certain, cautious, chary feeling already called forth in her the wish to see her son calm as he always was. She wanted this first joy in her life to remain fixed in her heart forever as live and strong as at first. In order to guard against the diminution of her happiness, she hastened to hide it, as a fowler secrets some rare bird that has happened to fall into his hands.

"Let's have dinner! Pasha, haven't you had anything to eat yet?" she asked with anxious haste.

"No. I learned yesterday from the warden that I was to be released, and I couldn't eat or drink anything to-day."

"The first person I met here was Sizov," Pavel communicated to Andrey. "He caught sight of me and crossed the street to greet me. I told him that he ought to be more careful now, as I was a dangerous man under the surveillance of the police. But he said: 'Never mind!' and you ought to have heard him inquire about his nephew! 'Did Fedor conduct himself properly in prison?' I wanted to know what is meant by proper behavior in prison, and he declared: 'Well, did he blab anything he shouldn't have against his comrades?' And when I told him that Fedya was an honest and wise young man, he stroked his beard and declared proudly: 'We, the Sizovs, have no trash in our family.'"

"He's a brainy old man!" said the Little Russian, nodding his head. "We often have talks with him. He's a fine peasant. Will they let Fedya out soon?"

"Yes, one of these days, I suppose. They'll let out all, I think. They have no evidence except Isay's, and what can he say?"

The mother walked up and down the room, and looked at her son. Andrey stood at the window with his hands clasped behind his back, listening to Pavel's narrative. Pavel also paced up and down the room. His beard had grown, and small ringlets of thin, dark hair curled in a dense growth around his cheeks, softening the swarthy color of his face. His dark eyes had their stern expression.

"Sit down!" said the mother, serving a hot dish.

At dinner Andrey told Pavel about Rybin. When he had concluded Pavel exclaimed regretfully:

"If I had been home, I would not have let him go that way. What did he take along with him? A feeling of discontent and a muddle in his head!"

"Well," said Andrey, laughing, "when a man's grown to the age of forty and has fought so long with the bears in his heart, it's hard to make him over."

Pavel looked at him sternly and asked:

"Do you think it's impossible for enlightenment to destroy all the rubbish that's been crammed into a man's brains?"

"Don't fly up into the air at once, Pavel! Your flight will knock you up against the belfry tower and break your wings," said the Little Russian in admonition.

And they started one of those discussions in which words were used that were unintelligible to the mother. The dinner was already at an end, but they still continued a vehement debate, flinging at each other veritable rattling hailstones of big words. Sometimes their language was simpler:

"We must keep straight on our path, turning neither to the right nor to the left!" Pavel asserted firmly.

"And run headlong into millions of people who will regard us as their enemies!"

"You can't avoid that!"

"And what, my dear sir, becomes of your enlightenment?"

The mother listened to the dispute, and understood that Pavel did not care for the peasants, but that the Little Russian stood up for them, and tried to show that the peasants, too, must be taught to comprehend the good. She understood Andrey better, and he seemed to her to be in the right; but every time he spoke she waited with strained ears and bated breath for her son's answer to find out whether the Little Russian had offended Pavel. But although they shouted at the top of their voices, they gave each other no offense.

Occasionally the mother asked:

"Is it so, Pavel?"

And he answered with a smile:

"Yes, it's so."

"Say, my dear sir," the Little Russian said with a good-natured sneer, "you have eaten well, but you have chewed your food up badly, and a piece has remained sticking in your throat. You had better gargle."

"Don't go fooling now!" said Pavel.

"I am as solemn as a funeral."

The mother laughed quietly and shook her head.

CHAPTER XV

Spring was rapidly drawing near; the snow melted and laid bare the mud and the soot of the factory chimneys. Mud, mud! Wherever the villagers looked—mud! Every day more mud! The entire village seemed unwashed and dressed in rags and tatters. During the day the water dripped monotonously from the roofs, and damp, weary exhalations emanated from the gray walls of the houses. Toward night whitish icicles glistened everywhere in dim outline. The sun appeared in the heavens more frequently, and the brooks began to murmur hesitatingly on their way to the marsh. At noon the throbbing song of spring hopes hung tremblingly and caressingly over the village.

They were preparing to celebrate the first of May. Leaflets appeared in the factory explaining the significance of this holiday, and even the young men not affected by the propaganda said, as they read them:

"Yes, we must arrange a holiday!"

Vyesovshchikov exclaimed with a sullen grin:

"It's time! Time we stopped playing hide and seek!"

Fedya Mazin was in high spirits. He had grown very thin. With his nervous, jerky gestures, and the trepidation in his speech, he was like a caged lark. He was always with Yakob Somov, taciturn and serious beyond his years.

Samoylov, who had grown still redder in prison, Vasily Gusev, curly-haired Dragunov, and a number of others argued that it was necessary to come out armed, but Pavel and the Little Russian, Somov, and others said it was not.

Yegor always came tired, perspiring, short of breath, but always joking.

"The work of changing the present order of things, comrades, is a great work, but in order to advance it more rapidly, I must buy myself a pair of boots!" he said, pointing to his wet, torn shoes. "My overshoes, too, are torn beyond the hope of redemption, and I get my feet wet every day. I have no intention of migrating from the earth even to the nearest planet before we have publicly and openly renounced the old order of things; and I am therefore absolutely opposed to comrade Samoylov's motion for an armed demonstration. I amend the motion to read that I be armed with a pair of strong boots, inasmuch as I am profoundly convinced that this will be of greater service for the ultimate triumph of socialism than even a grand exhibition of fisticuffs and black eyes!"

In the same playfully pretentious language, he told the workingmen the story of how in various foreign countries the people strove to lighten the burden of their lives. The mother loved to listen to his tales, and carried away a strange impression from them. She conceived the shrewdest enemies of the people, those who deceived them most frequently and most cruelly, as little, big-bellied, red-faced creatures, unprincipled and greedy, cunning and heartless. When life was hard for them under the domination of the czars, they would incite the common people against the ruler; and when the people arose and wrested the power from him, these little creatures got it into their own hands by deceit, and drove the people off to their holes; and if the people remonstrated, they killed them by the hundreds and thousands.

Once she summoned up courage and told him of the picture she had formed of life from his tales, and asked him:

"Is it so, Yegor Ivanovich?"

He burst into a guffaw, turned up his eyes, gasped for breath, and rubbed his chest.

"Exactly, granny! You caught the idea to a dot! Yes, yes! You've placed some ornaments on the canvas of history, you've added some flourishes, but that does not interfere with the correctness of the whole. It's these very little, pot-bellied creatures who are the chief sinners and deceivers and the most poisonous insects that harass the human race. The Frenchmen call them '*bourgeois.*' Remember that word, dear granny—*bourgeois*! Brr! How they chew us and grind us and suck the life out of us!"

"The rich, you mean?"

"Yes, the rich. And that's their misfortune. You see, if you keep adding copper bit by bit to a child's food, you prevent the growth of its bones, and he'll be a dwarf; and if from his youth up you poison a man with gold, you deaden his soul."

Once, speaking about Yegor, Pavel said:

"Do you know, Andrey, the people whose hearts are always aching are the ones who joke most?"

The Little Russian was silent a while, and then answered, blinking his eyes:

"No, that's not true. If it were, then the whole of Russia would split its sides with laughter."

Natasha made her appearance again. She, too, had been in prison, in another city, but she had not changed. The mother noticed that in her presence the Little Russian grew more cheerful, was full of jokes, poked fun at everybody, and kept her laughing merrily. But after she had left he would whistle his endless songs sadly, and pace up and down the room for a long time, wearily dragging his feet along the floor.

Sashenka came running in frequently, always gloomy, always in haste, and for some reason more and more angular and stiff. Once when Pavel accompanied her out onto the porch, the mother overheard their abrupt conversation.

"Will you carry the banner?" the girl asked in a low voice.

"Yes."

"Is it settled?"

"Yes, it's my right."

"To prison again?" Pavel was silent. "Is it not possible for you—" She stopped.

"What?"

"To give it up to somebody else?"

"No!" he said aloud.

"Think of it! You're a man of such influence; you are so much liked—you and Nakhodka are the two foremost revolutionary workers here. Think how much you could accomplish for the cause of freedom! You know that for this they'll send you off far, far, and for a long time!"

Nilovna thought she heard in the girl's voice the familiar sound of fear and anguish, and her words fell upon the mother's heart like heavy, icy drops of water.

"No, I have made up my mind. Nothing can make me give it up!"

"Not even if I beg you—if I—"

Pavel suddenly began to speak rapidly with a peculiar sternness. "You ought not to speak that way. Why you? You ought not!"

"I am a human being!" she said in an undertone.

"A good human being, too!" he said also in an undertone, and in a peculiar voice, as if unable to catch his breath. "You are a dear human being to me, yes! And that's why—why you mustn't talk that way!"

"Good-by!" said the girl.

The mother heard the sound of her departing footsteps, and knew that she was walking away very fast, nay, almost running. Pavel followed her into the yard.

A heavy oppressive fear fell like a load on the mother's breast. She did not understand what they had been talking about, but she felt that a new misfortune was in store for her, a great and sad misfortune. And her thoughts halted at the question, "What does he want to do?" Her thoughts halted, and were driven into her brain like a nail. She stood in the kitchen by the oven, and looked through the window into the profound, starry heaven.

Pavel walked in from the yard with Andrey, and the Little Russian said, shaking his head:

"Oh, Isay, Isay! What's to be done with him?"

"We must advise him to give up his project," said Pavel glumly.

"Then he'll hand over those who speak to him to the authorities," said the Little Russian, flinging his hat away in a corner.

"Pasha, what do you want to do?" asked the mother, drooping her head.

"When? Now?"

"The first of May—the first of May."

"Aha!" exclaimed Pavel, lowering his voice. "You heard! I am going to carry our banner. I will march with it at the head of the procession. I suppose they'll put me in prison for it again."

The mother's eyes began to burn. An unpleasant, dry feeling came into her mouth. Pavel took her hand and stroked it.

"I must do it! Please understand me! It is my happiness!"

"I'm not saying anything," she answered, slowly raising her head; but when her eyes met the resolute gleam in his, she again lowered it. He released her hand, and with a sigh said reproachfully:

"You oughtn't to be grieved. You ought to feel rejoiced. When are we going to have mothers who will rejoice in sending their children even to death?"

"Hopp! Hopp!" mumbled the Little Russian. "How you gallop away!"

"Why; do I say anything to you?" the mother repeated. "I don't interfere with you. And if I'm sorry for you—well, that's a mother's way."

Pavel drew away from her, and she heard his sharp, harsh words:

"There is a love that interferes with a man's very life."

She began to tremble, and fearing that he might deal another blow at her heart by saying something stern, she rejoined quickly:

"Don't, Pasha! Why should you? I understand. You can't act otherwise, you must do it for your comrades."

"No!" he replied. "I am doing it for myself. For their sake I can go without carrying the banner, but I'm going to do it!"

Andrey stationed himself in the doorway. It was too low for him, and he had to bend his knees oddly. He stood there as in a frame, one shoulder leaning against the jamb, his head and other shoulder thrust forward.

"I wish you would stop palavering, my dear sir," he said with a frown, fixing his protuberant eyes on Pavel's face. He looked like a lizard in the crevice of a stone wall.

The mother was overcome with a desire to weep, but she did not want her son to see her tears, and suddenly mumbled: "Oh, dear!—I forgot—" and walked out to the porch. There, her head in a corner, she wept noiselessly; and her copious tears weakened her, as though blood oozed from her heart along with them.

Through the door standing ajar the hollow sound of disputing voices reached her ear.

"Well, do you admire yourself for having tortured her?"

"You have no right to speak like that!" shouted Pavel.

"A fine comrade I'd be to you if I kept quiet when I see you making a fool of yourself. Why did you say all that to your mother?"

"A man must always speak firmly and without equivocation. He must be clear and definite when he says 'Yes.' He must be clear and definite when he says 'No.'"

"To her—to her must you speak that way?"

"To everybody! I want no love, I want no friendship which gets between my feet and holds me back."

"Bravo! You're a hero! Go say all this to Sashenka. You should have said that to her."

"I have!"

"You have! The way you spoke to your mother? You have not! To her you spoke softly; you spoke gently and tenderly to her. I did not hear you, but I know it! But you trot out your heroism before your mother. Of course! Your heroism is not worth a cent."

Vlasova began to wipe the tears from her face in haste. For fear a serious quarrel should break out between the Little Russian and Pavel, she quickly opened the door and entered the kitchen, shivering, terrified, and distressed.

"Ugh! How cold! And it's spring, too!"

She aimlessly removed various things in the kitchen from one place to another, and in order to drown the subdued voices in the room, she continued in a louder voice:

"Everything's changed. People have grown hotter and the weather colder. At this time of the year it used to get warm; the sky would clear, and the sun would be out."

Silence ensued in the room. The mother stood waiting in the middle of the floor.

"Did you hear?" came the low sound of the Little Russian's voice. "You must understand it, the devil take it! That's richer than yours."

"Will you have some tea?" the mother called with a trembling voice, and without waiting for an answer she exclaimed, in order to excuse the tremor in her voice:

"How cold I am!"

Pavel came up slowly to her, looking at her from the corners of his eyes, a guilty smile quivering on his lips.

"Forgive me, mother!" he said softly. "I am still a boy, a fool."

"You mustn't hurt me!" she cried in a sorrowful voice, pressing his head to her bosom. "Say nothing! God be with you. Your life is your own! But don't wound my heart. How can a mother help sorrowing for her son? Impossible! I am sorry for all of you. You are all dear to me as my own flesh and blood; you are all such good people! And who will be sorry for you if I am not? You go and others follow you. They have all left everything behind them, Pasha, and gone into this thing. It's just like a sacred procession."

A great ardent thought burned in her bosom, animating her heart with an exalted feeling of sad, tormenting joy; but she could find no words, and she waved her hands with the pang of muteness. She looked into her son's face with eyes in which a bright, sharp pain had lit its fires.

"Very well, mother! Forgive me. I see all now!" he muttered, lowering his head. Glancing at her with a light smile, he added, embarrassed but happy: "I will not forget this, mother, upon my word."

She pushed him from her, and looking into the room she said to Andrey in a good-natured tone of entreaty:

"Andriusha, please don't you shout at him so! Of course, you are older than he, and so you———"

The Little Russian was standing with his back toward her. He sang out drolly without turning around to face her:

"Oh, oh, oh! I'll bawl at him, be sure! And I'll beat him some day, too."

She walked up slowly to him, with outstretched hand, and said:

"My dear, dear man!"

The Little Russian turned around, bent his head like an ox, and folding his hands behind his back walked past her into the kitchen. Thence his voice issued in a tone of mock sullenness:

"You had better go away, Pavel, so I shan't bite your head off! I am only joking, mother; don't believe it! I want to prepare the samovar. What coals these are! Wet, the devil take them!"

He became silent, and when the mother walked into the kitchen he was sitting on the floor, blowing the coals in the samovar. Without looking at her the Little Russian began again:

"Yes, mother, don't be afraid. I won't touch him. You know, I'm a good-natured chap, soft as a stewed turnip. And then—you hero out there, don't listen—I love him! But I don't like the waistcoat he wears. You see, he has put on a new waistcoat, and he likes it very much, so he goes strutting about, and pushes everybody, crying: 'See, see what a waistcoat I have on!' It's true, it's a fine waistcoat. But what's the use of pushing people? It's hot enough for us without it."

Pavel smiled and asked:

"How long do you mean to keep up your jabbering? You gave me one thrashing with your tongue. That's enough!"

Sitting on the floor, the Little Russian spread his legs around the samovar, and regarded Pavel. The mother stood at the door, and fixed a sad, affectionate gaze at Andrey's long, bent neck and the round back of his head. He threw his body back, supporting himself with his hands on the floor, looked at the mother and at the son with his slightly reddened and blinking eyes, and said in a low, hearty voice:

"You are good people, yes, you are!"

Pavel bent down and grasped his hand.

"Don't pull my hand," said the Little Russian gruffly. "You'll let go and I'll fall. Go away!"

"Why are you so shy?" the mother said pensively. "You'd better embrace and kiss. Press hard, hard!"

"Do you want to?" asked Pavel softly.

"We—ell, why not?" answered the Little Russian, rising.

Pavel dropped on his knees, and grasping each other firmly, they sank for a moment into each other's embrace—two bodies and one soul passionately and evenly burning with a profound feeling of friendship.

Tears ran down the mother's face, but this time they were easy tears. Drying them she said in embarrassment:

"A woman likes to cry. She cries when she is in sorrow; she cries when she is in joy!"

The Little Russian pushed Pavel away, and with a light movement, also wiping his eyes with his fingers, he said:

"Enough! When the calves have had their frolic, they must go to the shambles. What beastly coal this is! I blew and blew on it, and got some of the dust in my eyes."

Pavel sat at the window with bent head, and said mildly:

"You needn't be ashamed of such tears."

The mother walked up to him, and sat down beside him. Her heart was wrapped in a soft, warm, daring feeling. She felt sad, but pleasant and at ease.

"It's all the same!" she thought, stroking her son's hand. "It can't be helped; it must be so!"

She recalled other such commonplace words, to which she had been accustomed for a long time; but they did not give adequate expression to all she had lived through that moment.

"I'll put the dishes on the table; you stay where you are, mother," said the Little Russian, rising from the floor, and going into the room. "Rest a while. Your heart has been worn out with such blows!"

And from the room his singing voice, raised to a higher pitch, was heard.

"It's not a nice thing to boast of, yet I must say we tasted the right life just now, real, human, loving life. It does us good."

"Yes," said Pavel, looking at the mother.

"It's all different now," she returned. "The sorrow is different, and the joy is different. I do not know anything, of course! I do not understand what it is I live by—and I can't express my feelings in words!"

"This is the way it ought to be!" said the Little Russian, returning. "Because, mark you, mother dear, a new heart is coming into existence, a new heart is growing up in life. All hearts are smitten in the conflict of interests, all are consumed with a blind greed, eaten up with envy, stricken, wounded, and dripping with filth, falsehood, and cowardice. All people are sick; they are afraid to live; they wander about as in a mist. Everyone feels only his own toothache. But lo, and behold! Here is a Man coming and illuminating life with the light of reason, and he shouts: 'Oh, ho! you straying roaches! It's time, high time, for you to understand that all your interests are one, that everyone has the need to live, everyone has the desire to grow!' The Man who shouts this is alone, and therefore he cries aloud; he needs comrades, he feels dreary in his loneliness, dreary and cold. And at his call the stanch hearts unite into one great, strong heart, deep and sensitive as a silver bell not yet cast. And hark! This bell rings forth the message: 'Men of all countries, unite into one family! Love is the mother of life, not hate!' My brothers! I hear this message sounding through the world!"

"And I do, too!" cried Pavel.

The mother compressed her lips to keep them from trembling, and shut her eyes tight so as not to cry.

"When I lie in bed at night or am out walking alone—everywhere I hear this sound, and my heart rejoices. And the earth, too—I know it—weary of injustice and sorrow, rings out like a bell, responding to the call, and trembles benignly, greeting the new sun arising in the breast of Man."

Pavel rose, lifted his hand, and was about to say something, but the mother took his other hand, and pulling him down whispered in his ear:

"Don't disturb him!"

"Do you know?" said the Little Russian, standing in the doorway, his eyes aglow with a bright flame, "there is still much suffering in store for the people, much of their blood will yet flow, squeezed out by the hands of greed; but all that—all my suffering, all my blood, is a small price for that which is already stirring in my breast, in my mind, in the marrow of my bones! I am already rich, as a star is rich in golden rays. And I will bear all, I will suffer all, because there is within me a joy which no one, which nothing can ever stifle! In this joy there is a world of strength!"

They drank tea and sat around the table until midnight, and

conversed heart to heart and harmoniously about life, about people, and about the future.

CHAPTER XVI

Whenever a thought was clear to the mother, she would find confirmation of the idea by drawing upon some of her rude, coarse experiences. She now felt as on that day when her father said to her roughly:

"What are you making a wry face about? A fool has been found who wants to marry you. Marry him! All girls must get husbands; all women must bear children, and all children become a burden to their parents!"

After these words she saw before her an unavoidable path running for some inexplicable reason through a dark, dreary waste. Thus it was at the present moment. In anticipation of a new approaching misfortune, she uttered speechless words, addressing some imaginary person.

This lightened her mute pain, which reverberated in her heart like a tight chord.

The next day, early in the morning, very soon after Pavel and Andrey had left, Korsunova knocked at the door alarmingly, and called out hastily:

"Isay is killed! Come, quick!"

The mother trembled; the name of the assassin flashed through her mind.

"Who did it?" she asked curtly, throwing a shawl over her shoulders.

"The man's not sitting out there mourning over Isay. He knocked him down and fled!"

On the street Marya said:

"Now they'll begin to rummage about again and look for the murderer. It's a good thing your folks were at home last night. I can bear witness to that. I walked past here after midnight and glanced into the window, and saw all of you sitting around the table."

"What are you talking about, Marya? Why, who could dream of such a thing about them?" the mother ejaculated in fright.

"Well, who killed him? Some one from among your people, of course!" said Korsunova, regarding the idea as a matter to be taken for granted. "Everybody knows he spied on them."

The mother stopped to fetch breath, and put her hand to her bosom.

"What are you going on that way for? Don't be afraid! Whoever it is will reap the harvest of his own rashness. Let's go quick, or else they'll take him away!"

The mother walked on without asking herself why she went, and shaken by the thought of Vyesovshchikov.

"There—he's done it!" Her mind was held fast by the one idea.

Not far from the factory walls, on the grounds of a building recently burned down, a crowd was gathered, tramping down the coal and stirring up ash dust. It hummed and buzzed like a swarm of bees. There were many women in the crowd, even more children, and storekeepers, tavern waiters, policemen, and the gendarme Petlin, a tall old man with a woolly, silvery beard, and decorations on his breast.

Isay half reclined on the ground, his back resting against a burned joist, his bare head hanging over his right shoulder, his right hand in his trousers' pocket, and the fingers of his left hand clutching the soil.

The mother looked at Isay's face. One eye, wide open, had its dim glance fixed upon his hat lying between his lazily outstretched legs. His mouth was half open in astonishment, his little shriveled body, with its pointed head and bony face, seemed to be resting. The mother crossed herself and heaved a sigh. He had been repulsive to her when alive, but now she felt a mild pity for him.

"No blood!" some one remarked in an undertone. "He was evidently knocked down with a fist blow."

A stout woman, tugging at the gendarme's hand, asked:

"Maybe he is still alive?"

"Go away!" the gendarme shouted not very loudly, withdrawing his hand.

"The doctor was here and said it was all over," somebody said to the woman.

A sarcastic, malicious voice cried aloud:

"They've choked up a denouncer's mouth. Serves him right!"

The gendarme pushed aside the women, who were crowded close about him, and asked in a threatening tone:

"Who was that? Who made that remark?"

The people scattered before him as he thrust them aside. A number took quickly to their heels, and some one in the crowd broke into a mocking laugh.

The mother went home.

"No one is sorry," she thought. The broad figure of Nikolay stood before her like a shadow, his narrow eyes had a cold, cruel look, and he wrung his right hand as if it had been hurt.

When Pavel and Andrey came to dinner, her first question was:

"Well? Did they arrest anybody for Isay's murder?"

"We haven't heard anything about it," answered the Little Russian.

She saw that they were both downhearted and sullen.

"Nothing is said about Nikolay?" the mother questioned again in a low voice.

Pavel fixed his stern eyes on the mother, and said distinctly:

"No, there is no talk of him. He is not even thought of in connection with this affair. He is away. He went off on the river yesterday, and hasn't returned yet. I inquired for him."

"Thank God!" said the mother with a sigh of relief. "Thank God!"

The Little Russian looked at her, and drooped his head.

"He lies there," the mother recounted pensively, "and looks as though he were surprised; that's the way his face looks. And no one pities him; no one bestows a good word on him. He is such a tiny bit of a fellow, such a wretched-looking thing, like a bit of broken china. It seems as if he had slipped on something and fallen, and there he lies!"

At dinner Pavel suddenly dropped his spoon and exclaimed:

"That's what I don't understand!"

"What?" asked the Little Russian, who had been sitting at the table dismal and silent.

"To kill anything living because one wants to eat, that's ugly enough. To kill a beast—a beast of prey—that I can understand. I think I myself could kill a man who had turned into a beast preying upon mankind. But to kill such a disgusting, pitiful creature—I don't understand how anyone could lift his hand for an act like that!"

The Little Russian raised his shoulders and dropped them again; then said:

"He was no less noxious than a beast."

"I know."

"We kill a mosquito for sucking just a tiny bit of our blood," the Little Russian added in a low voice.

"Well, yes, I am not saying anything about that. I only mean to say it's so disgusting."

"What can you do?" returned Andrey with another shrug of his shoulders.

After a long pause Pavel asked:

"Could you kill a fellow like that?"

The Little Russian regarded him with his round eyes, threw a glance at the mother, and said sadly, but firmly:

"For myself, I wouldn't touch a living thing. But for comrades, for the cause, I am capable of everything. I'd even kill. I'd kill my own son."

"Oh, Andriusha!" the mother exclaimed under her breath.

He smiled and said:

"It can't be helped! Such is our life!"

"Ye-es," Pavel drawled. "Such is our life."

With sudden excitement, as if obeying some impulse from within, Andrey arose, waved his hands, and said:

"How can a man help it? It so happens that we sometimes must abhor a certain person in order to hasten the time when it will be possible only to take delight in one another. You must destroy those who hinder the progress of life, who sell human beings for money in order to buy quiet or esteem for themselves. If a Judas stands in the way of honest people, lying in wait to betray them, I should be a Judas myself if I did not destroy him. It's sinful, you say? And do they, these masters of life, do they have the right to keep soldiers and executioners, public houses and prisons, places of penal servitude, and all that vile abomination by which they hold themselves in quiet security and in comfort? If it happens sometimes that I am compelled to take their stick into my own hands, what am I to do then? Why, I am going to take it, of course. I will not decline. They kill us out by the tens and hundreds. That gives me the right to raise my hand and level it against one of the enemy, against that one of their number who comes closest to me, and makes himself more directly noxious to the work of my life than the others. This is logic; but I go against logic for once. I do not need your logic now. I know that their blood can bring no results, I know that their blood is barren, fruitless! Truth grows well only on the soil irrigated with the copious rain of our own blood, and their putrid blood goes to waste, without a trace left. I know it! But I take the sin upon myself. I'll kill, if I see a need for it! I speak only for myself, mind you. My crime dies with me. It will not remain a blot upon the future. It will sully no one but myself—no one but myself."

He walked to and fro in the room, waving his hands in front of him, as if he were cutting something in the air out of his way. The mother looked at him with an expression of melancholy and alarm. She felt as though something had hit him, and that he was pained. The dangerous thoughts about murder left her. If Vyesovshchikov had not killed Isay, none of Pavel's comrades could have done the deed. Pavel listened to the Little Russian with drooping head, and Andrey stubbornly continued in a forceful tone:

"In your forward march it sometimes chances that you must go against your very own self. You must be able to give up everything—your heart and all. To give your life, to die for the cause—that's simple. Give more! Give that which is dearer to you than your life! Then you will see that grow with a vigorous growth which is dearest to you—your truth!"

He stopped in the middle of the room, his face grown pale and his eyes half closed. Raising his hand and shaking it, he began slowly in a solemn tone of assurance with faith and with strength:

"There will come a time, I know, when people will take delight in one another, when each will be like a star to the other, and when each will listen to his fellow as to music. The free men will walk upon the earth, men great in their freedom. They will walk with open hearts, and the heart of each will be pure of envy and greed, and therefore all mankind will be without malice, and there will be nothing to divorce the heart from reason. Then life will be one great service to man! His figure will be raised to lofty heights—for to free men all heights are attainable. Then we shall live in truth and freedom and in beauty, and those will be accounted the best who will the more widely embrace the world with their hearts, and whose love of it will be the profoundest; those will be the best who will be the freest; for in them is the greatest beauty. Then will life be great, and the people will be great who live that life."

He ceased and straightened himself. Then swinging to and fro like the tongue of a bell, he added in a resonant voice that seemed to issue from the depths of his breast:

"So for the sake of this life I am prepared for everything! I will tear my heart out, if necessary, and will trample it with my own feet!"

His face quivered and stiffened with excitement, and great, heavy tears rolled down one after the other.

Pavel raised his head and looked at him with a pale face and wide-open eyes. The mother raised herself a little over the table with a feeling that something great was growing and impending.

"What is the matter with you, Andrey?" Pavel asked softly.

The Little Russian shook his head, stretched himself like a violin string, and said, looking at the mother:

"I struck Isay."

She rose, and quickly walked up to him, all in a tremble, and seized his hands. He tried to free his right hand, but she held it firmly in her grasp and whispered hotly:

"My dear, my own, hush! It's nothing—it's nothing—nothing, Pasha! Andriushenka—oh, what a calamity! You sufferer! My darling heart!"

"Wait, mother," the Little Russian muttered hoarsely. "I'll tell you how it happened."

"Don't!" she whispered, looking at him with tears in her eyes. "Don't, Andriusha! It isn't our business. It's God's affair!"

Pavel came up to him slowly, looking at his comrade with moist eyes. He was pale, and his lips trembled. With a strange smile he said softly and slowly:

"Come, give me your hand, Andrey. I want to shake hands with you. Upon my word, I understand how hard it is for you!"

"Wait!" said the Little Russian without looking at them, shaking his head, and tearing himself away from their grasp. When he succeeded in freeing his right hand from the mother's, Pavel caught it, pressing it vigorously and wringing it.

"And you mean to tell me you killed that man?" said the mother. "No, *you* didn't do it! If I saw it with my own eyes I wouldn't believe it."

"Stop, Andrey! Mother is right. This thing is beyond our judgment."

With one hand pressing Andrey's, Pavel laid the other on his shoulder, as if wishing to stop the tremor in his tall body. The Little Russian bent his head down toward him, and said in a broken, mournful voice:

"I didn't want to do it, you know, Pavel. It happened when you walked ahead, and I remained behind with Ivan Gusev. Isay came from around a corner and stopped to look at us, and smiled at us. Ivan walked off home, and I went on toward the factory—Isay at my side!" Andrey stopped, heaved a deep sigh, and continued: "No one ever insulted me in such an ugly way as that dog!"

The mother pulled the Little Russian by the hand toward the table, gave him a shove, and finally succeeded in seating him on a chair. She sat down at his side close to him, shoulder to shoulder. Pavel stood in front of them, holding Andrey's hand in his and pressing it.

"I understand how hard it is for you," he said.

"He told me that they know us all, that we are all on the gendarme's record, and that we are going to be dragged in before the first of May. I didn't answer, I laughed, but my blood boiled. He began to tell me that I was a clever fellow, and that I oughtn't to go on the way I was going, but that I should rather———"

The Little Russian stopped, wiped his face with his right hand, shook his head, and a dry gleam flashed in his eyes.

"I understand!" said Pavel.

"Yes," he said, "I should rather enter the service of the law." The Little Russian waved his hand, and swung his clenched fist.

"The law!—curse his soul!" he hissed between his teeth. "It would have been better if he had struck me in the face. It would have been easier for me, and better for him, perhaps, too! But when he spit his dirty thought into my heart that way, I could not bear it."

Andrey pulled his hand convulsively from Pavel's, and said more hoarsely with disgust in his face:

"I dealt him a back-hand blow like that, downward and aslant, and walked away. I didn't even stop to look at him; I heard him fall. He dropped and was silent. I didn't dream of anything serious. I walked on peacefully, just as if I had done no more than kick a frog with my foot. And then—what's all this? I started to work, and I heard them shouting: 'Isay is killed!' I didn't even believe it, but my hand grew numb—and I felt awkward in working with it. It didn't hurt me, but it seemed to have grown shorter."

He looked at his hand obliquely and said:

"All my life, I suppose, I won't be able to wash off that dirty stain from it."

"If only your heart is pure, my dear boy!" the mother said softly, bursting into tears.

"I don't regard myself as guilty; no, I don't!" said the Little Russian firmly. "But it's disgust. It disgusts me to carry such dirt inside of me. I had no need of it. It wasn't called for."

"What do you think of doing?" asked Pavel, giving him a suspicious look.

"What am I going to do?" the Little Russian repeated thoughtfully, drooping his head. Then raising it again he said with a smile: "I am not afraid, of course, to say that it was I who struck him. But I am ashamed to say it. I am ashamed to go to prison, and even to hard labor, maybe, for such a—nothing. If some one else is accused, then I'll go and confess. But otherwise, go all of my own accord—I cannot!"

He waved his hands, rose, and repeated:

"I cannot! I am ashamed!"

The whistle blew. The Little Russian, bending his head to one side, listened to the powerful roar, and shaking himself, said:

"I am not going to work."

"Nor I," said Pavel.

"I'll go to the bath house," said the Little Russian, smiling. He got ready in silence and walked off, sullen and low-spirited.

The mother followed him with a compassionate look.

"Say what you please, Pasha, I cannot believe him! And even if I did believe him, I wouldn't lay any blame on him. No, I would not. I know it's sinful to kill a man; I believe in God and in the Lord Jesus Christ, but still I don't think Andrey guilty. I'm sorry for Isay. He's such a tiny bit of a manikin. He lies there in astonishment. When I looked at him I remembered how he threatened to have you hanged. And yet I neither felt hatred toward him nor joy because he was dead. I simply felt sorry. But now that I know by whose hand he fell I am not even sorry for him."

She suddenly became silent, reflected a while, and with a smile of surprise, exclaimed:

"Lord Jesus Christ! Do you hear what I am saying, Pasha?"

Pavel apparently had not heard her. Slowly pacing up and down the room with drooping head, he said pensively and with exasperation:

"Andrey won't forgive himself soon, if he'll forgive himself at all! There is life for you, mother. You see the position in which people are placed toward one another. You don't want to, but you must strike! And strike whom? Such a helpless being. He is more wretched even than you because he is stupid. The police, the gendarmes, the soldiers, the spies—they are all our enemies, and yet they are all such people as we are. Their blood is sucked out of them just as ours is, and they are no more regarded as human beings than we are. That's the way it is. But they have set one part of the people against the other, blinded them with fear, bound them all hand and foot, squeezed them, and drained their blood, and used some as clubs against the others. They've turned men into weapons, into sticks and stones, and called it civilization, government."

He walked up to his mother and said to her firmly:

"That's crime, mother! The heinous crime of killing millions of people, the murder of millions of souls! You understand—they kill the soul! You see the difference between them and us. He killed a man unwittingly. He feels disgusted, ashamed, sick—the main thing is he feels disgusted! But they kill off thousands calmly, without a qualm, without pity, without a shudder of the heart. They kill with pleasure and with delight. And why? They stifle everybody and everything to death merely to keep the timber of their houses secure, their furniture, their silver, their gold, their worthless papers—all that cheap trash which gives them control over the people. Think, it's not for their own selves, for their persons, that they protect themselves thus, using murder and the mutilation of souls as a means—it's not for themselves they do it, but for the sake of their possessions. They do not guard themselves from within, but from without."

He bent over to her, took her hands, and shaking them said:

"If you felt the abomination of it all, the disgrace and rottenness, you would understand our truth; you would then perceive how great it is, how glorious!"

The mother arose agitated, full of a desire to sink her heart into the heart of her son, and to join them in one burning, flaming torch.

"Wait, Pasha, wait!" she muttered, panting for breath. "I am a human being. I feel. Wait."

There was a loud noise of some one entering the porch. Both of them started and looked at each other.

"If it's the police coming for Andrey—" Pavel whispered.

"I know nothing—nothing!" the mother whispered back. "Oh, God!"

CHAPTER XVII

The door opened slowly, and bending to pass through, Rybin strode in heavily.

"Here I am!" he said, raising his head and smiling.

He wore a short fur overcoat, all stained with tar, a pair of dark mittens stuck from his belt, and his head was covered with a shaggy fur cap.

"Are you well? Have they let you out of prison, Pavel? So, how are you, Nilovna?"

"Why, you? How glad I am to see you!"

Slowly removing his overclothes, Rybin said:

"Yes, I've turned muzhik again. You're gradually turning gentlemen, and I am turning the other way. That's it!"

Pulling his ticking shirt straight, he passed through the room, examined it attentively, and remarked:

"You can see your property has not increased, but you've grown richer in books. So! That's the dearest possession, books are, it's true. Well, tell me how things are going with you."

"Things are going forward," said Pavel.

"Yes," said Rybin.

"We plow and we sow,
All high and low,
Boasting is cheap,
But the harvest we reap,
A feast we'll make,
And a rest we'll take."

"Will you have some tea?" asked the mother.

"Yes, I'll have some tea, and I'll take a sip of vodka, too; and if you'll give me something to eat, I won't decline it, either. I am glad to see you—that's what!"

"How's the world wagging with you, Mikhaïl Ivanych?" Pavel inquired, taking a seat opposite Rybin.

"So, so. Fairly well. I settled at Edilgeyev. Have you ever heard of Edilgeyev? It's a fine village. There are two fairs a year there; over two thousand inhabitants. The people are an evil pack. There's no land. It's leased out in lots. Poor soil!"

"Do you talk to them?" asked Pavel, becoming animated.

"I don't keep mum. You know I have all your leaflets with me. I grabbed them away from here—thirty-four of them. But I carry on my propaganda chiefly with the Bible. You can get something out of it. It's a thick book. It's a government book. It's published by the Holy Synod. It's easy to believe!" He gave Pavel a wink, and continued with a laugh: "But that's not enough! I have come here to you to get books. Yefim is here, too. We are transporting tar; and so we turned aside to stop at your house. You stock me up with books before Yefim comes. He doesn't have to know too much!"

"Mother," said Pavel, "go get some books! They'll know what to give you. Tell them it's for the country."

"All right. The samovar will be ready in a moment, and then I'll go."

"You have gone into this movement, too, Nilovna?" asked Rybin with a smile. "Very well. We have lots of eager candidates for books. There's a teacher there who creates a desire for them. He's a fine fellow, they say, although he belongs to the clergy. We have a woman teacher, too, about seven versts from the village. But they don't work with illegal books; they're a 'law and order' crowd out there; they're afraid. But I want forbidden books—sharp, pointed books. I'll slip them through their fingers. When the police commissioners or the priest see that they are illegal books, they'll think it's the teachers who circulate them. And in the meantime I'll remain in the background."

Well content with his hard, practical sense, he grinned merrily.

"Hm!" thought the mother. "He looks like a bear and behaves like a fox."

Pavel rose, and pacing up and down the room with even steps, said reproachfully:

"We'll let you have the books, but what you want to do is not right, Mikhaïl Ivanovich."

"Why is it not right?" asked Rybin, opening his eyes in astonishment.

"You yourself ought to answer for what you do. It is not right to manage matters so that others should suffer for what you do." Pavel spoke sternly.

Rybin looked at the floor, shook his head, and said:

"I don't understand you."

"If the teachers are suspected," said Pavel, stationing himself in front of Rybin, "of distributing illegal books, don't you think they'll be put in jail for it?"

"Yes. Well, what if they are?"

"But it's you who distribute the books, not they. Then it's you that ought to go to prison."

"What a strange fellow you are!" said Rybin with a smile,

striking his hand on his knee. "Who would suspect me, a muzhik, of occupying myself with such matters? Why, does such a thing happen? Books are affairs of the masters, and it's for them to answer for them."

The mother felt that Pavel did not understand Rybin, and she saw that he was screwing up his eyes—a sign of anger. So she interjected in a cautious, soft voice:

"Mikhaïl Ivanovich wants to fix it so that he should be able to go on with his work, and that others should take the punishment for it."

"That's it!" said Rybin, stroking his beard.

"Mother," Pavel asked dryly, "suppose some of our people, Andrey, for example, did something behind my back, and I were put in prison for it, what would you say to that?"

The mother started, looked at her son in perplexity, and said, shaking her head in negation:

"Why, is it possible to act that way toward a comrade?"

"Aha! Yes!" Rybin drawled. "I understand you, Pavel." And with a comical wink toward the mother, he added: "This is a delicate matter, mother." And again turning to Pavel he held forth in a didactic manner: "Your ideas on this subject are very green, brother. In secret work there is no honor. Think! In the first place, they'll put those persons in prison on whom they find the books, and not the teachers. That's number one! Secondly, even though the teachers give the people only legal books to read, you know that they contain prohibited things just the same as in the forbidden books; only they are put in a different language. The truths are fewer. That's number two. I mean to say, they want the same thing that I do; only they proceed by side paths, while I travel on the broad highway. And thirdly, brother, what business have I with them? How can a traveler on foot strike up friendship with a man on horseback? Toward a muzhik, maybe, I wouldn't want to act that way. But these people, one a clergyman, the other the daughter of a land proprietor, why they want to uplift the people, I cannot understand. Their ideas, the ideas of the masters, are unintelligible to me, a muzhik. What I do myself, I know, but what they are after I cannot tell. For thousands of years they have punctiliously and consistently pursued the business of being masters, and have fleeced and flayed the skins of the muzhiks; and all of a sudden they wake up and want to open the muzhik's eyes. I am not a man for fairy tales, brother, and that's in the nature of a fairy tale. That's why I can't get interested in them. The ways of the masters are strange to me. You travel in winter, and you see some living creature in front of you. But what it is—a wolf, a fox, or just a plain dog—you don't know."

The mother glanced at her son. His face wore a gloomy expression.

Rybin's eyes sparkled with a dark gleam. He looked at Pavel, combing down his beard with his fingers. His air was at once complacent and excited.

"I have no time to flirt," he said. "Life is a stern matter. We live in dog houses, not in sheep pens, and every pack barks after its own fashion."

"There are some masters," said the mother, recalling certain familiar faces, "who die for the people, and let themselves be tortured all their lives in prison."

"Their calculations are different, and their deserts are different," said Rybin. "The muzhik grown rich turns into a gentleman, and the gentleman grown poor goes to the muzhik. Willy-nilly, he must have a pure soul, if his purse is empty. Do you remember, Pavel, you explained to me that as a man lives, so he also thinks, and that if the workingman says 'Yes,' the master must say 'No,' and if the workingman says 'No,' the master, because of the nature of the beast, is bound to cry 'Yes.' So you see, their natures are different one from the other. The muzhik has his nature, and the gentleman has his. When the peasant has a full stomach, the gentleman passes sleepless nights. Of course, every fold has its black sheep, and I have no desire to defend the peasants wholesale."

Rybin rose to his feet somber and powerful. His face darkened, his beard quivered as if he ground his teeth inaudibly, and he continued in a lowered voice:

"For five years I beat about from factory to factory, and got unaccustomed to the village. Then I went to the village again, looked around, and I found I could not live like that any more! You understand? I *can't*. You live here, you don't know hunger, you don't see such outrages. There hunger stalks after a man all his life like a shadow, and he has no hope for bread—no hope! Hunger destroys the soul of the people; the very image of man is effaced from their countenances. They do not live, they rot in dire unavoidable want. And around them the government authorities watch like ravens to see if a crumb is not left over. And if they do find a crumb, they snatch that away, too, and give you a punch in the face besides."

Rybin looked around, bent down to Pavel, his hand resting on the table:

"I even got sick and faint when I saw that life again. I looked around me—but I couldn't! However, I conquered my repulsion. 'Fiddlesticks!' I said. 'I won't let my feelings get the better of me. I'll stay here. I won't get your bread for you; but I'll cook you a pretty mess, I will.' I carry within me the wrongs of my people and hatred of the oppressor. I feel these wrongs like a knife constantly cutting at my heart."

Perspiration broke out on his forehead; he shrugged his shoulders and slowly bent toward Pavel, laying a tremulous hand on his shoulder:

"Give me your help! Let me have books—such books that when a man has read them he will not be able to rest. Put a prickly hedgehog to his brains. Tell those city folks who write for you to write for the villagers also. Let them write such hot truth that it will scald the village, that the people will even rush to their death."

He raised his hand, and laying emphasis on each word, he said hoarsely:

"Let death make amends for death. That is, die so that the people should arise to life again. And let thousands die in order that hosts of people all over the earth may arise to life again. That's it! It's easy to die—but let the people rise to life again! That's a different thing! Let them rise up in rebellion!"

The mother brought in the samovar, looking askance at Rybin. His strong, heavy words oppressed her. Something in him reminded her of her husband. He, too, showed his teeth, waved his hands, and rolled up his sleeves; in him, too, there was that impatient wrath, impatient but dumb. Rybin was not dumb; he was not silent; he spoke, and therefore was less terrible.

"That's necessary," said Pavel, nodding his head. "We need a newspaper for the villages, too. Give us material, and we'll print you a newspaper."

The mother looked at her son with a smile, and shook her head. She had quietly put on her wraps and now went out of the house.

"Yes, do it. We'll give you everything. Write as simply as possible, so that even calves could understand," Rybin cried. Then, suddenly stepping back from Pavel, he said, as he shook his head:

"Ah, me, if I were a Jew! The Jew, my dear boy, is the most believing man in the world! Isaiah, the prophet, or Job, the patient, believed more strongly than Christ's apostles. They could say words to make a man's hair stand on end. But the apostles, you see, Pavel, couldn't. The prophets believed not in the church, but in themselves; they had their God in themselves. The apostles—they built churches; and the church is law. Man must believe in himself, not in law. Man carries the truth of God in his soul; he is not a police captain on earth, nor a slave! All the laws are in myself."

The kitchen door opened, and somebody walked in.

"It's Yefim," said Rybin, looking into the kitchen. "Come here, Yefim. As for you, Pavel, think! Think a whole lot. There is a great deal to think about. This is Yefim. And this man's name is Pavel. I told you about him."

A light-haired, broad-faced young fellow in a short fur overcoat, well built and evidently strong, stood before Pavel, holding his cap in both hands and looking at him from the corners of his gray eyes.

"How do you do?" he said hoarsely, as he shook hands with Pavel, and stroked his curly hair with both hands. He looked around the room, immediately spied the bookshelf, and walked over to it slowly.

"Went straight to them!" Rybin said, winking to Pavel.

Yefim started to examine the books, and said:

"A whole lot of reading here! But I suppose you haven't much time for it. Down in the village they have more time for reading."

"But less desire?" Pavel asked.

"Why? They have the desire, too," answered the fellow, rubbing his chin. "The times are so now that if you don't think, you might as well lie down and die. But the people don't want to die; and so they've begun to make their brains work. 'Geology'—what's that?"

Pavel explained.

"We don't need it!" Yefim said, replacing the book on the shelf.

Rybin sighed noisily, and said:

"The peasant is not so much interested to know where the land came from as where it's gone to, how it's been snatched from underneath his feet by the gentry. It doesn't matter to him whether it's fixed or whether it revolves—that's of no importance—you can hang it on a rope, if you want to, provided it feeds him; you can nail it to the skies, provided it gives him enough to eat."

"'The History of Slavery,'" Yefim read out again, and asked Pavel: "Is it about us?"

"Here's an account of Russian serfdom, too," said Pavel, giving him another book. Yefim took it, turned it in his hands, and putting it aside, said calmly:

"That's out of date."

"Have you an apportionment of land for yourself?" inquired Pavel.

"We? Yes, we have. We are three brothers, and our portion is about ten acres and a half—all sand—good for polishing brass, but poor for making bread." After a pause he continued: "I've freed myself from the soil. What's the use? It does not feed; it ties one's hands. This is the fourth year that I'm working as a hired man. I've got to become a soldier this fall. Uncle Mikhaïl says: 'Don't go. Now,' he says, 'the soldiers are being sent to beat the people.' However, I think I'll go. The army existed at the time of Stepan Timofeyevich Razin and Pugachev. The time has come to make an end of it. Don't you think so?" he asked, looking firmly at Pavel.

"Yes, the time has come." The answer was accompanied by a smile. "But it's hard. You must know what to say to soldiers, and how to say it."

"We'll learn; we'll know how," Yefim said.

"And if the superiors catch you at it, they may shoot you down," Pavel concluded, looking curiously at Yefim.

"They will show no mercy," the peasant assented calmly, and resumed his examination of the books.

"Drink your tea, Yefim; we've got to leave soon," said Rybin.

"Directly." And Yefim asked again: "Revolution is an uprising, isn't it?"

Andrey came, red, perspiring, and dejected. He shook Yefim's hand without saying anything, sat down by Rybin's side, and smiled as he looked at him.

"What's the trouble? Why so blue?" Rybin asked, tapping his knee.

"Nothing."

"Are you a workingman, too?" asked Yefim, nodding his head toward the Little Russian.

"Yes," Andrey answered. "Why?"

"This is the first time he's seen factory workmen," explained Rybin. "He says they're different from others."

"How so?" Pavel asked.

Yefim looked carefully at Andrey and said:

"You have sharp bones; peasants' bones are rounder."

"The peasant stands more firmly on his feet," Rybin supplemented. "He feels the ground under him although he does not possess it. Yet he feels the earth. But the factory workingman is something like a bird. He has no home. To-day he's here, to-morrow there. Even his wife can't attach him to the same spot. At the least provocation—farewell, my dear! and off he goes to look for something better. But the peasant wants to improve himself just where he is without moving off the spot. There's your mother!" And Rybin went out into the kitchen.

Yefim approached Pavel, and with embarrassment asked:

"Perhaps you will give me a book?"

"Certainly."

The peasant's eyes flashed, and he said rapidly:

"I'll return it. Some of our folks bring tar not far from here. They will return it for me. Thank you! Nowadays a book is like a candle in the night to us."

Rybin, already dressed and tightly girt, came in and said to Yefim:

"Come, it's time for us to go."

"Now, I have something to read!" exclaimed Yefim, pointing to the book and smiling inwardly. When he had gone, Pavel animatedly said, turning to Andrey:

"Did you notice those fellows?"

"Y-yes!" slowly uttered the Little Russian. "Like clouds in the sunset—thick, dark clouds, moving slowly."

"Mikhaïl!" exclaimed the mother. "He looks as if he had never been in a factory! A peasant again. And how formidable he looks!"

"I'm sorry you weren't here," said Pavel to Andrey, who was sitting at the table, staring gloomily into his glass of tea. "You could have seen the play of hearts. You always talk about the heart. Rybin got up a lot of steam; he upset me, crushed me. I couldn't even reply to him. How distrustful he is of people, and how cheaply he values them! Mother is right. That man has a formidable power in him."

"I noticed it," the Little Russian replied glumly. "They have poisoned people. When the peasants rise up, they'll overturn absolutely everything! They need bare land, and they will lay it bare, tear down everything." He spoke slowly, and it was evident that his mind was on something else. The mother cautiously tapped him on the shoulder.

"Pull yourself together, Andriusha."

"Wait a little, my dear mother, my own!" he begged softly and kindly. "All this is so ugly—although I didn't mean to do any harm. Wait!" And suddenly rousing himself, he said, striking the table with his hand: "Yes, Pavel, the peasant will lay the land bare for himself when he rises to his feet. He will burn everything up, as if after a plague, so that all traces of his wrongs will vanish in ashes."

"And then he will get in our way," Pavel observed softly.

"It's our business to prevent that. We are nearer to him; he trusts us; he will follow us."

"Do you know, Rybin proposes that we should publish a newspaper for the village?"

"We must do it, too. As soon as possible."

Pavel laughed and said:

"I feel bad I didn't argue with him."

"We'll have a chance to argue with him still," the Little Russian rejoined. "You keep on playing your flute; whoever has gay feet, if they haven't grown into the ground, will dance to your tune. Rybin would probably have said that we don't feel the ground under us, and need not, either. Therefore it's our business to shake it. Shake it once, and the people will be loosened from it; shake it once more, and they'll tear themselves away."

The mother smiled.

"Everything seems to be simple to you, Andriusha."

"Yes, yes, it's simple," said the Little Russian, and added gloomily: "Like life." A few minutes later he said: "I'll go take a walk in the field."

"After the bath? The wind will blow through you," the mother warned.

"Well, I need a good airing."

"Look out, you'll catch a cold," Pavel said affectionately. "You'd better lie down and try to sleep."

"No, I'm going." He put on his wraps, and went out without speaking.

"It's hard for him," the mother sighed.

"You know what?" Pavel observed to her. "It's very good that you started to say 'thou' to him after that."

She looked at him in astonishment, and after reflecting a moment, said:

"Um, I didn't even notice how it came. It came all of itself. He has grown so near to me. I can't tell you in words just how I feel. Oh, such a misfortune!"

"You have a good heart, mamma," Pavel said softly.

"I'm very glad if I have. If I could only help you in some way, all of you. If I only could!"

"Don't fear, you will."

She laughed softly:

"I can't help fearing; that's exactly what I can't help. But thank you for the good word, my dear son."

"All right, mother; don't let's talk about it any more. Know that I love you; and I thank you most heartily."

She walked into the kitchen in order not to annoy him with her tears.

CHAPTER XVIII

Several days later Vyesovshchikov came in, as shabby, untidy, and disgruntled as ever.

"Haven't you heard who killed Isay?" He stopped in his clumsy pacing of the room to turn to Pavel.

"No!" Pavel answered briefly.

"There you got a man who wasn't squeamish about the job! And I'd always been preparing to do it myself. It was my job—just the thing for me!"

"Don't talk nonsense, Nikolay," Pavel said in a friendly manner.

"Now, really, what's the matter with you?" interposed the mother kindly. "You have a soft heart, and yet you keep barking like a vicious dog. What do you go on that way for?"

At this moment she was actually pleased to see Nikolay. Even his pockmarked face looked more agreeable to her. She pitied him as never before.

"Well, I'm not fit for anything but jobs like that!" said Nikolay dully, shrugging his shoulders. "I keep thinking, and thinking where my place in the world is. There is no place for me! The people require to be spoken to, and I cannot. I see everything; I feel all the people's wrongs; but I cannot express myself: I have a dumb soul." He went over to Pavel with drooping head; and scraping his fingers on the table, he said plaintively, and so unlike himself, childishly, sadly: "Give me some hard work to do, comrade. I can't live this life any longer. It's so senseless, so useless. You are all working in the movement, and I see that it is growing, and I'm outside of it all. I haul boards and beams. Is it possible to live for the sake of hauling timber? Give me some hard work."

Pavel clasped his hand, pulling him toward himself.

"We will!"

From behind the curtains resounded the Little Russian's voice:

"Nikolay, I'll teach you typesetting, and you'll work as a compositor for us. Yes?"

Nikolay went over to him and said:

"If you'll teach me that, I'll give you my knife."

"To the devil with your knife!" exclaimed the Little Russian and burst out laughing.

"It's a good knife," Nikolay insisted. Pavel laughed, too.

Vyesovshchikov stopped in the middle of the room and asked: "Are you laughing at me?"

"Of course," replied the Little Russian, jumping out of bed. "I'll tell you what! Let's take a walk in the fields! The night is fine; there's bright moonshine. Let's go!"

"All right," said Pavel.

"And I'll go with you, too!" declared Nikolay. "I like to hear you laugh, Little Russian."

"And I like to hear you promise presents," answered the Little Russian, smiling.

While Andrey was dressing in the kitchen, the mother scolded him:

"Dress warmer! You'll get sick." And when they all had left, she watched them through the window; then looked at the ikon, and said softly: "God help them!"

She turned off the lamp and began to pray alone in the moonlit room.

◆

The days flew by in such rapid succession that the mother could not give much thought to the first of May. Only at night, when, exhausted by the noise and the exciting bustle of the day, she went to bed, tired and worn out, her heart would begin to ache.

"Oh, dear, if it would only be over soon!"

At dawn, when the factory whistle blew, the son and the Little Russian, after hastily drinking tea and snatching a bite, would go, leaving a dozen or so small commissions for the mother. The whole day long she would move around like a squirrel in a wheel, cook dinner, and boil lilac-colored gelatin and glue for the proclamations. Some people would come, leave notes with her to deliver to Pavel, and disappear, infecting her with their excitement.

The leaflets appealing to the working people to celebrate the first of May flooded the village and the factory. Every night they were posted on the fences, even on the doors of the police station; and every day they were found in the factory. In the mornings the police would go around, swearing, tearing down and scraping off the lilac-covered bills from the fences. At noon, however, these bills would fly over the streets again, rolling to the feet of the passers-by. Spies were sent from the city to stand at the street corners and carefully scan the working people on their gay passages from and to the factory at dinner time. Everybody was pleased to see the impotence of the police, and even the elder workingmen would smile at one another:

"Things are happening, aren't they?"

All over, people would cluster into groups hotly discussing the stirring appeals. Life was at boiling point. This spring it held more of interest to everybody, it brought forth something new to all; for some it was a good excuse to excite themselves—they could pour out their malicious oaths on the agitators; to others, it brought perplexed anxiety as well as hope; to others again, the minority, an acute delight in the consciousness of being the power that set the village astir.

Pavel and Andrey scarcely ever went to bed. They came home just before the morning whistle sounded, tired, hoarse, and pale. The mother knew that they held meetings in the woods and the marsh; that squads of mounted police galloped around the village, that spies were crawling all over, holding up and searching single workingmen, dispersing groups, and sometimes making an arrest. She understood that her son and Andrey might be arrested any night. Sometimes she thought that this would be the best thing for them.

Strangely enough, the investigation of the murder of Isay, the record clerk, suddenly ceased. For two days the local police questioned the people in regard to the matter, examining about ten men or so, and finally lost interest in the affair.

Marya Korsunova, in a chat with the mother, reflected the opinion of the police, with whom she associated as amicably as with everybody:

"How is it possible to find the guilty man? That morning some hundred people met Isay, and ninety of them, if not more, might have given him the blow. During these eight years he has galled everybody."

The Little Russian changed considerably. His face became hollow-cheeked; his eyelids got heavy and drooped over his round eyes, half covering them. His smiles were wrung from him unwillingly, and two thin wrinkles were drawn from his nostrils to the corners of his lips. He talked less about everyday matters; on the other hand, he was more frequently enkindled with a passionate fire; and he intoxicated his listeners with his ecstatic words about the future, about the bright, beautiful holiday, when they would celebrate the triumph of freedom and reason. Listening to his words, the mother felt that he had gone further than anybody else toward the great, glorious day, and that he saw the joys of that future more vividly than the rest. When the investigations of Isay's murder ceased, he said in disgust and smiling sadly:

"It's not only the people they treat like trash, but even the very men whom they set on the people like dogs. They have no concern for their faithful Judases, they care only for their shekels—only for them." And after a sullen silence, he added: "And I pity that man the more I think of him. I didn't intend to kill him—didn't want to!"

"Enough, Andrey," said Pavel severely.

"You happened to knock against something rotten, and it fell to pieces," added the mother in a low voice.

"You're right—but that's no consolation."

He often spoke in this way. In his mouth the words assumed a peculiar, universal significance, bitter and corrosive.

At last, it was the first of May! The whistle shrilled as usual, powerful and peremptory. The mother, who hadn't slept a minute during the night, jumped out of bed, made a fire in the samovar, which had been prepared the evening before, and was about, as always, to knock at the door of her son's and Andrey's room, when, with a wave of her hand she recollected the day, and went to seat herself at the window, leaning her cheek on her hand.

Clusters of light clouds, white and rosy, sailed swiftly across the pale blue sky, like huge birds frightened by the piercing shriek of the escaping steam. The mother watched the clouds, absorbed in herself. Her head was heavy, her eyes dry and inflamed from the sleepless night. A strange calm possessed her breast, her heart was beating evenly, and her mind dwelt on only common, everyday things.

"I prepared the samovar too early; it will boil away. Let them sleep longer to-day; they've worn themselves out, both of them."

A cheerful ray of sun looked into the room. She held her hand out to it, and with the other gently patted the bright young beam, smiling kindly and thoughtfully. Then she rose, removed the pipe from the samovar, trying not to make a noise, washed herself, and began to pray, crossing herself piously, and noiselessly moving her lips. Her face was radiant, and her right eyebrow kept rising gradually and suddenly dropping.

The second whistle blew more softly with less assurance, a tremor in its thick and mellow sound. It seemed to the mother that the whistle lasted longer to-day than ever. The clear, musical voice of the Little Russian sounded in the room:

"Pavel, do you hear? They're calling."

The mother heard the patter of bare feet on the floor and some one yawn with gusto.

"The samovar is ready," she cried.

"We're getting up," Pavel answered merrily.

"The sun is rising," said the Little Russian. "The clouds are racing; they're out of place to-day." He went into the kitchen all disheveled but jolly after his sleep. "Good morning, mother dear; how did you sleep?"

The mother went to him and whispered:

"Andriusha, keep close to him."

"Certainly. As long as it depends on us, we'll always stick to each other, you may be sure."

"What's that whispering about?" Pavel asked.

"Nothing. She told me to wash myself better, so the girls will look at me," replied the Little Russian, going out on the porch to wash himself.

"'Rise up, awake, you workingmen,'" Pavel sang softly.

As the day grew, the clouds dispersed, chased by the wind. The mother got the dishes ready for the tea, shaking her head over the thought of how strange it was for both of them to be joking and smiling all the time on this morning, when who knew what would befall them in the afternoon. Yet, curiously enough, she felt herself calm, almost happy.

They sat a long time over the tea to while away the hours of expectation. Pavel, as was his wont, slowly and scrupulously mixed the sugar in the glass with his spoon, and accurately salted his favorite crust from the end of the loaf. The Little Russian moved his feet under the table—he never could at once settle his feet comfortably—and looked at the rays of sunlight playing on the wall and ceiling.

"When I was a youngster of ten years," he recounted, "I wanted to catch the sun in a glass. So I took the glass, stole to the wall, and bang! I cut my hand and got a licking to boot. After the licking I went out in the yard and saw the sun in a puddle. So I started to trample the mud with my feet. I covered myself with mud, and got another drubbing. What was I to do? I screamed to the sun: 'It doesn't hurt me, you red devil; it doesn't hurt me!' and stuck out my tongue at him. And I felt comforted."

"Why did the sun seem red to you?" Pavel asked, laughing.

"There was a blacksmith opposite our house, with fine red cheeks, and a huge red beard. I thought the sun resembled him."

The mother lost patience and said:

"You'd better talk about your arrangements for the procession."

"Everything's been arranged," said Pavel.

"No use talking of things once decided upon. It only confuses the mind," the Little Russian added. "If we are all arrested, Nikolay Ivanovich will come and tell you what to do. He will help you in every way."

"All right," said the mother with a heavy sigh.

"Let's go out," said Pavel dreamily.

"No, rather stay indoors," replied Andrey. "No need to annoy the eyes of the police so often. They know you well enough."

Fedya Mazin came running in, all aglow, with red spots on his cheeks, quivering with youthful joy. His animation dispelled the tedium of expectation for them.

"It's begun!" he reported. "The people are all out on the street, their faces sharp as the edge of an ax. Vyesovshchikov, the Gusevs, and Samoylov have been standing at the factory gates all the time, and have been making speeches. Most of the people went back from the factory, and returned home. Let's go! It's just time! It's ten o'clock already."

"I'm going!" said Pavel decidedly.

"You'll see," Fedya assured them, "the whole factory will rise up after dinner."

And he hurried away, followed by the quiet words of the mother:

"Burning like a wax candle in the wind."

She rose and went into the kitchen to dress.

"Where are you going, mother?"

"With you," she said.

Andrey looked at Pavel pulling his mustache. Pavel arranged his hair with a quick gesture, and went to his mother.

"Mother, I will not tell you anything; and don't you tell me anything, either. Right, mother?"

"All right, all right! God bless you!" she murmured.

When she went out and heard the holiday hum of the people's voices—an anxious and expectant hum—when she saw everywhere, at the gates and windows, crowds of people staring at Andrey and her son, a blur quivered before her eyes, changes from a transparent green to a muddy gray.

People greeted them—there was something peculiar in their greetings. She caught whispered, broken remarks:

"Here they are, the leaders!"

"We don't know who the leaders are!"

"Why, I didn't say anything wrong."

At another place some one in a yard shouted excitedly:

"The police will get them, and that'll be the end of them!"

"What if they do?" retorted another voice.

Farther on a crying woman's voice leaped frightened from the window to the street:

"Consider! Are you a single man, are you? They are bachelors and don't care!"

When they passed the house of Zosimov, the man without legs, who received a monthly allowance from the factory because of his mutilation, he stuck his head through the window and cried out:

"Pavel, you scoundrel, they'll wring your head off for your doings, you'll see!"

The mother trembled and stopped. The exclamation aroused in her a sharp sensation of anger. She looked up at the thick, bloated face of the cripple, and he hid himself, cursing. Then she quickened her pace, overtook her son, and tried not to fall behind again. He and Andrey seemed not to notice anything, not to hear the outcries that pursued them. They moved calmly, without haste, and talked loudly about commonplaces. They were stopped by Mironov, a modest, elderly man, respected by everybody for his clean, sober life.

"Not working either, Daniïl Ivanovich?" Pavel asked.

"My wife is going to be confined. Well, and such an exciting day, too," Mironov responded, staring fixedly at the comrades. He said to them in an undertone:

"Boys, I hear you're going to make an awful row—smash the superintendent's windows."

"Why, are we drunk?" exclaimed Pavel.

"We are simply going to march along the streets with flags, and sing songs," said the Little Russian. "You'll have a chance to hear our songs. They're our confession of faith."

"I know your confession of faith," said Mironov thoughtfully. "I read your papers. You, Nilovna," he exclaimed, smiling at the mother with knowing eyes, "are you going to revolt, too?"

"Well, even if it's only before death, I want to walk shoulder to shoulder with the truth."

"I declare!" said Mironov. "I guess they were telling the truth when they said you carried forbidden books to the factory."

"Who said so?" asked Pavel.

"Oh, people. Well, good-by! Behave yourselves!"

The mother laughed softly; she was pleased to hear that such things were said of her. Pavel smilingly turned to her:

"Oh, you'll get into prison, mother!"

"I don't mind," she murmured.

The sun rose higher, pouring warmth into the bracing freshness of the spring day. The clouds floated more slowly, their shadows grew thinner and more transparent, and crawled gently over the streets and roofs. The bright sunlight seemed to clean the village, to wipe the dust and dirt from the walls and the tedium from the faces. Everything assumed a more cheerful aspect; the voices sounded louder, drowning the far-off rumble and heavings of the factory machines.

Again, from all sides, from the windows and the yards, different words and voices, now uneasy and malicious, now thoughtful and gay, found their way to the mother's ears. But this time she felt a desire to retort, to thank, to explain, to participate in the strangely variegated life of the day.

Off a corner of the main thoroughfare, in a narrow by-street, a crowd of about a hundred people had gathered, and from its depths resounded Vyesovshchikov's voice:

"They squeeze our blood like juice from huckleberries." His words fell like hammer blows on the people.

"That's true!" the resonant cry rang out simultaneously from a number of throats.

"The boy is doing his best," said the Little Russian. "I'll go help him." He bent low and before Pavel had time to stop him he twisted his tall, flexible body into the crowd like a corkscrew into a cork, and soon his singing voice rang out:

"Comrades! They say there are various races on the earth—Jews and Germans, English and Tartars. But I don't believe it. There are only two nations, two irreconcilable tribes—the rich and the poor. People dress differently and speak differently; but look at the rich Frenchman, the rich German, or the rich Englishman, you'll see that they are all Tartars in the way they treat their workingman—a plague on them!"

A laugh broke out in the crowd.

"On the other hand, we can see the French workingmen, the Tartar workingmen, the Turkish workingmen, all lead the same dog's life, as we—we, the Russian workingmen."

More and more people joined the crowd; one after the other they thronged into the by-street, silent, stepping on tiptoe, and craning their necks. Andrey raised his voice:

"The workingmen of foreign countries have already learned this simple truth, and to-day, on this bright first of May, the foreign working people fraternize with one another. They quit their work, and go out into the streets to look at themselves, to take stock of their immense power. On this day, the workingmen out there throb with one heart; for all hearts are lighted with the consciousness of the might of the working people; all hearts beat with comradeship, each and every one of them is ready to lay down his life in the war for the happiness of all, for freedom and truth to all—comrades!"

"The police!" some one shouted.

CHAPTER XIX

From the main street four mounted policemen flourishing their knouts came riding into the by-street directly at the crowd.

"Disperse!"

"What sort of talking is going on?"

"Who's speaking?"

The people scowled, giving way to the horses unwillingly. Some climbed up on fences; raillery was heard here and there.

"They put pigs on horses; they grunt: 'Here we are, leaders, too!'" resounded a sonorous, provoking voice.

The Little Russian was left alone in the middle of the street; two horses shaking their manes pressed at him. He stepped aside, and at the same time the mother grasped his hand, pulling him away grumbling:

"You promised to stick to Pasha; and here you are running up against the edge of a knife all by yourself."

"I plead guilty," said the Little Russian, smiling at Pavel. "Ugh! What a force of police there is in the world!"

"All right," murmured the mother.

An alarming, crushing exhaustion came over her. It rose from within her and made her dizzy. There was a strange alternation of sadness and joy in her heart. She wished the afternoon whistle would sound.

They reached the square where the church stood. Around the church within the paling a thick crowd was sitting and standing. There were some five hundred gay youth and bustling women with children darting around the groups like butterflies. The crowd swung from side to side. The people raised their heads and looked into the distance in different directions, waiting impatiently.

"Mitenka!" softly vibrated a woman's voice. "Have pity on yourself!"

"Stop!" rang out the response.

And the grave Sizov spoke calmly, persuasively:

"No, we mustn't abandon our children. They have grown wiser than ourselves; they live more boldly. Who saved our cent for the marshes? They did. We must remember that. For doing it they were dragged to prison; but we derived the benefit. The benefit was for all."

The whistle blew, drowning the talk of the crowd. The people started. Those sitting rose to their feet. For a moment the silence of death prevailed; all became watchful, and many faces grew pale.

"Comrades!" resounded Pavel's voice, ringing and firm.

A dry, hot haze burned the mother's eyes, and with a single movement of her body, suddenly strengthened, she stood behind her son. All turned toward Pavel, and drew up to him, like iron filings attracted by a magnet.

"Brothers! The hour has come to give up this life of ours, this life of greed, hatred, and darkness, this life of violence and falsehood, this life where there is no place for us, where we are no human beings."

He stopped, and everybody maintained silence, moving still closer to him. The mother stared at her son. She saw only his eyes, his proud, brave, burning eyes.

"Comrades! We have decided to declare openly who we are; we raise our banner to-day, the banner of reason, of truth, of liberty! And now I raise it!"

A flag pole, white and slender, flashed in the air, bent down, cleaving the crowd. For a moment it was lost from sight; then over the uplifted faces the broad canvas of the working people's flag spread its wings like a red bird.

Pavel raised his hand—the pole swung, and a dozen hands caught the smooth white rod. Among them was the mother's hand.

"Long live the working people!" he shouted.

Hundreds of voices responded to his sonorous call.

"Long live the Social Democratic Workingmen's Party, our party, comrades, our spiritual mother."

The crowd seethed and hummed. Those who understood the meaning of the flag squeezed their way up to it. Mazin, Samoylov, and the Gusevs stood close at Pavel's side. Nikolay with bent head pushed his way through the crowd. Some other people unknown to the mother, young and with burning eyes, jostled her.

"Long live the working people of all countries!" shouted Pavel.

And ever increasing in force and joy, a thousand-mouthed echo responded in a soul-stirring acclaim.

The mother clasped Pavel's hand, and somebody else's, too. She was breathless with tears, yet refrained from shedding them. Her legs trembled, and with quivering lips she cried:

"Oh, my dear boys, that's true. There you are now——"

A broad smile spread over Nikolay's pockmarked face; he stared at the flag and, stretching his hand toward it, roared out something; then caught the mother around the neck with the same hand, kissed her, and laughed.

"Comrades!" sang out the Little Russian, subduing the noise of the crowd with his mellow voice. "Comrades! We have now started a holy procession in the name of the new God, the God of Truth and Light, the God of Reason and Goodness. We march in this holy procession, comrades, over a long and hard road. Our goal is far, far away, and the crown of thorns is near! Those who don't believe in the might of truth, who have not the courage to stand up for it even unto death, who do not believe in themselves and are afraid of suffering—such of you, step aside! We call upon those only who believe in our triumph. Those who cannot see our goal, let them not walk with us; only misery is in store for them! Fall into line, comrades! Long live the first of May, the holiday of freemen!"

The crowd drew closer. Pavel waved the flag. It spread out in the air and sailed forward, sunlit, smiling, red, and glowing.

"Let us renounce the old world!" resounded Fedya Mazin's ringing voice; and scores of voices took up the cry. It floated as on a mighty wave.

"Let us shake its dust from our feet."

The mother marched behind Mazin with a smile on her dry lips, and looked over his head at her son and the flag. Everywhere, around her, was the sparkle of fresh young cheerful faces, the glimmer of many-colored eyes; and at the head of all—her son and Andrey. She heard their voices, Andrey's, soft and humid, mingled in friendly accord with the heavy bass of her son:

"Rise up, awake, you workingmen! On, on, to war, you hungry hosts!"

Men ran toward the red flag, raising a clamor; then joining the others, they marched along, their shouts lost in the broad sounds of the song of the revolution.

The mother had heard that song before. It had often been sung in a subdued tone; and the Little Russian had often whistled it. But now she seemed for the first time to hear this appeal to unite in the struggle.

"We march to join our suffering mates."

The song flowed on, embracing the people.

Some one's face, alarmed yet joyous, moved along beside the mother's, and a trembling voice spoke, sobbing:

"Mitya! Where are you going?"

The mother interfered without stopping:

"Let him go! Don't be alarmed! Don't fear! I myself was afraid at first, too. Mine is right at the head—he who bears the standard—that's my son!"

"Murderers! Where are you going? There are soldiers over there!" And suddenly clasping the mother's hand in her bony hands, the tall, thin woman exclaimed: "My dear! How they sing! Oh, the sectarians! And Mitya is singing!"

"Don't be troubled!" murmured the mother. "It's a sacred thing. Think of it! Christ would not have been, either, if men hadn't perished for his sake."

This thought had flashed across the mother's mind all of a sudden and struck her by its simple, clear truth. She stared at the woman, who held her hand firmly in her clasp, and repeated, smiling:

"Christ would not have been, either, if men hadn't suffered for his sake."

Sizov appeared at her side. He took off his hat and waving it to the measure of the song, said:

"They're marching openly, eh, mother? And composed a song, too! What a song, mother, eh?"

> "The Czar for the army soldiers must have,
> Then give him your sons———"

"They're not afraid of anything," said Sizov. "And my son is in the grave. The factory crushed him to death, yes!"

The mother's heart beat rapidly, and she began to lag behind. She was soon pushed aside hard against a fence, and the close-packed crowd went streaming past her. She saw that there were many people, and she was pleased.

> "Rise up, awake, you workingmen!"

It seemed as if the blare of a mighty brass trumpet were rousing men and stirring in some hearts the willingness to fight, in other hearts a vague joy, a premonition of something new, and a burning curiosity; in still others a confused tremor of hope and curiosity. The song was an outlet, too, for the stinging bitterness accumulated during years.

The people looked ahead, where the red banner was swinging and streaming in the air. All were saying something and shouting; but the individual voice was lost in the song—the new song, in which the old note of mournful meditation was absent. It was not the utterance of a soul wandering in solitude along the dark paths of melancholy perplexity, of a soul beaten down by want, burdened with fear, deprived of individuality, and colorless. It breathed no sighs of a strength hungering for space; it shouted no provoking cries of irritated courage ready to crush both the good and the bad indiscriminately. It did not voice the elemental instinct of the animal to snatch freedom for freedom's sake, nor the feeling of wrong or vengeance capable of destroying everything and powerless to build up anything. In this song there was nothing from the old, slavish world. It floated along directly, evenly; it proclaimed an iron virility, a calm threat. Simple, clear, it swept the people after it along an endless path leading to the far distant future; and it spoke frankly about the hardships of the way. In its steady fire a heavy clod seemed to burn and melt—the sufferings they had endured, the dark load of their habitual feelings, their cursed dread of what was coming.

"They all join in!" somebody roared exultantly. "Well done, boys!"

Apparently the man felt something vast, to which he could not give expression in ordinary words, so he uttered a stiff oath. Yet the malice, the blind dark malice of a slave also streamed hotly through his teeth. Disturbed by the light shed upon it, it hissed like a snake, writhing in venomous words.

"Heretics!" a man with a broken voice shouted from a window, shaking his fist threateningly.

A piercing scream importunately bored into the mother's ears—"Rioting against the emperor, against his Majesty the Czar? No, no?"

Agitated people flashed quickly past her, a dark lava stream of men and women, carried along by this song, which cleared every obstacle out of its path.

Growing in the mother's breast was the mighty desire to shout to the crowd:

"Oh, my dear people!"

There, far away from her, was the red banner—she saw her son without seeing him—his bronzed forehead, his eyes burning with the bright fire of faith. Now she was in the tail of the crowd among the people who walked without hurrying, indifferent, looking ahead with the cold curiosity of spectators who know beforehand how the show will end. They spoke softly with confidence.

"One company of infantry is near the school, and the other near the factory."

"The governor has come."

"Is that so?"

"I saw him myself. He's here."

Some one swore jovially and said:

"They've begun to fear our fellows, after all, haven't they? The soldiers have come and the governor——"

"Dear boys!" throbbed in the breast of the mother. But the words around her sounded dead and cold. She hastened her steps to get away from these people, and it was not difficult for her to outstrip their lurching gait.

Suddenly the head of the crowd, as it were, bumped against

something; its body swung backward with an alarming, low hum. The song trembled, then flowed on more rapidly and louder; but again the dense wave of sounds hesitated in its forward course. Voices fell out of the chorus one after the other. Here and there a voice was raised in the effort to bring the song to its previous height, to push it forward:

> "Rise up, awake, you workingmen!
> On, on, to war, you hungry hosts!"

Though she saw nothing and was ignorant of what was happening there in front, the mother divined, and elbowed her way rapidly through the crowd.

CHAPTER XX

"Comrades!" the voice of Pavel was heard. "Soldiers are people the same as ourselves. They will not strike us! Why should they beat us? Because we bear the truth necessary for all? This our truth is necessary to them, too. Just now they do not understand this; but the time is nearing when they will rise with us, when they will march, not under the banner of robbers and murderers, the banner which the liars and beasts order them to call the banner of glory and honor, but under our banner of freedom and goodness! We ought to go forward so that they should understand our truth the sooner. Forward, comrades! Ever forward!"

Pavel's voice sounded firm, the words rang in the air distinctly. But the crowd fell asunder; one after the other the people dropped off to the right or to the left, going toward their homes, or leaning against the fences. Now the crowd had the shape of a wedge, and its point was Pavel, over whose head the banner of the laboring people was burning red.

At the end of the street, closing the exit to the square, the mother saw a low, gray wall of men, one just like the other, without faces. On the shoulder of each a bayonet was smiling its thin, chill smile; and from this entire immobile wall a cold gust blew down on the workmen, striking the breast of the mother and penetrating her heart.

She forced her way into the crowd among people familiar to her, and, as it were, leaned on them.

She pressed closely against a tall, lame man with a clean-shaven face. In order to look at her, he had to turn his head stiffly.

"What do you want? Who are you?" he asked her.

"The mother of Pavel Vlasov," she answered, her knees trembling beneath her, her lower lip involuntarily dropping.

"Ha-ha!" said the lame man. "Very well!"

"Comrades!" Pavel cried. "Onward all your lives. There is no other way for us! Sing!"

The atmosphere grew tense. The flag rose and rocked and waved over the heads of the people, gliding toward the gray wall of soldiers. The mother trembled. She closed her eyes, and cried: "Oh—oh!"

None but Pavel, Andrey, Samoylov, and Mazin advanced beyond the crowd.

The limpid voice of Fedya Mazin slowly quivered in the air.

"'In mortal strife—'" he began the song.

"'You victims fell—'" answered thick, subdued voices. The words dropped in two heavy sighs. People stepped forward, each footfall audible. A new song, determined and resolute, burst out:

"You yielded up your lives for them."

Fedya's voice wreathed and curled like a bright ribbon.

"A-ha-ha-ha!" some one exclaimed derisively. "They've struck up a funeral song, the dirty dogs!"

"Beat him!" came the angry response.

The mother clasped her hands to her breast, looked about, and saw that the crowd, before so dense, was now standing irresolute, watching the comrades walk away from them with the banner, followed by about a dozen people, one of whom, however, at every forward move, jumped aside as if the path in the middle of the street were red hot and burned his soles.

"The tyranny will fall—" sounded the prophetic song from the lips of Fedya.

"And the people will rise!" the chorus of powerful voices

seconded confidently and menacingly.

But the harmonious flow of the song was broken by the quiet words:

"He is giving orders."

"Charge bayonets!" came the piercing order from the front.

The bayonets curved in the air, and glittered sharply; then fell and stretched out to confront the banner.

"Ma-arch!"

"They're coming!" said the lame man, and thrusting his hands into his pockets made a long step to one side.

The mother, without blinking, looked on. The gray line of soldiers tossed to and fro, and spread out over the entire width of the street. It moved on evenly, coolly, carrying in front of itself a fine-toothed comb of sparkling bayonets. Then it came to a stand. The mother took long steps to get nearer to her son. She saw how Andrey strode ahead of Pavel and fenced him off with his long body. "Get alongside of me!" Pavel shouted sharply. Andrey was singing, his hands clasped behind his back, his head uplifted. Pavel pushed him with his shoulder, and again cried:

"At my side! Let the banner be in front!"

"Disperse!" called a little officer in a thin voice, brandishing a white saber. He lifted his feet high, and without bending his knees struck his soles on the ground irritably. The high polish on his boots caught the eyes of the mother.

To one side and somewhat behind him walked a tall, clean-shaven man, with a thick, gray mustache. He wore a long gray overcoat with a red underlining, and yellow stripes on his trousers. His gait was heavy, and like the Little Russian, he clasped his hands behind his back. He regarded Pavel, raising his thick gray eyebrows.

The mother seemed to be looking into infinity. At each breath her breast was ready to burst with a loud cry. It choked her, but for some reason she restrained it. Her hands clutched at her bosom. She staggered from repeated thrusts. She walked onward without thought, almost without consciousness. She felt that behind her the crowd was getting thinner; a cold wind had blown on them and scattered them like autumn leaves.

The men around the red banner moved closer and closer

together. The faces of the soldiers were clearly seen across the entire width of the street, monstrously flattened, stretched out in a dirty yellowish band. In it were unevenly set variously colored eyes, and in front the sharp bayonets glittered crudely. Directed against the breasts of the people, although not yet touching them, they drove them apart, pushing one man after the other away from the crowd and breaking it up.

Behind her the mother heard the trampling noise of those who were running away. Suppressed, excited voices cried:

"Disperse, boys!"

"Vlasov, run!"

"Back, Pavel!"

"Drop the banner, Pavel!" Vyesovshchikov said glumly. "Give it to me! I'll hide it!"

He grabbed the pole with his hand; the flag rocked backward.

"Let go!" thundered Pavel.

Nikolay drew his hand back as if it had been burned. The song died away. Some persons crowded solidly around Pavel; but he cut through to the front. A sudden silence fell.

Around the banner some twenty men were grouped, not more, but they stood firmly. The mother felt drawn to them by awe and by a confused desire to say something to them.

"Take this thing away from him, lieutenant." The even voice of the tall old man was heard. He pointed to the banner. A little officer jumped up to Pavel, snatched at the flag pole, and shouted shrilly:

"Drop it!"

The red flag trembled in the air, moving to the right and to the left, then rose again. The little officer jumped back and sat down. Nikolay darted by the mother, shaking his outstretched fist.

"Seize them!" the old man roared, stamping his feet. A few soldiers jumped to the front, one of them flourishing the butt end of his gun. The banner trembled, dropped, and disappeared in a gray mass of soldiers.

"Oh!" somebody groaned aloud. And the mother yelled like a wild animal. But the clear voice of Pavel answered her from out of the crowd of soldiers:

"Good-by, mother! Good-by, dear!"

"He's alive! He remembered!" were the two strokes at the mother's heart.

"Good-by, mother dear!" came from Andrey.

Waving her hands, she raised herself on tiptoe, and tried to see them. There was the round face of Andrey above the soldiers' heads. He was smiling and bowing to her.

"Oh, my dear ones! Andriusha! Pasha!" she shouted.

"Good-by, comrades!" they called from among the soldiers.

A broken, manifold echo responded to them. It resounded from the windows and the roofs.

The mother felt some one pushing her breast. Through the mist in her eyes she saw the little officer. His face was red and strained, and he was shouting to her:

"Clear out of here, old woman!"

She looked down on him, and at his feet saw the flag pole broken in two parts, a piece of red cloth on one of them. She bent down and picked it up. The officer snatched it out of her hands, threw it aside, and shouted again, stamping his feet:

"Clear out of here, I tell you!"

A song sprang up and floated from among the soldiers:

"Arise, awake, you workingmen!"

Everything was whirling, rocking, trembling. A thick, alarming noise, resembling the dull hum of telegraph wires, filled the air. The officer jumped back, screaming angrily:

"Stop the singing, Sergeant Kraynov!"

The mother staggered to the fragment of the pole, which he had thrown down, and picked it up again.

"Gag them!"

The song became confused, trembled, expired. Somebody took the mother by the shoulders, turned her around, and shoved her from the back.

"Go, go! Clear the street!" shouted the officer.

About ten paces from her, the mother again saw a thick crowd of people. They were howling, grumbling, whistling, as they backed down the street. The yards were drawing in a number of them.

"Go, you devil!" a young soldier with a big mustache shouted right into the mother's ear. He brushed against her and shoved her onto the sidewalk. She moved away, leaning on the flag pole. She went quickly and lightly, but her legs bent under her. In order not to fall she clung to walls and fences. People in front were falling back alongside of her, and behind her were soldiers, shouting: "Go, go!"

The soldiers got ahead of her; she stopped and looked around. Down the end of the street she saw them again scattered in a thin chain, blocking the entrance to the square, which was empty. Farther down were more gray figures slowly moving against the people. She wanted to go back; but uncalculatingly went forward again, and came to a narrow, empty by-street into which she turned. She stopped again. She sighed painfully, and listened. Somewhere ahead she heard the hum of voices. Leaning on the pole she resumed her walk. Her eyebrows moved up and down, and she suddenly broke into a sweat; her lips quivered; she waved her hands, and certain words flashed up in her heart like sparks, kindling in her a strong, stubborn desire to speak them, to shout them.

The by-street turned abruptly to the left; and around the corner the mother saw a large, dense crowd of people. Somebody's voice was speaking loudly and firmly:

"They don't go to meet the bayonets from sheer audacity. Remember that!"

"Just look at them. Soldiers advance against them, and they stand before them without fear. Y-yes!"

"Think of Pasha Vlasov!"

"And how about the Little Russian?"

"Hands behind his back and smiling, the devil!"

"My dear ones! My people!" the mother shouted, pushing into the crowd. They cleared the way for her respectfully. Somebody laughed:

"Look at her with the flag in her hand!"

"Shut up!" said another man sternly.

The mother with a broad sweep of her arms cried out:

"Listen for the sake of Christ! You are all dear people, you are all good people. Open up your hearts. Look around without fear, without terror. Our children are going into the world. Our children are going, our blood is going for the truth; with honesty in their hearts they open the gates of the new road—a straight, wide road for all. For all of you, for the sake of your young ones, they have devoted themselves to the sacred cause. They seek the sun of new days that shall always be bright. They want another life, the life of truth and justice, of goodness for all."

Her heart was rent asunder, her breast contracted, her throat was hot and dry. Deep inside of her, words were being born, words of a great, all-embracing love. They burned her tongue, moving it more powerfully and more freely. She saw that the people were listening to her words. All were silent. She felt that they were thinking as they surrounded her closely; and the desire grew in her, now a clear desire, to drive these people to follow her son, to follow Andrey, to follow all those who had fallen into the soldiers' hands, all those who were left entirely alone, all those who were abandoned. Looking at the sullen, attentive faces around her, she resumed with soft force:

"Our children are going in the world toward happiness. They went for the sake of all, and for Christ's truth—against all with which our malicious, false, avaricious ones have captured, tied, and crushed us. My dear ones—why it is for you that our young blood rose—for all the people, for all the world, for all the workingmen, they went! Then don't go away from them, don't renounce, don't forsake them, don't leave your children on a lonely path—they went just for the purpose of showing you all the path to truth, to take all on that path! Pity yourselves! Love them! Understand the children's hearts. Believe your sons' hearts; they have brought forth the truth; it burns in them; they perish for it. Believe them!"

Her voice broke down, she staggered, her strength gone. Somebody seized her under the arms.

"She is speaking God's words!" a man shouted hoarsely and excitedly. "God's words, good people! Listen to her!"

Another man said in pity of her:

"Look how she's hurting herself!"

"She's not hurting herself, but hitting us, fools, understand that!" was the reproachful reply.

A high-pitched, quavering voice rose up over the crowd:

"Oh, people of the true faith! My Mitya, pure soul, what has he done? He went after his dear comrades. She speaks truth—why did we forsake our children? What harm have they done us?"

The mother trembled at these words and replied with soft tears.

"Go home, Nilovna! Go, mother! You're all worn out," said Sizov loudly.

He was pale, his disheveled beard shook. Suddenly knitting his brows he threw a stern glance about him on all, drew himself up to his full height, and said distinctly:

"My son Matvey was crushed in the factory. You know it! But were he alive, I myself would have sent him into the lines of those— along with them. I myself would have told him: 'Go you, too, Matvey! That's the right cause, that's the honest cause!'"

He stopped abruptly, and a sullen silence fell on all, in the powerful grip of something huge and new, but something that no longer frightened them. Sizov lifted his hand, shook it, and continued:

"It's an old man who is speaking to you. You know me! I've been working here thirty-nine years, and I've been alive fifty-three years. To-day they've arrested my nephew, a pure and intelligent boy. He, too, was in the front, side by side with Vlasov; right at the banner." Sizov made a motion with his hand, shrank together, and said as he took the mother's hand: "This woman spoke the truth. Our children want to live honorably, according to reason, and we have abandoned them; we walked away, yes! Go, Nilovna!"

"My dear ones!" she said, looking at them all with tearful eyes. "The life is for our children and the earth is for them."

"Go, Nilovna, take this staff and lean upon it!" said Sizov, giving her the fragment of the flag pole.

All looked at the mother with sadness and respect. A hum of sympathy accompanied her. Sizov silently put the people out of her way, and they silently moved aside, obeying a blind impulse to follow her. They walked after her slowly, exchanging brief, subdued remarks on the way. Arrived at the gate of her house, she turned to them, leaning on the fragment of the flag pole, and bowed in gratitude.

"Thank you!" she said softly. And recalling the thought which she fancied had been born in her heart, she said: "Our Lord Jesus Christ would not have been, either, if people had not perished for his sake."

The crowd looked at her in silence.

She bowed to the people again, and went into her house, and Sizov, drooping his head, went in with her.

The people stood at the gates and talked. Then they began to depart slowly and quietly.

PART II

CHAPTER I

The day passed in a motley blur of recollections, in a depressing state of exhaustion, which tightly clutched at the mother's body and soul. The faces of the young men flashed before her mental vision, the banner blazed, the songs clamored at her ear, the little officer skipped about, a gray stain before her eyes, and through the whirlwind of the procession she saw the gleam of Pavel's bronzed face and the smiling sky-blue eyes of Andrey.

She walked up and down the room, sat at the window, looked out into the street, and walked away again with lowered eyebrows. Every now and then she started, and looked about in an aimless search for something. She drank water, but could not slake her thirst, nor quench the smoldering fire of anguish and injury in her bosom. The day was chopped in two. It began full of meaning and content, but now it dribbled away into a dismal waste, which stretched before her endlessly. The question swung to and fro in her barren, perplexed mind:

"What now?"

Korsunova came in. Waving her hands, she shouted, wept, and went into raptures; stamped her feet, suggested this and that, made promises, and threw out threats against somebody. All this failed to impress the mother.

"Aha!" she heard the squeaking voice of Marya. "So the people have been stirred up! At last the whole factory has arisen! All have arisen!"

"Yes, yes!" said the mother in a low voice, shaking her head. Her eyes were fixed on something that had already fallen into the past, had departed from her along with Andrey and Pavel. She was unable to weep. Her heart was dried up, her lips, too, were dry, and her mouth was parched. Her hands shook, and a cold, fine shiver ran down her back, setting her skin aquiver.

In the evening the gendarmes came. She met them without surprise and without fear. They entered noisily, with a peculiarly jaunty air, and with a look of gayety and satisfaction in their faces. The yellow-faced officer said, displaying his teeth:

"Well, how are you? The third time I have the honor, eh?"

She was silent, passing her dry tongue along her lips. The officer talked a great deal, delivering a homily to her. The mother realized what pleasure he derived from his words. But they did not reach her; they did not disturb her; they were like the insistent chirp of a cricket. It was only when he said: "It's your own fault, little mother, that you weren't able to inspire your son with reverence for God and the Czar," that she answered dully, standing at the door and looking at him: "Yes, our children are our judges. They visit just punishment upon us for abandoning them on such a road."

"Wha-at?" shouted the officer. "Louder!"

"I say, the children are our judges," the mother repeated with a sigh.

He said something quickly and angrily, but his words buzzed around her without touching her. Marya Korsunova was a witness. She stood beside the mother, but did not look at her; and when the officer turned to her with a question, she invariably answered with a hasty, low bow: "I don't know, your Honor. I am just a simple, ignorant woman. I make my living by peddling, stupid as I am, and I know nothing."

"Shut up, then!" commanded the officer.

She was ordered to search Vlasova. She blinked her eyes, then opened them wide on the officer, and said in fright:

"I can't, your Honor!"

The officer stamped his feet and began to shout. Marya lowered her eyes, and pleaded with the mother softly:

"Well, what can be done? You have to submit, Pelagueya Nilovna."

As she searched and felt the mother's dress, the blood mounting to her face, she murmured:

"Oh, the dogs!"

"What are you jabbering about there?" the officer cried rudely, looking into the corner where she was making the search.

"It's about women's affairs, your Honor," mumbled Marya, terrorized.

On his order to sign the search warrant the mother, with unskilled hand, traced on the paper in printed shining letters:

"Pelagueya Nilovna, widow of a workingman."

They went away, and the mother remained standing at the window. With her hands folded over her breast, she gazed into vacancy without winking, her eyebrows raised. Her lips were compressed, her jaws so tightly set that her teeth began to pain her. The oil burned down in the lamp, the light flared up for a moment, and then went out. She blew on it, and remained in the dark. She felt no malice, she harbored no sense of injury in her heart. A dark, cold cloud of melancholy settled on her breast, and impeded the beating of her heart. Her mind was a void. She stood at the window a long time; her feet and eyes grew weary. She heard Marya stop at the window, and shout: "Are you asleep, Pelagueya? You unfortunate, suffering woman, sleep! They abuse everybody, the heretics!" At last she dropped into bed without undressing, and quickly fell into a heavy sleep, as if she had plunged into a deep abyss.

She dreamed she saw a yellow sandy mound beyond the marsh on the road to the city. At the edge, which descended perpendicularly to the ditch, from which sand was being taken, stood Pavel singing softly and sonorously with the voice of Andrey:

"Rise up, awake, you workingmen!"

She walked past the mound along the road to the city, and putting her hand to her forehead looked at her son. His figure was clearly and sharply outlined against the sky. She could not make up her mind to go up to him. She was ashamed because she was pregnant. And she held an infant in her arms, besides. She walked farther on. Children were playing ball in the field. There were many of them, and the ball was a red one. The infant threw himself forward out of her arms toward them, and began to cry aloud. She gave him the breast, and turned back. Now soldiers were already at the mound, and they turned the bayonets against her. She ran quickly to the church standing in the middle of the field, the white, light church that seemed to be constructed out of clouds, and was immeasurably high. A funeral was going on there. The coffin was wide, black, and tightly covered with a lid. The priest and deacon walked around in white canonicals and sang:

"Christ has arisen from the dead."

The deacon carried the incense, bowed to her, and smiled. His hair was glaringly red, and his face jovial, like Samoylov's. From the top of the dome broad sunbeams descended to the ground. In both choirs the boys sang softly:

"Christ has arisen from the dead."

"Arrest them!" the priest suddenly cried, standing up in the middle of the church. His vestments vanished from his body, and a gray, stern mustache appeared on his face. All the people started to run, and the deacon, flinging the censer aside, rushed forward, seizing his head in his hands like the Little Russian. The mother dropped the infant on the ground at the feet of the people. They ran to the side of her, timidly regarding the naked little body. She fell on her knees and shouted to them: "Don't abandon the child! Take it with you!"

"Christ has arisen from the dead," the Little Russian sang, holding his hands behind his back, and smiling. He bent down, took the child, and put it on the wagon loaded with timber, at the side of which Nikolay was walking slowly, shaking with laughter. He said:

"They have given me hard work."

The street was muddy, the people thrust their faces from the windows of the houses, and whistled, shouted, waved their hands. The day was clear, the sun shone brightly, and there was not a single shadow anywhere.

"Sing, mother!" said the Little Russian. "Oh, what a life!"

And he sang, drowning all the other sounds with his kind, laughing voice. The mother walked behind him, and complained:

"Why does he make fun of me?"

But suddenly she stumbled and fell in a bottomless abyss. Fearful shrieks met her in her descent.

She awoke, shivering and yet perspiring. She put her ear, as it were, to her own breast, and marveled at the emptiness that prevailed there. The whistle blew insistently. From its sound she realized that it was already the second summons. The room was all in disorder; the books and clothes lay about in confusion; everything was turned upside down, and dirt was trampled over the entire floor.

She arose, and without washing or praying began to set the room in order. In the kitchen she caught sight of the stick with the piece of red cloth. She seized it angrily, and was about to throw it away under the oven, but instead, with a sigh, removed the remnant of the flag from the pole, folded it carefully, and put it in her pocket. Then she began to wash the windows with cold water, next the floor, and finally herself; then dressed herself and prepared the samovar. She sat down at the window in the kitchen, and once more the question came to her:

"What now? What am I to do now?"

Recollecting that she had not yet said her prayers, she walked up to the images, and after standing before them for a few seconds, she sat down again. Her heart was empty.

The pendulum, which always beat with an energy seeming to say: "I must get to the goal! I must get to the goal!" slackened its hasty ticking. The flies buzzed irresolutely, as if pondering a certain plan of action.

Suddenly she recalled a picture she had once seen in the days of her youth. In the old park of the Zansaylovs, there was a large pond densely overgrown with water lilies. One gray day in the fall, while walking along the pond, she had seen a boat in the middle of it. The pond was dark and calm, and the boat seemed glued to the black water, thickly strewn with yellow leaves. Profound sadness and a vague sense of misfortune were wafted from that boat without a rower and without oars, standing alone and motionless out there on the dull water amid the dead leaves. The mother had stood a long time at the edge of the pond meditating as to who had pushed the boat from the shore and why. Now it seemed to her that she herself was like that boat, which at the time had reminded her of a coffin waiting for its dead. In the evening of the same day she had learned that the wife of one of Zansaylov's clerks had been drowned in the pond—a little woman with black disheveled hair, who always walked at a brisk gait.

The mother passed her hands over her eyes as if to rub her reminiscences away, and her thoughts fluttered like a varicolored ribbon. Overcome by her impressions of the day before, she sat for a long time, her eyes fixed upon the cup of tea grown cold. Gradually the desire came to see some wise, simple person, speak to him, and ask him many things.

As if in answer to her wish, Nikolay Ivanovich came in after dinner. When she saw him, however, she was suddenly seized with alarm, and failed to respond to his greeting.

"Oh, my friend," she said softly, "there was no use for you to come here. If they arrest you here, too, then that will be the end of Pasha altogether. It's very careless of you! They'll take you without fail if they see you here."

He clasped her hand tightly, adjusted his glasses on his nose, and bending his face close to her, explained to her in haste:

"I made an agreement with Pavel and Andrey, that if they were arrested, I must see that you move over to the city the very next day." He spoke kindly, but with a troubled air. "Did they make a search in your house?"

"They did. They rummaged, searched, and nosed around. Those people have no shame, no conscience!" exclaimed the mother indignantly.

"What do they need shame for?" said Nikolay with a shrug of his shoulders, and explained to her the necessity of her going to the city.

His friendly, solicitous talk moved and agitated her. She looked at him with a pale smile, and wondered at the kindly feeling of confidence he inspired in her.

"If Pasha wants it, and I'll be no inconvenience to you——"

"Don't be uneasy on that score. I live all alone; my sister comes over only rarely."

"I'm not going to eat my head off for nothing," she said, thinking aloud.

"If you want to work, you'll find something to do."

Her conception of work was now indissolubly connected with

the work that her son, Andrey, and their comrades were doing. She moved a little toward Nikolay, and looking in his eyes, asked:

"Yes? You say work will be found for me?"

"My household is a small one, I am a bachelor——"

"I'm not talking about that, not about housework," she said quietly. "I mean world work."

And she heaved a melancholy sigh, stung and repelled by his failure to understand her. He rose, and bending toward her, with a smile in his nearsighted eyes, he said thoughtfully, "You'll find a place for yourself in the work world, too, if you want it."

Her mind quickly formulated the simple and clear thought: "Once I was able to help Pavel; perhaps I will succeed again. The greater the number of those who work for his cause, the clearer will his truth come out before the people."

But these thoughts did not fully express the whole force and complexity of her desire.

"What could I do?" she asked quietly.

He thought a while, and then began to explain the technical details of the revolutionary work. Among other things, he said:

"If, when you go to see Pavel in prison, you tried to find out from him the address of the peasant who asked for a newspaper——"

"I know it!" exclaimed the mother in delight. "I know where they are, and who they are. Give me the papers, I'll deliver them. I'll find the peasants, and do everything just as you say. Who will think that I carry illegal books? I carried books to the factory. I smuggled in more than a hundred pounds, Heaven be praised!"

The desire came upon her to travel along the road, through forests and villages, with a birch-bark sack over her shoulders, and a staff in her hand.

"Now, you dear, dear man, you just arrange it for me, arrange it so that I can work in this movement. I'll go everywhere for you! I'll keep going summer and winter, down to my very grave, a pilgrim for the sake of truth. Why, isn't that a splendid lot for a woman like me? The wanderer's life is a good life. He goes about through the world, he has nothing, he needs nothing except bread, no one abuses him, and so, quietly, unnoticed, he roves over the earth. And so I'll go, too; I'll go to Andrey, to Pasha, wherever they live."

She was seized with sadness when she saw herself homeless, begging for alms, in the name of Christ, at the windows of the village cottages.

Nikolay took her hand gently, and stroked it with his warm hand. Then, looking at the watch, he said:

"We'll speak about that later. You are taking a dangerous burden upon your shoulders. You must consider very carefully what you intend doing."

"My dear man, what have I to consider? What have I to live for if not for this cause? Of what use am I to anybody? A tree grows, it gives shade; it's split into wood, and it warms people. Even a mere dumb tree is helpful to life, and I am a human being. The children, the best blood of man, the best there is of our hearts, give up their liberty and their lives, perish without pity for themselves! And I, a mother—am I to stand by and do nothing?"

The picture of her son marching at the head of the crowd with the banner in his hands flashed before her mind.

"Why should I lie idle when my son gives up his life for the sake of truth? I know now—I know that he is working for the truth. It's the fifth year now that I live beside the woodpile. My heart has melted and begun to burn. I understand what you are striving for. I see what a burden you all carry on your shoulders. Take me to you, too, for the sake of Christ, that I may be able to help my son! Take me to you!"

Nikolay's face grew pale; he heaved a deep sigh, and smiling, said, looking at her with sympathetic attention:

"This is the first time I've heard such words."

"What can I say?" she replied, shaking her head sadly, and spreading her hands in a gesture of impotence. "If I had the words to express my mother's heart—" She arose, lifted by the power that waxed in her breast, intoxicated her, and gave her the words to express her indignation. "Then many and many a one would weep, and even the wicked, the men without conscience would tremble! I would make them taste gall, even as they made Christ drink of the cup of bitterness, and as they now do our children. They have bruised a mother's heart!"

Nikolay rose, and pulling his little beard with trembling fingers, he said slowly in an unfamiliar tone of voice:

"Some day you will speak to them, I think!"

He started, looked at his watch again, and asked in a hurry:

"So it's settled? You'll come over to me in the city?"

She silently nodded her head.

"When? Try to do it as soon as possible." And he added in a tender voice: "I'll be anxious for you; yes, indeed!"

She looked at him in surprise. What was she to him? With bent head, smiling in embarrassment, he stood before her, dressed in a simple black jacket, stooping, nearsighted.

"Have you money?" he asked, dropping his eyes.

"No."

He quickly whipped his purse out of his pocket, opened it, and handed it to her.

"Here, please take some."

She smiled involuntarily, and shaking her head, observed:

"Everything about all of you is different from other people. Even money has no value for you. People do anything to get money; they kill their souls for it. But for you money is so many little pieces of paper, little bits of copper. You seem to keep it by you just out of kindness to people."

Nikolay Ivanovich laughed softly.

"It's an awfully bothersome article, money is. Both to take it and to give it is embarrassing."

He caught her hand, pressed it warmly, and asked again:

"So you will try to come soon, won't you?"

And he walked away quietly, as was his wont.

She got herself ready to go to him on the fourth day after his visit. When the cart with her two trunks rolled out of the village into the open country, she turned her head back, and suddenly had the feeling that she was leaving the place forever—the place where she had passed the darkest and most burdensome period of her life, the place where that other varied life had begun, in which the next day swallowed up the day before, and each was filled by an abundance of new sorrows and new joys, new thoughts and new feelings.

The factory spread itself like a huge, clumsy, dark-red spider, raising its lofty smokestacks high up into the sky. The small one-storied houses pressed against it, gray, flattened out on the soot-covered ground, and crowded up in close clusters on the edge of the marsh. They looked sorrowfully at one another with their little dull windows. Above them rose the church, also dark red like the factory. The belfry, it seemed to her, was lower than the factory chimneys.

The mother sighed, and adjusted the collar of her dress, which choked her. She felt sad, but it was a dry sadness like the dust of the hot day.

"Gee!" mumbled the driver, shaking the reins over the horse. He was a bow-legged man of uncertain height, with sparse, faded hair on his face and head, and faded eyes. Swinging from side to side he walked alongside the wagon. It was evidently a matter of indifference to him whether he went to the right or the left.

"Gee!" he called in a colorless voice, with a comical forward stride of his crooked legs clothed in heavy boots, to which clods of mud were clinging. The mother looked around. The country was as bleak and dreary as her soul.

"You'll never escape want, no matter where you go, auntie," the driver said dully. "There's no road leading away from poverty; all roads lead to it, and none out of it."

Shaking its head dejectedly the horse sank its feet heavily into the deep sun-dried sand, which crackled softly under its tread. The rickety wagon creaked for lack of greasing.

CHAPTER II

Nikolay Ivanovich lived on a quiet, deserted street, in a little green wing annexed to a black two-storied structure swollen with age. In front of the wing was a thickly grown little garden, and branches of lilac bushes, acacias, and silvery young poplars looked benignly and freshly into the windows of the three rooms occupied by Nikolay. It was quiet and tidy in his place. The shadows trembled mutely on the floor, shelves closely set with books stretched across the walls, and portraits of stern, serious persons hung over them.

"Do you think you'll find it convenient here?" asked Nikolay, leading the mother into a little room with one window giving on the garden and another on the grass-grown yard. In this room, too, the walls were lined with bookcases and bookshelves.

"I'd rather be in the kitchen," she said. "The little kitchen is bright and clean."

It seemed to her that he grew rather frightened. And when she yielded to his awkward and embarrassed persuasions to take the room, he immediately cheered up.

There was a peculiar atmosphere pervading all the three rooms. It was easy and pleasant to breathe in them; but one's voice involuntarily dropped a note in the wish not to speak aloud and intrude upon the peaceful thoughtfulness of the people who sent down a concentrated look from the walls.

"The flowers need watering," said the mother, feeling the earth in the flowerpots in the windows.

"Yes, yes," said the master guiltily. "I love them very much, but I have no time to take care of them."

The mother noticed that Nikolay walked about in his own comfortable quarters just as carefully and as noiselessly as if he were a stranger, and as if all that surrounded him were remote from him. He would pick up and examine some small article, such as a bust, bring it close to his face, and scrutinize it minutely, adjusting his glasses with the thin finger of his right hand, and screwing up his eyes. He had the appearance of just having entered the rooms for the first time, and everything seemed as unfamiliar and strange to him as to the mother. Consequently, the mother at once felt herself at home. She followed Nikolay, observing where each thing stood, and inquiring about his ways and habits of life. He answered with the guilty air of a man who knows he is all the time doing things as they ought not to be done, but cannot help himself.

After she had watered the flowers and arranged the sheets of music scattered in disorder over the piano, she looked at the samovar, and remarked, "It needs polishing."

Nikolay ran his finger over the dull metal, then stuck the finger close to his nose. He looked at the mother so seriously that she could not restrain a good-natured smile.

When she lay down to sleep and thought of the day just past, she raised her head from the pillow in astonishment and looked around. For the first time in her life she was in the house of a stranger, and she did not experience the least constraint. Her mind dwelt solicitously on Nikolay. She had a distinct desire to do the best she could for him, and to introduce more warmth into his lonely life. She was stirred and affected by his embarrassed awkwardness and droll ignorance, and smiled to herself with a sigh. Then her thoughts leaped to her son and to Andrey. She recalled the high-pitched, sparkling voice of Fedya, and gradually the whole day of the first of May unrolled itself before her, clothed in new sounds, reflecting new thoughts. The trials of the day were peculiar as the day itself. They did not bring her head to the ground as with the dull, stunning blow of the fist. They stabbed the heart with a thousand pricks, and called forth in her a quiet wrath, opening her eyes and straightening her backbone.

"Children go in the world," she thought as she listened to the unfamiliar nocturnal sounds of the city. They crept through the open window like a sigh from afar, stirring the leaves in the garden and faintly expiring in the room.

Early in the morning she polished up the samovar, made a fire in it, and filled it with water, and noiselessly placed the dishes on the table. Then she sat down in the kitchen and waited for Nikolay to rise. Presently she heard him cough. He appeared at the door, holding his glasses in one hand, the other hand at his throat. She responded to his greeting, and brought the samovar into the room. He began to wash himself, splashing the water on the floor, dropping the soap and his toothbrush, and grumbling in dissatisfaction at himself.

When they sat down to drink tea, he said to the mother:

"I am employed in the Zemstvo board—a very sad occupation. I see the way our peasants are going to ruin."

And smiling he repeated guiltily: "It's literally so—I see! People go hungry, they lie down in their graves prematurely, starved to death, children are born feeble and sick, and drop like flies in autumn—we know all this, we know the causes of this wretchedness, and for observing it we receive a good salary. But that's all we do, really; truly all we do."

"And what are you, a student?"

"No. I'm a village teacher. My father was superintendent in a mill in Vyatka, and I became a teacher. But I began to give books to the peasants in the village, and was put in prison for it. When I came out of prison I became clerk in a bookstore, but not behaving carefully enough I got myself into prison again, and was then exiled to Archangel. There I also got into trouble with the governor, and they sent me to the White Sea coast, where I lived for five years."

His talk sounded calm and even in the bright room flooded with sunlight. The mother had already heard many such stories; but she could never understand why they were related with such composure, why no blame was laid on anybody for the suffering the people had gone through, why these sufferings were regarded as so inevitable.

"My sister is coming to-day," he announced.

"Is she married?"

"She's a widow. Her husband was exiled to Siberia; but he escaped, caught a severe cold on the way, and died abroad two years ago."

"Is she younger than you?"

"Six years older. I owe a great deal to her. Wait, and you'll hear how she plays. That's her piano. There are a whole lot of her things here, my books——"

"Where does she live?"

"Everywhere," he answered with a smile. "Wherever a brave soul is needed, there's where you'll find her."

"Also in this movement?"

"Yes, of course."

He soon left to go to work, and the mother fell to thinking of "that movement" for which the people worked, day in, day out, calmly and resolutely. When confronting them she seemed to stand before a mountain looming in the dark.

About noon a tall, well-built lady came. When the mother opened the door for her she threw a little yellow valise on the floor, and quickly seizing Vlasova's hand, asked:

"Are you the mother of Pavel Mikhaylovich?"

"Yes, I am," the mother replied, embarrassed by the lady's rich appearance.

"That's the way I imagined you," said the lady, removing her hat in front of the mirror. "We have been friends of Pavel Mikhaylovich a long time. He spoke about you often."

Her voice was somewhat dull, and she spoke slowly; but her movements were quick and vigorous. Her large, limpid gray eyes smiled youthfully; on her temples, however, thin radiate wrinkles were already limned, and silver hairs glistened over her ears.

"I'm hungry; can I have a cup of coffee?"

"I'll make it for you at once." The mother took down the coffee apparatus from the shelf and quietly asked:

"*Did* Pasha speak about me?"

"Yes, indeed, a great deal." The lady took out a little leather cigarette case, lighted a cigarette, and inquired: "You're extremely uneasy about him, aren't you?"

The mother smiled, watching the blue, quivering flame of the spirit lamp. Her embarrassment at the presence of the lady vanished in the depths of her joy.

"So he talks about me, my dear son!" she thought.

"You asked me whether I'm uneasy? Of course, it's not easy for me. But it would have been worse some time ago; now I know that he's not alone, and that even I am not alone." Looking into the lady's face, she asked: "What is your name?"

"Sofya," the lady answered, and began to speak in a businesslike way. "The most important thing is that they should not stay in prison long, but that the trial should come off very soon. The moment they are exiled, we'll arrange an escape for Pavel Mikhaylovich. There's nothing for him to do in Siberia, and he's indispensable here."

The mother incredulously regarded Sofya, who was searching about for a place into which to drop her cigarette stump, and finally threw it in a flowerpot.

"That'll spoil the flowers," the mother remarked mechanically.

"Excuse me," said Sofya simply. "Nikolay always tells me the same thing." She picked up the stump and threw it out of the window. The mother looked at her in embarrassment, and said guiltily:

"You must excuse me. I said it without thinking. Is it in my place to teach you?"

"Why not? Why not teach me, if I'm a sloven?" Sofya calmly queried with a shrug. "I know it; but I always forget—the worse for me. It's an ugly habit—to throw cigarette stumps any and everywhere, and to litter up places with ashes—particularly in a woman. Cleanliness in a room is the result of work, and all work ought to be respected. Is the coffee ready? Thank you! Why one cup? Won't you have any?" Suddenly seizing the mother by the shoulder, she drew her to herself, and looking into her eyes asked in surprise: "Why, are you embarrassed?"

The mother answered with a smile:

"I just blamed you for throwing the cigarette stump away—does that look as if I were embarrassed?" Her surprise was unconcealed. "I came to your house only yesterday, but I behave as if I were at home, and as if I had known you a long time. I'm afraid of nothing; I say anything. I even find fault."

"That's the way it ought to be."

"My head's in a whirl. I seem to be a stranger to myself. Formerly I didn't dare speak out from my heart until I'd been with a person a long, long time. And now my heart is always open, and I at once say things I wouldn't have dreamed of before, and a lot of things, too." Sofya lit another cigarette, turning the kind glance of her gray eyes on the mother. "Yes, you speak of arranging an escape. But how will he be able to live as a fugitive?" The mother finally gave expression to the thought that was agitating her.

"That's a trifle," Sofya remarked, pouring out a cup of coffee for herself. "He'll live as scores of other fugitives live. I just met one, and saw him off. Another very valuable man, who worked for the movement in the south. He was exiled for five years, but remained only three and a half months. That's why I look such a *grande dame*. Do you think I always dress this way? I can't bear this fine toggery, this sumptuous rustle. A human being is simple by nature, and should dress simply—beautifully but simply."

The mother looked at her fixedly, smiled, and shaking her head meditatively said:

"No, it seems that day, the first of May, has changed me. I feel awkward somehow or other, as if I were walking on two roads at the same time. At one moment I understand everything; the next moment I am plunged into a mist. Here are you! I see you a lady; you occupy yourself with this movement, you know Pasha, and you esteem him. Thank you!"

"Why, you ought to be thanked!" Sofya laughed.

"I? I didn't teach him about the movement," the mother said with a sigh. "As I speak now," she continued stubbornly, "everything seems simple and near. Then, all of a sudden, I cannot understand this simplicity. Again, I'm calm. In a second I grow fearful, because I *am* calm. I always used to be afraid, my whole life long; but now that there's a great deal to be afraid of, I have very little fear. Why is it? I cannot understand." She stopped, at a loss for words. Sofya looked at her seriously, and waited; but seeing that the mother was agitated, unable to find the expression she wanted, she herself took up the conversation.

"A time will come when you'll understand everything. The chief thing that gives a person power and faith in himself is when he begins to love a certain cause with all his heart, and knows it is a good cause of use to everybody. There is such a love. There's everything. There's no human being too mean to love. But it's time for me to be getting out of all this magnificence."

Putting the stump of her cigarette in the saucer, she shook her head. Her golden hair fell back in thick waves. She walked away smiling. The mother followed her with her eyes, sighed, and looked around. Her thoughts came to a halt, and in a half-drowsy, oppressive condition of quiet, she began to get the dishes together.

At four o'clock Nikolay appeared. Then they dined. Sofya, laughing at times, told how she met and concealed the fugitive, how she feared the spies, and saw one in every person she met, and how comically the fugitive conducted himself. Something in her tone reminded the mother of the boasting of a workingman who had completed a difficult piece of work to his own satisfaction. She was now dressed in a flowing, dove-colored robe, which fell from her shoulders to her feet in warm waves. The effect was soft and noiseless. She appeared to be taller in this dress; her eyes seemed darker, and her movements less nervous.

"Now, Sofya," said Nikolay after dinner, "here's another job for you. You know we undertook to publish a newspaper for the village.

But our connection with the people there was broken, thanks to the latest arrests. No one but Pelagueya Nilovna can show us the man who will undertake the distribution of the newspapers. You go with her. Do it as soon as possible."

"Very well," said Sofya. "We'll go, Pelagueya Nilovna."

"Yes, we'll go."

"Is it far?"

"About fifty miles."

"Splendid! And now I'm going to play a little. Do you mind listening to music, Pelagueya Nilovna?"

"Don't bother about me. Act as if I weren't here," said the mother, seating herself in the corner of the sofa. She saw that the brother and the sister went on with their affairs without giving heed to her; yet, at the same time, she seemed involuntarily to mix in their conversation, imperceptibly drawn into it by them.

"Listen to this, Nikolay. It's by Grieg. I brought it to-day. Shut the window."

She opened the piano, and struck the keys lightly with her left hand. The strings sang out a thick, juicy melody. Another note, breathing a deep, full breath, joined itself to the first, and together they formed a vast fullness of sound that trembled beneath its own weight. Strange, limpid notes rang out from under the fingers of her right hand, and darted off in an alarming flight, swaying and rocking and beating against one another like a swarm of frightened birds. And in the dark background the low notes sang in measured, harmonious cadence like the waves of the sea exhausted by the storm. Some one cried out, a loud, agitated, woeful cry of rebellion, questioned and appealed in impotent anguish, and, losing hope, grew silent; and then again sang his rueful plaints, now resonant and clear, now subdued and dejected. In response to this song came the thick waves of dark sound, broad and resonant, indifferent and hopeless. They drowned by their depth and force the swarm of ringing wails; questions, appeals, groans blended in the alarming song. At times the music seemed to take a desperate upward flight, sobbing and lamenting, and again precipitated itself, crept low, swung hither and thither on the dense, vibratory current of bass notes, foundered, and disappeared in them; and once more breaking through to an even cadence, in a hopeless, calm rumble, it grew in volume, pealed forth, and melted and dissolved in the broad flourish of humid notes—which continued to sigh with equal force and calmness, never wearying.

At first the sounds failed to touch the mother. They were incomprehensible to her, nothing but a ringing chaos. Her ear could not gather a melody from the intricate mass of notes. Half asleep she looked at Nikolay sitting with his feet crossed under him at the other end of the long sofa, and at the severe profile of Sofya with her head enveloped in a mass of golden hair. The sun shone into the room. A single ray, trembling pensively, at first lighted up her hair and shoulder, then settled upon the keys of the piano, and quivered under the pressure of her fingers. The branches of the acacia rocked to and fro outside the window. The room became music-filled, and unawares to her, the mother's heart was stirred. Three notes of nearly the same pitch, resonant as the voice of Fedya Mazin, sparkled in the stream of sounds, like three silvery fish in a brook. At times another note united with these in a simple song, which enfolded the heart in a kind yet sad caress. She began to watch for them, to await their warble, and she heard only their music, distinguished from the tumultuous chaos of sound, to which her ears gradually became deaf.

And for some reason there rose before her out of the obscure depths of her past, wrongs long forgotten.

Once her husband came home late, extremely intoxicated. He grasped her hand, threw her from the bed to the floor, kicked her in the side with his foot, and said:

"Get out! I'm sick of you! Get out!"

In order to protect herself from his blows, she quickly gathered her two-year-old son into her arms, and kneeling covered herself with his body as with a shield. He cried, struggled in her arms, frightened, naked, and warm.

"Get out!" bellowed her husband.

She jumped to her feet, rushed into the kitchen, threw a jacket over her shoulders, wrapped the baby in a shawl, and silently, without outcries or complaints, barefoot, in nothing but a shirt under her jacket, walked out into the street. It was in the month of May, and the night was fresh. The cold, damp dust of the street stuck to her feet, and got between her toes. The child wept and struggled. She opened her breast, pressed her son to her body, and pursued by fear walked down the street, quietly lulling the baby.

It began to grow light. She was afraid and ashamed lest some one come out on the street and see her half naked. She turned toward the marsh, and sat down on the ground under a thick group of aspens. She sat there for a long time, embraced by the night, motionless, looking into the darkness with wide-open eyes, and timidly wailing a lullaby—a lullaby for her baby, which had fallen asleep, and a lullaby for her outraged heart.

A gray bird darted over her head, and flew far away. It awakened her, and brought her to her feet. Then, shivering with cold, she walked home to confront the horror of blows and new insults.

For the last time a heavy and resonant chord heaved a deep breath, indifferent and cold; it sighed and died away.

Sofya turned around, and asked her brother softly:

"Did you like it?"

"Very much," he said, nodding his head. "Very much."

Sofya looked at the mother's face, but said nothing.

"They say," said Nikolay thoughtfully, throwing himself deeper back on the sofa, "that you should listen to music without thinking. But I can't."

"Nor can I," said Sofya, striking a melodious chord.

"I listened, and it seemed to me that people were putting their questions to nature, that they grieved and groaned, and protested angrily, and shouted, 'Why?' Nature does not answer, but goes on calmly creating, incessantly, forever. In her silence is heard her answer: 'I do not know.'"

The mother listened to Nikolay's quiet words without understanding them, and without desiring to understand. Her bosom echoed with her reminiscences, and she wanted more music. Side by side with her memories the thought unfolded itself before her: "Here live people, a brother and sister, in friendship; they live peacefully and calmly—they have music and books—they don't swear at each other—they don't drink whisky—they don't quarrel for a relish—they have no desire to insult each other, the way all the people at the bottom do."

Sofya quickly lighted a cigarette; she smoked almost without intermission.

"This used to be the favorite piece of Kostya," she said, as a veil of smoke quickly enveloped her. She again struck a low mournful chord. "How I used to love to play for him! You remember how well he translated music into language?" She paused and smiled. "How sensitive he was! What fine feelings he had—so responsive to everything—so fully a man!"

"She must be recalling memories of her husband," the mother noted, "and she smiles!"

"How much happiness that man gave me!" said Sofya in a low voice, accompanying her words with light sounds on the keys. "What a capacity he had for living! He was always aglow with joy, buoyant, childlike joy!"

"Childlike," repeated the mother to herself, and shook her head as if agreeing with something.

"Ye-es," said Nikolay, pulling his beard, "his soul was always singing."

"When I played this piece for him the first time, he put it in these words." Sofya turned her face to her brother, and slowly stretched out her arms. Encircled with blue streaks of smoke, she spoke in a low, rapturous voice. "In a barren sea of the far north, under the gray canopy of the cold heavens, stands a lonely black island, an unpeopled rock, covered with ice; the smoothly polished shore descends abruptly into the gray, foaming billows. The transparently blue blocks of ice inhospitably float on the shaking cold water and press against the dark rock of the island. Their knocking resounds mournfully in the dead stillness of the barren sea. They have been floating a long time on the bottomless depths, and the waves splashing about them have quietly borne them toward the lonely rock in the midst of the sea. The sound is grewsome as they break against the shore and against one another, sadly inquiring: 'Why?'"

Sofya flung away the cigarette she had begun to smoke, turned to the piano, and again began to play the ringing plaints, the plaints of the lonely blocks of ice by the shore of the barren island in the sea of the far north.

The mother was overcome with unendurable sadness as she listened to the simple sketch. It blended strangely with her past, into which her recollections kept boring deeper and deeper.

"In music one can hear everything," said Nikolay quietly.

Sofya turned toward the mother, and asked:

"Do you mind my noise?"

The mother was unable to restrain her slight irritation.

"I told you not to pay any attention to me. I sit here and listen and think about myself."

"No, you ought to understand," said Sofya. "A woman can't help understanding music, especially when in grief."

She struck the keys powerfully, and a loud shout went forth, as if some one had suddenly heard horrible news, which pierced him to the heart, and wrenched from him this troubled sound. Young voices trembled in affright, people rushed about in haste, pellmell. Again a loud, angry voice shouted out, drowning all other sounds. Apparently a catastrophe had occurred, in which the chief source of pain was an affront offered to some one. It evoked not complaints, but wrath. Then some kindly and powerful person appeared, who began to sing, just like Andrey, a simple beautiful song, a song of exhortation and summons to himself. The voices of the bass notes grumbled in a dull, offended tone.

Sofya played a long time. The music disquieted the mother, and aroused in her a desire to ask of what it was speaking. Indistinct sensations and thoughts passed through her mind in quick succession. Sadness and anxiety gave place to moments of calm joy. A swarm of unseen birds seemed to be flying about in the room, penetrating everywhere, touching the heart with caressing wings, soothing and at the same time alarming it. The feelings in the mother's breast could not be fixed in words. They emboldened her heart with perplexed hopes, they fondled it in a fresh and firm embrace.

A kindly impulse came to her to say something good both to these two persons and to all people in general. She smiled softly, intoxicated by the music, feeling herself capable of doing work helpful to the brother and sister. Her eyes roved about in search of something to do for them. She saw nothing but to walk out into the kitchen quietly, and prepare the samovar. But this did not satisfy her desire. It struggled stubbornly in her breast, and as she poured out the tea she began to speak excitedly with an agitated smile. She seemed to bestow the words as a warm caress impartially on Sofya and Nikolay and on herself.

"We people at the bottom feel everything; but it is hard for us to speak out our hearts. Our thoughts float about in us. We are ashamed because, although we understand, we are not able to express them; and often from shame we are angry at our thoughts, and at those who inspire them. We drive them away from ourselves. For life, you see, is so troublesome. From all sides we get blows and beatings; we want rest, and there come the thoughts that rouse our souls and demand things of us."

Nikolay listened, and nodded his head, rubbing his eyeglasses briskly, while Sofya looked at her, her large eyes wide open and the forgotten cigarette burning to ashes. She sat half turned from the piano, supple and shapely, at times touching the keys lightly with the slender fingers of her right hand. The pensive chord blended delicately with the speech of the mother, as she quickly invested her new feelings and thoughts in simple, hearty words.

"Now I am able to say something about myself, about my people, because I understand life. I began to understand it when I was able to make comparisons. Before that time there was nobody to compare myself with. In our state, you see, all lead the same life, and now that I see how others live, I look back at my life, and the recollection is hard and bitter. But it is impossible to return, and even if you could, you wouldn't find your youth again. And I think I understand a great deal. Here, I am looking at you, and I recollect all your people whom I've seen." She lowered her voice and continued: "Maybe I don't say things right, and I needn't say them, because you know them yourself; but I'm just speaking for myself. You at once set me alongside of you. You don't need anything of me; you can't make use of me; you can't get any enjoyment out of me, I know it. And day after day my heart grows, thank God! It grows in goodness, and I wish good for everybody. This is my thanks that I'm saying to you." Tears of happy gratitude affected her voice, and looking at them with a smile in her eyes, she went on: "I want to open my heart before you, so that you may see how I wish your welfare."

"We see it," said Nikolay in a low voice. "You're making a holiday for us."

"What do you think I imagined?" the mother asked with a smile and lowering her voice. "I imagined I found a treasure, and became rich, and I could endow everybody. Maybe it's only my stupidity that's run away with me."

"Don't speak like that," said Sofya seriously. "You mustn't be ashamed."

The mother began to speak again, telling Sofya and Nikolay of herself, her poor life, her wrongs, and patient sufferings. Suddenly she stopped in her narrative. It seemed to her that she was turning aside, away from herself, and speaking about somebody else. In simple words, without malice, with a sad smile on her lips, she drew the monotonous, gray sketch of sorrowful days. She enumerated the beatings she had received from her husband; and herself marveled at the trifling causes that led to them and her own inability to avert them.

The brother and sister listened to her in attentive silence, impressed by the deep significance of the unadorned story of a human being, who was regarded as cattle are regarded, and who, without a murmur, for a long time felt herself to be that which she was held to be. It seemed to them as if thousands, nay millions, of lives spoke through her mouth. Her existence had been commonplace and simple; but such is the simple, ordinary existence of multitudes, and her story, assuming ever larger proportions in their eyes, took on the significance of a symbol. Nikolay, his elbows on the table, and his head leaning on his hands, looked at her through his glasses without moving, his eyes screwed up intently. Sofya flung herself back on her chair. Sometimes she trembled, and at times muttered to herself, shaking her head in disapproval. Her face grew paler. Her eyes deepened.

"Once I thought myself unhappy. My life seemed a fever," said Sofya, inclining her head. "That was when I was in exile. It was in a small district town. There was nothing to do, nothing to think about except myself. I swept all my misfortunes together into one heap, and weighed them, from lack of anything better to do. Then I quarreled with my father, whom I loved. I was expelled from the gymnasium, and insulted—the prison, the treachery of a comrade near to me, the arrest of my husband, again prison and exile, the death of my husband. But all my misfortunes, and ten times their number, are not worth a month of your life, Pelagueya Nilovna. Your torture continued daily through years. From where do the people draw their power to suffer?"

"They get used to it," responded the mother with a sigh.

"I thought I knew that life," said Nikolay softly. "But when I hear it spoken of—not when my books, not when my incomplete impressions speak about it, but she herself with a living tongue—it is horrible. And the details are horrible, the inanities, the seconds of which the years are made."

The conversation sped along, thoughtfully and quietly. It branched out and embraced the whole of common life on all sides. The mother became absorbed in her recollections. From her dim past she drew to light each daily wrong, and gave a massive picture of the huge, dumb horror in which her youth had been sunk. Finally she said:

"Oh! How I've been chattering to you! It's time for you to rest. I'll never be able to tell you all."

The brother and sister took leave of her in silence. Nikolay seemed to the mother to bow lower to her than ever before and to press her hand more firmly. Sofya accompanied her to her room, and stopping at the door said softly: "Now rest. I hope you have a good night."

Her voice blew a warm breath on the mother, and her gray eyes embraced the mother's face in a caress. She took Sofya's hand and pressing it in hers, answered: "Thank you! You are good people."

CHAPTER III

Three days passed in incessant conversations with Sofya and Nikolay. The mother continued to recount tales of the past, which stubbornly arose from the depths of her awakened soul, and disturbed even herself. Her past demanded an explanation. The attention with which the brother and sister listened to her opened her heart more and more widely, freeing her from the narrow, dark cage of her former life.

On the fourth day, early in the morning, she and Sofya appeared before Nikolay as burgher women, poorly clad in worn chintz skirts and blouses, with birch-bark sacks on their shoulders, and canes in their hands. This costume reduced Sofya's height and gave a yet sterner appearance to her pale face.

"You look as if you had walked about monasteries all your life," observed Nikolay on taking leave of his sister, and pressed her hand warmly. The mother again remarked the simplicity and calmness of their relation to each other. It was hard for her to get used to it. No kissing, no affectionate words passed between them; but they behaved so sincerely, so amicably and solicitously toward each other. In the life she had been accustomed to, people kissed a great deal and uttered many sentimental words, but always bit at one another like hungry dogs.

The women walked down the street in silence, reached the open country, and strode on side by side along the wide beaten road between a double row of birches.

"Won't you get tired?" the mother asked.

"Do you think I haven't done much walking? All this is an old story to me."

With a merry smile, as if speaking of some glorious childhood frolics, Sofya began to tell the mother of her revolutionary work. She had had to live under a changed name, use counterfeit documents, disguise herself in various costumes in order to hide from spies, carry hundreds and hundreds of pounds of illegal books through various cities, arrange escapes for comrades in exile, and escort them abroad. She had had a printing press fixed up in her quarters, and when on learning of it the gendarmes appeared to make a search, she succeeded in a minute's time before their arrival in dressing as a servant, and walking out of the house just as her guests were entering at the gate. She met them there. Without an outer wrap, a light kerchief on her head, a tin kerosene can in her hand, she traversed the city from one end to the other in the biting cold of a winter's day. Another time she had just arrived in a strange city to pay a visit to friends. When she was already on the stairs leading to their quarters, she noticed that a search was being conducted in their apartments. To turn back was too late. Without a second's hesitation she boldly rang the bell at the door of a lower floor, and walked in with her traveling bag to unknown people. She frankly explained the position she was in.

"You can hand me over to the gendarmes if you want to; but I don't think you will," she said confidently.

The people were greatly frightened, and did not sleep the whole night. Every minute they expected the sound of the gendarmes knocking at the door. Nevertheless, they could not make up their minds to deliver her over to them, and the next morning they had a hearty laugh with her over the gendarmes.

And once, dressed as a nun, she traveled in the same railroad coach, in fact, sat on the very same seat, with a spy, then in search of her. He boasted of his skill, and told her how he was conducting his search. He was certain she was riding on the same train as himself, in a second-class coach; but at every stop, after walking out, he came back saying: "Not to be seen. She must have gone to bed. They, too, get tired. Their life is a hard one, just like ours."

The mother listening to her stories laughed, and regarded her affectionately. Tall and dry, Sofya strode along the road lightly and firmly, at an even gait. In her walk, her words, and the very sound of her voice—although a bit dull, it was yet bold—in all her straight and stolid figure, there was much of robust strength, jovial daring, and thirst for space and freedom. Her eyes looked at everything with a youthful glance. She constantly spied something that gladdened her heart with childlike joy.

"See what a splendid pine!" she exclaimed, pointing out a tree to the mother.

The mother looked and stopped. It was a pine neither higher nor thicker than others.

"Ye-es, ye-es, a good tree," she said, smiling.

"Do you hear? A lark!" Sofya raised her head, and looked into the blue expanse of the sky for the merry songster. Her gray eyes flashed with a fond glance, and her body seemed to rise from the ground to meet the music ringing from an unseen source in the far-distant height. At times bending over, she plucked a field flower, and with light touches of her slender, agile fingers, she fondly stroked the quivering petals and hummed quietly and prettily.

Over them burned the kindly spring sun. The blue depths flashed softly. At the sides of the road stretched a dark pine forest. The fields were verdant, birds sang, and the thick, resinous atmosphere stroked the face warmly and tenderly.

All this moved the mother's heart nearer to the woman with the bright eyes and the bright soul; and, trying to keep even pace with her, she involuntarily pressed close to Sofya, as if desiring to draw into herself her hearty boldness and freshness.

"How young you are!" the mother sighed.

"I'm thirty-two years old already!"

Vlasova smiled. "I'm not talking about that. To judge by your face, one would say you're older; but one wonders that your eyes, your voice are so fresh, so springlike, as if you were a young girl. Your life is so hard and troubled, yet your heart is smiling."

"The heart is smiling," repeated Sofya thoughtfully. "How well you speak—simple and good. A hard life, you say? But I don't feel that it is hard, and I cannot imagine a better, a more interesting life than this."

"What pleases me more than anything else is to see how you all know the roads to a human being's heart. Everything in a person opens itself out to you without fear or caution—just so, all of itself, the heart throws itself open to meet you. I'm thinking of all of you. You overcome the evil in the world—overcome it absolutely."

"We shall be victorious, because we are with the working people," said Sofya with assurance. "Our power to work, our faith in the victory of truth we obtain from you, from the people; and the people is the inexhaustible source of spiritual and physical strength.

In the people are vested all possibilities, and with them everything is attainable. It's necessary only to arouse their consciousness, their soul, the great soul of a child, who is not given the liberty to grow." She spoke softly and simply, and looked pensively before her down the winding depths of the road, where a bright haze was quivering.

Sofya's words awakened a complex feeling in the mother's heart. For some reason she felt sorry for her. Her pity, however, was not offensive; not bred of familiarity. She marveled that here was a lady walking on foot and carrying a dangerous burden on her back.

"Who's going to reward you for your labors?"

Sofya answered the mother's thought with pride:

"We are already rewarded for everything. We have found a life that satisfies us; we live broadly and fully, with all the power of our souls. What else can we desire?"

Filling their lungs with the aromatic air, they paced along, not swiftly, but at a good, round gait. The mother felt she was on a pilgrimage. She recollected her childhood, the fine joy with which she used to leave the village on holidays to go to a distant monastery, where there was a wonder-working icon.

Sometimes Sofya would hum some new unfamiliar songs about the sky and about love, or suddenly she would begin to recite poems about the fields and forests and the Volga. The mother listened, a smile on her face, swinging her head to the measure of the tune or rhythm, involuntarily yielding to the music. Her breast was pervaded by a soft, melancholy warmth, like the atmosphere in a little old garden on a summer night.

On the third day they arrived at the village, and the mother inquired of a peasant at work in the field where the tar works were. Soon they were descending a steep woody path, on which the exposed roots of the trees formed steps through a small, round glade, which was choked up with coal and chips of wood caked with tar.

Outside a shack built of poles and branches, at a table formed simply of three unplaned boards laid on a trestle stuck firmly into the ground, sat Rybin, all blackened, his shirt open at his breast, Yefim, and two other young men. They were just dining. Rybin was the first to notice the women. Shading his eyes with his hand, he waited in silence.

"How do you do, brother Mikhaïl?" shouted the mother from afar.

He arose and leisurely walked to meet them. When he recognized the mother, he stopped and smiled and stroked his beard with his black hand.

"We are on a pilgrimage," said the mother, approaching him. "And so I thought I would stop in and see my brother. This is my friend Anna."

Proud of her resourcefulness she looked askance at Sofya's serious, stern face.

"How are you?" said Rybin, smiling grimly. He shook her hand, bowed to Sofya, and continued: "Don't lie. This isn't the city. No need of lies. These are all our own people, good people."

Yefim, sitting at the table, looked sharply at the pilgrims, and whispered something to his comrades. When the women walked up to the table, he arose and silently bowed to them. His comrades didn't stir, seeming to take no notice of the guests.

"We live here like monks," said Rybin, tapping the mother lightly on the shoulder. "No one comes to us; our master is not in the village; the mistress was taken to the hospital. And now I'm a sort of superintendent. Sit down at the table. Maybe you're hungry. Yefim, bring some milk."

Without hurrying, Yefim walked into the shack. The travelers removed the sacks from their shoulders, and one of the men, a tall, lank fellow, rose from the table to help them. Another one, resting his elbows thoughtfully on the table, looked at them, scratching his head and quietly humming a song.

The pungent odor of the fresh tar blended with the stifling smell of decaying leaves dizzied the newcomers.

"This fellow is Yakob," said Rybin, pointing to the tall man, "and that one Ignaty. Well, how's your son?"

"He's in prison," the mother sighed.

"In prison again? He likes it, I suppose."

Ignaty stopped humming; Yakob took the staff from the mother's hand, and said:

"Sit down, little mother."

"Yes, why don't you sit down?" Rybin extended the invitation to Sofya.

She sat down on the stump of a tree, scrutinizing Rybin seriously and attentively.

"When did they take him?" asked Rybin, sitting down opposite the mother, and shaking his head. "You've bad luck, Nilovna."

"Oh, well!"

"You're getting used to it?"

"I'm not used to it, but I see it's not to be helped."

"That's right. Well, tell us the story."

Yefim brought a pitcher of milk, took a cup from the table, rinsed it with water, and after filling it shoved it across the table to Sofya. He moved about noiselessly, listening to the mother's narrative. When the mother had concluded her short account, all were silent for a moment, looking at one another. Ignaty, sitting at the table, drew a pattern with his nails on the boards. Yefim stood behind Rybin, resting his elbows on his shoulders. Yakob leaned against the trunk of a tree, his hands folded over his chest, his head inclined. Sofya observed the peasants from the corner of her eye.

"Yes," Rybin drawled sullenly. "That's the course of action they've decided on—to go out openly."

"If we were to arrange such a parade here," said Yefim, with a surly smile, "they'd hack the peasants to death."

"They certainly would," Ignaty assented, nodding his head. "No, I'll go to the factory. It's better there."

"You say Pavel's going to be tried?" asked Rybin.

"Yes. They've decided on a trial."

"Well, what'll he get? Have you heard?"

"Hard labor, or exile to Siberia for life," answered the mother softly. The three young men simultaneously turned their look on her, and Rybin, lowering his head, asked slowly:

"And when he got this affair up, did he know what was in store for him?"

"I don't know. I suppose he did."

"He did," said Sofya aloud.

All were silent, motionless, as if congealed by one cold thought.

"So," continued Rybin slowly and gravely. "I, too, think he knew. A serious man looks before he leaps. There, boys, you see, the man knew that he might be struck with a bayonet, or exiled to hard labor; but he went. He felt it was necessary for him to go, and he went. If his mother had lain across his path, he would have stepped over her body and gone his way. Wouldn't he have stepped over you, Nilovna?"

"He would," said the mother shuddering and looking around. She heaved a heavy sigh. Sofya silently stroked her hand.

"There's a man for you!" said Rybin in a subdued voice, his dark eyes roving about the company. They all became silent again. The thin rays of the sun trembled like golden ribbons in the thick, odorous atmosphere. Somewhere a crow cawed with bold assurance. The mother looked around, troubled by her recollections of the first of May, and grieving for her son and Andrey.

Broken barrels lay about in confusion in the small, crowded glade. Uprooted stumps stretched out their dead, scraggy roots, and chips of wood littered the ground. Dense oaks and birches encircled the clearing, and drooped over it slightly on all sides as if desiring to sweep away and destroy this offensive rubbish and dirt.

Suddenly Yakob moved forward from the tree, stepped to one side, stopped, and shaking his head observed dryly:

"So, when we're in the army with Yefim, it's on such men as Pavel Mikhaylovich that they'll set us."

"Against whom did you think they'd make you go?" retorted Rybin glumly. "They choke us with our own hands. That's where the jugglery comes in."

"I'll join the army all the same," announced Yefim obstinately.

"Who's trying to dissuade you?" exclaimed Ignaty. "Go!" He looked Yefim straight in the face, and said with a smile: "If you're going to shoot at me, aim at the head. Don't just wound me; kill me at once."

"I hear what you're saying," Yefim replied sharply.

"Listen, boys," said Rybin, letting his glance stray about the little assembly with a deliberate, grave gesture of his raised hand. "Here's a woman," pointing to the mother, "whose son is surely done for now."

"Why are you saying this?" the mother asked in a low, sorrowful voice.

"It's necessary," he answered sullenly. "It's necessary that your hair shouldn't turn gray in vain, that your heart shouldn't ache for nothing. Behold, boys! She's lost her son, but what of it? Has it killed her? Nilovna, did you bring books?"

The mother looked at him, and after a pause said:

"I did."

"That's it," said Rybin, striking the table with the palm of his hand. "I knew it at once when I saw you. Why need you have come here, if not for that?" He again measured the young men with his eyes, and continued, solemnly knitting his eyebrows: "Do you see? They thrust the son out of the ranks, and the mother drops into his place."

He suddenly struck the table with both hands, and straightening himself said with an air that seemed to augur ill:

"Those———"—here he flung out a terrible oath—"those people don't know what their blind hands are sowing. They *will* know when our power is complete and we begin to mow down their cursed grass. They'll know it then!"

The mother was frightened. She looked at him, and saw that Mikhaïl's face had changed greatly. He had grown thinner; his beard was roughened, and his cheek bones seemed to have sharpened. The bluish whites of his eyes were threaded with thin red fibers, as if he had gone without sleep for a long time. His nose, less fleshy than formerly, had acquired a rapacious crook. His open, tar-saturated collar, attached to a shirt that had once been red, exposed his dry collar bones and the thick black hair on his breast. About his whole figure there was something more tragic than before. Red sparks seemed to fly from his inflamed eyes and light the lean, dark face with the fire of unconquerable, melancholy rage. Sofya paled and was silent, her gaze riveted on the peasant. Ignaty shook his head and screwed up his eyes, and Yakob, standing at the wall again, angrily tore splinters from the boards with his blackened fingers. Yefim, behind the mother, slowly paced up and down along the length of the table.

"The other day," continued Rybin, "a government official called me up, and, says he, 'You blackguard, what did you say to the priest?' 'Why am I a blackguard?' I say. 'I earn my bread in the sweat of my brow, and I don't do anything bad to people.' That's what I said. He bawled out at me, and hit me in the face. For three days and three nights I sat in the lockup." Rybin grew infuriated. "That's the way you speak to the people, is it?" he cried. "Don't expect pardon, you devils. My wrong will be avenged, if not by me, then by another, if not on you, then on your children. Remember! The greed in your breasts has harrowed the people with iron claws. You have sowed malice; don't expect mercy!"

The wrath in Rybin seethed and bubbled; his voice shook with sounds that frightened the mother.

"And what had I said to the priest?" he continued in a lighter tone. "After the village assembly he sits with the peasants in the street, and tells them something. 'The people are a flock,' says he, 'and they always need a shepherd.' And I joke. 'If,' I say, 'they make the fox the chief in the forest, there'll be lots of feathers but no birds.' He looks at me sidewise and speaks about how the people ought to be patient and pray more to God to give them the power to be patient. And I say that the people pray, but evidently God has no time, because he doesn't listen to them. The priest begins to cavil with me as to what prayers I pray. I tell him I use one prayer, like all the people, 'O Lord, teach the masters to carry bricks, eat stones, and spit wood.' He wouldn't even let me finish my sentence.—Are you a lady?" Rybin asked Sofya, suddenly breaking off his story.

"Why do you think I'm a lady?" she asked quickly, startled by the unexpectedness of his question.

"Why?" laughed Rybin. "That's the star under which you were born. That's why. You think a chintz kerchief can conceal the blot of the nobleman from the eyes of the people? We'll recognize a priest even if he's wrapped in sackcloth. Here, for instance, you put your elbows on a wet table, and you started and frowned. Besides, your back is too straight for a working woman."

Fearing he would insult Sofya with his heavy voice and his raillery, the mother said quickly and sternly:

"She's my friend, Mikhaïl Ivanovich. She's a good woman.

Working in this movement has turned her hair gray. You're not very——"

Rybin fetched a deep breath.

"Why, was what I said insulting?"

Sofya looked at him dryly and queried:

"You wanted to say something to me?"

"I? Not long ago a new man came here, a cousin of Yakob. He's sick with consumption; but he's learned a thing or two. Shall we call him?"

"Call him! Why not?" answered Sofya.

Rybin looked at her, screwing up his eyes.

"Yefim," he said in a lowered voice, "you go over to him, and tell him to come here in the evening."

Yefim went into the shack to get his cap; then silently, without looking at anybody, he walked off at a leisurely pace and disappeared in the woods. Rybin nodded his head in the direction he was going, saying dully:

"He's suffering torments. He's stubborn. He has to go into the army, he and Yakob, here. Yakob simply says, 'I can't.' And that fellow can't either; but he wants to; he has an object in view. He thinks he can stir the soldiers. My opinion is, you can't break through a wall with your forehead. Bayonets in their hands, off they go—where? They don't see—they're going against themselves. Yes, he's suffering. And Ignaty worries him uselessly."

"No, not at all!" said Ignaty. He knit his eyebrows, and kept his eyes turned away from Rybin. "They'll change him, and he'll become just like all the other soldiers."

"No, hardly," Rybin answered meditatively. "But, of course, it's better to run away from the army. Russia is large. Where will you find the fellow? He gets himself a passport, and goes from village to village."

"That's what I'm going to do, too," remarked Yakob, tapping his foot with a chip of wood. "Once you've made up your mind to go against the government, go straight."

The conversation dropped off. The bees and wasps circled busily around humming in the stifling atmosphere. The birds chirped, and somewhere at a distance a song was heard straying through the fields.

After a pause Rybin said:

"Well, we've got to get to work. Do you want to rest? There are boards inside the shanty. Pick up some dry leaves for them, Yakob. And you, mother, give us the books. Where are they?"

The mother and Sofya began to untie their sacks. Rybin bent down over them, and said with satisfaction:

"That's it! Well, well—not a few, I see. Have you been in this business a long time? What's your name?" he turned toward Sofya.

"Anna Ivanovna. Twelve years. Why?"

"Nothing."

"Have you been in prison?"

"I have."

He was silent, taking a pile of books in his hand, and said to her, showing his teeth:

"Don't take offense at the way I speak. A peasant and a nobleman are like tar and water. It's hard for them to mix. They jump away from each other."

"I'm not a lady. I'm a human being," Sofya retorted with a quiet laugh.

"That may be. It's hard for me to believe it; but they say it happens. They say that a dog was once a wolf. Now I'll hide these books."

Ignaty and Yakob walked up to him, and both stretched out their hands.

"Give us some."

"Are they all the same?" Rybin asked of Sofya.

"No, they're different. There's a newspaper here, too."

"Oh!"

The three men quickly walked into the shack.

"The peasant is on fire," said the mother in a low voice, looking after Rybin thoughtfully.

"Yes," answered Sofya. "I've never seen such a face as his—such a martyrlike face. Let's go inside, too. I want to look at them."

When the women reached the door they found the men already engrossed in the newspapers. Ignaty was sitting on the board, the newspaper spread on his knees, and his fingers run through his hair. He raised his head, gave the women a rapid glance, and bent over his paper again. Rybin was standing to let the ray of sun that penetrated a chink in the roof fall on his paper. He moved his lips as he read. Ignaty read kneeling, with his breast against the edge of the board.

Sofya felt the eagerness of the men for the word of truth. Her face brightened with a joyful smile. Walking carefully over to a corner, she sat down next to the mother, her arm on the mother's shoulder, and gazed about silently.

"Uncle Mikhaïl, they're rough on us peasants," muttered Yakob without turning.

Rybin looked around at him, and answered with a smile:

"For love of us. He who loves does not insult, no matter what he says."

Ignaty drew a deep breath, raised his head, smiled satirically, and closing his eyes said with a scowl:

"Here it says: 'The peasant has ceased to be a human being.' Of course he has." Over his simple, open face glided a shadow of offense. "Well, try to wear my skin for a day or so, and turn around in it, and then we'll see what you'll be like, you wiseacre, you!"

"I'm going to lie down," said the mother quietly. "I got tired, after all. My head is going around. And you?" she asked Sofya.

"I don't want to."

The mother stretched herself on the board and soon fell asleep. Sofya sat over her looking at the people reading. When the bees buzzed about the mother's face, she solicitously drove them away.

Rybin came up and asked:

"Is she asleep?"

"Yes."

He was silent for a moment, looked fixedly at the calm sleeping face, and said softly:

"She is probably the first mother who has followed in the footsteps of her son—the first."

"Let's not disturb her; let's go away," suggested Sofya.

"Well, we have to work. I'd like to have a chat with you; but we'll put it off until evening. Come, boys."

CHAPTER IV

The three men walked away, leaving Sofya in the cabin. Then from a distance came the sound of the ax blows, the echo straying through the foliage. In a half-dreamy condition of repose, intoxicated with the spicy odor of the forest, Sofya sat just outside the door, humming a song, and watching the approach of evening, which gradually enfolded the forest. Her gray eyes smiled softly at some one. The reddening rays of the sun fell more and more aslant. The busy chirping of the birds died away. The forest darkened, and seemed to grow denser. The trees moved in more closely about the choked-up glade, and gave it a more friendly embrace, covering it with shadows. Cows were lowing in the distance. The tar men came, all four together, content that the work was ended.

Awakened by their voices the mother walked out from the cabin, yawning and smiling. Rybin was calmer and less gloomy. The surplus of his excitement was drowned in exhaustion.

"Ignaty," he said, "let's have our tea. We do housekeeping here by turns. To-day Ignaty provides us with food and drink."

"To-day I'd be glad to yield my turn," remarked Ignaty, gathering up pieces of wood and branches for an open-air fire.

"We're all interested in our guests," said Yefim, sitting down by Sofya's side.

"I'll help you," said Yakob softly.

He brought out a big loaf of bread baked in hot ashes, and began to cut it and place the pieces on the table.

"Listen!" exclaimed Yefim. "Do you hear that cough?"

Rybin listened, and nodded.

"Yes, he's coming," he said to Sofya. "The witness is coming. I would lead him through cities, put him in public squares, for the people to hear him. He always says the same thing. But everybody ought to hear it."

The shadows grew closer, the twilight thickened, and the voices sounded softer. Sofya and the mother watched the actions of the peasants. They all moved slowly and heavily with a strange sort of cautiousness. They, too, constantly followed the women with their eyes, listening attentively to their conversation.

A tall, stooping man came out of the woods into the glade, and walked slowly, firmly supporting himself on a cane. His heavy, raucous breathing was audible.

"There is Savely!" exclaimed Yakob.

"Here I am," said the man hoarsely. He stopped, and began to cough.

A shabby coat hung over him down to his very heels. From under his round, crumpled hat straggled thin, limp tufts of dry, straight, yellowish hair. His light, sparse beard grew unevenly upon his yellow, bony face; his mouth stood half-open; his eyes were sunk deep beneath his forehead, and glittered feverishly in their dark hollows.

When Rybin introduced him to Sofya he said to her:

"I heard you brought books for the people."

"I did."

"Thank you in the name of the people. They themselves cannot yet understand the book of truth. They cannot yet thank; so I, who have learned to understand it, render you thanks in their behalf." He breathed quickly, with short, eager breaths, strangely drawing in the air through his dry lips. His voice broke. The bony fingers of his feeble hands crept along his breast trying to button his coat.

"It's bad for you to be in the woods so late; it's damp and close here," remarked Sofya.

"Nothing is good for me any more," he answered, out of breath. "Only death!"

It was painful to listen to him. His entire figure inspired a futile pity that recognized its own powerlessness, and gave way to a sullen feeling of discomfort.

The wood pile blazed up; everything round about trembled and shook; the scorched shadows flung themselves into the woods in fright. The round face of Ignaty with its inflated cheeks shone over the fire. The flames died down, and the air began to smell of smoke. Again the trees seemed to draw close and unite with the mist on the glade, listening in strained attention to the hoarse words of the sick man.

"But as a witness of the crime, I can still bring good to the people. Look at me! I'm twenty-eight years old; but I'm dying. About ten years ago I could lift five hundred pounds on my shoulders without an effort. With such strength I thought I could go on for seventy years without dropping into the grave, and I've lived for only ten years, and can't go on any more. The masters have robbed me; they've torn forty years of my life from me; they've stolen forty years from me."

"There, that's his song," said Rybin dully.

The fire blazed up again, but now it was stronger and more vivid. Again the shadows leaped into the woods, and again darted back to the fire, quivering about it in a mute, astonished dance. The wood crackled, and the leaves of the trees rustled softly. Alarmed by the waves of the heated atmosphere, the merry, vivacious tongues of fire, yellow and red, in sportive embrace, soared aloft, sowing sparks. The burning leaves flew, and the stars in the sky smiled to the sparks, luring them up to themselves.

"That's not *my* song. Thousands of people sing it. But they sing it to themselves, not realizing what a salutary lesson their unfortunate lives hold for all. How many men, tormented to death by work, miserable cripples, maimed, die silently from hunger! It is necessary to shout it aloud, brothers, it is necessary to shout it aloud!" He fell into a fit of coughing, bending and all a-shiver.

"Why?" asked Yefim. "My misery is my own affair. Just look at my joy."

"Don't interrupt," Rybin admonished.

"You yourself said a man mustn't boast of his misfortune," observed Yefim with a frown.

"That's a different thing. Savely's misfortune is a general affair, not merely his own. It's very different," said Rybin solemnly. "Here you have a man who has gone down to the depths and been suffocated. Now he shouts to the world, 'Look out, don't go there!'"

Yakob put a pail of cider on the table, dropped a bundle of green branches, and said to the sick man:

"Come, Savely, I've brought you some milk."

Savely shook his head in declination, but Yakob took him under the arm, lifted him, and made him walk to the table.

"Listen," said Sofya softly to Rybin. She was troubled and

reproached him. "Why did you invite him here? He may die any minute."

"He may," retorted Rybin. "Let him die among people. That's easier than to die alone. In the meantime let him speak. He lost his life for trifles. Let him suffer a little longer for the sake of the people. It's all right!"

"You seem to take particular delight in it," exclaimed Sofya.

"It's the masters who take pleasure in Christ as he groans on the cross. But what we want is to learn from a man, and make you learn something, too."

At the table the sick man began to speak again:

"They destroy lives with work. What for? They rob men of their lives. What for, I ask? My master—I lost my life in the textile mill of Nefidov—my master presented one prima donna with a golden wash basin. Every one of her toilet articles was gold. That basin holds my life-blood, my very life. That's for what my life went! A man killed me with work in order to comfort his mistress with my blood. He bought her a gold wash basin with my blood."

"Man is created in the image of God," said Yefim, smiling. "And that's the use to which they put the image. Fine!"

"Well, then don't be silent!" exclaimed Rybin, striking his palm on the table.

"Don't suffer it," added Yakob softly.

Ignaty laughed. The mother observed that all three men spoke little, but listened with the insatiable attention of hungry souls, and every time that Rybin spoke they looked into his face with watchful eyes. Savely's talk produced a strange, sharp smile on their faces. No feeling of pity for the sick man was to be detected in their manner.

Bending toward Sofya the mother whispered:

"Is it possible that what he says is true?"

Sofya answered aloud:

"Yes, it's true. The newspapers tell about such gifts. It happened in Moscow."

"And the man wasn't executed for it?" asked Rybin dully. "But he should have been executed, he should have been led out before the people and torn to pieces. His vile, dirty flesh should have been thrown to the dogs. The people will perform great executions when once they arise. They'll shed much blood to wash away their wrongs. This blood is theirs; it has been drained from their veins; they are its masters."

"It's cold," said the sick man. Yakob helped him to rise, and led him to the fire.

The wood pile burned evenly and glaringly, and the faceless shadows quivered around it. Savely sat down on a stump, and stretched his dry, transparent hands toward the fire, coughing. Rybin nodded his head to one side, and said to Sofya in an undertone:

"That's sharper than books. That ought to be known. When they tear a workingman's hand in a machine or kill him, you can understand—the workingman himself is at fault. But in a case like this, when they suck a man's blood out of him and throw him away like a carcass—that can't be explained in any way. I can comprehend every murder; but torturing for mere sport I can't comprehend. And why do they torture the people? To what purpose do they torture us all? For fun, for mere amusement, so that they can live pleasantly on the earth; so that they can buy everything with the blood of the people, a prima donna, horses, silver knives, golden dishes, expensive toys for their children. *You* work, work, work, work more and more, and *I'll* hoard money by your labor and give my mistress a golden wash basin."

The mother listened, looked, and once again, before her in the darkness, stretched the bright streak of the road that Pavel was going, and all those with whom he walked.

When they had concluded their supper, they sat around the fire, which consumed the wood quickly. Behind them hung the darkness, embracing forest and sky. The sick man with wide-open eyes looked into the fire, coughed incessantly, and shivered all over. The remnants of his life seemed to be tearing themselves from his bosom impatiently, hastening to forsake the dry body, drained by sickness.

"Maybe you'd better go into the shanty, Savely?" Yakob asked, bending over him.

"Why?" he answered with an effort. "I'll sit here. I haven't much time left to stay with people, very little time." He paused, let his eyes rove about the entire group, then with a pale smile, continued:

"I feel good when I'm with you. I look at you, and think, 'Maybe you will avenge the wrongs of all who were robbed, of all the people destroyed because of greed.'"

No one replied, and he soon fell into a doze, his head limply hanging over his chest. Rybin looked at him, and said in a dull voice:

"He comes to us, sits here, and always speaks of the same thing, of this mockery of man. This is his entire soul; he feels nothing else."

"What more do you want?" said the mother thoughtfully. "If people are killed by the thousands day after day working so that their masters may throw money away for sport, what else do you want?"

"It's endlessly wearying to listen to him," said Ignaty in a low voice. "When you hear this sort of thing once, you never forget it, and he keeps harping on it all the time."

"But everything is crowded into this one thing. It's his entire life, remember," remarked Rybin sullenly.

The sick man turned, opened his eyes, and lay down on the ground. Yakob rose noiselessly, walked into the cabin, brought out two short overcoats, and wrapped them about his cousin. Then he sat down beside Sofya.

The merry, ruddy face of the fire smiled irritatingly as it illumined the dark figures about it; and the voices blended mournfully with the soft rustle and crackle of the flames.

Sofya began to tell about the universal struggle of the people for the right to life, about the conflicts of the German peasants in the olden times, about the misfortunes of the Irish, about the great exploits of the workingmen of France in their frequent battling for freedom.

In the forest clothed in the velvet of night, in the little glade bounded by the dumb trees, before the sportive face of the fire, the events that shook the world rose to life again; one nation of the earth after the other passed in review, drained of its blood, exhausted by combats; the names of the great soldiers for freedom and truth were recalled.

The somewhat dull voice of the woman seemed to echo softly from the remoteness of the past. It aroused hope, it carried conviction; and the company listened in silence to its music, to the great story of their brethren in spirit. They looked into her face, lean and pale, and smiled in response to the smile of her gray eyes. Before them the cause of all the people of the world, the endless war for freedom and equality, became more vivid and assumed a greater holiness. They saw their desires and thoughts in the distance, overhung with the dark, bloody curtain of the past, amid strangers unknown to them; and inwardly, both in mind and heart, they became united with the world, seeing in it friends even in olden times, friends who had unanimously resolved to obtain right upon the earth, and had consecrated their resolve with measureless suffering, and shed rivers of their own blood. With this blood, mankind dedicated itself to a new life, bright and cheerful. A feeling arose and grew of the spiritual nearness of each unto each. A new heart was born on the earth, full of hot striving to embrace all and to unite all in itself.

"A day is coming when the workingmen of all countries will raise their heads, and firmly declare, 'Enough! We want no more of this life.'" Sofya's low but powerful voice rang with assurance. "And then the fantastic power of those who are mighty by their greed will crumble; the earth will vanish from under their feet, and their support will be gone."

"That's how it will be," said Rybin, bending his head. "Don't pity yourselves, and you will conquer everything."

The men listened in silence, motionless, endeavoring in no way to break the even flow of the narrative, fearing to cut the bright thread that bound them to the world. Only occasionally some one would carefully put a piece of wood in the fire, and when a stream of sparks and smoke rose from the pile he would drive them away from the woman with a wave of his hand.

Once Yakob rose and said:

"Wait a moment, please." He ran into the shack and brought out wraps. With Ignaty's help he folded them about the shoulders and feet of the women.

And again Sofya spoke, picturing the day of victory, inspiring people with faith in their power, arousing in them a consciousness of their oneness with all who give away their lives to barren toil for the amusement of the satiated.

At break of dawn, exhausted, she grew silent, and smiling she looked around at the thoughtful, illumined faces.

"It's time for us to go," said the mother.

"Yes, it's time," said Sofya wearily.

Some one breathed a noisy sigh.

"I am sorry you're going," said Rybin in an unusually mild tone. "You speak well. This great cause will unite people. When you know that millions want the same as you do, your heart becomes better, and in goodness there is great power."

"You offer goodness, and get the stake in return," said Yefim with a low laugh, and quickly jumped to his feet. "But they ought to go, Uncle Mikhaïl, before anybody sees them. We'll distribute the books among the people; the authorities will begin to wonder where they came from; then some one will remember having seen the pilgrims here."

"Well, thank you, mother, for your trouble," said Rybin, interrupting Yefim. "I always think of Pavel when I look at you, and you've gone the right way."

He stood before the mother, softened, with a broad, good-natured smile on his face. The atmosphere was raw, but he wore only one shirt, his collar was unbuttoned, and his breast was bared low. The mother looked at his large figure, and smiling also, advised:

"You'd better put on something; it's cold."

"There's a fire inside of me."

The three young men standing at the burning pile conversed in a low voice. At their feet the sick man lay as if dead, covered with the short fur coats. The sky paled, the shadows dissolved, the leaves shivered softly, awaiting the sun.

"Well, then, we must say good-by," said Rybin, pressing Sofya's hand. "How are you to be found in the city?"

"You must look for me," said the mother.

The young men in a close group walked up to Sofya, and silently pressed her hand with awkward kindness. In each of them was evident grateful and friendly satisfaction, though they attempted to conceal the feeling which apparently embarrassed them by its novelty. Smiling with eyes dry with the sleepless night, they looked in silence into Sofya's eyes, shifting from one foot to the other.

"Won't you drink some milk before you go?" asked Yakob.

"Is there any?" queried Yefim.

"There's a little."

Ignaty, stroking his hair in confusion, announced:

"No, there isn't; I spilled it."

All three laughed. They spoke about milk, but the mother and Sofya felt that they were thinking of something else, and without words were wishing them well. This touched Sofya, and produced in her, too, embarrassment and modest reserve, which prevented her from saying anything more than a quiet and warm "Thank you, comrades."

They exchanged glances, as if the word "comrade" had given them a mild shock. The dull cough of the sick man was heard. The embers of the burning woodpile died out.

"Good-by," the peasants said in subdued tones; and the sad word rang in the women's ears a long time.

They walked without haste, in the twilight of the dawn, along the wood path. The mother striding behind Sofya said:

"All this is good, just as in a dream—so good! People want to know the truth, my dear; yes, they want to know the truth. It's like being in a church on the morning of a great holiday, when the priest has not yet arrived, and it's dark and quiet; then it's raw, and the people are already gathering. Here the candles are lighted before the images, and there the lamps are lighted; and little by little, they drive away the darkness, illumining the House of God."

"True," answered Sofya. "Only here the House of God is the whole earth."

"The whole earth," the mother repeated, shaking her head thoughtfully. "It's so good that it's hard to believe."

They walked and talked about Rybin, about the sick man, about the young peasants who were so attentively silent, and who so awkwardly but eloquently expressed a feeling of grateful friendship by little attentions to the women. They came out into the open field; the sun rose to meet them. As yet invisible, he spread out over the sky a transparent fan of rosy rays, and the dewdrops in the grass glittered with the many-colored gems of brave spring joy. The birds awoke fresh from their slumber, vivifying the morning with their merry, impetuous voices. The crows flew about croaking, and flapping their wings heavily. The black rooks jumped about in the winter wheat, conversing in abrupt accents. Somewhere the orioles whistled mournfully, a note of alarm in their song. The larks sang, soaring up to meet the sun. The distance opened up, the nocturnal shadows lifting from the hills.

"Sometimes a man will speak and speak to you, and you won't understand him until he succeeds in telling you some simple word; and this one word will suddenly lighten up everything," the mother said thoughtfully. "There's that sick man, for instance; I've heard and known myself how the workingmen in the factories and everywhere are squeezed; but you get used to it from childhood on, and it doesn't touch your heart much. But he suddenly tells you such an outrageous, vile thing! O Lord! Can it be that people give their whole lives away to work in order that the masters may permit themselves pleasure? That's without justification."

The thoughts of the mother were arrested by this fact. Its dull, impudent gleam threw light upon a series of similar facts, at one time known to her, but now forgotten.

"It's evident that they are satiated with everything. I know one country officer who compelled the peasants to salute his horse when it was led through the village; and he arrested everyone who failed to salute it. Now, what need had he of that? It's impossible to understand." After a pause she sighed: "The poor people are stupid from poverty, and the rich from greed."

Sofya began to hum a song bold as the morning.

CHAPTER V

The life of Nilovna flowed on with strange placidity. This calmness sometimes astonished her. There was her son immured in prison. She knew that a severe sentence awaited him, yet every time the idea of it came to her mind her thoughts strayed to Andrey, Fedya, and an endless series of other people she had never seen, but only heard of. The figure of her son appeared to her absorbing all the people into his own destiny. The contemplative feeling aroused in her involuntarily and unnoticeably diverted her inward gaze away from him to all sides. Like thin, uneven rays it touched upon everything, tried to throw light everywhere, and make one picture of the whole. Her mind was hindered from dwelling upon some one thing.

Sofya soon went off somewhere, and reappeared in about five days, merry and vivacious. Then, in a few hours, she vanished again, and returned within a couple of weeks. It seemed as if she were borne along in life in wide circles.

Nikolay, always occupied, lived a monotonous, methodical existence. At eight o'clock in the morning he drank tea, read the newspapers, and recounted the news to the mother. He repeated the speeches of the merchants in the Douma without malice, and clearly depicted the life in the city.

Listening to him the mother saw with transparent clearness the mechanism of this life pitilessly grinding the people in the millstones of money. At nine o'clock he went off to the office.

She tidied the rooms, prepared dinner, washed herself, put on a clean dress, and then sat in her room to examine the pictures and the books. She had already learned to read, but the effort of reading quickly exhausted her; and she ceased to understand the meaning of the words. But the pictures were a constant astonishment to her. They opened up before her a clear, almost tangible world of new and marvelous things. Huge cities arose before her, beautiful structures, machines, ships, monuments, and infinite wealth, created by the people, overwhelming the mind by the variety of nature's products. Life widened endlessly; each day brought some new, huge wonders. The awakened hungry soul of the woman was more and more strongly aroused to the multitude of riches in the world, its countless beauties. She especially loved to look through the great folios of the zoölogical atlas, and although the text was written in a foreign language, it gave her the clearest conception of the beauty, wealth, and vastness of the earth.

"It's an immense world," she said to Nikolay at dinner.

"Yes, and yet the people are crowded for space."

The insects, particularly the butterflies, astonished her most.

"What beauty, Nikolay Ivanovich," she observed. "And how much of this fascinating beauty there is everywhere, but all covered up from us; it all flies by without our seeing it. People toss about, they know nothing, they are unable to take delight in anything, they have no inclination for it. How many could take happiness to themselves if they knew how rich the earth is, how many wonderful things live in it!"

Nikolay listened to her raptures, smiled, and brought her new illustrated books.

In the evening visitors often gathered in his house—Alexey Vasilyevich, a handsome man, pale-faced, black-bearded, sedate, and taciturn; Roman Petrovich, a pimply, round-headed individual always smacking his lips regretfully; Ivan Danilovich, a short, lean fellow with a pointed beard and thin hair, impetuous, vociferous, and sharp as an awl, and Yegor, always joking with his comrades about his sickness. Sometimes other people were present who had come from various distant cities. The long conversations always turned on one and the same thing, on the working people of the world. The comrades discussed the workingmen, got into arguments about them, became heated, waved their hands, and drank much tea; while Nikolay, in the noise of the conversation, silently composed proclamations. Then he read them to the comrades, who copied them on the spot in printed letters. The mother carefully collected the pieces of the torn, rough copies, and burned them.

She poured out tea for them, and wondered at the warmth with which they discussed life and the working-people, the means whereby to sow truth among them the sooner and the better, and how to elevate their spirit. These problems were always agitating the comrades; their lives revolved about them. Often they angrily disagreed, blamed one another for something, got offended, and again discussed.

The mother felt that she knew the life of the workingmen better than these people, and saw more clearly than they the enormity of the task they assumed. She could look upon them with the somewhat melancholy indulgence of a grown-up person toward children who play man and wife without understanding the drama of the relation.

Sometimes Sashenka came. She never stayed long, and always spoke in a businesslike way without smiling. She did not once fail to ask on leaving how Pavel Mikhaylovich was.

"Is he well?" she would ask.

"Thank God! So, so. He's in good spirits."

"Give him my regards," the girl would request, and then disappear.

Sometimes the mother complained to Sashenka because Pavel was detained so long and no date was yet set for his trial. Sashenka looked gloomy, and maintained silence, her fingers twitching. Nilovna was tempted to say to her: "My dear girl, why, I know you love him, I know." But Sashenka's austere face, her compressed lips, and her dry, businesslike manner, which seemed to betoken a desire for silence as soon as possible, forbade any demonstration of sentiment. With a sigh the mother mutely clasped the hand that the girl extended to her, and thought: "My unhappy girl!"

Once Natasha came. She showed great delight at seeing the mother, kissed her, and among other things announced to her quietly, as if she had just thought of the thing:

"My mother died. Poor woman, she's dead!" She wiped her eyes with a rapid gesture of her hands, and continued: "I'm sorry for her. She was not yet fifty. She had a long life before her still. But when you look at it from the other side you can't help thinking that death is easier than such a life—always alone, a stranger to everybody, needed by no one, scared by the shouts of my father. Can you call that living? People live waiting for something good, and she had nothing to expect except insults."

"You're right, Natasha," said the mother musingly. "People live expecting some good, and if there's nothing to expect, what sort of a life is it?" Kindly stroking Natasha's hand, she asked: "So you're alone now?"

"Alone!" the girl rejoined lightly.

The mother was silent, then suddenly remarked with a smile:

"Never mind! A good person does not live alone. People will always attach themselves to a good person."

Natasha was now a teacher in a little town where there was a textile mill, and Nilovna occasionally procured illegal books, proclamations, and newspapers for her. The distribution of literature, in fact, became the mother's occupation. Several times a month, dressed as a nun or as a peddler of laces or small linen articles, as a rich merchant's wife or a religious pilgrim, she rode or walked about with a sack on her back, or a valise in her hand. Everywhere, in the train, in the steamers, in hotels and inns, she behaved simply and unobtrusively. She was the first to enter into conversations with strangers, fearlessly drawing attention to herself by her kind, sociable talk and the confident manner of an experienced person who has seen and heard much.

She liked to speak to people, liked to listen to their stories of life, their complaints, their perplexities, and lamentations. Her heart was bathed in joy each time she noticed in anybody poignant discontent with life, that discontent which, protesting against the blows of fate, earnestly seeks to find an answer to its questions. Before her the picture of human life unrolled itself ever wider and more varicolored, that restless, anxious life passed in the struggle to fill the stomach. Everywhere she clearly saw the coarse, bare striving, insolent in its openness, deceiving man, robbing him, pressing out of him as much sap as possible, draining him of his very life-blood. She realized that there was plenty of everything upon earth, but that the people were in want, and lived half starved, surrounded by inexhaustible wealth. In the cities stood churches filled with gold and silver, not needed by God, and at the entrance to the churches shivered the beggars vainly awaiting a little copper coin to be thrust into their hands. Formerly she had seen this, too—rich churches, priestly vestments sewed with gold threads, and the hovels of the poor, their ignominious rags. But at that time the thing had seemed natural; now the contrast was irreconcilable and insulting to the poor, to whom, she knew, the churches were both nearer and more necessary than to the rich.

From the pictures and stories of Christ, she knew also that he was a friend of the poor, that he dressed simply. But in the churches, where poverty came to him for consolation, she saw him nailed to the cross with insolent gold, she saw silks and satins flaunting in the face of want. The words of Rybin occurred to her: "They have mutilated even our God for us, they have turned everything in their hands against us. In the churches they set up a scarecrow before us. They have dressed God up in falsehood and calumny; they have distorted His face in order to destroy our souls!"

Without being herself aware of it, she prayed less; yet, at the same time, she meditated more and more upon Christ and the people who, without mentioning his name, as though ignorant of him, lived, it seemed to her, according to his will, and, like him, regarded the earth as the kingdom of the poor, and wanted to divide all the wealth of the earth among the poor. Her reflections grew in her soul, deepening and embracing everything she saw and heard. They grew and assumed the bright aspect of a prayer, suffusing an even glow over the entire dark world, the whole of life, and all people.

And it seemed to her that Christ himself, whom she had always loved with a perplexed love, with a complicated feeling in which fear was closely bound up with hope, and joyful emotion with melancholy, now came nearer to her, and was different from what he had been. His position was loftier, and he was more clearly visible to her. His aspect turned brighter and more cheerful. Now his eyes smiled on her with assurance, and with a live inward power, as if he had in reality risen to life for mankind, washed and vivified by the hot blood lavishly shed in his name. Yet those who had lost their blood modestly refrained from mentioning the name of the unfortunate friend of the people.

The mother always returned to Nikolay from her travels delightfully exhilarated by what she had seen and heard on the road, bold and satisfied with the work she had accomplished.

"It's good to go everywhere, and to see much," she said to Nikolay in the evening. "You understand how life is arranged. They brush the people aside and fling them to the edge. The people, hurt and wounded, keep moving about, even though they don't want to, and though they keep thinking: 'What for? Why do they drive us away? Why must we go hungry when there is so much of everything? And how much intellect there is everywhere! Nevertheless, we must remain in stupidity and darkness. And where is He, the merciful God, in whose eyes there are no rich nor poor, but all are children dear to His heart.' The people are gradually revolting against this life. They feel that untruth will stifle them if they don't take thought of themselves."

And in her leisure hours she sat down to the books, and again looked over the pictures, each time finding something new, ever widening the panorama of life before her eyes, unfolding the beauties of nature and the vigorous creative capacity of man. Nikolay often found her poring over the pictures. He would smile and always tell her something wonderful. Struck by man's daring, she would ask him incredulously, "Is it possible?"

Quietly, with unshakable confidence in the truth of his prophecies, Nikolay peered with his kind eyes through his glasses into the mother's face, and told her stories of the future.

"There is no measure to the desires of man; and his power is inexhaustible," he said. "But the world, after all, is still very slow in acquiring spiritual wealth. Because nowadays everyone desiring to free himself from dependence is compelled to hoard, not knowledge but money. However, when the people will have exterminated greed and will have freed themselves from the bondage of enslaving labor—"

She listened to him with strained attention. Though she but rarely understood the meaning of his words, yet the calm faith animating them penetrated her more and more deeply.

"There are extremely few free men in the world—that's its misfortune," he said.

This the mother understood. She knew men who had emancipated themselves from greed and evil; she understood that if there were more such people, the dark, incomprehensible, and awful face of life would become more kindly and simple, better and brighter.

"A man must perforce be cruel," said Nikolay dismally.

The mother nodded her head in confirmation. She recalled the sayings of the Little Russian.

CHAPTER VI

Once Nikolay, usually so punctual, came from his work much later than was his wont, and said, excitedly rubbing his hands: "Do you know, Nilovna, to-day at the visiting hour one of our comrades disappeared from prison? But we have not succeeded in finding out who."

The mother's body swayed, overpowered by excitement. She sat down on a chair and asked with forced quiet:

"Maybe it's Pasha?"

"Possibly. But the question is how to find him, how to help him keep in concealment. Just now I was walking about the streets to see if I couldn't detect him. It was a stupid thing of me to do, but I had to do something. I'm going out again."

"I'll go, too," said the mother, rising.

"You go to Yegor, and see if he doesn't know anything about it," Nikolay suggested, and quickly walked away.

She threw a kerchief on her head, and, seized with hope, swiftly sped along the streets. Her eyes dimmed and her heart beat faster. Her head drooped; she saw nothing about her. It was hot. The mother lost breath, and when she reached the stairway leading to Yegor's quarters, she stopped, too faint to proceed farther. She turned around and uttered an amazed, low cry, closing her eyes for a second. It seemed to her that Nikolay Vyesovshchikov was standing at the gate, his hands thrust into his pockets, regarding her with a smile. But when she looked again nobody was there.

"I imagined I saw him," she said to herself, slowly walking up the steps and listening. She caught the sound of slow steps, and stopping at a turn in the stairway, she bent over to look below, and again saw the pockmarked face smiling up at her.

"Nikolay! Nikolay!" she whispered, and ran down to meet him. Her heart, stung by disappointment, ached for her son.

"Go, go!" he answered in an undertone, waving his hand.

She quickly ran up the stairs, walked into Yegor's room, and found him lying on the sofa. She gasped in a whisper:

"Nikolay is out of prison!"

"Which Nikolay?" asked Yegor, raising his head from the pillow. "There are two there."

"Vyesovshchikov. He's coming here!"

"Fine! But I can't rise to meet him."

Vyesovshchikov had already come into the room. He locked the door after him, and taking off his hat laughed quietly, stroking his hair. Yegor raised himself on his elbows.

"Please, signor, make yourself at home," he said with a nod.

Without saying anything, a broad smile on his face, Nikolay walked up to the mother and grasped her hand.

"If I had not seen you I might as well have returned to prison. I know nobody in the city. If I had gone to the suburbs they would have seized me at once. So I walked about, and thought what a fool I was—why had I escaped? Suddenly I see Nilovna running; off I am, after you."

"How did you make your escape?"

Vyesovshchikov sat down awkwardly on the edge of the sofa and pressed Yegor's hand.

"I don't know how," he said in an embarrassed manner. "Simply a chance. I was taking my airing, and the prisoners began to beat the overseer of the jail. There's one overseer there who was expelled from the gendarmerie for stealing. He's a spy, an informer, and tortures the life out of everybody. They gave him a drubbing, there was a hubbub, the overseers got frightened and blew their whistles. I noticed the gates open. I walked up and saw an open square and the city. It drew me forward and I went away without haste, as if in sleep. I walked a little and bethought myself: 'Where am I to go?' I looked around and the gates of the prison were already closed. I began to feel awkward. I was sorry for the comrades in general. It was stupid somehow. I hadn't thought of going away."

"Hm!" said Yegor. "Why, sir, you should have turned back, respectfully knocked at the prison door, and begged for admission. 'Excuse me,' you should have said,'I was tempted; but here I am.'"

"Yes," continued Nikolay, smiling; "that would have been stupid, too, I understand. But for all that, it's not nice to the other comrades. I walk away without saying anything to anybody. Well, I kept on going, and I came across a child's funeral. I followed the hearse with my head bent down, looking at nobody. I sat down in the cemetery and enjoyed the fresh air. One thought came into my head——"

"One?" asked Yegor. Fetching breath, he added: "I suppose it won't feel crowded there."

Vyesovshchikov laughed without taking offense, and shook his head.

"Well, my brain's not so empty now as it used to be. And you, Yegor Ivanovich, still sick?"

"Each one does what he can. No one has a right to interfere with him." Yegor evaded an answer; he coughed hoarsely. "Continue."

"Then I went to a public museum. I walked about there, looked around, and kept thinking all the time: 'Where am I to go next?' I even began to get angry with myself. Besides, I got dreadfully hungry. I walked into the street and kept on trotting. I felt very down in the mouth. And then I saw police officers looking at everybody closely. 'Well,' thinks I to myself, 'with my face I'll arrive at God's judgment seat pretty soon.' Suddenly Nilovna came running opposite me. I turned about, and off I went after her. That's all."

"And I didn't even see you," said the mother guiltily.

"The comrades are probably uneasy about me. They must be wondering where I am," said Nikolay, scratching his head.

"Aren't you sorry for the officials? I guess they're uneasy, too," teased Yegor. He moved heavily on the sofa, and said seriously and solicitously: "However, jokes aside, we must hide you—by no means as easy as pleasant. If I could get up—" His breath gave out. He clapped his hand to his breast, and with a weak movement began to rub it.

"You've gotten very sick, Yegor Ivanovich," said Nikolay gloomily, drooping his head. The mother sighed and cast an anxious glance about the little, crowded room.

"That's my own affair. Granny, you ask about Pavel. No reason to feign indifference," said Yegor.

Vyesovshchikov smiled broadly.

"Pavel's all right; he's strong; he's like an elder among us; he converses with the officials and gives commands; he's respected. There's good reason for it."

Vlasova nodded her head, listening, and looked sidewise at the swollen, bluish face of Yegor, congealed to immobility, devoid of expression. It seemed strangely flat, only the eyes flashed with animation and cheerfulness.

"I wish you'd give me something to eat. I'm frightfully hungry," Nikolay cried out unexpectedly, and smiled sheepishly.

"Granny, there's bread on the shelf—give it to him. Then go out in the corridor, to the second door on the left, and knock. A woman will open it, and you'll tell her to snatch up everything she has to eat and come here."

"Why everything?" protested Nikolay.

"Don't get excited. It's not much—maybe nothing at all."

The mother went out and rapped at the door. She strained her ears for an answering sound, while thinking of Yegor with dread and grief. He was dying, she knew.

"Who is it?" somebody asked on the other side of the door.

"It's from Yegor Ivanovich," the mother whispered. "He asked you to come to him."

"I'll come at once," the woman answered without opening the door. The mother waited a moment, and knocked again. This time the door opened quickly, and a tall woman wearing glasses stepped out into the hall, rapidly tidying the ruffled sleeves of her waist. She asked the mother harshly:

"What do you want?"

"I'm from Yegor Ivanovich."

"Aha! Come! Oh, yes, I know you!" the woman exclaimed in a low voice. "How do you do? It's dark here."

Nilovna looked at her and remembered that this woman had come to Nikolay's home on rare occasions.

"All comrades!" flashed through her mind.

The woman compelled Nilovna to walk in front.

"Is he feeling bad?"

"Yes; he's lying down. He asked you to bring something to eat."

"Well, he doesn't need anything to eat."

When they walked into Yegor's room they were met by the words:

"I'm preparing to join my forefathers, my friend. Liudmila Vasilyevna, this man walked away from prison without the permission of the authorities—a bit of shameless audacity. Before all, feed him, then hide him somewhere for a day or two."

The woman nodded her head and looked carefully at the sick man's face.

"Stop your chattering, Yegor," she said sternly. "You know it's bad for you. You ought to have sent for me at once, as soon as they came. And I see you didn't take your medicine. What do you mean by such negligence? You yourself say it's easier for you to breathe after a dose. Comrade, come to my place. They'll soon call for Yegor from the hospital."

"So I'm to go to the hospital, after all?" asked Yegor, puckering up his face.

"Yes, I'll be there with you."

"There, too?"

"Hush!"

As she talked she adjusted the blanket on Yegor's breast, looked fixedly at Nikolay, and with her eyes measured the quantity of medicine in the bottle. She spoke evenly, not loud, but in a resonant voice. Her movements were easy, her face was pale, with large blue circles around her eyes. Her black eyebrows almost met at the bridge of the nose, deepening the setting of her dark, stern eyes. Her face did not please the mother; it seemed haughty in its sternness and immobility, and her eyes were rayless. She always spoke in a tone of command.

"We are going away," she continued. "I'll return soon. Give Yegor a tablespoon of this medicine."

"Very well," said the mother.

"And don't let him speak." She walked away, taking Nikolay with her.

"Admirable woman!" said Yegor with a sigh. "Magnificent woman! You ought to be working with her, granny. You see, she gets very much worn out. It's she that does all the printing for us."

"Don't speak. Here, you'd better take this medicine," the mother said gently.

He swallowed the medicine and continued, for some reason screwing up one eye:

"I'll die all the same, even if I don't speak."

He looked into the mother's face with his other eye, and his lips slowly formed themselves into a smile. The mother bent her head, a sharp sensation of pity bringing tears into her eyes.

"Never mind, granny. It's natural. The pleasure of living carries with it the obligation to die."

The mother put her hand on his, and again said softly:

"Keep quiet, please!"

He shut his eyes as if listening to the rattle in his breast, and went on stubbornly.

"It's senseless to keep quiet, granny. What'll I gain by keeping quiet? A few superfluous seconds of agony. And I'll lose the great pleasure of chattering with a good person. I think that in the next world there aren't such good people as here."

The mother uneasily interrupted him.

"The lady will come, and she'll scold me because you talk."

"She's no lady. She's a revolutionist, the daughter of a village scribe, a teacher. She is sure to scold you anyhow, granny. She scolds everybody always." And, slowly moving his lips with an effort, Yegor began to relate the life history of his neighbor. His eyes smiled. The mother saw that he was bantering her purposely. As she regarded his face, covered with a moist blueness, she thought distressfully that he was near to death.

Liudmila entered, and carefully closing the door after her, said, turning to Vlasova:

"Your friend ought to change his clothes without fail, and leave here as soon as possible. So go at once; get him some clothes, and bring them here. I'm sorry Sofya's not here. Hiding people is her specialty."

"She's coming to-morrow," remarked Vlasova, throwing her shawl over her shoulders. Every time she was given a commission the strong desire seized her to accomplish it promptly and well, and she was unable to think of anything but the task before her. Now, lowering her brows with an air of preoccupation, she asked zealously:

"How should we dress him, do you think?"

"It's all the same. It's night, you know."

"At night it's worse. There are less people on the street, and the police spy around more; and, you know, he's rather awkward."

Yegor laughed hoarsely.

"You're a young girl yet, granny."

"May I visit you in the hospital?"

He nodded his head, coughing. Liudmila glanced at the mother with her dark eyes and suggested:

"Do you want to take turns with me in attending him? Yes? Very well. And now go quickly."

She vigorously seized Vlasova by the hand, with perfect good nature, however, and led her out of the door.

"You mustn't be offended," she said softly, "because I dismiss you so abruptly. I know it's rude; but it's harmful for him to speak, and I still have hopes of his recovery." She pressed her hands together until the bones cracked. Her eyelids drooped wearily over her eyes.

The explanation disturbed the mother. She murmured:

"Don't talk that way. The idea! Who thought of rudeness? I'm going; good-by."

"Look out for the spies!" whispered the woman.

"I know," the mother answered with some pride.

She stopped for a minute outside the gate to look around sharply under the pretext of adjusting her kerchief. She was already able to distinguish spies in a street crowd almost immediately. She recognized the exaggerated carelessness of their gait, their strained attempt to be free in their gestures, the expression of tedium on their faces, the wary, guilty glimmer of their restless, unpleasantly sharp gaze badly hidden behind their feigned candor.

This time she did not notice any familiar faces, and walked along the street without hastening. She took a cab, and gave orders to be driven to the market place. When buying the clothes for Nikolay she bargained vigorously with the salespeople, all the while scolding at her drunken husband whom she had to dress anew every month. The tradespeople paid little attention to her talk, but she herself was greatly pleased with her ruse. On the road she had calculated that the police would, of course, understand the necessity for Nikolay to change his clothes, and would send spies to the market. With such naïve precautions, she returned to Yegor's quarters; then she had to escort Nikolay to the outskirts of the city. They took different sides of the street, and it was amusing to the mother to see how Vyesovshchikov strode along heavily, with bent head, his legs getting tangled in the long flaps of his russet-colored coat, his hat falling over his nose. In one of the deserted streets, Sashenka met them, and the mother, taking leave of Vyesovshchikov with a nod of her head, turned toward home with a sigh of relief.

"And Pasha is in prison with Andriusha!" she thought sadly.

Nikolay met her with an anxious exclamation:

"You know that Yegor is in a very bad way, very bad! He was

taken to the hospital. Liudmila was here. She asks you to come to her there."

"At the hospital?"

Adjusting his eyeglasses with a nervous gesture, Nikolay helped her on with her jacket and pressed her hand in a dry, hot grasp. His voice was low and tremulous. "Yes. Take this package with you. Have you disposed of Vyesovshchikov all right?"

"Yes, all right."

"I'll come to Yegor, too!"

The mother's head was in a whirl with fatigue, and Nikolay's emotion aroused in her a sad premonition of the drama's end.

"So he's dying—he's dying!" The dark thought knocked at her brain heavily and dully.

But when she entered the bright, tidy little room of the hospital and saw Yegor sitting on the pallet propped against the wide bosom of the pillow, and heard him laugh with zest, she was at once relieved. She paused at the door, smiling, and listened to Yegor talk with the physician in a hoarse but lively voice.

"A cure is a reform."

"Don't talk nonsense!" the physician cried officiously in a thin voice.

"And I'm a revolutionist! I detest reforms!"

The physician, thoughtfully pulling his beard, felt the dropsical swelling on Yegor's face. The mother knew him well. He was Ivan Danilovich, one of the close comrades of Nikolay. She walked up to Yegor, who thrust forth his tongue by way of welcome to her. The physician turned around.

"Ah, Nilovna! How are you? Sit down. What have you in your hand?"

"It must be books."

"He mustn't read."

"The doctor wants to make an idiot of me," Yegor complained.

"Keep quiet!" the physician commanded, and began to write in a little book.

The short, heavy breaths, accompanied by rattling in his throat, fairly tore themselves from Yegor's breast, and his face became covered with thin perspiration. Slowly raising his swollen hand, he wiped his forehead with the palm. The strange immobility of his swollen cheeks denaturalized his broad, good face, all the features of which disappeared under the dead, bluish mask. Only his eyes, deeply sunk beneath the swellings, looked out clear and smiling benevolently.

"Oh, Science, I'm tired! May I lie down?"

"No, you mayn't."

"But I'm going to lie down after you go."

"Nilovna, please don't let him. It's bad for him."

The mother nodded. The physician hurried off with short steps. Yegor threw back his head, closed his eyes and sank into a torpor, motionless save for the twitching of his fingers. The white walls of the little room seemed to radiate a dry coldness and a pale, faceless sadness. Through the large window peered the tufted tops of the lime trees, amid whose dark, dusty foliage yellow stains were blazing, the cold touches of approaching autumn.

"Death is coming to me slowly, reluctantly," said Yegor without moving and without opening his eyes. "He seems to be a little sorry for me. I was such a fine, sociable chap."

"You'd better keep quiet, Yegor Ivanovich!" the mother bade, quietly stroking his hand.

"Wait, granny, I'll be silent soon."

Losing breath every once in a while, enunciating the words with a mighty effort, he continued his talk, interrupted by long spells of faintness.

"It's splendid to have you with me. It's pleasant to see your face, granny, and your eyes so alert, and your *naïveté*. 'How will it end?' I ask myself. It's sad to think that the prison, exile, and all sorts of vile outrages await you as everybody else. Are you afraid of prison?"

"No," answered the mother softly.

"But after all the prison is a mean place. It's the prison that knocked me up. To tell you the truth, I don't want to die."

"Maybe you won't die yet," the mother was about to say, but a look at his face froze the words on her lips.

"If I hadn't gotten sick I could have worked yet, not badly; but if you can't work there's nothing to live for, and it's stupid to live."

"That's true, but it's no consolation." Andrey's words flashed into the mother's mind, and she heaved a deep sigh. She was greatly fatigued by the day, and hungry. The monotonous, humid, hoarse whisper of the sick man filled the room and crept helplessly along the smooth, cold, shining walls. At the windows the dark tops of the lime trees trembled quietly. It was growing dusk, and Yegor's face on the pillow turned dark.

"How bad I feel," he said. He closed his eyes and became silent. The mother listened to his breathing, looked around, and sat for a few minutes motionless, seized by a cold sensation of sadness. Finally she dozed off.

The muffled sound of a door being carefully shut awakened her, and she saw the kind, open eyes of Yegor.

"I fell asleep; excuse me," she said quietly.

"And you excuse me," he answered, also quietly. At the door was heard a rustle and Liudmila's voice.

"They sit in the darkness and whisper. Where is the knob?"

The room trembled and suddenly became filled with a white, unfriendly light. In the middle of the room stood Liudmila, all black, tall, straight, and serious. Yegor transferred his glance to her, and making a great effort to move his body, raised his hand to his breast.

"What's the matter?" exclaimed Liudmila, running up to him. He looked at the mother with fixed eyes, and now they seemed large and strangely bright.

"Wait!" he whispered.

Opening his mouth wide, he raised his head and stretched his hand forward. The mother carefully held it up and caught her breath as she looked into his face. With a convulsive and powerful movement of his neck he flung his head back, and said aloud:

"Give me air!"

A quiver ran through his body; his head dropped limply on his shoulder, and in his wide open eyes the cold light of the lamp burning over the bed was reflected dully.

"My darling!" whispered the mother, firmly pressing his hand, which suddenly grew heavy.

Liudmila slowly walked away from the bed, stopped at the window and stared into space.

"He's dead!" she said in an unusually loud voice unfamiliar to Vlasova. She bent down, put her elbows on the window sill, and repeated in dry, startled tones: "He's dead! He died calmly, like a man, without complaint." And suddenly, as if struck a blow on the head, she dropped faintly on her knees, covered her face, and gave vent to dull, stifled groans.

CHAPTER VII

The mother folded Yegor's hands over his breast and adjusted his head, which was strangely warm, on the pillow. Then silently wiping her eyes, she went to Liudmila, bent over her, and quietly stroked her thick hair. The woman slowly turned around to her, her dull eyes widened in a sickly way. She rose to her feet, and with trembling lips whispered:

"I've known him for a long time. We were in exile together. We went there together on foot, we sat in prison together; at times it was intolerable, disgusting; many fell in spirit."

Her dry, loud groans stuck in her throat. She overcame them with an effort, and bringing her face nearer to the mother's she continued in a quick whisper, moaning without tears:

"Yet he was unconquerably jolly. He joked and laughed, and covered up his suffering in a manly way, always striving to encourage the weak. He was always good, alert, kind. There, in Siberia, idleness depraves people, and often calls forth ugly feelings toward life. How he mastered such feelings! What a comrade he was! If you only knew. His own life was hard and tormented; but I know that nobody ever heard him complain, not a soul—never! Here was I, nearer to him than others. I'm greatly indebted to his heart, to his mind. He gave me all he could of it; and though exhausted, he never asked either kindness or attention in return."

She walked up to Yegor, bent down and kissed him. Her voice was husky as she said mournfully:

"Comrade, my dear, dear friend, I thank you with all my heart! Good-by. I shall work as you worked—unassailed by doubt—all my life—good-by!"

The dry, sharp groans shook her body, and gasping for breath she laid her head on the bed at Yegor's feet. The mother wept silent tears which seared her cheeks. For some reason she tried to restrain them. She wanted to fondle Liudmila, and wanted to speak about Yegor with words of love and grief. She looked through her tears at his swollen face, at his eyes calmly covered by his drooping eyelids as in sleep, and at his dark lips set in a light, serene smile. It was quiet, and a bleak brightness pervaded the room.

Ivan Danilovich entered, as always, with short, hasty steps. He suddenly stopped in the middle of the room, and thrust his hands into his pockets with a quick gesture.

"Did it happen long ago?" His voice was loud and nervous.

Neither woman replied. He quietly swung about, and wiping his forehead went to Yegor, pressed his hand, and stepped to one side.

"It's not strange—with his heart. It might have happened six months ago."

His voice, high-pitched and jarringly loud for the occasion, suddenly broke off. Leaning his back against the wall, he twisted his beard with nimble fingers, and winking his eyes, rapidly looked at the group by the bed.

"One more!" he muttered.

Liudmila rose and walked over to the window. The mother raised her head and glanced around with a sigh. A minute afterwards they all three stood at the open window, pressing close against one another, and looked at the dusky face of the autumn night. On the black tops of the trees glittered the stars, endlessly deepening the distance of the sky.

Liudmila took the mother by the hand, and silently pressed her head to her shoulders. The physician nervously bit his lips and wiped his eyeglasses with his handkerchief. In the stillness beyond the window the nocturnal noise of the city heaved wearily, and cold air blew on their faces and shoulders. Liudmila trembled; the mother saw tears running down her cheeks. From the corridor of the hospital floated confused, dismal sounds. The three stood motionless at the window, looking silently into the darkness.

The mother felt herself not needed, and carefully freeing her hand, went to the door, bowing to Yegor.

"Are you going?" the physician asked softly without looking around.

"Yes."

In the street she thought with pity of Liudmila, remembering her scant tears. She couldn't even have a good cry. Then she pictured to herself Liudmila and the physician in the extremely light white room, the dead eyes of Yegor behind them. A compassion for all people oppressed her. She sighed heavily, and hastened her pace, driven along by her tumultuous feelings.

"I must hurry," she thought in obedience to a sad but encouraging power that jostled her from within.

The whole of the following day the mother was busy with preparations for the funeral. In the evening when she, Nikolay, and Sofya were drinking tea, quietly talking about Yegor, Sashenka appeared, strangely brimming over with good spirits, her cheeks brilliantly red, her eyes beaming happily. She seemed to be filled with some joyous hope. Her animation contrasted sharply with the mournful gloom of the others. The discordant note disturbed them and dazzled them like a fire that suddenly flashes in the darkness. Nikolay thoughtfully struck his fingers on the table and smiled quietly.

"You're not like yourself to-day, Sasha."

"Perhaps," she laughed happily.

The mother looked at her in mute remonstrance, and Sofya observed in a tone of admonishment:

"And we were talking about Yegor Ivanovich."

"What a wonderful fellow, isn't he?" she exclaimed. "Modest, proof against doubt, he probably never yielded to sorrow. I have never seen him without a joke on his lips; and what a worker! He is an artist of the revolution, a great master, who skillfully manipulates revolutionary thoughts. With what simplicity and power he always draws his pictures of falsehood, violence and untruth! And what a capacity he has for tempering the horrible with his gay humor which does not diminish the force of facts but only the more brightly illumines his inner thought! Always droll! I am greatly indebted to him, and I shall never forget his merry eyes, his fun. And I shall always feel the effect of his ideas upon me in the time of my doubts—I love him!"

She spoke in a moderated voice, with a melancholy smile in her eyes. But the incomprehensible fire of her gaze was not extinguished; her exultation was apparent to everybody.

People love their own feelings—sometimes the very feelings that are harmful to them—are enamored of them, and often derive keen pleasure even from grief, a pleasure that corrodes the heart. Nikolay, the mother, and Sofya were unwilling to let the sorrowful mood produced by the death of their comrade give way to the joy brought in by Sasha. Unconsciously defending their melancholy right to feed on their sadness, they tried to impose their feelings on the girl.

"And now he's dead," announced Sofya, watching her carefully.

Sasha glanced around quickly, with a questioning look. She knit her eyebrows and lowered her head. She was silent for a short time, smoothing her hair with slow strokes of her hand.

"He's dead?" She again cast a searching glance into their faces. "It's hard for me to reconcile myself to the idea."

"But it's a fact," said Nikolay with a smile.

Sasha arose, walked up and down the room, and suddenly stopping, said in a strange voice:

"What does 'to die' signify? What died? Did my respect for Yegor die? My love for him, a comrade? The memory of his mind's labor? Did that labor die? Did all our impressions of him as of a hero disappear without leaving a trace? Did all this die? This best in him will never die out of me, I know. It seems to me we're in too great a hurry to say of a man 'he's dead.' That's the reason we too soon forget that a man never dies if we don't wish our impressions of his manhood, his self-denying toil for the triumph of truth and happiness to disappear. We forget that everything should always be alive in living hearts. Don't be in a hurry to bury the eternally alive, the ever luminous, along with a man's body. The church is destroyed, but God is immortal."

Carried away by her emotions she sat down, leaning her elbows on the table, and continued more thoughtfully in a lower voice, looking smilingly through mist-covered eyes at the faces of the comrades:

"Maybe I'm talking nonsense. But life intoxicates me by its wonderful complexity, by the variety of its phenomena, which at times seem like a miracle to me. Perhaps we are too sparing in the expenditure of our feelings. We live a great deal in our thoughts, and that spoils us to a certain extent. We estimate, but we don't feel."

"Did anything good happen to you?" asked Sofya with a smile.

"Yes," said Sasha, nodding her head. "I had a whole night's talk with Vyesovshchikov. I didn't use to like him. He seemed rude and dull. Undoubtedly that's what he was. A dark, immovable irritation at everybody lived in him. He always used to place himself, as it were, like a dead weight in the center of things, and wrathfully say, 'I, I, I.' There was something bourgeois in this, low, and exasperating." She smiled, and again took in everybody with her burning look.

"Now he says: 'Comrades'—and you ought to hear how he says it, with what a stirring, tender love. He has grown marvelously simple and open-hearted, and possessed with a desire to work. He has found himself, he has measured his power, and knows what he is not. But the main thing is, a true comradely feeling has been born in him, a broad, loving comradeship, which smiles in the face of every difficulty in life."

Vlasova listened to Sasha attentively. She was glad to see this girl, always so stern, now softened, cheerful, and happy. Yet from some deeps of her soul arose the jealous thought: "And how about Pasha?"

"He's entirely absorbed in thoughts of the comrades," continued Sasha. "And do you know of what he assures me? Of the necessity of arranging an escape for them. He says it's a very simple, easy matter."

Sofya raised her head, and said animatedly:

"And what do *you* think, Sasha? Is it feasible?"

The mother trembled as she set a cup of tea on the table. Sasha knit her brows, her animation gone from her. After a moment's silence, she said in a serious voice, but smiling in joyous confusion:

"*He's* convinced. If everything is really as he says, we ought to try. It's our duty." She blushed, dropped into a chair, and lapsed into silence.

"My dear, dear girl!" the mother thought, smiling. Sofya also smiled, and Nikolay, looking tenderly into Sasha's face, laughed quietly. The girl raised her head with a stern glance for all. Then she paled, and her eyes flashed, and she said dryly, the offense she felt evident in her voice:

"You're laughing. I understand you. You consider me personally interested in the case, don't you?"

"Why, Sasha?" asked Sofya, rising and going over to her.

Agitated, pale, the girl continued:

"But I decline. I'll not take any part in deciding the question if you consider it."

"Stop, Sasha," said Nikolay calmly.

The mother understood the girl. She went to her and kissed her silently on her head. Sasha seized her hand, leaned her cheek on it, and raised her reddened face, looking into the mother's eyes, troubled and happy. The mother silently stroked her hair. She felt sad at heart. Sofya seated herself at Sasha's side, her arm over her shoulder, and said, smiling into the girl's eyes:

"You're a strange person."

"Yes, I think I've grown foolish," Sasha acknowledged. "But I don't like shadows."

"That'll do," said Nikolay seriously, but immediately followed up the admonition by the businesslike remark: "There can't be two opinions as to the escape, if it's possible to arrange it. But before everything, we must know whether the comrades in prison want it."

Sasha drooped her head. Sofya, lighting a cigarette, looked at her brother, and with a broad sweep of her arm dropped the match in a corner.

"How is it possible they should not want it?" asked the mother with a sigh. Sofya nodded to her, smiling, and walked over to the window. The mother could not understand the failure of the others to respond, and looked at them in perplexity. She wanted so much to hear more about the possibility of an escape.

"I must see Vyesovshchikov," said Nikolay.

"All right. To-morrow I'll tell you when and where," replied Sasha.

"What is he going to do?" asked Sofya, pacing through the room.

"It's been decided to make him compositor in a new printing place. Until then he'll stay with the forester."

Sasha's brow lowered. Her face assumed its usual severe expression. Her voice sounded caustic. Nikolay walked up to the mother, who was washing cups, and said to her:

"You'll see Pasha day after to-morrow. Hand him a note when you're there. Do you understand? We must know."

"I understand. I understand," the mother answered quickly. "I'll deliver it to him all right. That's my business."

"I'm going," Sasha announced, and silently shook hands with everybody. She strode away, straight and dry-eyed, with a peculiarly heavy tread.

"Poor girl!" said Sofya softly.

"Ye-es," Nikolay drawled. Sofya put her hand on the mother's shoulder and gave her a gentle little shake as she sat in the chair.

"Would you love such a daughter?" and Sofya looked into the mother's face.

"Oh! If I could see them together, if only for one day!" exclaimed Nilovna, ready to weep.

"Yes, a bit of happiness is good for everybody."

"But there are no people who want only a bit of happiness," remarked Nikolay; "and when there's much of it, it becomes cheap."

Sofya sat herself at the piano, and began to play something low and doleful.

CHAPTER VIII

The next morning a number of men and women stood at the gate of the hospital waiting for the coffin of their comrade to be carried out to the street. Spies watchfully circled about, their ears alert to catch each sound, noting faces, manners, and words. From the other side of the street a group of policemen with revolvers at their belts looked on. The impudence of the spies, the mocking smiles of the police ready to show their power, were strong provocatives to the crowd. Some joked to cover their excitement; others looked down on the ground sullenly, trying not to notice the affronts; still others, unable to restrain their wrath, laughed in sarcasm at the government, which feared people armed with nothing but words. The pale blue sky of autumn gleamed upon the round, gray paving stones of the streets, strewn with yellow leaves, which the wind kept whirling about under the people's feet.

The mother stood in the crowd. She looked around at the familiar faces and thought with sadness: "There aren't many of you, not many."

The gate opened, and the coffin, decorated with wreaths tied with red ribbons, was carried out. The people, as if inspired with one will, silently raised their hats. A tall officer of police with a thick black mustache on a red face unceremoniously jostled his way through the crowd, followed by the soldiers, whose heavy boots trampled loudly on the stones. They made a cordon around the coffin, and the officer said in a hoarse, commanding voice:

"Remove the ribbons, please!"

The men and women pressed closely about him. They called to him, waving their hands excitedly and trying to push past one another. The mother caught the flash of pale, agitated countenances, some of them with quivering lips and tears.

"Down with violence!" a young voice shouted nervously. But the lonely outcry was lost in the general clamor.

The mother also felt bitterness in her heart. She turned in indignation to her neighbor, a poorly dressed young man.

"They don't permit a man's comrades even to bury him as they want to. What do they mean by it?"

The hubbub increased and hostility waxed strong. The coffin rocked over the heads of the people. The silken rustling of the ribbons fluttering in the wind about the heads and faces of the carriers could be heard amid the noise of the strife.

The mother was seized with a shuddering dread of the possible collision, and she quickly spoke in an undertone to her neighbors on the right and on the left:

"Why not let them have their way if they're like that? The comrades ought to yield and remove the ribbons. What else can they do?"

A loud, sharp voice subdued all the other noises:

"We demand not to be disturbed in accompanying on his last journey one whom you tortured to death!"

Somebody—apparently a girl—sang out in a high, piping voice:

"In mortal strife your victims fell."

"Remove the ribbons, please, Yakovlev! Cut them off!"

A saber was heard issuing from its scabbard. The mother closed her eyes, awaiting shouts; but it grew quieter.

The people growled like wolves at bay; then silently drooping their heads, crushed by the consciousness of impotence, they moved forward, filling the street with the noise of their tramping. Before them swayed the stripped cover of the coffin with the crumpled wreaths, and swinging from side to side rode the mounted police. The mother walked on the pavement; she was unable to see the coffin through the dense crowd surrounding it, which imperceptibly grew and filled the whole breadth of the street. Back of the crowd also rose the gray figures of the mounted police; at their sides, holding their hands on their sabers, marched the policemen on foot, and everywhere were the sharp eyes of the spies, familiar to the mother, carefully scanning the faces of the people.

"Good-by, comrade, good-by!" plaintively sang two beautiful voices.

"Don't!" a shout was heard. "We will be silent, comrades—for the present."

The shout was stern and imposing; it carried an assuring threat, and it subdued the crowd. The sad songs broke off; the talking became lower; only the noise of heavy tramping on the stones filled the street with its dull, even sound. Over the heads of the people, into the transparent sky, and through the air it rose like the first peal of distant thunder. People silently bore grief and revolt in their breasts. Was it possible to carry on the war for freedom peacefully? A vain illusion! Hatred of violence, love of freedom blazed up and burned the last remnants of the illusion to ashes in the hearts that still cherished it. The steps became heavier, heads were raised, eyes looked cold and firm, and feeling, outstripping thought, brought forth resolve. The cold wind, waxing stronger and stronger, carried an unfriendly cloud of dust and street litter in front of the people. It blew through their garments and their hair, blinded their eyes and struck against their breasts.

The mother was pained by these silent funerals without priests and heart-oppressing chants, with thoughtful faces, frowning brows, and the heavy tramp of the feet. Her slowly circling thoughts formulated her impression in the melancholy phrase:

"There are not many of you who stand up for the truth, not many; and yet they fear you, they fear you!"

Her head bent, she strode along without looking around. It seemed to her that they were burying, not Yegor, but something else unknown and incomprehensible to her.

At the cemetery the procession for a long time moved in and out along the narrow paths amid the tombs until an open space was reached, which was sprinkled with wretched little crosses. The people gathered about the graves in silence. This austere silence of the living among the dead promised something strange, which caused the mother's heart to tremble and sink with expectation. The wind whistled and sighed among the graves. The flowers trembled on the lid of the coffin.

The police, stretching out in a line, assumed an attitude of guard, their eyes on their captain. A tall, long-haired, black-browed, pale young man without a hat stood over the fresh grave. At the same time the hoarse voice of the captain was heard:

"Ladies and gentlemen!"

"Comrades!" began the black-browed man sonorously.

"Permit me!" shouted the police captain. "In pursuance of the order of the chief of police I announce to you that I cannot permit a speech!"

"I will say only a few words," the young man said calmly. "Comrades! over the grave of our teacher and friend let us vow in silence never to forget his will; let each one of us continue without ceasing to dig the grave for the source of our country's misfortune, the evil power that crushes it—the autocracy!"

"Arrest him!" shouted the police captain. But his voice was drowned in the confused outburst of shouts.

"Down with the autocracy!"

The police rushed through the crowd toward the orator who, closely surrounded on all sides, shouted, waving his hand:

"Long live liberty! We will live and die for it!"

The mother shut her eyes in momentary fear. The boisterous

tempest of confused sounds deafened her. The earth rocked under her feet; terror impeded her breathing. The startling whistles of the policemen pierced the air. The rude, commanding voice of the captain was heard; the women cried hysterically. The wooden fences cracked, and the heavy tread of many feet sounded dully on the dry ground. A sonorous voice, subduing all the other voices, blared like a war trumpet:

"Comrades! Calm yourselves! Have more respect for yourselves! Let me go! Comrades, I insist, let me go!"

The mother looked up, and uttered a low exclamation. A blind impulse carried her forward with outstretched hands. Not far from her, on a worn path between the graves, the policemen were surrounding the long-haired man and repelling the crowd that fell upon them from all sides. The unsheathed bayonets flashed white and cold in the air, flying over the heads of the people, and falling quickly again with a spiteful hiss. Broken bits of the fence were brandished; the baleful shouts of the struggling people rose wildly.

The young man lifted his pale face, and his firm, calm voice sounded above the storm of irritated outcries:

"Comrades! Why do you spend your strength? Our task is to arm the heads."

He conquered. Throwing away their sticks, the people dropped out of the throng one after the other; and the mother pushed forward. She saw how Nikolay, with his hat fallen back on his neck, thrust aside the people, intoxicated with the commotion, and heard his reproachful voice:

"Have you lost your senses? Calm yourselves!"

It seemed to her that one of his hands was red.

"Nikolay Ivanovich, go away!" she shouted, rushing toward him.

"Where are you going? They'll strike you there!"

She stopped. Seizing her by the shoulder, Sofya stood at her side, hatless, her jacket open, her other hand grasping a young, light-haired man, almost a boy. He held his hands to his bruised face, and he muttered with tremulous lips: "Let me go! It's nothing."

"Take care of him! Take him home to us! Here's a handkerchief. Bandage his face!" Sofya gave the rapid orders, and putting his hand into the mother's ran away, saying:

"Get out of this place quickly, else they'll arrest you!"

The people scattered all over the cemetery. After them the policemen strode heavily among the graves, clumsily entangling themselves in the flaps of their military coats, cursing, and brandishing their bayonets.

"Let's hurry!" said the mother, wiping the boy's face with the handkerchief. "What's your name?"

"Ivan." Blood spurted from his mouth. "Don't be worried; I don't feel hurt. He hit me over the head with the handle of his saber, and I gave him such a blow with a stick that he howled," the boy concluded, shaking his blood-stained fist. "Wait—it'll be different. We'll choke you without a fight, when we arise, all the working people."

"Quick—hurry!" The mother urged him on, walking swiftly toward the little wicket gate. It seemed to her that there, behind the fence in the field, the police were lying in wait for them, ready to pounce on them and beat them as soon as they went out. But on carefully opening the gate, and looking out over the field clothed in the gray garb of autumn dusk, its stillness and solitude at once gave her composure.

"Let me bandage your face."

"Never mind. I'm not ashamed to be seen with it as it is. The fight was honorable—he hit me—I hit him———"

The mother hurriedly bandaged his wound. The sight of fresh, flowing blood filled her breast with terror and pity. Its humid warmth on her fingers sent a cold, fine tremor through her body. Then, holding his hand, she silently and quickly conducted the wounded youth through the field. Freeing his mouth of the bandage, he said with a smile:

"But where are you taking me, comrade? I can go by myself."

But the mother perceived that he was reeling with faintness, that his legs were unsteady, and his hands twitched. He spoke to her in a weak voice, and questioned her without waiting for an answer:

"I'm a tinsmith, and who are you? There were three of us in Yegor Ivanovich's circle—three tinsmiths—and there were twelve men in all. We loved him very much—may he have eternal life!—although I don't believe in God—it's they, the dogs, that dupe us with God, so that we should obey the authorities and suffer life patiently without kicking."

In one of the streets the mother hailed a cab and put Ivan into it. She whispered, "Now be silent," and carefully wrapped his face up in the handkerchief. He raised his hand to his face, but was no longer able to free his mouth. His hand fell feebly on his knees; nevertheless he continued to mutter through the bandages:

"I won't forget those blows; I'll score them against you, my dear sirs! With Yegor there was another student, Titovich, who taught us political economy—he was a very stern, tedious fellow—he was arrested."

The mother, drawing the boy to her, put his head on her bosom in order to muffle his voice. It was not necessary, however, for he suddenly grew heavy and silent. In awful fear, she looked about sidewise out of the corners of her eyes. She felt that the policemen would issue from some corner, would see Ivan's bandaged head, would seize him and kill him.

"Been drinking?" asked the driver, turning on the box with a benignant smile.

"Pretty full."

"Your son?"

"Yes, a shoemaker. I'm a cook."

Shaking the whip over the horse, the driver again turned, and continued in a lowered voice:

"I heard there was a row in the cemetery just now. You see, they were burying one of the politicals, one of those who are against the authorities. They have a crow to pick with the authorities. He was buried by fellows like him, his friends, it must be; and they up and begin to shout: 'Down with the authorities! They ruin the people.' The police began to beat them. It's said some were hewed down and killed. But the police got it, too." He was silent, shaking his head as if afflicted by some sorrow, and uttered in a strange voice: "They don't even let the dead alone; they even bother people in their graves."

The cab rattled over the stones. Ivan's head jostled softly against the mother's bosom. The driver, sitting half-turned from his horse, mumbled thoughtfully:

"The people are beginning to boil. Every now and then some disorder crops out. Yes! Last night the gendarmes came to our neighbors, and kept up an ado till morning, and in the morning they led away a blacksmith. It's said they'll take him to the river at night and drown him. And the blacksmith—well—he was a wise man—he understood a great deal—and to understand, it seems, is forbidden. He used to come to us and say: 'What sort of life is the cabman's life?' 'It's true,' we say, 'the life of a cabman is worse than a dog's.'"

"Stop!" the mother said.

Ivan awoke from the shock of the sudden halt, and groaned softly.

"It shook him up!" remarked the driver. "Oh, whisky, whisky!"

Ivan shifted his feet about with difficulty. His whole body swaying, he walked through the entrance, and said:

"Nothing—comrade, I can get along."

CHAPTER IX

Sofya was already at home when they reached the house. She met the mother with a cigarette in her teeth. She was somewhat ruffled, but, as usual, bold and assured of manner. Putting the wounded man on the sofa, she deftly unbound his head, giving orders and screwing up her eyes from the smoke of her cigarette.

"Ivan Danilovich!" she called out. "He's been brought here. You are tired, Nilovna. You've had enough fright, haven't you? Well, rest now. Nikolay, quick, give Nilovna some tea and a glass of port."

Dizzied by her experience, the mother breathing heavily and feeling a sickly pricking in her breast, said: "Don't bother about me."

But her entire anxious being begged for attention and kindnesses.

From the next room entered Nikolay with a bandaged hand, and the doctor, Ivan Danilovich, all disheveled, his hair standing on end like the spines of a hedgehog. He quickly stepped to Ivan, bent over him, and said:

"Water, Sofya Ivanovich, more water, clean linen strips, and cotton."

The mother walked toward the kitchen; but Nikolay took her by the arm with his left hand, and led her into the dining room.

"He didn't speak to you; he was speaking to Sofya. You've had enough suffering, my dear woman, haven't you?"

The mother met Nikolay's fixed, sympathetic glance, and, pressing his head, exclaimed with a groan she could not restrain:

"Oh, my darling, how fearful it was! They mowed the comrades down! They mowed them down!"

"I saw it," said Nikolay, giving her a glass of wine, and nodding his head. "Both sides grew a little heated. But don't be uneasy; they used the flats of their swords, and it seems only one was seriously wounded. I saw him struck, and I myself carried him out of the crowd."

His face and voice, and the warmth and brightness of the room quieted Vlasova. Looking gratefully at him, she asked:

"Did they hit you, too?"

"It seems to me that I myself through carelessness knocked my hand against something and tore off the skin. Drink some tea. The weather is cold and you're dressed lightly."

She stretched out her hand for the cup and saw that her fingers were stained with dark clots of blood. She instinctively dropped her hands on her knees. Her skirt was damp. Ivan Danilovich came in in his vest, his shirt sleeves rolled up, and in response to Nikolay's mute question, said in his thin voice:

"The wound on his face is slight. His skull, however, is fractured, but not very badly. He's a strong fellow, but he's lost a lot of blood. We'll take him over to the hospital."

"Why? Let him stay here!" exclaimed Nikolay.

"To-day he may; and—well—to-morrow, too; but after that it'll be more convenient for us to have him at the hospital. I have no time to pay visits. You'll write a leaflet about the affair at the cemetery, won't you?"

"Of course!"

The mother rose quietly and walked into the kitchen.

"Where are you going, Nilovna?" Nikolay stopped her with solicitude. "Sofya can get along by herself."

She looked at him and started and smiled strangely.

"I'm all covered with blood."

While changing her dress she once again thought of the calmness of these people, of their ability to recover from the horrible, an ability which clearly testified to their manly readiness to meet any demand made on them for work in the cause of truth. This thought, steadying the mother, drove fear from her heart.

When she returned to the room where the sick man lay, she heard Sofya say, as she bent over him:

"That's nonsense, comrade!"

"Yes, I'll incommode you," he said faintly.

"You keep still. That's better for you."

The mother stood back of Sofya, and putting her hand on her shoulders peered with a smile into the face of the sick man. She related how he had raved in the presence of the cabman and frightened her by his lack of caution. Ivan heard her; his eyes turned feverishly, he smacked his lips, and at times exclaimed in a confused low voice: "Oh, what a fool I am!"

"We'll leave you here," Sofya said, straightening out the blanket. "Rest."

The mother and Sofya went to the dining room and conversed there in subdued voices about the events of the day. They already regarded the drama of the burial as something remote, and looked with assurance toward the future in deliberating on the work of the morrow. Their faces wore a weary expression, but their thoughts were bold.

They spoke of their dissatisfaction with themselves. Nervously moving in his chair and gesticulating animatedly the physician, dulling his thin, sharp voice with an effort, said:

"Propaganda! propaganda! There's too little of it now. The young workingmen are right. We must extend the field of agitation. The workingmen are right, I say."

Nikolay answered somberly:

"From everywhere come complaints of not enough literature, and we still cannot get a good printing establishment. Liudmila is wearing herself out. She'll get sick if we don't see that she gets assistance."

"And Vyesovshchikov?" asked Sofya.

"He cannot live in the city. He won't be able to go to work until he can enter the new printing establishment. And one man is still needed for it."

"Won't I do?" the mother asked quietly.

All three looked at her in silence for a short while.

"No, it's too hard for you, Nilovna," said Nikolay. "You'll have to live outside the city and stop your visits to Pavel, and in general——"

With a sigh the mother said:

"For Pasha it won't be a great loss. And so far as I am concerned these visits, too, are a torment; they tear out my heart. I'm not allowed to speak of anything; I stand opposite my son like a fool. And they look into my mouth and wait to see something come out that oughtn't."

Sofya groped for the mother's hand under the table and pressed it warmly with her thin fingers. Nikolay looked at the mother fixedly while explaining to her that she would have to serve in the new printing establishment as a protection to the workers.

"I understand," she said. "I'll be a cook. I'll be able to do it; I can imagine what's needed."

"How persistent you are!" remarked Sofya.

The events of the last few days had exhausted the mother; and now as she heard of the possibility of living outside the city, away from its bustle, she greedily grasped at the chance.

But Nikolay changed the subject of conversation.

"What are you thinking about, Ivan?" He turned to the physician.

Raising his head from the table, the physician answered sullenly:

"There are too few of us. That's what I'm thinking of. We positively must begin to work more energetically, and we must persuade Pavel and Andrey to escape. They are both too invaluable to be sitting there idle."

Nikolay lowered his brows and shook his head in doubt, darting a glance at the mother.

As she realized the embarrassment they must feel in speaking of her son in her presence, she walked out into her own room.

There, lying in bed with open eyes, the murmur of low talking in her ears, she gave herself up to anxious thoughts. She wanted to see her son at liberty, but at the same time the idea of freeing him frightened her. She felt that the struggle around her was growing keener and that a sharp collision was threatening. The silent patience of the people was wearing away, yielding to a strained expectation of something new. The excitement was growing perceptibly. Bitter words were tossed about. Something novel and stirring was wafted from all quarters; every proclamation evoked lively discussions in the market place, in the shops, among servants, among workingmen. Every arrest aroused a timid, uncomprehending, and sometimes unconscious sympathy when judgment regarding the causes of the arrest was expressed. She heard the words that had once frightened her—riot, socialism, politics—uttered more and more frequently among the simple folk, though accompanied by derision. However, behind their ridicule it was impossible to conceal an eagerness to understand, mingled with fear and hope, with hatred of the masters and threats against them.

Agitation disturbed the settled, dark life of the people in slow but wide circles. Dormant thoughts awoke, and men were shaken from their usual forced calm attitude toward daily events. All this the mother saw more clearly than others, because she, better than they, knew the dismal, dead face of existence; she stood nearer to it, and now saw upon it the wrinkles of hesitation and turmoil, the vague hunger for the new. She both rejoiced over the change and feared it. She rejoiced because she regarded this as the cause of her son; she feared because she knew that if he emerged from prison he would stand at the head of all, in the most dangerous place, and—he would perish.

She often felt great thoughts needful to everybody stirring in her bosom, but scarcely ever was able to make them live in words; and they oppressed her heart with a dumb, heavy sadness. Sometimes the image of her son grew before her until it assumed the proportions of a giant in the old fairy tales. He united within himself all the honest thoughts she had heard spoken, all the people that she liked, everything heroic of which she knew. Then, moved with delight in him, she exulted in quiet rapture. An indistinct hope filled her. "Everything will be well—everything!" Her love, the love of a mother, was fanned into a flame, a veritable pain to her heart. Then the motherly affection hindered the growth of the broader human feeling, burned it; and in place of a great sentiment a small, dismal thought beat faint-heartedly in the gray ashes of alarm: "He will perish; he will fall!"

Late that night the mother sank into a heavy sleep, but rose early, her bones stiff, her head aching. At midday she was sitting in the prison office opposite Pavel and looking through a mist in her eyes at his bearded, swarthy face. She was watching for a chance to deliver to him the note she held tightly in her hand.

"I am well and all are well," said Pavel in a moderated voice. "And how are you?"

"So so. Yegor Ivanovich died," she said mechanically.

"Yes?" exclaimed Pavel, and dropped his head.

"At the funeral the police got up a fight and arrested one man," the mother continued in her simple-hearted way.

The thin-lipped assistant overseer of the prison jumped from his chair and mumbled quickly:

"Cut that out; it's forbidden! Why don't you understand? You know politics are prohibited."

The mother also rose from her chair, and as if failing to comprehend him, she said guiltily:

"I wasn't discussing politics. I was telling about a fight—and they did fight; that's true. They even broke one fellow's head."

"All the same, please keep quiet—that is to say, keep quiet about everything that doesn't concern you personally—your family; in general, your home."

Aware that his speech was confused, he sat down in his chair and arranged papers.

"I'm responsible for what you say," he said sadly and wearily.

The mother looked around and quickly thrust the note into Pavel's hand. She breathed a deep sigh of relief.

"I don't know what to speak about."

Pavel smiled:

"I don't know either."

"Then why pay visits?" said the overseer excitedly. "They have nothing to say, but they come here anyhow and bother me."

"Will the trial take place soon?" asked the mother after a pause.

"The procurator was here the other day, and he said it will come off soon."

"You've been in prison half a year already!"

They spoke to each other about matters of no significance to either. The mother saw Pavel's eyes look into her face softly and lovingly. Even and calm as before, he had not changed, save that his wrists were whiter, and his beard, grown long, made him look older. The mother experienced a strong desire to do something pleasant for him—tell him about Vyesovshchikov, for instance. So, without changing her tone, she continued in the same voice in which she spoke of the needless and uninteresting things.

"I saw your godchild." Pavel fixed a silent questioning look on her eyes. She tapped her fingers on her cheeks to picture to him the pockmarked face of Vyesovshchikov.

"He's all right! The boy is alive and well. He'll soon get his position—you remember how he always asked for hard work?"

Pavel understood, and gratefully nodded his head. "Why, of course I remember!" he answered, with a cheery smile in his eyes.

"Very well!" the mother uttered in a satisfied tone, content with herself and moved by his joy.

On parting with her he held her hand in a firm clasp.

"Thank you, mamma!" The joyous feeling of hearty nearness to him mounted to her head like a strong drink. Powerless to answer in words, she merely pressed his hand.

At home she found Sasha. The girl usually came to Nilovna on the days when the mother had visited Pavel.

"Well, how is he?"

"He's well."

"Did you hand him the note?"

"Of course! I stuck it into his hands very cleverly."

"Did he read it?"

"On the spot? How could he?"

"Oh, yes; I forgot! Let us wait another week, one week longer. Do you think he'll agree to it?"

"I don't know—I think he will," the mother deliberated. "Why shouldn't he if he can do so without danger?"

Sasha shook her head.

"Do you know what the sick man is allowed to eat? He's asked for some food."

"Anything at all. I'll get him something at once." The mother walked into the kitchen, slowly followed by Sasha.

"Can I help you?"

"Thank you! Why should you?"

The mother bent at the oven to get a pot. The girl said in a low voice:

"Wait!"

Her face paled, her eyes opened sadly and her quivering lips whispered hotly with an effort:

"I want to beg you—I know he will not agree—try to persuade him. He's needed. Tell him he's essential, absolutely necessary for the cause—tell him I fear he'll get sick. You see the date of the trial hasn't been set yet, and six months have already passed—I beg of you!"

It was apparent that she spoke with difficulty. She stood up straight, in a tense attitude, and looked aside. Her voice sounded uneven, like the snapping of a taut string. Her eyelids drooping wearily, she bit her lips, and the fingers of her compressed hand cracked.

The mother was ruffled by her outburst; but she understood it, and a sad emotion took possession of her. Softly embracing Sasha, she answered:

"My dear, he will never listen to anybody except himself—never!"

For a short while they were both silent in a close embrace. Then Sasha carefully removed the mother's hands from her shoulders.

"Yes, you're right," she said in a tremble. "It's all stupidity and nerves. One gets so tired." And, suddenly growing serious, she concluded: "Anyway, let's give the sick man something to eat."

In an instant she was sitting at Ivan's bed, kindly and solicitously inquiring, "Does your head ache badly?"

"Not very. Only everything is muddled up, and I'm weak," answered Ivan in embarrassment. He pulled the blanket up to his chin, and screwed up his eyes as if dazzled by too brilliant a light. Noticing that she embarrassed him by her presence and that he could not make up his mind to eat, Sasha rose and walked away. Then Ivan sat up in bed and looked at the door through which she had left.

"Be-au-tiful!" he murmured.

His eyes were bright and merry; his teeth fine and compact; his young voice was not yet steady as an adult's.

"How old are you?" the mother asked thoughtfully.

"Seventeen years."

"Where are your parents?"

"In the village. I've been here since I was ten years old. I got through school and came here. And what is your name, comrade?"

This word, when applied to her, always brought a smile to the mother's face and touched her.

"Why do you want to know?"

The youth, after an embarrassed pause, explained:

"You see, a student of our circle, that is, a fellow who used to read to us, told us about Pavel's mother—a workingman, you know—and about the first of May demonstration."

She nodded her head and pricked up her ears.

"He was the first one who openly displayed the banner of our party," the youth declared with pride—a pride which found a response in the mother's heart.

"I wasn't present; we were then thinking of making our own demonstration here in the city, but it fizzled out; we were too few of us then. But this year we will—you'll see!"

He choked from agitation, having a foretaste of the future event. Then waving his spoon in the air, he continued:

"So Vlasova—the mother, as I was telling you—she, too, got into the party after that. They say she's a wonder of an old woman."

The mother smiled broadly. It was pleasant for her to hear the boy's enthusiastic praise—pleasant, yet embarrassing. She even had to restrain herself from telling him that she was Vlasova, and she thought sadly, in derision of herself: "Oh, you old fool!"

"Eat more! Get well sooner for the sake of the cause!" She burst out all of a sudden, in agitation, bending toward him: "It awaits powerful young hands, clean hearts, honest minds. It lives by these forces! With them it holds aloof everything evil, everything mean!"

The door opened, admitting a cold, damp, autumn draught.

Sofya entered, bold, a smile on her face, reddened by the cold.

"Upon my word, the spies are as attentive to me as a bridegroom to a rich bride! I must leave this place. Well, how are you, Vanya? All right? How's Pavel, Nilovna? What! is Sasha here?"

Lighting a cigarette, she showered questions without waiting for answers, caressing the mother and the youth with merry glances of her gray eyes. The mother looked at her and smiled inwardly. "What good people I'm among!" she thought. She bent over Ivan again and gave him back his kindness twofold:

"Get well! Now I must give you wine." She rose and walked into the dining room, where Sofya was saying to Sasha:

"She has three hundred copies prepared already. She'll kill herself working so hard. There's heroism for you! Unseen, unnoticed, it finds its reward and its praise in itself. Do you know, Sasha, it's the greatest happiness to live among such people, to be their comrade, to work with them?"

"Yes," answered the girl softly.

In the evening at tea Sofya said to the mother:

"Nilovna, you have to go to the village again."

"Well, what of it? When?"

"It would be good if you could go to-morrow. Can you?"

"Yes."

"Ride there," advised Nikolay. "Hire post horses, and please take a different route from before—across the district of Nikolsk." Nikolay's somber expression was alarming.

"The way by Nikolsk is long, and it's expensive if you hire horses."

"You see, I'm against this expedition in general. It's already begun to be unquiet there—some arrests have been made, a teacher was taken. Rybin escaped, that's certain. But we must be more careful. We ought to have waited a little while still."

"That can't be avoided," said Nilovna.

Sofya, tapping her fingers on the table, remarked:

"It's important for us to keep spreading literature all the time. You're not afraid to go, are you, Nilovna?"

The mother felt offended. "When have I ever been afraid? I was without fear even the first time. And now all of a sudden—"

She drooped her head. Each time she was asked whether she was afraid, whether the thing was convenient for her, whether she could do this or that—she detected an appeal to her which placed her apart from the comrades, who seemed to behave differently toward her than toward one another. Moreover, when fuller days came, although at first disquieted by the commotion, by the rapidity of events, she soon grew accustomed to the bustle and responded, as it were, to the jolts she received from her impressions. She became filled with a zealous greed for work. This was her condition to-day; and, therefore, Sofya's question was all the more displeasing to her.

"There's no use for you to ask me whether or not I'm afraid and various other things," she sighed. "I've nothing to be afraid of. Those people are afraid who have something. What have I? Only a son. I used to be afraid for him, and I used to fear torture for his sake. And if there is no torture—well, then?"

"Are you offended?" exclaimed Sofya.

"No. Only you don't ask each other whether you're afraid."

Nikolay removed his glasses, adjusted them to his nose again, and looked fixedly at his sister's face. The embarrassed silence that followed disturbed the mother. She rose guiltily from her seat, wishing to say something to them, but Sofya stroked her hand, and said quietly:

"Forgive me! I won't do it any more."

The mother had to laugh, and in a few minutes the three were speaking busily and amicably about the trip to the village.

CHAPTER X

The next day, early in the morning, the mother was seated in the post chaise, jolting along the road washed by the autumn rain. A damp wind blew on her face, the mud splashed, and the coachman on the box, half-turned toward her, complained in a meditative snuffle:

"I say to him—my brother, that is—let's go halves. We began to divide"—he suddenly whipped the left horse and shouted angrily:

"Well, well, play, your mother is a witch."

The stout autumn crows strode with a businesslike air through the bare fields. The wind whistled coldly, and the birds caught its buffets on their backs. It blew their feathers apart, and even lifted them off their feet, and, yielding to its force, they lazily flapped their wings and flew to a new spot.

"But he cheated me; I see I have nothing——"

The mother listened to the coachman's words as in a dream. A dumb thought grew in her heart. Memory brought before her a long series of events through which she had lived in the last years. On an examination of each event, she found she had actively participated in it. Formerly, life used to happen somewhere in the distance, remote from where she was, uncertain for whom and for what. Now, many things were accomplished before her eyes, with her help. The result in her was a confused feeling, compounded of distrust of herself, complacency, perplexity, and sadness.

The scenery about her seemed to be slowly moving. Gray clouds floated in the sky, chasing each other heavily; wet trees flashed along the sides of the road, swinging their bare tops; little hills appeared and swam asunder. The whole turbid day seemed to be hastening to meet the sun—to be seeking it.

The drawling voice of the coachman, the sound of the bells, the humid rustle and whistle of the wind, blended in a trembling, tortuous stream, which flowed on with a monotonous force, and roused the wind.

"The rich man feels crowded, even in Paradise. That's the way it is. Once he begins to oppress, the government authorities are his friends," quoth the coachman, swaying on his seat.

While unhitching the horses at the station he said to the mother in a hopeless voice:

"If you gave me only enough for a drink——"

She gave him a coin, and tossing it in the palm of his hand, he informed her in the same hopeless tone:

"I'll take a drink for three coppers, and buy myself bread for two."

In the afternoon the mother, shaken up by the ride and chilled, reached the large village of Nikolsk. She went to a tavern and asked for tea. After placing her heavy valise under the bench, she sat at a window and looked out into an open square, covered with yellow, trampled grass, and into the town hall, a long, old building with an overhanging roof. Swine were straggling about in the square, and on the steps of the town hall sat a bald, thin-bearded peasant smoking a pipe. The clouds swam overhead in dark masses, and piled up, one absorbing the other. It was dark, gloomy, and tedious. Life seemed to be in hiding.

Suddenly the village sergeant galloped up to the square, stopped his sorrel at the steps of the town hall, and waving his whip in the air, shouted to the peasant. The shouts rattled against the window panes, but the words were indistinguishable. The peasant rose and stretched his hand, pointing to something. The sergeant jumped to the ground, reeled, threw the reins to the peasant, and seizing the rails with his hands, lifted himself heavily up the steps, and disappeared behind the doors of the town hall.

Quiet reigned again. Only the horse struck the soft earth with the iron of his shoes.

A girl came into the room. A short yellow braid lay on her neck, her face was round, and her eyes kind. She bit her lips with the effort of carrying a ragged-edged tray, with dishes, in her outstretched hands. She bowed, nodding her head.

"How do you do, my good girl?" said the mother kindly.

"How do you do?"

Putting the plates and the china dishes on the table, she announced with animation:

"They've just caught a thief. They're bringing him here."

"Indeed? What sort of a thief?"

"I don't know."

"What did he do?"

"I don't know. I only heard that they caught him. The watchman of the town hall ran off for the police commissioner, and shouted: 'They've caught him. They're bringing him here.'"

The mother looked through the window. Peasants gathered in the square; some walked slowly, some quickly, while buttoning their overcoats. They stopped at the steps of the town hall, and all looked to the left. It was strangely quiet. The girl also went to the window to see the street, and then silently ran from the room, banging the door after her. The mother trembled, pushed her valise farther under the bench, and throwing her shawl over her head, hurried to the door. She had to restrain a sudden, incomprehensible desire to run.

When she walked up the steps of the town hall a sharp cold struck her face and breast. She lost breath, and her legs stiffened. There, in the middle of the square, walked Rybin! His hands were bound behind his back, and on each side of him a policeman, rhythmically striking the ground with his club. At the steps stood a crowd waiting in silence.

Unconscious of the bearing of the thing, the mother's gaze was riveted on Rybin. He said something; she heard his voice, but the words did not reach the dark emptiness of her heart.

She recovered her senses, and took a deep breath. A peasant with a broad light beard was standing at the steps looking fixedly into her face with his blue eyes. Coughing and rubbing her throat with her hands, weak with fear, she asked him with an effort:

"What's the matter?"

"Well, look." The peasant turned away. Another peasant came up to her side.

"Oh, thief! How horrible you look!" shouted a woman's voice.

The policemen stepped in front of the crowd, which increased in size. Rybin's voice sounded thick:

"Peasants, I'm not a thief; I don't steal; I don't set things on fire. I only fight against falsehood. That's why they seized me. Have you heard of the true books in which the truth is written about our peasant life? Well, it's because of these writings that I suffer. It's I who distributed them among the people."

The crowd surrounded Rybin more closely. His voice steadied the mother.

"Did you hear?" said a peasant in a low voice, nudging a blue-eyed neighbor, who did not answer but raised his head and again looked into the mother's face. The other peasant also looked at her. He was younger than he of the blue eyes, with a dark, sparse beard, and a lean freckled face. Then both of them turned away to the side of the steps.

"They're afraid," the mother involuntarily noted. Her attention grew keener. From the elevation of the stoop she clearly saw the dark face of Rybin, distinguished the hot gleam of his eyes. She wanted that he, too, should see her, and raised herself on tiptoe and craned her neck.

The people looked at him sullenly, distrustfully, and were silent. Only in the rear of the crowd subdued conversation was heard.

"Peasants!" said Rybin aloud, in a peculiar full voice. "Believe these papers! I shall now, perhaps, get death on account of them. The authorities beat me, they tortured me, they wanted to find out from where I got them, and they're going to beat me more. For in these writings the truth is laid down. An honest world and the truth ought to be dearer to us than bread. That's what I say."

"Why is he doing this?" softly exclaimed one of the peasants near the steps. He of the blue eyes answered:

"Now it's all the same. He won't escape death, anyhow. And a man can't die twice."

The sergeant suddenly appeared on the steps of the town hall, roaring in a drunken voice:

"What is this crowd? Who's the fellow speaking?"

Suddenly precipitating himself down the steps, he seized Rybin by the hair, and pulled his head backward and forward. "Is it you speaking, you damned scoundrel? Is it you?"

The crowd, giving way, still maintained silence. The mother, in impotent grief, bowed her head; one of the peasants sighed. Rybin spoke again:

"There! Look, good people!"

"Silence!" and the sergeant struck his face.

Rybin reeled.

"They bind a man's hands and then torment him, and do with him whatever they please."

"Policemen, take him! Disperse, people!" The sergeant, jumping and swinging in front of Rybin, struck him in his face, breast, and stomach.

"Don't beat him!" some one shouted dully.

"Why do you beat him?" another voice upheld the first.

"Lazy, good-for-nothing beast!"

"Come!" said the blue-eyed peasant, motioning with his head; and without hastening, the two walked toward the town hall, accompanied by a kind look from the mother. She sighed with relief. The sergeant again ran heavily up the steps, and shaking his fists in menace, bawled from his height vehemently:

"Bring him here, officers, I say! I say——"

"Don't!" a strong voice resounded in the crowd, and the mother knew it came from the blue-eyed peasant. "Boys! don't permit it! They'll take him in there and beat him to death, and then they'll say we killed him. Don't permit it!"

"Peasants!" the powerful voice of Rybin roared, drowning the shouts of the sergeant. "Don't you understand your life? Don't you understand how they rob you—how they cheat you—how they drink your blood? You keep everything up; everything rests on you; you are all the power that is at the bottom of everything on earth—its whole power. And what rights have you? You have the right to starve—it's your only right!"

"He's speaking the truth, I tell *you*!"

Some men shouted:

"Call the commissioner of police! Where is the commissioner of police?"

"The sergeant has ridden away for him!"

"It's not our business to call the authorities!"

The noise increased as the crowd grew louder and louder.

"Speak! We won't let them beat you!"

"Officers, untie his hands!"

"No, brothers; that's not necessary!"

"Untie him!"

"Look out you don't do something you'll be sorry for!"

"I am sorry for my hands!" Rybin said evenly and resonantly, making himself heard above all the other voices. "I'll not escape, peasants. I cannot hide from my truth; it lives inside of me!"

Several men walked away from the crowd, formed different circles, and with earnest faces and shaking their heads carried on conversations. Some smiled. More and more people came running up—excited, bearing marks of having dressed quickly. They seethed like black foam about Rybin, and he rocked to and fro in their midst. Raising his hands over his head and shaking them, he called into the crowd, which responded now by loud shouts, now by silent, greedy attention, to the unfamiliar, daring words:

"Thank you, good people! Thank you! I stood up for you, for your lives!" He wiped his beard and again raised his blood-covered hand. "There's my blood! It flows for the sake of truth!"

The mother, without considering, walked down the steps, but immediately returned, since on the ground she couldn't see Mikhaïl, hidden by the close-packed crowd. Something indistinctly joyous trembled in her bosom and warmed it.

"Peasants! Keep your eyes open for those writings; read them. Don't believe the authorities and the priests when they tell you those people who carry truth to us are godless rioters. The truth travels over the earth secretly; it seeks a nest among the people. To the authorities it's like a knife in the fire. They cannot accept it. It will cut them and burn them. Truth is your good friend and a sworn enemy of the authorities—that's why it hides itself."

"That's so; he's speaking the gospel!" shouted the blue-eyed peasant.

"Ah, brother! You will perish—and soon, too!"

"Who betrayed you?"

"The priest!" said one of the police.

Two peasants gave vent to hard oaths.

"Look out, boys!" a somewhat subdued cry was heard in warning.

The commissioner of police walked into the crowd—a tall, compact man, with a round, red face. His cap was cocked to one side; his mustache with one end turned up the other drooping made his face seem crooked, and it was disfigured by a dull, dead grin. His left hand held a saber, his right waved broadly in the air. His heavy, firm tramp was audible. The crowd gave way before him. Something sullen and crushed appeared in their faces, and the noise died away as if it had sunk into the ground.

"What's the trouble?" asked the police commissioner, stopping in front of Rybin and measuring him with his eyes. "Why are his hands not bound? Officers, why? Bind them!" His voice was high and resonant, but colorless.

"They were tied, but the people unbound them," answered one of the policemen.

"The people! What people?" The police commissioner looked

at the crowd standing in a half-circle before him. In the same monotonous, blank voice, neither elevating nor lowering it, he continued: "Who are the people?"

With a back stroke he thrust the handle of his saber against the breast of the blue-eyed peasant.

"Are you the people, Chumakov? Well, who else? You, Mishin?" and he pulled somebody's beard with his right hand.

"Disperse, you curs!"

Neither his voice nor face displayed the least agitation or threat. He spoke mechanically, with a dead calm, and with even movements of his strong, long hands, pushed the people back. The semicircle before him widened. Heads drooped, faces were turned aside.

"Well," he addressed the policeman, "what's the matter with you? Bind him!" He uttered a cynical oath and again looked at Rybin, and said nonchalantly: "Your hands behind your back, you!"

"I don't want my hands to be bound," said Rybin. "I'm not going to run away, and I'm not fighting. Why should my hands be bound?"

"What?" exclaimed the police commissioner, striding up to him.

"It's enough that you torture the people, you beasts!" continued Rybin in an elevated voice. "The red day will soon come for you, too. You'll be paid back for everything."

The police commissioner stood before him, his mustached upper lip twitching. Then he drew back a step, and with a whistling voice sang out in surprise:

"Um! you damned scoundrel! Wha-at? What do you mean by your words? People, you say? A-a——"

Suddenly he dealt Rybin a quick, sharp blow in the face.

"You won't kill the truth with your fist!" shouted Rybin, drawing on him. "And you have no right to beat me, you dog!"

"I won't dare, I suppose?" the police commissioner drawled.

Again he waved his hand, aiming at Rybin's head; Rybin ducked; the blow missed, and the police commissioner almost toppled over. Some one in the crowd gave a jeering snort, and the angry shout of Mikhaïl was heard:

"Don't you dare to beat me, I say, you infernal devil! I'm no weaker than you! Look out!"

The police commissioner looked around. The people shut down

on him in a narrower circle, advancing sullenly.

"Nikita!" the police commissioner called out, looking around. "Nikita, hey!" A squat peasant in a short fur overcoat emerged from the crowd. He looked on the ground, with his large disheveled head drooping.

"Nikita," the police commissioner said deliberately, twirling his mustache, "give him a box on the ear—a good one!"

The peasant stepped forward, stopped in front of Rybin and raised his hand. Staring him straight in the face, Rybin stammered out heavily:

"Now look, people, how the beasts choke you with your own hands! Look! Look! Think! Why does he want to beat me—why? I ask."

The peasant raised his hand and lazily struck Mikhaïl's face.

"Ah, Nikita! don't forget God!" subdued shouts came from the crowd.

"Strike, I say!" shouted the police commissioner, pushing the peasant on the back of his neck.

The peasant stepped aside, and inclining his head, said sullenly:

"I won't do it again."

"What?" The face of the police commissioner quivered. He stamped his feet, and, cursing, suddenly flung himself upon Rybin. The blow whizzed through the air; Rybin staggered and waved his arms; with the second blow the police commissioner felled him to the ground, and, jumping around with a growl, he began to kick him on his breast, his side, and his head.

The crowd set up a hostile hum, rocked, and advanced upon the police commissioner. He noticed it and jumped away, snatching his saber from its scabbard.

"So that's what you're up to! You're rioting, are you?"

His voice trembled and broke; it had grown husky. And he lost his composure along with his voice. He drew his shoulders up about his head, bent over, and turning his blank, bright eyes on all sides, he fell back, carefully feeling the ground behind him with his feet. As he withdrew he shouted hoarsely in great excitement:

"All right; take him! I'm leaving! But now, do you know, you cursed dogs, that he is a political criminal; that he is going against our Czar; that he stirs up riots—do you know it?—against the Emperor, the Czar? And you protect him; you, too, are rebels. Aha—a—"

Without budging, without moving her eyes, the strength of reason gone from her, the mother stood as if in a heavy sleep, overwhelmed by fear and pity. The outraged, sullen, wrathful shouts of the people buzzed like bees in her head.

"If he has done something wrong, lead him to court."

"And don't beat him!"

"Forgive him, your Honor!"

"Now, really, what does it mean? Without any law whatever!"

"Why, is it possible? If they begin to beat everybody that way, what'll happen then?"

"The devils! Our torturers!"

The people fell into two groups—the one surrounding the police commissioner shouted and exhorted him; the other, less numerous, remained about the beaten man, humming and sullen. Several men lifted him from the ground. The policemen again wanted to bind his hands.

"Wait a little while, you devils!" the people shouted.

Rybin wiped the blood from his face and beard and looked about in silence. His gaze glided by the face of the mother. She started, stretched herself out to him, and instinctively waved her hand. He turned away; but in a few minutes his eyes again rested on her face. It seemed to her that he straightened himself and raised his head, that his blood-covered cheeks quivered.

"Did he recognize me? I wonder if he did?"

She nodded her head to him and started with a sorrowful, painful joy. But the next moment she saw that the blue-eyed peasant was standing near him and also looking at her. His gaze awakened her to the consciousness of the risk she was running.

"What am I doing? They'll take me, too."

The peasant said something to Rybin, who shook his head.

"Never mind!" he exclaimed, his voice tremulous, but clear and bold. "I'm not alone in the world. They'll not capture all the truth. In the place where I was the memory of me will remain. That's it! Even though they destroy the nest, aren't there more friends and comrades there?"

"He's saying this for me," the mother decided quickly.

"The people will build other nests for the truth; and a day will come when the eagles will fly from them into freedom. The people will emancipate themselves."

A woman brought a pail of water and, wailing and groaning, began to wash Rybin's face. Her thin, piteous voice mixed with Mikhaïl's words and hindered the mother from understanding them. A throng of peasants came up with the police commissioner in front of them. Some one shouted aloud:

"Come; I'm going to make an arrest! Who's next?"

Then the voice of the police commissioner was heard. It had changed—mortification now evident in its altered tone.

"I may strike you, but you mayn't strike me. Don't you dare, you dunce!"

"Is that so? And who are you, pray? A god?"

A confused but subdued clamor drowned Rybin's voice.

"Don't argue, uncle. You're up against the authorities."

"Don't be angry, your Honor. The man's out of his wits."

"Keep still, you funny fellow!"

"Here, they'll soon take you to the city!"

"There's more law there!"

The shouts of the crowd sounded pacificatory, entreating; they blended into a thick, indistinct babel, in which there was something hopeless and pitiful. The policemen led Rybin up the steps of the town hall and disappeared with him behind the doors. People began to depart in a hurry. The mother saw the blue-eyed peasant go across the square and look at her sidewise. Her legs trembled under her knees. A dismal feeling of impotence and loneliness gnawed at her heart sickeningly.

"I mustn't go away," she thought. "I mustn't!" and holding on to the rails firmly, she waited.

The police commissioner walked up the steps of the town hall and said in a rebuking voice, which had assumed its former blankness and soullessness:

"You're fools, you damned scoundrels! You don't understand a thing, and poke your noses into an affair like this—a government affair. Cattle! You ought to thank me, fall on your knees before me for my goodness! If I were to say so, you would all be put to hard labor."

About a score of peasants stood with bared heads and listened in silence. It began to grow dusk; the clouds lowered. The blue-eyed peasant walked up to the steps, and said with a sigh:

"That's the kind of business we have here!"

"Ye-es," the mother rejoined quietly.

He looked at her with an open gaze.

"What's your occupation?" he asked after a pause.

"I buy lace from the women, and linen, too."

The peasant slowly stroked his beard. Then looking up at the town hall he said gloomily and softly:

"You won't find anything of that kind here."

The mother looked down on him, and waited for a more suitable moment to depart for the tavern. The peasant's face was thoughtful and handsome and his eyes were sad. Broad-shouldered and tall, he was dressed in a patched-up coat, in a clean chintz shirt, and reddish homespun trousers. His feet were stockingless.

The mother for some reason drew a sigh of relief, and suddenly obeying an impulse from within, yielding to an instinct that got the better of her reason, she surprised herself by asking him:

"Can I stay in your house overnight?"

At the question everything in her muscles, her bones, tightened stiffly. She straightened herself, holding her breath, and fixed her eyes on the peasant. Pricking thoughts quickly flashed through her mind: "I'll ruin everybody—Nikolay Ivanovich, Sonyushka—I'll not see Pasha for a long time—they'll kill him——"

Looking on the ground, the peasant answered deliberately, folding his coat over his breast:

"Stay overnight? Yes, you can. Why not? Only my home is very poor!"

"Never mind; I'm not used to luxury," the mother answered uncalculatingly.

"You can stay with me overnight," the peasant repeated, measuring her with a searching glance.

It had already grown dark, and in the twilight his eyes shone cold, his face seemed very pale. The mother looked around, and as if dropping under distress, she said in an undertone:

"Then I'll go at once, and you'll take my valise."

"All right!" He shrugged his shoulders, again folded his coat and said softly:

"There goes the wagon!"

In a few moments, after the crowd had begun to disperse, Rybin appeared again on the steps of the town hall. His hands were bound; his head and face were wrapped up in a gray cloth, and he was pushed into a waiting wagon.

"Farewell, good people!" his voice rang out in the cold evening twilight. "Search for the truth. Guard it! Believe the man who will bring you the clean word; cherish him. Don't spare yourselves in the cause of truth!"

"Silence, you dog!" shouted the voice of the police commissioner. "Policeman, start the horses up, you fool!"

"What have you to be sorry for? What sort of life have you?"

The wagon started. Sitting in it with a policeman on either side, Rybin shouted dully:

"For the sake of what are you perishing—in hunger? Strive for freedom—it'll give you bread and—truth. Farewell, good people!"

The hasty rumble of the wheels, the tramp of the horses, the shout of the police officer, enveloped his speech and muffled it.

"It's done!" said the peasant, shaking his head. "You wait at the station a little while, and I'll come soon."

CHAPTER XI

The mother went to the room in the tavern, sat herself at the table in front of the samovar, took a piece of bread in her hand, looked at it, and slowly put it back on the plate. She was not hungry; the feeling in her breast rose again and flushed her with nausea. She grew faint and dizzy; the blood was sucked from her heart. Before her stood the face of the blue-eyed peasant. It was a face that expressed nothing and failed to arouse confidence. For some reason the mother did not want to tell herself in so many words that he would betray her. The suspicion lay deep in her breast—a dead weight, dull and motionless.

"He scented me!" she thought idly and faintly. "He noticed—he guessed." Further than this her thoughts would not go, and she sank into an oppressive despondency. The nausea, the spiritless stillness beyond the window that replaced the noise, disclosed something huge, but subdued, something frightening, which sharpened her feeling of solitude, her consciousness of powerlessness, and filled her heart with ashen gloom.

The young girl came in and stopped at the door.

"Shall I bring you an omelette?"

"No, thank you, I don't want it; the shouts frightened me."

The girl walked up to the table and began to speak excitedly in hasty, terror-stricken tones:

"How the police commissioner beat him! I stood near and could see. All his teeth were broken. He spit out and his teeth fell on the ground. The blood came thick—thick and dark. You couldn't see his eyes at all; they were swollen up. He's a tar man. The sergeant is in there in our place drunk, but he keeps on calling for whisky. They say there was a whole band of them, and that this bearded man was their elder, the hetman. Three were captured and one escaped. They seized a teacher, too; he was also with them. They don't believe in God, and they try to persuade others to rob all the churches. That's the kind of people they are; and our peasants, some of them pitied him—that fellow—and others say they should have settled him for good and all. We have such mean peasants here! Oh, my! oh, my!"

The mother, by giving the girl's disconnected, rapid talk her fixed attention, tried to stifle her uneasiness, to dissipate her dismal forebodings. As for the girl, she must have rejoiced in an auditor. Her words fairly choked her and she babbled on in lowered voice with greater and greater animation:

"Papa says it all comes from the poor crop. This is the second year we've had a bad harvest. The people are exhausted. That's the reason we have such peasants springing up now. What a shame! You ought to hear them shout and fight at the village assemblies. The other day when Vosynkov was sold out for arrears he dealt the starosta (bailiff) a cracking blow on the face. 'There are my arrears for you!' he says."

Heavy steps were heard at the door. The mother rose to her feet with difficulty. The blue-eyed peasant came in, and taking off his hat asked:

"Where is the baggage?"

He lifted the valise lightly, shook it, and said:

"Why, it's empty! Marya, show the guest the way to my house," and he walked off without looking around.

"Are you going to stay here overnight?" asked the girl.

"Yes. I'm after lace; I buy lace."

"They don't make lace here. They make lace in Tinkov and in Daryina, but not among us."

"I'm going there to-morrow; I'm tired."

On paying for the tea she made the girl very happy by handing her three kopecks. On the road the girl's feet splashed quickly in the mud.

"If you want to, I'll run over to Daryina, and I'll tell the women to bring their lace here. That'll save your going there. It's about eight miles."

"That's not necessary, my dear."

The cold air refreshed the mother as she stepped along beside the girl. A resolution slowly formulated itself in her mind—confused, but fraught with a promise. She wished to hasten its growth, and asked herself persistently: "How shall I behave? Suppose I come straight out with the truth?"

It was dark, damp, and cold. The windows of the peasants' huts shone dimly with a motionless reddish light; the cattle lowed drowsily in the stillness, and short halloos reverberated through the fields. The village was clothed in darkness and an oppressive melancholy.

"Here!" said the girl, "you've chosen a poor lodging for yourself. This peasant is very poor." She opened the door and shouted briskly into the hut: "Aunt Tatyana, a lodger has come!" She ran away, her "Good-by!" flying back from the darkness.

The mother stopped at the threshold and peered about with her palm above her eyes. The hut was very small, but its cleanness and neatness caught the eye at once. From behind the stove a young woman bowed silently and disappeared. On a table in a corner toward the front of the room burned a lamp. The master of the hut sat at the table, tapping his fingers on its edge. He fixed his glance on the mother's eyes.

"Come in!" he said, after a deliberate pause.

"Tatyana, go call Pyotr. Quick!"

The woman hastened away without looking at her guest. The mother seated herself on the bench opposite the peasant and looked around—her valise was not in sight. An oppressive stillness filled the hut, broken only by the scarcely audible sputtering of the lamplight. The face of the peasant, preoccupied and gloomy, wavered in vague outline before the eyes of the mother, and for some reason caused her dismal annoyance.

"Well, why doesn't he say something? Quick!"

"Where's my valise?" Her loud, stern question coming suddenly was a surprise to herself. The peasant shrugged his shoulders and thoughtfully gave the indefinite answer:

"It's safe." He lowered his voice and continued gloomily: "Just now, in front of the girl, I said on purpose that it was empty. No, it's not empty. It's very heavily loaded."

"Well, what of it?"

The peasant rose, approached her, bent over her, and whispered: "Do you know that man?"

The mother started, but answered firmly:

"I do."

Her laconic reply, as it were, kindled a light within her which rendered everything outside clear. She sighed in relief. Shifting her position on the bench, she settled herself more firmly on it, while the peasant laughed broadly.

"I guessed it—when you made the sign—and he, too. I asked him, whispering in his ear, whether he knows the woman standing on the steps."

"And what did he say?"

"He? He says 'there are a great many of us.' Yes—'there are a great many of us,' he says."

The peasant looked into the eyes of his guest questioningly, and, smiling again, he continued:

"He's a man of great force, he is brave, he speaks straight out. They beat him, and he keeps on his own way."

The peasant's uncertain, weak voice, his unfinished, but clear face, his open eyes, inspired the mother with more and more confidence. Instead of alarm and despondency, a sharp, shooting pity for Rybin filled her bosom. Overwhelmed by her feelings, unable to restrain herself, she suddenly burst out in bitter malice:

"Robbers, bigots!" and she broke into sobs.

The peasant walked away from her, sullenly nodding his head.

"The authorities have hired a whole lot of assistants to do their dirty work for them. Yes, yes." He turned abruptly toward the mother again and said softly: "Here's what I guessed—that you have papers in the valise. Is that true?"

"Yes," answered the mother simply, wiping away her tears. "I was bringing them to him."

He lowered his brows, gathered his beard into his hand, and looking on the floor was silent for a time.

"The papers reached us, too; some books, also. We need them all. They are so true. I can do very little reading myself, but I have a friend—he can. My wife also reads to me." The peasant pondered for a moment. "Now, then, what are you going to do with them—with the valise?"

The mother looked at him.

"I'll leave it to you."

He was not surprised, did not protest, but only said curtly, "To us," and nodded his head in assent. He let go of his beard, but continued to comb it with his fingers as he sat down.

With inexorable, stubborn persistency the mother's memory held up before her eyes the scene of Rybin's torture. His image extinguished all thoughts in her mind. The pain and injury she felt for the man obscured every other sensation. Forgotten was the valise with the books and newspapers. She had feelings only for Rybin. Tears flowed constantly; her face was gloomy; but her voice did not tremble when she said to her host:

"They rob a man, they choke him, they trample him in the mud—the accursed! And when he says, 'What are you doing, you godless men?' they beat and torture him."

"Power," returned the peasant. "They have great power."

"From where do they get it?" exclaimed the mother, thoroughly aroused. "From us, from the people—they get everything from us."

"Ye-es," drawled the peasant. "It's a wheel." He bent his head toward the door, listening attentively. "They're coming," he said softly.

"Who?"

"Our people, I suppose."

His wife entered. A freckled peasant, stooping, strode into the hut after her. He threw his cap into a corner, and quickly went up to their host.

"Well?"

The host nodded in confirmation.

"Stepan," said the wife, standing at the oven, "maybe our guest wants to eat something."

"No, thank you, my dear."

The freckled peasant moved toward the mother and said quietly, in a broken voice:

"Now, then, permit me to introduce myself to you. My name is Pyotr Yegorov Ryabinin, nicknamed Shilo—the Awl. I understand something about your affairs. I can read and write. I'm no fool, so to speak." He grasped the hand the mother extended to him, and wringing it, turned to the master of the house.

"There, Stepan, see, Varvara Nikolayevna is a good lady, true. But in regard to all this, she says it is nonsense, nothing but dreams. Boys and different students, she says, muddle the people's mind with absurdities. However, you saw just now a sober, steady man, as he ought to be, a peasant, arrested. Now, here is she, an elderly woman, and as to be seen, not of blue blood. Don't be offended—what's your station in life?"

He spoke quickly and distinctly, without taking breath. His little beard shook nervously, and his dark eyes, which he screwed up, rapidly scanned the mother's face and figure. Ragged, crumpled, his hair disheveled, he seemed just to have come from a fight, in which he had vanquished his opponent, and still to be flushed with the joy of victory. He pleased the mother with his sprightliness and his simple talk, which at once went straight to the point. She gave him a kind look as she answered his question. He once more shook her hand vigorously, and laughed softly.

"You see, Stepan, it's a clean business, an excellent business. I told you so. This is the way it is: the people, so to speak, are beginning to take things into their own hands. And as to the lady—she won't tell you the truth; it's harmful to her. I respect her, I must say; she's a good person, and wishes us well—well, a little bit, and provided it won't harm her any. But the people want to go straight, and they fear no loss and no harm—you see?—all life is harmful to them; they have no place to turn to; they have nothing all around except 'Stop!' which is shouted at them from all sides."

"I see," said Stepan, nodding and immediately adding: "She's uneasy about her baggage."

Pyotr gave the mother a shrewd wink, and again reassured her:

"Don't be uneasy; it's all right. Everything will be all right, mother. Your valise is in my house. Just now when he told me about you—that you also participate in this work and that you know that man—I said to him: 'Take care, Stepan! In such a serious business you must keep your mouth shut.' Well, and you, too, mother, seem to have scented us when we stood near you. The faces of honest people can be told at once. Not many of them walk the streets, to speak frankly. Your valise is in my house." He sat down alongside of her and looked entreatingly into her eyes. "If you wish to empty it we'll help you, with pleasure. We need books."

"She wants to give us everything," remarked Stepan.

"First rate, mother! We'll find a place for all of it." He jumped to his feet, burst into a laugh, and quickly pacing up and down the room said contentedly: "The matter is perfectly simple: in one place it snaps, and in another it is tied up. Very well! And the newspaper, mother, is a good one, and does its work—it peels the people's eyes open; it's unpleasant to the masters. I do carpentry work for a lady about five miles from here—a good woman, I must admit. She gives me various books, sometimes very simple books. I read them over—I might as well fall asleep. In general we're thankful to her. But I showed her one book and a number of a newspaper; she was somewhat offended. 'Drop it, Pyotr!' she said. 'Yes, this,' she says, 'is the work of senseless youngsters; from such a business your troubles can only increase; prison and Siberia for this,' she says."

He grew abruptly silent, reflected for a moment, and asked: "Tell me, mother, this man—is he a relative of yours?"

"A stranger."

Pyotr threw his head back and laughed noiselessly, very well satisfied with something. To the mother, however, it seemed the very next instant that, in reference to Rybin, the word "stranger" was not in place; it jarred upon her.

"I'm not a relative of his; but I've known him for a long time, and I look up to him as to an elder brother."

She was pained and displeased not to find the word she wanted, and she could not suppress a quiet groan. A sad stillness pervaded the hut. Pyotr leaned his head upon one shoulder; his little beard, narrow and sharp, stuck out comically on one side, and gave his shadow swinging on the wall the appearance of a man sticking out his tongue teasingly. Stepan sat with his elbows on the table, and beat a tattoo on the boards. His wife stood at the oven without stirring; the mother felt her look riveted upon herself and often glanced at the woman's face—oval, swarthy, with a straight nose, and a chin cut off short; her dark and thick eyebrows joined sternly, her eyelids drooped, and from under them her greenish eyes shone sharply and intently.

"A friend, that is to say," said Pyotr quietly. "He has character, indeed he has; he esteems himself highly, as he ought to; he has put a high price on himself, as he ought to. There's a man, Tatyana! You say——"

"Is he married?" Tatyana interposed, and compressed the thin lips of her small mouth.

"He's a widower," answered the mother sadly.

"That's why he's so brave," remarked Tatyana. Her utterance was low and difficult. "A married man like him wouldn't go—he'd be afraid."

"And I? I'm married and everything, and yet—" exclaimed Pyotr.

"Enough!" she said without looking at him and twisting her lips. "Well, what are you? You only talk a whole lot, and on rare occasions you read a book. It doesn't do people much good for you and Stepan to whisper to each other on the corners."

"Why, sister, many people hear me," quietly retorted the peasant, offended. "I act as a sort of yeast here. It isn't fair in you to speak that way."

Stepan looked at his wife silently and again drooped his head.

"And why should a peasant marry?" asked Tatyana. "He needs a worker, they say. What work?"

"You haven't enough? You want more?" Stepan interjected dully.

"But what sense is there in the work we do? We go half-hungry from day to day anyhow. Children are born; there's no time to look after them on account of the work that doesn't give us bread." She walked up to the mother, sat down next to her, and spoke on stubbornly, no plaint nor mourning in her voice. "I had two children; one, when he was two years old, was boiled to death in hot water; the other was born dead—from this thrice-accursed work. Such a happy life! I say a peasant has no business to marry. He only binds his hands. If he were free he would work up to a system of life needed by everybody. He would come out directly and openly for the truth. Am I right, mother?"

"You are. You're right, my dear. Otherwise we can't conquer life."

"Have you a husband?"

"He died. I have a son."

"And where is he? Does he live with you?"

"He's in prison." The mother suddenly felt a calm pride in these words, usually painful to her. "This is the second time—all because he came to understand God's truth and sowed it openly without sparing himself. He's a young man, handsome, intelligent; he planned a newspaper, and gave Mikhaïl Ivanovich a start on his way, although he's only half of Mikhaïl's age. Now they're going to try my son for all this, and sentence him; and he'll escape from Siberia and continue with his work."

Her pride waxed as she spoke. It created the image of a hero, and demanded expression in words. The mother needed an offset—something fine and bright—to balance the gloomy incident she had witnessed that day, with its senseless horror and shameless cruelty. Instinctively yielding to this demand of a healthy soul, she reached out for everything she had seen that was pure and shining and heaped it into one dazzling, cleansing fire.

"Many such people have already been born, more and more are being born, and they will all stand up for the freedom of the people, for the truth, to the very end of their lives."

She forgot precaution, and although she did not mention names, she told everything known to her of the secret work for the emancipation of the people from the chains of greed. In depicting the personalities she put all her force into her words, all the abundance of love awakened in her so late by her rousing experiences. And she herself became warmly enamored of the images rising up in her memory, illumined and beautified by her feeling.

"The common cause advances throughout the world in all the cities. There's no measuring the power of the good people. It keeps growing and growing, and it will grow until the hour of our victory, until the resurrection of truth."

Her voice flowed on evenly, the words came to her readily, and she quickly strung them, like bright, varicolored beads, on strong threads of her desire to cleanse her heart of the blood and filth of that day. She saw that the three people were as if rooted to the spot where her speech found them, and that they looked at her without stirring. She heard the intermittent breathing of the woman sitting by her side, and all this magnified the power of her faith in what she said, and in what she promised these people.

"All those who have a hard life, whom want and injustice crush—it's the rich and the servitors of the rich who have overpowered them. The whole people ought to go out to meet those who perish in the dungeons for them, and endure mortal torture. Without gain to themselves they show where the road to happiness for all people lies. They frankly admit it is a hard road, and they force no one to follow them. But once you take your position by their side you will never leave them. You will see it is the true, the right road. With such persons the people may travel. Such persons will not be reconciled to small achievements; they will not stop until they will vanquish all deceit, all evil and greed. They will not fold their hands until the people are welded into one soul, until the people will say in one voice: 'I am the ruler, and I myself will make the laws equal for all.'"

She ceased from exhaustion, and looked about. Her words would not be wasted here, she felt assured. The silence lasted for a minute, while the peasants regarded her as if expecting more. Pyotr stood in the middle of the hut, his hands clasped behind his back, his eyes screwed up, a smile quivering on his freckled face. Stepan was leaning one hand on the table; with his neck and entire body forward, he seemed still to be listening. A shadow on his face gave it more finish. His wife, sitting beside the mother, bent over, her elbows on her knees, and studied her feet.

"That's how it is," whispered Pyotr, and carefully sat on the bench, shaking his head.

Stepan slowly straightened himself, looked at his wife, and threw his hands in the air, as if grasping for something.

"If a man takes up this work," he began thoughtfully in a moderated voice, "then his entire soul is needed."

Pyotr timidly assented:

"Yes, he mustn't look back."

"The work has spread very widely," continued Stepan.

"Over the whole earth," added Pyotr.

They both spoke like men walking in darkness, groping for the way with their feet. The mother leaned against the wall, and throwing back her head listened to their careful utterances. Tatyana arose, looked around, and sat down again. Her green eyes gleamed dryly as she looked into the peasants' faces with dissatisfaction and contempt.

"It seems you've been through a lot of misery," she said, suddenly turning to the mother.

"I have."

"You speak well. You draw—you draw the heart after your talk. It makes me think, it makes me think, 'God! If I could only take a peep at such people and at life through a chink!' How does one live? What life has one? The life of sheep. Here am I; I can read and write; I read books, I think a whole lot. Sometimes I don't even sleep the entire night because I think. And what sense is there in it? If I don't think, my existence is a purposeless existence; and if I do, it is also purposeless. And everything seems purposeless. There are the peasants, who work and tremble over a piece of bread for their homes, and they have nothing. It hurts them, enrages them; they drink, fight, and work again—work, work, work. But what comes of it? Nothing."

She spoke with scorn in her eyes and in her voice, which was low and even, but at times broke off like a taut thread overstrained. The peasants were silent, the wind glided by the window panes, buzzed through the straw of the roofs, and at times whined softly down the chimney. A dog barked, and occasional drops of rain pattered on the window. Suddenly the light flared in the lamp, dimmed, but in a second sprang up again even and bright.

"I listened to your talk, and I see what people live for now. It's so strange—I hear you, and I think, 'Why, I know all this.' And yet, until you said it, I hadn't heard such things, and I had no such thoughts. Yes."

"I think we ought to take something to eat, and put out the lamp," said Stepan, somberly and slowly. "People will notice that at the Chumakovs' the light burned late. It's nothing for us, but it might turn out bad for the guest."

Tatyana arose and walked to the oven.

"Ye-es," Pyotr said softly, with a smile. "Now, friend, keep your ears pricked. When the papers appear among the people—"

"I'm not speaking of myself. If they arrest me, it's no great matter."

The wife came up to the table and asked Stepan to make room.

He arose and watched her spread the table as he stood to one side.

"The price of fellows of our kind is a nickel a bundle, a hundred in a bundle," he said with a smile.

The mother suddenly pitied him. He now pleased her more.

"You don't judge right, host," she said. "A man mustn't agree to the price put upon him by people from the outside, who need nothing of him except his blood. You, knowing yourself within, must put your own estimate on yourself—your price, not for your enemies, but for your friends."

"What friends have we?" the peasant exclaimed softly. "Up to the first piece of bread."

"And I say that the people have friends."

"Yes, they have, but not here—that's the trouble," Stepan deliberated.

"Well, then create them here."

Stepan reflected a while. "We'll try."

"Sit down at the table," Tatyana invited her.

At supper, Pyotr, who had been subdued by the talk of the mother and appeared to be at a loss, began to speak again with animation:

"Mother, you ought to get out of here as soon as possible, to escape notice. Go to the next station, not to the city—hire the post horses."

"Why? I'm going to see her off!" said Stepan.

"You mustn't. In case anything happens and they ask you whether she slept in your house—'She did.' 'When did she go?' 'I saw her off.' 'Aha! You did? Please come to prison!' Do you understand? And no one ought to be in a hurry to get into prison; everybody's turn will come. 'Even the Czar will die,' as the saying goes. But the other way: she simply spent the night in your house, hired horses, and went away. And what of it? Somebody passing through the village sleeps with somebody in the village. There's nothing in that."

"Where did you learn to be afraid, Pyotr?" Tatyana scoffed.

"A man must know everything, friend!" Pyotr exclaimed, striking his knee—"know how to fear, know how to be brave. You remember how a policeman lashed Vaganov for that newspaper? Now you'll not persuade Vaganov for any amount of money to take a book in his hand. Yes; you believe me, mother, I'm a sharp fellow for every sort of a trick—everybody knows it. I'm going to scatter these books and papers for you in the best shape and form, as much as you please. Of course, the people here are not educated; they've been intimidated. However, the times squeeze a man and wide open go his eyes, 'What's the matter?' And the book answers him in a perfectly simple way: 'That's what's the matter—Think! Unite! Nothing else is left for you to do!' There are examples of men who can't read or write and can understand more than the educated ones—especially if the educated ones have their stomachs full. I go about here everywhere; I see much. Well? It's possible to live; but you want brains and a lot of cleverness in order not to sit down in the cesspool at once. The authorities, too, smell a rat, as though a cold wind were blowing on them from the peasants. They see the peasant smiles very little, and altogether is not very kindly disposed and wants to disaccustom himself to the authorities. The other day in Smolyakov, a village not far from here, they came to extort the taxes; and your peasants got stubborn and flew into a passion. The police commissioner said straight out: 'Oh, you damned scoundrels! why, this is disobedience to the Czar!' There was one little peasant there, Spivakin, and says he: 'Off with you to the evil mother with your Czar! What kind of a Czar is he if he pulls the last shirt off your body?' That's how far it went, mother. Of course, they snatched Spivakin off to prison. But the word remained, and even the little boys know it. It lives! It shouts! And perhaps in our days the word is worth more than a man. People are stupefied and deadened by their absorption in breadwinning. Yes."

Pyotr did not eat, but kept on talking in a quick whisper, his dark, roguish eyes gleaming merrily. He lavishly scattered before the mother innumerable little observations on the village life—they rolled from him like copper coins from a full purse.

Stepan several times reminded him: "Why don't you eat?" Pyotr would then seize a piece of bread and a spoon and fall to talking and sputtering again like a goldfinch. Finally, after the meal, he jumped to his feet and announced:

"Well, it's time for me to go home. Good-by, mother!" and he shook her hand and nodded his head. "Maybe we shall never see each other again. I must say to you that all this is very good—to meet you and hear your speeches—very good! Is there anything in your valise beside the printed matter? A shawl? Excellent! A shawl, remember, Stepan. He'll bring you the valise at once. Come, Stepan. Good-by. I wish everything good to you."

After he had gone the crawling sound of the roaches became audible in the hut, the blowing of the wind over the roof and its knocking against the door in the chimney. A fine rain dripped monotonously on the window. Tatyana prepared a bed for the mother on the bench with clothing brought from the oven and the storeroom.

"A lively man!" remarked the mother.

The hostess looked at her sidewise.

"A light fellow," she answered. "He rattles on and rattles on; you can't but hear the rattling at a great distance."

"And how is your husband?" asked the mother.

"So so. A good peasant; he doesn't drink; we live peacefully. So so. Only he has a weak character." She straightened herself, and after a pause asked:

"Why, what is it that's wanted nowadays? What's wanted is that the people should be stirred up to revolt. Of course! Everybody thinks about it, but privately, for himself. And what's necessary is that he should speak out aloud. Some one person must be the first to decide to do it." She sat down on the bench and suddenly asked: "Tell me, do young ladies also occupy themselves with this? Do they go about with the workingmen and read? Aren't they squeamish and afraid?" She listened attentively to the mother's reply and fetched a deep sigh; then drooping her eyelids and inclining her head, she said: "In one book I read the words 'senseless life.' I understood them very well at once. I know such a life. Thoughts there are, but they're not connected, and they stray like stupid sheep without a shepherd. They stray and stray, with no one to bring them together. There's no understanding in people of what must be done. That's what a senseless life is. I'd like to run away from it without even looking around—such a severe pang one suffers when one understands something!"

The mother perceived the pang in the dry gleam of the woman's green eyes, in her wizened face, in her voice. She wanted to pet and soothe her.

"You understand, my dear, what to do—"

Tatyana interrupted her softly:

"A person must be able— The bed's ready for you. Lie down and sleep."

She went over to the oven and remained standing there erect, in silence, sternly centered in herself. The mother lay down without undressing. She began to feel the weariness in her bones and groaned softly. Tatyana walked up to the table, extinguished the lamp, and when darkness descended on the hut she resumed speech in her low, even voice, which seemed to erase something from the flat face of the oppressive darkness.

"You do not pray? I, too, think there is no God, there are no miracles. All these things were contrived to frighten us, to make us stupid."

The mother turned about on the bench uneasily; the dense darkness looked straight at her from the window, and the scarcely audible crawling of the roaches persistently disturbed the quiet. She began to speak almost in a whisper and fearfully:

"In regard to God, I don't know; but I do believe in Christ, in the Little Father. I believe in his words, 'Love thy neighbor as thyself.' Yes, I believe in them." And suddenly she asked in perplexity: "But if there is a God, why did He withdraw his good power from us? Why did He allow the division of people into two worlds? Why, if He is merciful, does He permit human torture—the mockery of one man by another, all kinds of evil and beastliness?"

Tatyana was silent. In the darkness the mother saw the faint outline of her straight figure—gray on the black background. She stood motionless. The mother closed her eyes in anguish. Then the groaning, cold voice sullenly broke in upon the stillness again:

"The death of my children I will never forgive, neither God nor man—I will never forgive—*never*!"

Nilovna uneasily rose from her bed; her heart understood the mightiness of the pain that evoked such words.

"You are young; you will still have children," she said kindly.

The woman did not answer immediately. Then she whispered:

"No, no. I'm spoiled. The doctor says I'll never be able to have a child again."

A mouse ran across the floor, something cracked—a flash of sound flaring up in the noiselessness. The autumn rain again rustled on the thatch like light thin fingers running over the roof. Large drops of water dismally fell to the ground, marking the slow course of the autumn night. Hollow steps on the street, then on the porch, awoke the mother from a heavy slumber. The door opened carefully.

"Tatyana!" came the low call. "Are you in bed already?"

"No."

"Is she asleep?"

"It seems she is."

A light flared up, trembled, and sank into the darkness.

The peasant walked over to the mother's bed, adjusted the sheepskin over her, and wrapped up her feet. The attention touched the mother in its simplicity. She closed her eyes again and smiled. Stepan undressed in silence, crept up to the loft, and all became quiet.

CHAPTER XII

The mother lay motionless, with ears strained in the drowsy stillness, and before her in the darkness wavered Rybin's face covered with blood. In the loft a dry whisper could be heard.

"You see what sort of people go into this work? Even elderly people who have drunk the cup of misery to the bottom, who have worked, and for whom it is time to rest. And there they are! But you are young, sensible! Ah, Stepan!"

The thick, moist voice of the peasant responded:

"Such an affair—you mustn't take it up without thinking over it. Just wait a little while!"

"I've heard you say so before." The sounds dropped, and rose again. The voice of Stepan rang out:

"You must do it this way—at first you must take each peasant aside and speak to him by himself—for instance, to Makov Alesha, a lively man—can read and write—was wronged by the police; Shorin Sergey, also a sensible peasant; Knyazev, an honest, bold man, and that'll do to begin with. Then we'll get a group together, we look about us—yes. We must learn how to find her; and we ourselves must take a look at the people about whom she spoke. I'll shoulder my ax and go off to the city myself, making out I'm going there to earn money by splitting wood. You must proceed carefully in this matter. She's right when she says that the price a man has is according to his own estimate of himself—and this is an affair in which you must set a high value on yourself when once you take it up. There's that peasant! See! You can put him even before God, not to speak of before a police commissioner. He won't yield. He stands for his own firmly—up to his knees in it. And Nikita, why his honor was suddenly pricked—a marvel? No. If the people will set out in a friendly way to do something together, they'll draw everybody after them."

"Friendly! They beat a man in front of your eyes, and you stand with your mouths wide open."

"You just wait a little while. He ought to thank God we didn't beat him ourselves, that man. Yes, indeed. Sometimes the authorities compel you to beat, and you do beat. Maybe you weep inside yourself with pity, but still you beat. People don't dare to decline from beastliness—they'll be killed themselves for it. They command you, 'Be what I want you to be—a wolf, a pig'—but to be a man is prohibited. And a bold man they'll get rid of—send to the next world. No. You must contrive for many to get bold at once, and for all to arise suddenly."

He whispered for a long time, now lowering his voice so that the mother scarcely could hear, and now bursting forth powerfully. Then the woman would stop him. "S-sh, you'll wake her."

The mother fell into a heavy dreamless sleep.

Tatyana awakened her in the early twilight, when the dusk still peered through the window with blank eyes, and when brazen sounds of the church bell floated and melted over the village in the gray, cold stillness.

"I have prepared the samovar. Take some tea or you'll be cold if you go out immediately after getting up."

Stepan, combing his tangled beard, asked the mother solicitously how to find her in the city. To-day the peasant's face seemed more finished to her. While they drank tea he remarked, smiling:

"How wonderfully things happen!"

"What?" asked Tatyana.

"Why, this acquaintance—so simply."

The mother said thoughtfully, but confidently:

"In this affair there's a marvelous simplicity in everything."

The host and hostess restrained themselves from demonstrativeness in parting with her; they were sparing of words, but lavish in little attentions for her comfort.

Sitting in the post, the mother reflected that this peasant would begin to work carefully, noiselessly, like a mole, without cease, and that at his side the discontented voice of his wife would always sound, and the dry burning gleam in her green eyes would never die out of her so long as she cherished the revengeful wolfish anguish of a mother for lost children.

The mother recalled Rybin—his blood, his face, his burning eyes, his words. Her heart was compressed again with a bitter feeling of impotence; and along the entire road to the city the powerful figure of black-bearded Mikhaïl with his torn shirt, his hands bound behind his back, his disheveled head, clothed in wrath and faith in his truth, stood out before her on the drab background of the gray day. And as she regarded the figure, she thought of the numberless villages timidly pressed to the ground; of the people, faint-heartedly and secretly awaiting the coming of truth; and of the thousands of people who senselessly and silently work their whole lifetime without awaiting the coming of anything.

Life represented itself to her as an unplowed, hilly field, which mutely awaits the workers and promises a harvest to free and honest hands: "Fertilize me with seeds of reason and truth; I will return them to you a hundredfold."

When from afar she saw the roofs and spires of the city, a warm joy animated and eased her perturbed, worn heart. The preoccupied faces of those people flashed up in her memory who, from day to day, without cease, in perfect confidence kindle the fire of thought and scatter the sparks over the whole earth. Her soul was flooded by the serene desire to give these people her entire force, and—doubly the love of a mother, awakened and animated by their thoughts.

At home Nikolay opened the door for the mother. He was disheveled and held a book in his hand.

"Already?" he exclaimed joyfully. "You've returned very quickly. Well, I'm glad, very glad."

His eyes blinked kindly and briskly behind his glasses. He quickly helped her off with her wraps, and said with an affectionate smile:

"And here in my place, as you see, there was a search last night.

And I wondered what the reason for it could possibly be—whether something hadn't happened to you. But you were not arrested. If they had arrested you they wouldn't have let me go either."

He led her into the dining room, and continued with animation: "However, they suggested that I should be discharged from my position. That doesn't distress me. I was sick, anyway, of counting the number of horseless peasants, and ashamed to receive money for it, too; for the money actually comes from them. It would have been awkward for me to leave the position of my own accord. I am under obligations to the comrades in regard to work. And now the matter has found its own solution. I'm satisfied!"

The mother sat down and looked around. One would have supposed that some powerful man in a stupid fit of insolence had knocked the walls of the house from the outside until everything inside had been jolted down. The portraits were scattered on the floor; the wall paper was torn away and stuck out in tufts; a board was pulled out of the flooring; a window sill was ripped away; the floor by the oven was strewn with ashes. The mother shook her head at the sight of this familiar picture.

"They wanted to show that they don't get money for nothing," remarked Nikolay.

On the table stood a cold samovar, unwashed dishes, sausages, and cheese on paper, along with plates, crumbs of bread, books, and coals from the samovar. The mother smiled. Nikolay also laughed in embarrassment, following the look of her eyes.

"It was I who didn't waste time in completing the picture of the upset. But never mind, Nilovna, never mind! I think they're going to come again. That's the reason I didn't pick it all up. Well, how was your trip?"

The mother started at the question. Rybin arose before her; she felt guilty at not having told of him immediately. Bending over a chair, she moved up to Nikolay and began her narrative. She tried to preserve her calm in order not to omit something as a result of excitement.

"They caught him!"

A quiver shot across Nikolay's face.

"They did? How?"

The mother stopped his questions with a gesture of her hand,

and continued as if she were sitting before the very face of justice and bringing in a complaint regarding the torture of a man. Nikolay threw himself back in his chair, grew pale, and listened, biting his lips. He slowly removed his glasses, put them on the table, and ran his hand over his face as if wiping away invisible cobwebs. The mother had never seen him wear so austere an expression.

When she concluded he arose, and for a minute paced the floor in silence, his fists thrust deep into his pockets. Conquering his agitation he looked almost calmly with a hard gleam in his eyes into the face of the mother, which was covered with silent tears.

"Nilovna, we mustn't waste time! Let us try, dear comrade, to take ourselves in hand." Then he remarked through his teeth:

"He must be a remarkable fellow—such nobility! It'll be hard for him in prison. Men like him feel unhappy there." Stepping in front of the mother he exclaimed in a ringing voice: "Of course, all the commissioners and sergeants are nothings. They are sticks in the hands of a clever villain, a trainer of animals. But I would kill an animal for allowing itself to be turned into a brute!" He restrained his excitement, which, however, made itself felt to the mother's perceptions. Again he strode through the room, and spoke in wrath: "See what horror! A gang of stupid people, protesting their pernicious power over the people, beat, stifle, oppress everybody. Savagery grows apace; cruelty becomes the law of life. A whole nation is depraved. Think of it! One part beats and turns brute; from immunity to punishment, sickens itself with a voluptuous greed of torture—that disgusting disease of slaves licensed to display all the power of slavish feelings and cattle habits. Others are poisoned with the desire for vengeance. Still others, beaten down to stupidity, become dumb and blind. They deprave the nation, the whole nation!" He stopped, leaning his elbows against the doorpost. He clasped his head in both hands, and was silent, his teeth set.

"You involuntarily turn a beast yourself in this beastly life!"

Smiling sadly, he walked up to her, and bending over her asked, pressing her hand: "Where is your valise?"

"In the kitchen."

"A spy is standing at our gate. We won't be able to get such a big mass of papers out of the way unnoticed. There's no place to hide them in and I think they'll come again to-night. I don't want you to be arrested. So, however sorry we may be for the lost labor, let's burn the papers."

"What?"

"Everything in the valise!"

She finally understood; and though sad, her pride in her success brought a complacent smile to her face.

"There's nothing in it—no leaflets." With gradually increasing animation she told how she had placed them in the hands of sympathetic peasants after Rybin's departure. Nikolay listened, at first with an uneasy frown, then in surprise, and finally exclaimed, interrupting her story:

"Say, that's capital! Nilovna, do you know—" He stammered, embarrassed, and pressing her hand, exclaimed quietly: "You touch me so by your faith in people, by your faith in the cause of their emancipation! You have such a good soul! I simply love you as I didn't love my own mother!"

Embracing his neck, she burst into happy sobs, and pressed his head to her lips.

"Maybe," he muttered, agitated and embarrassed by the newness of his feeling, "maybe I'm speaking nonsense; but, upon my honest word, you are a beautiful person, Nilovna—yes!"

"My darling, I love you, too; and I love you all with my whole soul, every drop of my blood!" she said, choking with a wave of hot joy.

The two voices blended into one throbbing speech, subdued and pulsating with the great feeling that was seizing the people.

"Such a large, soft power is in you; it draws the heart toward you imperceptibly. How brightly you describe people! How well you see them!"

"I see your life; I understand it, my dear!"

"One loves you. And it's such a marvelous thing to love a person—it's so good, you know!"

"It is you, you who raise the people from the dead to life again; you!" the mother whispered hotly, stroking his head. "My dear, I think I see there's much work for you, much patience needed. Your power must not be wasted. It's so necessary for life. Listen to what else happened: there was a woman there, the wife of that man—"

Nikolay sat near her, his happy face bent aside in embarrassment, and stroked his hair. But soon he turned around again, and looking at the mother, listened greedily to her simple and clear story.

"A miracle! Every possibility of your getting into prison and suddenly— Yes, it's evident that the peasants, too, are beginning to stir. After all, it's natural. We ought to get special people for the villages. People! We haven't enough—nowhere. Life demands hundreds of hands!"

"Now, if Pasha could be free—and Andriusha," said the mother softly. Nikolay looked at her and drooped his head.

"You see, Nilovna, it'll be hard for you to hear; but I'll say it, anyway—I know Pavel well; he won't leave prison. He wants to be tried; he wants to rise in all his height. He won't give up a trial, and he needn't either. He will escape from Siberia."

The mother sighed and answered softly:

"Well, he knows what's best for the cause."

Nikolay quickly jumped to his feet, suddenly seized with joy again.

"Thank you, Nilovna! I've just lived through a magnificent moment—maybe the best moment of my life. Thank you! Now, come, let's give each other a good, strong kiss!"

They embraced, looking into each other's eyes. And they gave each other firm, comradely kisses.

"That's good!" he said softly.

The mother unclasped her hands from about his neck and laughed quietly and happily.

"Um!" said Nikolay the next minute. "If your peasant there would hurry up and come here! You see, we must be sure to write a leaflet about Rybin for the village. It won't hurt him once he's come out so boldly, and it will help the cause. I'll surely do it to-day. Liudmila will print it quickly. But then arises the question—how will it get to the village?"

"I'll take it!"

"No, thank you!" Nikolay exclaimed quietly. "I'm wondering whether Vyesovshchikov won't do for it. Shall I speak to him?"

"Yes; suppose you try and instruct him."

"What'll I do then?"

"Don't worry!"

Nikolay sat down to write, while the mother put the table in order, from time to time casting a look at him. She saw how his pen trembled in his hand. It traveled along the paper in straight lines. Sometimes the skin on his neck quivered; he threw back his head and shut his eyes. All this moved her.

"Execute them!" she muttered under her breath. "Don't pity the villains!"

"There! It's ready!" he said, rising. "Hide the paper somewhere on your body. But know that when the gendarmes come they'll search you, too!"

"The dogs take them!" she answered calmly.

In the evening Dr. Ivan Danilovich came.

"What's gotten into the authorities all of a sudden?" he said, running about the room. "There were seven searches last night. Where's the patient?"

"He left yesterday. To-day, you see, Saturday, he reads to working people. He couldn't bring it over himself to omit the reading."

"That's stupid—to sit at readings with a fractured skull!"

"I tried to prove it to him, but unsuccessfully."

"He wanted to do a bit of boasting before the comrades," observed the mother. "Look! I've already shed my blood!"

The physician looked at her, made a fierce face, and said with set teeth:

"Ugh! ugh! you bloodthirsty person!"

"Well, Ivan, you've nothing to do here, and we're expecting guests. Go away! Nilovna, give him the paper."

"Another paper?"

"There, take it and give it to the printer."

"I've taken it; I'll deliver it. Is that all?"

"That's all. There's a spy at the gate."

"I noticed. At my door, too. Good-by! Good-by, you fierce woman! And do you know, friends, a squabble in a cemetery is a fine thing after all! The whole city's talking about it. It stirs the people up and compels them to think. Your article on that subject was excellent, and it came in time. I always said that a good fight is better than a bad peace."

"All right. Go away now!"

"You're polite! Let's shake hands, Nilovna. And that fellow—he certainly behaved stupidly. Do you know where he lives?"

Nikolay gave him the address.

"I must go to him to-morrow. He's a fine fellow, eh?"

"Very!"

"We must keep him alive; he has good brains. It's from just such fellows that the real proletarian intellectuals ought to grow up—men to take our places when we leave for the region where evidently there are no class antagonisms. But, after all, who knows?"

"You've taken to chattering, Ivan."

"I feel happy, that's why. Well, I'm going! So you're expecting prison? I hope you get a good rest there!"

"Thank you, I'm not tired!"

The mother listened to their conversation. Their solicitude in regard to the workingmen was pleasant to her; and, as always, the calm activity of these people which did not forsake them even before the gates of the prison, astonished her.

After the physician left, Nikolay and the mother conversed quietly while awaiting their evening visitors. Then Nikolay told her at length of his comrades living in exile; of those who had already escaped and continued their work under assumed names. The bare walls of the room echoed the low sounds of his voice, as if listening in incredulous amazement to the stories of modest heroes who disinterestedly devoted all their powers to the great cause of liberty.

A shadow kindly enveloped the woman, warming her heart with love for the unseen people, who in her imagination united into one huge person, full of inexhaustible, manly force. This giant slowly but incessantly strides over the earth, cleansing it, laying bare before the eyes of the people the simple and clear truth of life—the great truth that raises humanity from the dead, welcomes all equally, and promises all alike freedom from greed, from wickedness, and falsehood, the three monsters which enslaved and intimidated the whole world. The image evoked in the mother's soul a feeling similar to that with which she used to stand before an ikon. After she had offered her joyful, grateful prayer, the day had then seemed lighter than the other days of her life. Now she forgot those days. But the feeling left by them had broadened, had become brighter and better, had grown more deeply into her soul. It was more keenly alive and burned more luminously.

"But the gendarmes aren't coming!" Nikolay exclaimed suddenly, interrupting his story.

The mother looked at him, and after a pause answered in vexation:

"Oh, well, let them go to the dogs!"

"Of course! But it's time for you to go to bed, Nilovna. You must be desperately tired. You're wonderfully strong, I must say. So much commotion and disturbance, and you live through it all so lightly. Only your hair is turning gray very quickly. Now go and rest."

They pressed each other's hand and parted.

CHAPTER XIII

The mother fell quickly into a calm sleep, and rose early in the morning, awakened by a subdued tap at the kitchen door. The knock was incessant and patiently persistent. It was still dark and quiet, and the rapping broke in alarmingly on the stillness. Dressing herself rapidly, she walked out into the kitchen, and standing at the door asked:

"Who's there?"

"I," answered an unfamiliar voice.

"Who?"

"Open." The quiet word was spoken in entreaty.

The mother lifted the hook, pushed the door with her foot, and Ignaty entered, saying cheerfully:

"Well, so I'm not mistaken. I'm at the right place."

He was spattered with mud up to his belt. His face was gray, his eyes fallen.

"We've gotten into trouble in our place," he whispered, locking the door behind him.

"I know it."

The reply astonished the young man. He blinked and asked: "How? Where from?"

She explained in a few rapid words, and asked:

"Did they take the other comrades, too?"

"They weren't there. They had gone off to be recruited. Five were captured, including Rybin."

He snuffled and said, smiling:

"And I was left over. I guess they're looking for me. Let them look. I'm not going back there again, not for anything. There are other people there yet, some seven young men and a girl. Never mind! They're all reliable."

"How did you find this place?" The mother smiled.

The door from the room opened quietly.

"I?" Seating himself on a bench and looking around, Ignaty exclaimed: "They crawled up at night, straight to the tar works. Well, a minute before they came the forester ran up to us and knocked on the window. 'Look out, boys,' says he, 'they're coming on you.'"

He laughed softly, wiped his face with the flap of his coat, and continued:

"Well, they can't stun Uncle Mikhaïl even with a hammer. At once he says to me, 'Ignaty, run away to the city, quick! You remember the elderly woman.' And he himself writes a note. 'There, go! Good-by, brother.' He pushed me in the back. I flung out of the hut. I scrambled along on all fours through the bushes, and I hear them coming. There must have been a lot of them. You could hear the rustling on all sides, the devils—like a moose around the tar works. I lay in the bushes. They passed by me. Then I rose and off I went; and for two nights and a whole day I walked without stopping. My feet'll ache for a week."

He was evidently satisfied with himself. A smile shone in his hazel eyes. His full red lips quivered.

"I'll set you up with some tea soon. You wash yourself while I get the samovar ready."

"I'll give you the note." He raised his leg with difficulty, and frowning and groaning put his foot on the bench and began to untie the leg wrappings.

"I got frightened. 'Well,' thinks I, 'I'm a goner.'"

Nikolay appeared at the door. Ignaty in embarrassment dropped his foot to the floor and wanted to rise, but staggered and fell heavily on the bench, catching himself with his hands.

"You sit still!" exclaimed the mother.

"How do you do, comrade?" said Nikolay, screwing up his eyes good-naturedly and nodding his head. "Allow me, I'll help you."

Kneeling on the floor in front of the peasant, he quickly unwound the dirty, damp wrappings.

"Well!" the fellow exclaimed quietly, pulling back his foot and blinking in astonishment. He regarded the mother, who said, without paying attention to his look:

"His legs ought to be rubbed down with alcohol."

"Of course!" said Nikolay.

Ignaty snorted in embarrassment. Nikolay found the note, straightened it out, looked at it, and handed the gray, crumpled piece of paper to the mother.

"For you."

"Read it."

"'Mother, don't let the affair go without your attention. Tell the tall lady not to forget to have them write more for our cause, I beg of you. Good-by. Rybin.'"

"My darling!" said the mother sadly. "They've already seized him by the throat, and he——"

Nikolay slowly dropped his hand holding the note.

"That's magnificent!" he said slowly and respectfully. "It both touches and teaches."

Ignaty looked at them, and quietly shook his bared feet with his dirty hands. The mother, covering her tearful face, walked up to him with a basin of water, sat down on the floor, and stretched out her hands to his feet. But he quickly thrust them under the bench, exclaiming in fright:

"What are you going to do?"

"Give me your foot, quick!"

"I'll bring the alcohol at once," said Nikolay.

The young man shoved his foot still farther under the bench and mumbled:

"What *are* you going to do? It's not proper."

Then the mother silently unbared his other foot. Ignaty's round face lengthened in amazement. He looked around helplessly with his wide-open eyes.

"Why, it's going to tickle me!"

"You'll be able to bear it," answered the mother, beginning to wash his feet.

Ignaty snorted aloud, and moving his neck awkwardly looked down at her, comically drooping his under lip.

"And do you know," she said tremulously, "that they beat Mikhaïl Ivanovich?"

"What?" the peasant exclaimed in fright.

"Yes; he had been beaten when they led him to the village, and in Nikolsk the sergeant beat him, the police commissioner beat him in the face and kicked him till he bled." The mother became silent, overwhelmed by her recollections.

"They can do it," said the peasant, lowering his brows sullenly. His shoulders shook. "That is, I fear them like the devils. And the peasants—didn't the peasants beat him?"

"One beat him. The police commissioner ordered him to. All the others were so so—they even took his part. 'You mustn't beat him!' they said."

"Um! Yes, yes! The peasants are beginning to realize where a man stands, and for what he stands."

"There are sensible people there, too."

"Where can't you find sensible people? Necessity! They're everywhere; but it's hard to get at them. They hide themselves in chinks and crevices, and suck their hearts out each one for himself. Their resolution isn't strong enough to make them gather into a group."

Nikolay brought a bottle of alcohol, put coals in the samovar, and walked away silently. Ignaty accompanied him with a curious look.

"A gentleman?"

"In this business there are no masters; they're all comrades!"

"It's strange to me," said Ignaty with a skeptical but embarrassed smile.

"What's strange?"

"This: at one end they beat you in the face; at the other they wash your feet. Is there a middle of any kind?"

The door of the room was flung open and Nikolay, standing on the threshold, said:

"And in the middle stand the people who lick the hands of those who beat you in the face and suck the blood of those whose faces are beaten. That's the middle!"

Ignaty looked at him respectfully, and after a pause said: "That's it!"

The mother sighed. "Mikhaïl Ivanovich also always used to say, 'That's it!' like an ax blow."

"Nilovna, you're evidently tired. Permit me—I——"

The peasant pulled his feet uneasily.

"That'll do;" said the mother, rising. "Well, Ignaty, now wash yourself."

The young man arose, shifted his feet about, and stepped firmly on the floor.

"They seem like new feet. Thank you! Many, many thanks!"

He drew a wry face, his lips trembled, and his eyes reddened. After a pause, during which he regarded the basin of black water, he whispered softly:

"I don't even know how to thank you!"

Then they sat down to the table to drink tea. And Ignaty soberly began:

"I was the distributer of literature, a very strong fellow at walking. Uncle Mikhaïl gave me the job. 'Distribute!' says he; 'and if you get caught you're alone.'"

"Do many people read?" asked Nikolay.

"All who can. Even some of the rich read. Of course, they don't get it from us. They'd clap us right into chains if they did! They understand that this is a slipknot for them in all ages."

"Why a slipknot?"

"What else!" exclaimed Ignaty in amazement. "Why, the peasants are themselves going to take the land from everyone else. They'll wash it out with their blood from under the gentry and the rich; that is to say, they themselves are going to divide it, and divide it so that there won't be masters or workingmen anymore. How then?

What's the use of getting into a scrap if not for that?"

Ignaty even seemed to be offended. He looked at Nikolay mistrustfully and skeptically. Nikolay smiled.

"Don't get angry," said the mother jokingly.

Nikolay thoughtfully exclaimed:

"How shall we get the leaflets about Rybin's arrest to the village?" Ignaty grew attentive.

"I'll speak to Vyesovshchikov to-day."

"Is there a leaflet already?" asked Ignaty.

"Yes."

"Give it to me. I'll take it." Ignaty rubbed his hands at the suggestion, his eyes flashing. "I know where and how. Let me."

The mother laughed quietly, without looking at him.

"Why, you're tired and afraid, and you said you'd never go there again!"

Ignaty smacked his lips and stroked his curly hair with his broad palm.

"I'm tired; I'll rest; and of course I'm afraid!" His manner was businesslike and calm. "They beat a man until the blood comes, as you yourself say—then who wants to be mutilated? But I'll pull through somehow at night. Never mind! Give me the leaflets; this evening I'll get on the go." He was silent, thought a while, his eyebrows working. "I'll go to the forest; I'll hide the literature, and then I'll notify our fellows: 'Go get it.' That's better. If I myself should distribute them I might fall into the hands of the police, and it would be a pity for the leaflets. You must act carefully here. There are not many such leaflets!"

"And how about your fear?" the mother observed again with a smile. This curly-haired, robust fellow put her into a good humor by his sincerity, which sounded in his every word, and shone from his round, determined face.

"Fear is fear, and business is business!" he answered with a grin. "Why are you laughing at me, eh? You, too! Why, isn't it natural to be afraid in this matter? Well, and if it's necessary a man'll go into a fire. Such an affair, it requires it."

"Ah, you, my child!"

Ignaty, embarrassed, smiled. "Well, there you are—child!" he said.

Nikolay began to speak, all the time looking good-naturedly with screwed-up eyes at the young peasant.

"You're not going there!"

"Then what'll I do? Where am I to be?" Ignaty asked uneasily.

"Another fellow will go in place of you. And you'll tell him in detail what to do and how to do it."

"All right!" said Ignaty. But his consent was not given at once, and then only reluctantly.

"And for you we'll obtain a good passport and make you a forester."

The young fellow quickly threw back his head and asked uneasily:

"But if the peasants come there for wood, or there—in general—what'll I do? Bind them? That doesn't suit me."

The mother laughed, and Nikolay, too. This again confused and vexed Ignaty.

"Don't be uneasy!" Nikolay soothed him. "You won't have to bind peasants. You trust us."

"Well, well," said Ignaty, set at ease, smiling at Nikolay with confidence and merriness in his eyes. "If you could get me to the factory. There, they say, the fellows are mighty smart."

A fire seemed to be ever burning in his broad chest, unsteady as yet, not confident in its own power. It flashed brightly in his eyes, forced out from within; but suddenly it would nearly expire in fright and flicker behind the smoke of perplexed alarm and embarrassment.

The mother rose from behind the table, and looking through the window reflected:

"Ah, life! Five times in the day you laugh and five times you weep. All right. Well, are you through, Ignaty? Go to bed and sleep."

"But I don't want to."

"Go on, go on!"

"You're stern in this place. Thank you for the tea, for the sugar, for the kindness."

Lying down in the mother's bed he mumbled, scratching his head:

"Now everything'll smell of tar in your place. Ah, it's all for nothing all this—plain coddling! I don't want to sleep. You're good people, yes. It's more than I can understand—as if I'd gotten a hundred thousand miles away from the village—how he hit it off about the middle—and in the middle are the people who lick the hands—of those who beat the faces—um, yes."

And suddenly he gave a loud short snore and dropped off to sleep, with eyebrows raised high and half-open mouth.

◆

Late at night he sat in a little room of a basement at a table opposite Vyesovshchikov. He said in a subdued tone, knitting his brows:

"On the middle window, four times."

"Four."

"At first three times like this"—he counted aloud as he tapped thrice on the table with his forefinger. "Then waiting a little, once again."

"I understand."

"A red-haired peasant will open the door for you, and will ask you for the midwife. You'll tell him, 'Yes, from the boss.' Nothing else. He'll understand your business."

They sat with heads bent toward each other, both robust fellows, conversing in half tones. The mother, with her arms folded on her bosom, stood at the table looking at them. All the secret tricks and passwords compelled her to smile inwardly as she thought, "Mere children still."

A lamp burned on the wall, illuminating a dark spot of dampness and pictures from journals. On the floor old pails were lying around, fragments of slate iron. A large, bright star out in the high darkness shone into the window. The odor of mildew, paint, and damp earth filled the room.

Ignaty was dressed in a thick autumn overcoat of shaggy material. It pleased him; the mother observed how he stroked it admiringly with the palm of his hand, how he looked at himself, clumsily turning his powerful neck. Her bosom beat tenderly with, "My dears, my children, my own."

"There!" said Ignaty, rising. "You'll remember, then? First you go to Muratov and ask for grandfather."

"I remember."

But Ignaty was still distrustful of Nikolay's memory, and reiterated all the instructions, words, and signs, and finally extended his hand to him, saying:

"That's all now. Good-by, comrade. Give my regards to them. I'm alive and strong. The people there are good—you'll see." He cast a satisfied glance down at himself, stroked the overcoat, and asked the mother, "Shall I go?"

"Can you find the way?"

"Yes. Good-by, then, dear comrades."

He walked off, raising his shoulders high, thrusting out his chest, with his new hat cocked to one side, and his hands deep in his pockets in most dignified fashion. On his forehead and temples his bright, boyish curls danced gayly.

"There, now, I have work, too," said Vyesovshchikov, going over to the mother quietly. "I'm bored already—jumped out of prison—what for? My only occupation is hiding—and there I was learning. Pavel so pressed your brains—it was one pure delight. And Andrey, too, polished us fellows zealously. Well, Nilovna, did you hear how they decided in regard to the escape? Will they arrange it?"

"They'll find out day after to-morrow," she repeated, sighing involuntarily. "One day still—day after to-morrow."

Laying his heavy hand on her shoulder, and bringing his face close to hers, Nikolay said animatedly:

"You tell them, the older ones there—they'll listen to you. Why, it's very easy. You just see for yourself. There's the wall of the prison near the lamp-post; opposite is an empty lot, on the left the cemetery, on the right the streets—the city. The lamplighter goes to the lamp-post; by day he cleans the lamp; he puts the ladder against the wall, climbs up, screws hooks for a rope ladder onto the top of the wall, lets the rope ladder down into the prison yard, and off he goes. There inside the walls they know the time when this will be done, and will ask the criminals to arrange an uproar, or they'll arrange it themselves, and those who need it will go up the ladder over the wall—one, two, it's done. And they calmly proceed to the city because the chase throws itself first of all on the vacant lot and the cemetery."

He gesticulated rapidly in front of the mother's face, drawing his plan, the details of which were clear, simple, and clever. She had known him as a clumsy fellow, and it was strange to her to see the pockmarked face with the high cheek bones, usually so gloomy, now lively and alert. The narrow gray eyes, formerly harsh and cold, looking at the world sullenly with malice and distrust, seemed to be chiseled anew, assuming an oval form and shining with an even, warm light that convinced and moved the mother.

"You think of it—by day, without fail by day. To whom would it occur that a prisoner would make up his mind to escape by day in the eyes of the whole prison?"

"And they'll shoot him down," the woman said trembling.

"Who? There are no soldiers, and the overseers of the prison use their revolvers to drive nails in."

"Why, it's very simple—all this."

"And you'll see it'll all come out all right. No. You speak to them. I have everything prepared already—the rope ladder, the screw hooks; I spoke to my host, he'll be the lamplighter."

Somebody stirred noisily at the door and coughed, and iron clanked.

"There he is!" exclaimed Nikolay.

At the open door a tin bathtub was thrust in, and a hoarse voice said:

"Get in, you devil."

Then a round, gray, hatless head appeared. It had protruding eyes and a mustache, and wore a good-natured expression. Nikolay helped the man in with the tub. A tall, stooping figure strode through the door. The man coughed, his shaven cheeks puffing up; he spat out and greeted hoarsely:

"Good health to you!"

"There! Ask him!"

"Me? What about?"

"About the escape."

"Ah, ah!" said the host, wiping his mustache with black fingers.

"There, Yakob Vasilyevich! She doesn't believe it's a simple matter!"

"Hm! she doesn't believe! Not to believe means not to want to believe. You and I want to, and so we believe." The old man suddenly bent over and coughed hoarsely, rubbed his breast for a long time, while he stood in the middle of the room panting for breath and scanning the mother with wide-open eyes.

"I'm not the one to decide, Nikolay."

"But, mother, you talk with them. Tell them everything is ready. Ah, if I could only see them! I'd force them!" He threw out his hands with a broad gesture and pressed them together as if embracing something firmly, and his voice rang with hot feeling that astounded the mother by its power.

"Hm! what a fellow you are!" she thought; but said aloud: "It's for Pasha and the comrades to decide."

Nikolay thoughtfully inclined his head.

"Who's this Pasha?" asked the host, seating himself.

"My son."

"What's the family?"

"Vlasov."

He nodded his head, got his tobacco pouch, whipped out his pipe and filled it with tobacco. He spoke brokenly:

"I've heard of him. My nephew knows him. He, too, is in prison—my nephew Yevchenko. Have you heard of him? And my family is Godun. They'll soon shut all the young people in prison, and then there'll be plenty and comfort for us old folks. The gendarme assures me that my nephew will even be sent to Siberia. They'll exile him—the dogs!"

Lighting his pipe, he turned to Nikolay, spitting frequently on the floor:

"So she doesn't want to? Well, that's her affair! A person is free to feel as he wants to. Are you tired of sitting in prison? Go. Are you tired of going? Sit. They robbed you? Keep still. They beat you? Bear it. They have killed you? Stay dead. That's certain. And I'll carry off Savka; I'll carry him off!" His curt, barking phrases, full of good-natured irony, perplexed the mother. But his last words aroused envy in her.

While walking along the street in the face of a cold wind and rain, she thought of Nikolay, "What a man he's become! Think of it!" And remembering Godun, she almost prayerfully reflected, "It seems I'm not the only one who lives for the new. It's a big fire if it so cleanses and burns all who see it." Then she thought of her son, "If he only agreed!"

On Sunday, taking leave of Pavel in the waiting room of the prison, she felt a little lump of paper in her hand. She started as if it burned her skin, and cast a look of question and entreaty into her son's face. But she found no answer there. Pavel's blue eyes smiled with the usual composed smile familiar to her.

"Good-by!" she sighed.

The son again put out his hand to her, and a certain kindness and tenderness for her quivered on his face. "Good-by, mamma!"

She waited without letting go of his hand. "Don't be uneasy—don't be angry," he said.

These words and the stubborn folds between his brows answered her question. "Well, what do you mean?" she muttered, drooping her head. "What of it?" And she quickly walked away without looking at him, in order not to betray her feelings by the tears in her eyes and the quiver of her lips. On the road she thought that the bones of the hand which had pressed her son's hand ached and grew heavy, as if she had been struck on the shoulder.

At home, after thrusting the note into Nikolay's hand, she stood before him, and waited while he smoothed out the tight little roll. She felt a tremor of hope again; but Nikolay said:

"Of course, this is what he writes: 'We will not go away, comrade; we cannot, not one of us. We should lose respect for ourselves. Take into consideration the peasant recently arrested. He has merited your solicitude; he deserves that you expend much time and energy on him. It's very hard for him here—daily collisions with the authorities. He's already had the twenty-four hours of the dark cell. They torture him to death. We all intercede for him. Soothe and be kind to my mother; tell her; she'll understand all. Pavel.'"

The mother straightened herself easily, and proudly tossed her head.

"Well, what is there to tell me?" she said firmly. "I understand—they want to go straight at the authorities again—'there! condemn the truth!'"

Nikolay quickly turned aside, took out his handkerchief, blew his nose aloud, and mumbled: "I've caught a cold, you see!" Covering his eyes with his hands, under the pretext of adjusting his glasses, he paced up and down the room, and said: "We shouldn't have been successful anyway."

"Never mind; let the trial come off!" said the mother frowning.

"Here, I've received a letter from a comrade in St. Petersburg———"

"He can escape from Siberia, too, can't he?"

"Of course! The comrade writes: 'The trial is appointed for the near future; the sentence is certain—exile for everybody!' You see, these petty cheats convert their court into the most trivial comedy. You understand? Sentence is pronounced in St. Petersburg before the trial."

"Stop!" the mother said resolutely. "You needn't comfort me or explain to me. Pasha won't do what isn't right—he won't torture himself for nothing." She paused to catch breath. "Nor will he torture others, and he loves me, yes. You see, he thinks of me. 'Explain to her,' he writes; 'soothe her and comfort her,' eh?"

Her heart beat quickly but boldly, and her head whirled slightly from excitement.

"Your son's a splendid man! I respect and love him very much."

"I tell you what—let's think of something in regard to Rybin," she suggested.

She wanted to do something forthwith—go somewhere, walk till she dropped from exhaustion, and then fall asleep, content with the day's work.

"Yes—very well!" said Nikolay, pacing through the room. "Why not? We ought to have Sashenka here!"

"She'll be here soon. She always comes on my visiting day to Pasha."

Thoughtfully drooping his head, biting his lips and twisting his beard, Nikolay sat on the sofa by the mother's side.

"I'm sorry my sister isn't here. She ought to occupy herself with Rybin's case."

"It would be well to arrange it at once, while Pasha is there. It would be pleasant for him."

The bell rang. They looked at each other.

"That's Sasha," Nikolay whispered.

"How will you tell her?" the mother whispered back.

"Yes—um!—it's hard!"

"I pity her very much."

The bell rang again, not so loud, as if the person on the other side of the door had also fallen to thinking and hesitated. Nikolay and the mother rose simultaneously, but at the kitchen door Nikolay turned aside.

"You'd better do it," he said.

"He's not willing?" the girl asked the moment the mother opened the door.

"No."

"I knew it!" Sasha's face paled. She unbuttoned her coat, fastened two buttons again, then tried to remove her coat, unsuccessfully, of course. "Dreadful weather—rain, wind; it's disgusting! Is he well?"

"Yes."

"Well and happy; always the same, and only this—" Her tone was disconsolate, and she regarded her hands.

"He writes that Rybin ought to be freed." The mother kept her eyes turned from the girl.

"Yes? It seems to me we ought to make use of this plan."

"I think so, too," said Nikolay, appearing at the door. "How do you do, Sasha?"

The girl asked, extending her hand to him:

"What's the question about? Aren't all agreed that the plan is practicable? I know they are."

"And who'll organize it? Everybody's occupied."

"Give it to me," said Sasha, quickly jumping to her feet. "I have time!"

"Take it. But you must ask others."

"Very well, I will. I'll go at once."

She began to button up her coat again with sure, thin fingers.

"You ought to rest a little," the mother advised.

Sasha smiled and answered in a softer voice:

"Don't worry about me. I'm not tired." And silently pressing their hands, she left once more, cold and stern.

CHAPTER XIV

The mother and Nikolay, walking up to the window, watched the girl pass through the yard and disappear beyond the gate. Nikolay whistled quietly, sat down at the table and began to write.

"She'll occupy herself with this affair, and it'll be easier for her," the mother reflected.

"Yes, of course!" responded Nikolay, and turning around to the mother with a kind smile on his face, asked: "And how about you, Nilovna—did this cup of bitterness escape you? Did you never know the pangs for a beloved person?"

"Well!" exclaimed the mother with a wave of her hand. "What sort of a pang? The fear they had whether they won't marry me off to this man or that man?"

"And you liked no one?"

She thought a little, and answered:

"I don't recall, my dear! How can it be that I didn't like anybody? I suppose there was somebody I was fond of, but I don't remember."

She looked at him, and concluded simply, with sad composure: "My husband beat me a lot; and everything that was before him was effaced from my soul."

Nikolay turned back to the table; the mother walked out of the room for a minute. On her return Nikolay looked at her kindly and began to speak softly and lovingly. His reminiscences stroked her like a caress.

"And I, you see, was like Sashenka. I loved a girl: a marvelous being, a wonder, a—guiding star; she was gentle and bright for me. I met her about twenty years ago, and from that time on I loved her. And I love her now, too, to speak the truth. I love her all so—with my whole soul—gratefully—forever!"

Standing by his side the mother saw his eyes lighted from within by a clear, warm light. His hands folded over the back of the chair, and his head leaning on them, he looked into the distance; his whole body, lean and slender, but powerful, seemed to strive upward, like the stalk of a plant toward the sun.

"Why didn't you marry? You should have!"

"Oh, she's been married five years!"

"And before that—what was the matter? Didn't she love you?"

He thought a while, and answered:

"Yes, apparently she loved me; I'm certain she did. But, you see, it was always this way: I was in prison, she was free; I was free, she was in prison or in exile. That's very much like Sasha's position, really. Finally they exiled her to Siberia for ten years. I wanted to follow her, but I was ashamed and she was ashamed, and I remained here. Then she met another man—a comrade of mine, a very good fellow, and they escaped together. Now they live abroad. Yes——"

Nikolay took off his glasses, wiped them, held them up to the light and began to wipe them again.

"Ah, you, my dear!" the mother exclaimed lovingly, shaking her head. She was sorry for him; at the same time something compelled her to smile a warm, motherly smile. He changed his pose, took the pen in his hand, and said, punctuating the rhythm of his speed with waves of his hand:

"Family life always diminishes the energy of a revolutionist. Children must be maintained in security, and there's the need to work a great deal for one's bread. The revolutionist ought without cease to develop every iota of his energy; he must deepen and broaden it; but this demands time. He must always be at the head, because we—the workingmen—are called by the logic of history to destroy the old world, to create the new life; and if we stop, if we yield to exhaustion, or are attracted by the possibility of a little immediate conquest, it's bad—it's almost treachery to the cause. No revolutionist can adhere closely to an individual—walk through life side by side with another individual—without distorting his faith; and we must never forget that our aim is not little conquests, but only complete victory!"

His voice became firm, his face paled, and his eyes kindled with the force that characterized him. The bell sounded again. It was Liudmila. She wore an overcoat too light for the season, her cheeks were purple with the cold. Removing her torn overshoes, she said in a vexed voice:

"The date of the trial is appointed—in a week!"

"Really?" shouted Nikolay from the room.

The mother quickly walked up to him, not understanding whether fright or joy agitated her. Liudmila, keeping step with her, said, with irony in her low voice:

"Yes, really! The assistant prosecuting attorney, Shostak, just now brought the incriminating acts. In the court they say, quite openly, that the sentence has already been fixed. What does it mean? Do the authorities fear that the judges will deal too mercifully with the enemies of the government? Having so long and so assiduously kept corrupting their servants, is the government still unassured of their readiness to be scoundrels?"

Liudmila sat on the sofa, rubbing her lean cheeks with her palms; her dull eyes burned contemptuous scorn, and her voice filled with growing wrath.

"You waste your powder for nothing, Liudmila!" Nikolay tried to soothe her. "They don't hear you."

"Some day I'll compel them to hear me!"

The black circles under her eyes trembled and threw an ominous shadow on her face. She bit her lips.

"You go against me—that's your right; I'm your enemy. But in defending your power don't corrupt people; don't compel me to have instinctive contempt for them; don't dare to poison my soul with your cynicism!"

Nikolay looked at her through his glasses, and screwing up his eyes, shook his head sadly. But she continued to speak as if those whom she detested stood before her. The mother listened with strained attention, understanding nothing, and instinctively repeating to herself one and the same words, "The trial—the trial will come off in a week!"

She could not picture to herself what it would be like; how the judges would behave toward Pavel. Her thoughts muddled her brain, covered her eyes with a gray mist, and plunged her into something sticky, viscid, chilling and paining her body. The feeling grew, entered her blood, took possession of her heart, and weighed it down heavily, poisoning in it all that was alive and bold.

Thus, in a cloud of perplexity and despondency under the load of painful expectations, she lived through one day, and a second day; but on the third day Sasha appeared and said to Nikolay:

"Everything is ready—to-day, in an hour!"

"Everything ready? So soon?" He was astonished.

"Why shouldn't everything be ready? The only thing I had to do was to get a hiding place and clothes for Rybin. All the rest Godun took on himself. Rybin will have to go through only one ward of the city. Vyesovshchikov will meet him on the street, all disguised, of course. He'll throw an overcoat over him, give him a hat, and show him the way. I'll wait for him, change his clothes and lead him off."

"Not bad! And who's this Godun?"

"You've seen him! You gave talks to the locksmiths in his place."

"Oh, I remember! A droll old man."

"He's a soldier who served his time—a roofer, a man of little education, but with an inexhaustible fund of hatred for every kind of violence and for all men of violence. A bit of a philosopher!"

The mother listened in silence to her, and something indistinct slowly dawned upon her.

"Godun wants to free his nephew—you remember him? You liked Yevchenko, a blacksmith, quite a dude." Nikolay nodded his head. "Godun has arranged everything all right. But I'm beginning to doubt his success. The passages in the prison are used by all the inmates, and I think when the prisoners see the ladder many will want to run—" She closed her eyes and was silent for a while. The mother moved nearer to her. "They'll hinder one another."

They all three stood before the window, the mother behind Nikolay and Sasha. Their rapid conversation roused in her a still stronger sense of uneasiness and anxiety.

"I'm going there," the mother said suddenly.

"Why?" asked Sasha.

"Don't go, darling! Maybe you'll get caught. You mustn't!" Nikolay advised.

The mother looked at them and softly, but persistently, repeated: "No; I'm going! I'm going!"

They quickly exchanged glances, and Sasha, shrugging her shoulders, said:

"Of course—hope is tenacious!"

Turning to the mother she took her by the hand, leaned her head on her shoulder, and said in a new, simple voice, near to the heart of the mother:

"But I'll tell you after all, mamma, you're waiting in vain—he won't try to escape!"

"My dear darling!" exclaimed the mother, pressing Sasha to her tremulously. "Take me; I won't interfere with you; I don't believe it is possible—to escape!"

"She'll go," said the girl simply to Nikolay.

"That's your affair!" he answered, bowing his head.

"We mustn't be together, mamma. You go to the garden in the lot. From there you can see the wall of the prison. But suppose they ask you what you are doing there?"

Rejoiced, the mother answered confidently:

"I'll think of what to say."

"Don't forget that the overseers of the prison know you," said Sasha; "and if they see you there——"

"They won't see me!" the mother laughed softly.

An hour later she was in the lot by the prison. A sharp wind blew about her, pulled her dress, and beat against the frozen earth, rocked the old fence of the garden past which the woman walked, and rattled against the low wall of the prison; it flung up somebody's shouts from the court, scattered them in the air, and carried them up to the sky. There the clouds were racing quickly, little rifts opening in the blue height.

Behind the mother lay the city; in front the cemetery; to the right, about seventy feet from her, the prison. Near the cemetery a soldier was leading a horse by a rein, and another soldier tramped noisily alongside him, shouted, whistled, and laughed. There was no one else near the prison. On the impulse of the moment the mother walked straight up to them. As she came near she shouted:

"Soldiers! didn't you see a goat anywhere around here?"

One of them answered:

"No."

She walked slowly past them, toward the fence of the cemetery, looking slantwise to the right and the back. Suddenly she felt her feet tremble and grow heavy, as if frozen to the ground. From the corner of the prison a man came along, walking quickly, like a lamplighter. He was a stooping man, with a little ladder on his shoulder. The mother, blinking in fright, quickly glanced at the soldiers; they were stamping their feet on one spot, and the horse was running around them. She looked at the ladder—he had already placed it against the wall and was climbing up without haste. He waved his hand in the courtyard, quickly let himself down, and disappeared around the corner. That very second the black head of Mikhaïl appeared on the wall, followed by his entire body. Another head, with a shaggy hat, emerged alongside of his. Two black lumps rolled to the ground; one disappeared around the corner; Mikhaïl straightened himself up and looked about.

"Run, run!" whispered the mother, treading impatiently. Her ears were humming. Loud shouts were wafted to her. There on the wall appeared a third head. She clasped her hands in faintness. A light-haired head, without a beard, shook as if it wanted to tear itself away, but it suddenly disappeared behind the wall. The shouts came louder and louder, more and more boisterous. The wind scattered the thin trills of the whistles through the air. Mikhaïl walked along the wall—there! he was already beyond it, and traversed the open space between the prison and the houses of the city. It seemed to her as if he were walking very, very slowly, that he raised his head to no purpose. "Everyone who sees his face will remember it forever," and she whispered, "Faster! faster!" Behind the wall of the prison something slammed, the thin sound of broken glass was heard. One of the soldiers, planting his feet firmly on the ground, drew the horse to him, and the horse jumped. The other one, his fist at his mouth, shouted something in the direction of the prison, and as he shouted he turned his head sidewise, with his ear cocked.

All attention, the mother turned her head in all directions, her eyes seeing everything, believing nothing. This thing which she had pictured as terrible and intricate was accomplished with extreme simplicity and rapidity, and the simpleness of the happenings stupefied her. Rybin was no longer to be seen—a tall man in a thin overcoat was walking there—a girl was running along. Three wardens jumped out from a corner of the prison; they ran side by side, stretching out their right hands. One of the soldiers rushed in front of them; the other ran around the horse, unsuccessfully trying to vault on the refractory animal, which kept jumping about. The whistles incessantly cut the air, their alarming, desperate shrieks aroused a consciousness of danger in the woman. Trembling, she walked along the fence of the cemetery, following the wardens; but they and the soldiers ran around the other corner of the prison and disappeared. They were followed at a run by the assistant overseer of the prison, whom she knew; his coat was unbuttoned. From somewhere policemen appeared, and people came running.

The wind whistled, leaped about as if rejoicing, and carried the broken, confused shouts to the mother's ears.

"It stands here all the time."

"The ladder?"

"What's the matter with you then? The devil take you!"

"Arrest the soldiers!"

"Policeman!"

Whistles again. This hubbub delighted her and she strode on more boldly, thinking, "So, it's possible—*he* could have done it!"

But now pain for her son no longer entered her heart without pride in him also. And only fear for him weighed and oppressed her to stupefaction as before.

From the corner of the fence opposite her a constable with a black, curly beard, and two policemen emerged.

"Stop!" shouted the constable, breathing heavily. "Did you see—a man—with a beard—didn't he run by here?"

She pointed to the garden and answered calmly:

"He went that way!"

"Yegorov, run! Whistle! Is it long ago?"

"Yes—I should say—about a minute!"

But the whistle drowned her voice. The constable, without waiting for an answer, precipitated himself in a gallop along the hillocky ground, waving his hands in the direction of the garden. After him, with bent head, and whistling, the policemen darted off.

The mother nodded her head after them, and, satisfied with herself, went home. When she walked out of the field into the street a cab crossed her way. Raising her head she saw in the vehicle a young man with light mustache and a pale, worn face. He, too, regarded her. He sat slantwise. It must have been due to his position that his right shoulder was higher than his left.

At home Nikolay met her joyously.

"Alive? How did it go?"

"It seems everything's been successful!"

And slowly trying to reinstate all the details in her memory, she began to tell of the escape. Nikolay, too, was amazed at the success.

"You see, we're lucky!" said Nikolay, rubbing his hands. "But how frightened I was on your account only God knows. You know what, Nilovna, take my friendly advice: don't be afraid of the trial. The sooner it's over and done with the sooner Pavel will be free. Believe me. I've already written to my sister to try to think what can be done for Pavel. Maybe he'll even escape on the road. And the trial is approximately like this." He began to describe to her the session of the court. She listened, and understood that he was afraid of something—that he wanted to inspirit her.

"Maybe you think I'll say something to the judges?" she suddenly inquired. "That I'll beg them for something?"

He jumped up, waved his hands at her, and said in an offended tone:

"What are you talking about? You're insulting me!"

"Excuse me, please; excuse me! I really *am* afraid—of what I don't know."

She was silent, letting her eyes wander about the room.

"Sometimes it seems to me that they'll insult Pasha—scoff at him. 'Ah, you peasant!' they'll say. 'You son of a peasant! What's this mess you've cooked up?' And Pasha, proud as he is, he'll answer them so—! Or Andrey will laugh at them—and all the comrades there are hot-headed and honest. So I can't help thinking that something will suddenly happen. One of them will lose his patience, the others will support him, and the sentence will be so severe—you'll never see them again."

Nikolay was silent, pulling his beard glumly as the mother continued:

"It's impossible to drive this thought from my head. The trial is terrible to me. When they'll begin to take everything apart and weigh it—it's awful! It's not the sentence that's terrible, but the trial—I can't express it." She felt that Nikolay didn't understand her fear; and his inability to comprehend kept her from further analysis of her timidities, which, however, only increased and broadened during the three following days. Finally, on the day of the trial, she carried into the hall of the session a heavy dark load that bent her back and neck.

In the street, acquaintances from the suburbs had greeted her. She had bowed in silence, rapidly making her way through the dense crowd in the corridor of the courthouse. In the hall she was met by relatives of the defendants, who also spoke to her in undertones. All the words seemed needless; she didn't understand them. Yet all the people were sullen, filled with the same mournful feeling which infected the mother and weighed her down.

"Let's sit next to each other," suggested Sizov, going to a bench.

She sat down obediently, settled her dress, and looked around. Green and crimson specks, with thin yellow threads between, slowly swam before her eyes.

"Your son has ruined our Vasya," a woman sitting beside her said quietly.

"You keep still, Natalya!" Sizov chided her angrily.

Nilovna looked at the woman; it was the mother of Samoylov. Farther along sat her husband—bald-headed, bony-faced, dapper, with a large, bushy, reddish beard which trembled as he sat looking in front of himself, his eyes screwed up.

A dull, immobile light entered through the high windows of the hall, outside of which snow glided and fell lingeringly on the ground. Between the windows hung a large portrait of the Czar in a massive frame of glaring gilt. Straight, austere folds of the heavy crimson window drapery dropped over either side of it. Before the portrait, across almost the entire breadth of the hall, stretched the table covered with green cloth. To the right of the wall, behind the grill, stood two wooden benches; to the left two rows of crimson armchairs. Attendants with green collars and yellow buttons on their abdomens ran noiselessly about the hall. A soft whisper hummed in the turbid atmosphere, and the odor was a composite of many odors as in a drug shop. All this—the colors, the glitter, the sounds and odors—pressed on the eyes and invaded the breast with each inhalation. It forced out live sensations, and filled the desolate heart with motionless, dismal awe.

Suddenly one of the people said something aloud. The mother trembled. All arose; she, too, rose, seizing Sizov's hand.

In the left corner of the hall a high door opened and an old man emerged, swinging to and fro. On his gray little face shook white, sparse whiskers; he wore eyeglasses; the upper lip, which was shaven, sank into his mouth as by suction; his sharp jawbones and his chin were supported by the high collar of his uniform; apparently there was no neck under the collar. He was supported under the arm from behind by a tall young man with a porcelain face, red and round. Following him three more men in uniforms embroidered in gold, and three garbed in civilian wear, moved in slowly. They stirred about the table for a long time and finally took seats in the armchairs. When they had sat down, one of them in unbuttoned uniform, with a sleepy, clean-shaven face, began to say something to the little old man, moving his puffy lips heavily and soundlessly. The old man listened, sitting strangely erect and immobile. Behind the glasses of his *pince-nez* the mother saw two little colorless specks.

At the end of the table, at the desk, stood a tall, bald man, who coughed and shoved papers about.

The little old man swung forward and began to speak. He pronounced clearly the first words, but what followed seemed to creep without sound from his thin, gray lips.

"I open——"

"See!" whispered Sizov, nudging the mother softly and arising.

In the wall behind the grill the door opened, a soldier came out with a bared saber on his shoulder; behind him appeared Pavel, Andrey, Fedya Mazin, the two Gusevs, Samoylov, Bukin, Somov, and five more young men whose names were unknown to the mother. Pavel smiled kindly; Andrey also, showing his teeth as he nodded to her. The hall, as it were, became lighter and simpler from their smile; the strained, unnatural silence was enlivened by their faces and movements. The greasy glitter of gold on the uniforms dimmed and softened. A waft of bold assurance, the breath of living power, reached the mother's heart and roused it. On the benches behind her, where up to that time the people had been waiting in crushed silence, a responsive, subdued hum was audible.

"They're not trembling!" she heard Sizov whisper; and at her right side Samoylov's mother burst into soft sobs.

"Silence!" came a stern shout.

"I warn you beforehand," said the old man, "I shall have to——"

CHAPTER XV

Pavel and Andrey sat side by side; along with them on the first bench were Mazin, Samoylov, and the Gusevs. Andrey had shaved his beard, but his mustache had grown and hung down, and gave his round head the appearance of a seacow or walrus. Something new lay on his face; something sharp and biting in the folds about his mouth; something black in his eyes. On Mazin's upper lip two black streaks were limned, his face was fuller. Samoylov was just as curly-haired as before; and Ivan Gusev smiled just as broadly.

"Ah, Fedka, Fedka!" whispered Sizov, drooping his head.

The mother felt she could breathe more freely. She heard the indistinct questions of the old man, which he put without looking at the prisoners; and his head rested motionless on the collar of his uniform. She heard the calm, brief answers of her son. It seemed to her that the oldest judge and his associates could be neither evil nor cruel people. Looking carefully at their faces she tried to guess something, softly listening to the growth of a new hope in her breast.

The porcelain-faced man read a paper indifferently; his even voice filled the hall with weariness, and the people, enfolded by it, sat motionless as if benumbed. Four lawyers softly but animatedly conversed with the prisoners. They all moved powerfully, briskly, and called to mind large blackbirds.

On one side of the old man a judge with small, bleared eyes filled the armchair with his fat, bloated body. On the other side sat a stooping man with reddish mustache on his pale face. His head was wearily thrown on the back of the chair, his eyes, half-closed, he seemed to be reflecting over something. The face of the prosecuting attorney was also worn, bored, and unexpectant. Behind the judge sat the mayor of the city, a portly man, who meditatively stroked his cheek; the marshal of the nobility, a gray-haired, large-bearded, ruddy-faced man, with large, kind eyes; and the district elder, who wore a sleeveless peasant overcoat, and possessed a huge belly which apparently embarrassed him; he endeavored to cover it with the folds of his overcoat, but it always slid down and showed again.

"There are no criminals here and no judges," Pavel's vigorous voice was heard. "There are only captives here, and conquerors!"

Silence fell. For a few seconds the mother's ears heard only the thin, hasty scratch of the pen on the paper and the beating of her own heart.

The oldest judge also seemed to be listening to something from afar. His associates stirred. Then he said:

"Hm! yes—Andrey Nakhodka, do you admit——"

Somebody whispered, "Rise!"

Andrey slowly rose, straightened himself, and pulling his mustache looked at the old man from the corners of his eyes.

"Yes! To what can I confess myself guilty?" said the Little Russian in his slow, surging voice, shrugging his shoulders. "I did not murder nor steal; I simply am not in agreement with an order of life in which people are compelled to rob and kill one another."

"Answer briefly—yes or no?" the old man said with an effort, but distinctly.

On the benches back of her the mother felt there was animation; the people began to whisper to one another about something and stirred, sighing as if freeing themselves from the cobweb spun about them by the gray words of the porcelain-faced man.

"Do you hear how they speak?" whispered Sizov.

"Yes."

"Fedor Mazin, answer!"

"I don't want to!" said Fedya clearly, jumping to his feet. His face reddened with excitation, his eyes sparkled. For some reason he hid his hands behind his back.

Sizov groaned softly, and the mother opened her eyes wide in astonishment.

"I declined a defense—I'm not going to say anything—I don't regard your court as legal! Who are you? Did the people give you the right to judge us? No, they did not! I don't know you." He sat down and concealed his heated face behind Andrey's shoulders.

The fat judge inclined his head to the old judge and whispered something. The old judge, pale-faced, raised his eyelids and slanted his eyes at the prisoners, then extended his hand on the table, and wrote something in pencil on a piece of paper lying before him. The district elder swung his head, carefully shifting his feet, rested his abdomen on his knees, and his hands on his abdomen. Without moving his head the old judge turned his body to the red-mustached judge, and began to speak to him quickly. The red-mustached judge inclined his head to listen. The marshal of the nobility conversed with the prosecuting attorney; the mayor of the city listened and smiled, rubbing his cheek. Again the dull speech of the old judge was heard. All four lawyers listened attentively. The prisoners exchanged whispers with one another, and Fedya, smiling in confusion, hid his face.

"How he cut them off! Straight, downright, better than all!" Sizov whispered in amazement in the ear of the mother. "Ah, you little boy!"

The mother smiled in perplexity. The proceedings seemed to be nothing but the necessary preliminary to something terrible, which would appear and at once stifle everybody with its cold horror. But the calm words of Pavel and Andrey had sounded so fearless and firm, as if uttered in the little house of the suburb, and not in the presence of the court. Fedya's hot, youthful sally amused her; something bold and fresh grew up in the hall, and she guessed from the movement of the people back of her that she was not the only one who felt this.

"Your opinion," said the old judge.

The bald-headed prosecuting attorney arose, and, steadying himself on the desk with one hand, began to speak rapidly, quoting figures. In his voice nothing terrible was heard.

At the same time, however, a sudden dry, shooting attack disturbed the heart of the mother. It was an uneasy suspicion of something hostile to her, which did not threaten, did not shout, but unfolded itself unseen, soundless, intangible. It swung lazily and dully about the judges, as if enveloping them with an impervious cloud, through which nothing from the outside could reach them. She looked at them. They were incomprehensible to her. They were not angry at Pavel or at Fedya; they did not shout at the young men, as she had expected; they did not abuse them in words, but put all their questions reluctantly, with the air of "What's the use?". It cost them an effort to hear the answers to the end. Apparently they lacked interest because they knew everything beforehand.

There before her stood the gendarme, and spoke in a bass voice:
"Pavel Vlasov was named as the ringleader."
"And Nakhodka?" asked the fat judge in his lazy undertone.
"He, too."
"May I——"
The old judge asked a question of somebody:
"You have nothing?"

All the judges seemed to the mother to be worn out and ill. A sickened weariness marked their poses and voices, a sickened weariness and a bored, gray *ennui*. It was an evident nuisance to them, all this—the uniforms, the hall, the gendarmes, the lawyers, the obligation to sit in armchairs, and to put questions concerning things perforce already known to them. The mother in general was but little acquainted with the masters; she had scarcely ever seen them; and now she regarded the faces of the judges as something altogether new and incomprehensible, deserving pity, however, rather than inspiring horror.

The familiar, yellow-faced officer stood before them, and told about Pavel and Andrey, stretching the words with an air of importance. The mother involuntarily laughed, and thought: "You don't know much, my little father."

And now, as she looked at the people behind the grill, she ceased to feel dread for them; they did not evoke alarm, pity was not for them; they one and all called forth in her only admiration and love, which warmly embraced her heart; the admiration was calm, the love joyously distinct. There they sat to one side, by the wall, young, sturdy, scarcely taking any part in the monotonous talk of the witnesses and judges, or in the disputes of the lawyers with the prosecuting attorney. They behaved as if the talk did not concern them in the least. Sometimes somebody would laugh contemptuously, and say something to the comrades, across whose faces, then, a sarcastic smile would also quickly pass. Andrey and Pavel conversed almost the entire time with one of their lawyers, whom the mother had seen the day before at Nikolay's, and had heard Nikolay address as comrade. Mazin, brisker and more animated than the others, listened to the conversation. Now and then Samoylov said something to Ivan Gusev; and the mother noticed that each time Ivan gave a slight elbow nudge to a comrade, he could scarcely restrain a laugh; his face would grow red, his cheeks would puff up, and he would have to incline his head. He had already sniffed a couple of times, and for several minutes afterward sat with blown cheeks trying to be serious. Thus, in each comrade his youth played and sparkled after his fashion, lightly bursting the restraint he endeavored to put upon its lively effervescence. She looked, compared, and reflected. She was unable to understand or express in words her uneasy feeling of hostility.

Sizov touched her lightly with his elbow; she turned to him, and found a look of contentment and slight preoccupation on his face.

"Just see how they've intrenched themselves in their defiance! Fine stuff in 'em! Eh? Barons, eh? Well, and yet they're going to be sentenced!"

The mother listened, unconsciously repeating to herself:

"Who will pass the sentence? Whom will they sentence?"

The witnesses spoke quickly, in their colorless voices, the judges reluctantly and listlessly. Their bloodless, worn-out faces stared into space unconcernedly. They did not expect to see or hear anything new. At times the fat judge yawned, covering his smile with his puffy hand, while the red-mustached judge grew still paler, and sometimes raised his hand to press his finger tightly on the bone of his temple, as he looked up to the ceiling with sorrowful, widened eyes. The prosecuting attorney infrequently scribbled on his paper, and then resumed his soundless conversation with the marshal of the nobility, who stroked his gray beard, rolled his large, beautiful eyes, and smiled, nodding his head with importance. The city mayor sat with crossed legs, and beat a noiseless tattoo on his knee, giving the play of his fingers concentrated attention. The only one who listened to the monotonous murmur of the voices seemed to be the district elder, who sat with inclined head, supporting his abdomen on his knees and solicitously holding it up with his hands. The old judge, deep in his armchair, stuck there immovably. The proceedings continued to drag on in this way for a long, long time; and *ennui* again numbed the people with its heavy, sticky embrace.

The mother saw that this large hall was not yet pervaded by that cold, threatening justice which sternly uncovers the soul, examines it, and seeing everything estimates its value with incorruptible eyes, weighing it rigorously with honest hands. Here was nothing to frighten her by its power or majesty.

"I declare—" said the old judge clearly, and arose as he crushed the following words with his thin lips.

The noise of sighs and low exclamations, of coughing and scraping of feet, filled the hall as the court retired for a recess. The prisoners were led away. As they walked out, they nodded their heads to their relatives and familiars with a smile, and Ivan Gusev shouted to somebody in a modulated voice:

"Don't lose courage, Yegor."

The mother and Sizov walked out into the corridor.

"Will you go to the tavern with me to take some tea?" the old man asked her solicitously. "We have an hour and a half's time."

"I don't want to."

"Well, then I won't go, either. No, say! What fellows those are! They act as if they were the only real people, and the rest nothing at all. They'll all go scot-free, I'm sure. Look at Fedka, eh?"

Samoylov's father came up to them holding his hat in his hand. He smiled sullenly and said:

"My Vasily! He declined a defense, and doesn't want to palaver. He was the first to have the idea. Yours, Pelagueya, stood for lawyers; and mine said: 'I don't want one.' And four declined after him. Hm, ye-es."

At his side stood his wife. She blinked frequently, and wiped her nose with the end of her handkerchief. Samoylov took his beard in his hand, and continued looking at the floor.

"Now, this is the queer thing about it: you look at them, those devils, and you think they got up all this at random—they're ruining themselves for nothing. And suddenly you begin to think: 'And maybe they're right!' You remember that in the factory more like them keep on coming, keep on coming. They always get caught; but they're not destroyed, no more than common fish in the river get destroyed. No. And again you think, 'And maybe power is with them, too.'"

"It's hard for us, Stepan Petrov, to understand this affair," said Sizov.

"It's hard, yes," agreed Samoylov.

His wife noisily drawing in air through her nose remarked:

"They're all strong, those imps!" With an unrestrained smile on her broad, wizened face, she continued: "You, Nilovna, don't be angry with me because I just now slapped you, when I said that your son is to blame. A dog can tell who's the more to blame, to tell you the truth. Look at the gendarmes and the spies, what they said about our Vasily! He has shown what he can do too!"

She apparently was proud of her son, perhaps even without understanding her feeling; but the mother did understand her feeling, and answered with a kind smile and quiet words:

"A young heart is always nearer to the truth."

People rambled about the corridor, gathered into groups, speaking excitedly and thoughtfully in hollow voices. Scarcely anybody stood alone; all faces bore evidence of a desire to speak, to ask, to listen. In the narrow white passageway the people coiled about in sinuous curves, like dust carried in circles before a powerful wind. Everybody seemed to be seeking something hard and firm to stand upon.

The older brother of Bukin, a tall, red-faced fellow, waved his hands and turned about rapidly in all directions.

"The district elder Klepanov has no place in this case," he declared aloud.

"Keep still, Konstantin!" his father, a little old man, tried to dissuade him, and looked around cautiously.

"No; I'm going to speak out! There's a rumor afloat about him that last year he killed a clerk of his on account of the clerk's wife. What kind of a judge is he? permit me to ask. He lives with the wife of his clerk—what have you got to say to that? Besides, he's a well-known thief!"

"Oh, my little father—Konstantin!"

"True!" said Samoylov. "True, the court is not a very just one."

Bukin heard his voice and quickly walked up to him, drawing the whole crowd after him. Red with excitement, he waved his hands and said:

"For thievery, for murder, jurymen do the trying. They're common people, peasants, merchants, if you please; but for going against the authorities you're tried by the authorities. How's that?"

"Konstantin! Why are they against the authorities? Ah, you! They——"

"No, wait! Fedor Mazin said the truth. If you insult me, and I land you one on your jaw, and you try me for it, of course I'm going to turn out guilty. But the first offender—who was it? You? Of course, you!"

The watchman, a gray man with a hooked nose and medals on his chest, pushed the crowd apart, and said to Bukin, shaking his finger at him:

"Hey! don't shout! Don't you know where you are? Do you think this is a saloon?"

"Permit me, my cavalier, I know where I am. Listen! If I strike you and you me, and I go and try you, what would you think?"

"And I'll order you out," said the watchman sternly.

"Where to? What for?"

"Into the street, so that you shan't bawl."

"The chief thing for them is that people should keep their mouths shut."

"And what do you think?" the old man bawled. Bukin threw out his hands, and again measuring the public with his eyes, began to speak in a lower voice:

"And again—why are the people not permitted to be at the trial, but only the relatives? If you judge righteously, then judge in front of everybody. What is there to be afraid of?"

Samoylov repeated, but this time in a louder tone:

"The trial is not altogether just, that's true."

The mother wanted to say to him that she had heard from Nikolay of the dishonesty of the court; but she had not wholly comprehended Nikolay, and had forgotten some of his words.

While trying to recall them she moved aside from the people, and noticed that somebody was looking at her—a young man with a light mustache. He held his right hand in the pocket of his trousers, which made his left shoulder seem lower than the right, and this peculiarity of his figure seemed familiar to the mother. But he turned from her, and she again lost herself in the endeavor to recollect, and forgot about him immediately. In a minute, however, her ear was caught by the low question:

"This woman on the left?"

And somebody in a louder voice cheerfully answered:

"Yes."

She looked around. The man with the uneven shoulders stood sidewise toward her, and said something to his neighbor, a black-bearded fellow with a short overcoat and boots up to his knees.

Again her memory stirred uneasily, but did not yield any distinct results.

The watchman opened the door of the hall, and shouted:

"Relatives, enter; show your tickets!"

A sullen voice said lazily:

"Tickets! Like a circus!"

All the people now showed signs of a dull excitement, an uneasy passion. They began to behave more freely, and hummed and disputed with the watchman.

Sitting down on the bench, Sizov mumbled something to the mother.

"What is it?" asked the mother.

"Oh, nothing—the people are fools! They know nothing; they live groping about and groping about."

The bellman rang; somebody announced indifferently:

"The session has begun!"

Again all arose, and again, in the same order, the judges filed in and sat down; then the prisoners were led in.

"Pay attention!" whispered Sizov; "the prosecuting attorney is going to speak."

The mother craned her neck and extended her whole body. She yielded anew to expectation of the horrible.

Standing sidewise toward the judges, his head turned to them, leaning his elbow on the desk, the prosecuting attorney sighed, and abruptly waving his right hand in the air, began to speak:

The mother could not make out the first words. The prosecuting attorney's voice was fluent, thick; it sped on unevenly, now a bit slower, now a bit faster. His words stretched out in a thin line, like a gray seam; suddenly they burst out quickly and whirled like a flock of black flies around a piece of sugar. But she did not find anything horrible in them, nothing threatening. Cold as snow, gray as ashes, they fell and fell, filling the hall with something which recalled a slushy day in early autumn. Scant in feeling, rich in words, the speech seemed not to reach Pavel and his comrades. Apparently it touched none of them; they all sat there quite composed, smiling at times as before, and conversed without sound. At times they frowned to cover up their smiles.

"He lies!" whispered Sizov.

She could not have said it. She understood that the prosecuting attorney charged all the comrades with guilt, not singling out any one of them. After having spoken about Pavel, he spoke about Fedya, and having put him side by side with Pavel, he persistently thrust Bukin up against them. It seemed as if he packed and sewed them into a sack, piling them up on top of one another. But the external sense of his words did not satisfy, did not touch, did not frighten her. She still waited for the horrible, and rigorously sought something beyond his words—something in his face, his eyes, his voice, in his white hand, which slowly glided in the air. Something terrible must be there; she felt it, but it was impalpable; it did not yield to her consciousness, which again covered her heart with a dry, pricking dust.

She looked at the judges. There was no gainsaying that they were bored at having to listen to this speech. The lifeless, yellow faces expressed nothing. The sickly, the fat, or the extremely lean, motionless dead spots all grew dimmer and dimmer in the dull *ennui* that filled the hall. The words of the prosecuting attorney spurted into the air like a haze imperceptible to the eye, growing and thickening around the judges, enveloping them more closely in a cloud of dry indifference, of weary waiting. At times one of them changed his pose; but the lazy movement of the tired body did not rouse their drowsy souls. The oldest judge did not stir at all; he was congealed in his erect position, and the gray blots behind the eyeglasses at times disappeared, seeming to spread over his whole face. The mother realized this dead indifference, this unconcern without malice in it, and asked herself in perplexity, "Are they judging?"

The question pressed her heart, and gradually squeezed out of it her expectation of the horrible. It pinched her throat with a sharp feeling of wrong.

The speech of the prosecuting attorney snapped off unexpectedly. He made a few quick, short steps, bowed to the judges, and sat down, rubbing his hands. The marshal of the nobility nodded his head to him, rolling his eyes; the city mayor extended his hand, and the district elder stroked his belly and smiled.

But the judges apparently were not delighted by the speech, and did not stir.

"The scabby devil!" Sizov whispered the oath.

"Next," said the old judge, bringing the paper to his face, "lawyers for the defendants, Fedoseyev, Markov, Zagarov."

The lawyer whom the mother had seen at Nikolay's arose. His face was broad and good-natured; his little eyes smiled radiantly and seemed to thrust out from under his eyebrows two sharp blades, which cut the air like scissors. He spoke without haste, resonantly, and clearly; but the mother was unable to listen to his speech. Sizov whispered in her ear:

"Did you understand what he said? Did you understand? 'People,' he says, 'are poor, they are all upset, insensate.' Is that Fedor? He says they don't understand anything; they're savages."

The feeling of wrong grew, and passed into revolt. Along with the quick, loud voice of the lawyer, time also passed more quickly.

"A live, strong man having in his breast a sensitive, honest heart cannot help rebelling with all his force against this life so full of open cynicism, corruption, falsehood, and so blunted by vapidity. The eyes of honest people cannot help seeing such glaring contradictions——"

The judge with the green face bent toward the president and whispered something to him; then the old man said dryly:

"Please be more careful!"

"Ha!" Sizov exclaimed softly.

"Are they judging?" thought the mother, and the word seemed hollow and empty as an earthen vessel. It seemed to make sport of her fear of the terrible.

"They're a sort of dead body," she answered the old man.

"Don't fear; they're livening up."

She looked at them, and she actually saw something like a shadow of uneasiness on the faces of the judges. Another man was already speaking, a little lawyer with a sharp, pale, satiric face. He spoke very respectfully:

"With all due respect, I permit myself to call the attention of the court to the solid manner of the honorable prosecuting attorney, to the conduct of the safety department, or, as such people are called in common parlance, spies———"

The judge with the green face again began to whisper something to the president. The prosecuting attorney jumped up. The lawyer continued without changing his voice:

"The spy Gyman tells us about the witness: 'I frightened him.' The prosecuting attorney also, as the court has heard, frightened witnesses; as a result of which act, at the insistence of the defense, he called forth a rebuke from the presiding judge."

The prosecuting attorney began to speak quickly and angrily; the old judge followed suit; the lawyer listened to them respectfully, inclining his head. Then he said:

"I can even change the position of my words if the prosecuting attorney deems it is not in the right place; but that will not change the plan of my defense. However, I cannot understand the excitement of the prosecuting attorney."

"Go for him!" said Sizov. "Go for him, tooth and nail! Pick him open down to his soul, wherever that may be!"

The hall became animated; a fighting passion flared up; the defense attacked from all sides, provoking and disturbing the judges, driving away the cold haze that enveloped them, pricking the old skin of the judges with sharp words. The judges had the air of moving more closely to one another, or suddenly they would puff and swell, repulsing the sharp, caustic raps with the mass of their soft, mellow bodies. They acted as if they feared that the blow of the opponent might call forth an echo in their empty bosoms, might shake their resolution, which sprang not from their own will but from a will strange to them. Feeling this conflict, the people on the benches back of the mother sighed and whispered.

But suddenly Pavel arose; tense quiet prevailed. The mother stretched her entire body forward.

"A party man, I recognize only the court of my party and will not speak in my defense. According to the desire of my comrades, I, too, declined a defense. I will merely try to explain to you what you don't understand. The prosecuting attorney designated our coming out under the banner of the Social Democracy as an uprising against the superior power, and regarded us as nothing but rebels against the Czar. I must declare to you that to us the Czar is not the only chain that fetters the body of the country. We are obliged to tear off only the first and nearest chain from the people."

The stillness deepened under the sound of the firm voice; it seemed to widen the space between the walls of the hall. Pavel, by his words, removed the people to a distance from himself, and thereby grew in the eyes of the mother. His stony, calm, proud face with the beard, his high forehead, and blue eyes, somewhat stern, all became more dazzling and more prominent.

The judges began to stir heavily and uneasily; the marshal of the nobility was the first to whisper something to the judge with the indolent face. The judge nodded his head and turned to the old man; on the other side of him the sick judge was talking. Rocking back and forth in the armchair, the old judge spoke to Pavel, but his voice was drowned in the even, broad current of the young man's speech.

"We are Socialists! That means we are enemies to private property, which separates people, arms them against one another, and brings forth an irreconcilable hostility of interests; brings forth lies that endeavor to cover up, or to justify, this conflict of interests, and corrupt all with falsehood, hypocrisy and malice. We maintain that a society that regards man only as a tool for its enrichment is anti-human; it is hostile to us; we cannot be reconciled to its morality; its double-faced and lying cynicism. Its cruel relation to individuals is repugnant to us. We want to fight, and will fight, every form of the physical and moral enslavement of man by such a society; we will fight every measure calculated to disintegrate society for the gratification of the interests of gain. We are workers—men by whose labor everything is created, from gigantic machines to childish toys. We are people devoid of the right to fight for our human dignity. Everyone strives to utilize us, and may utilize us, as tools for the attainment of his ends. Now we want to have as much freedom as will give us the possibility in time to come to conquer all the power. Our slogan is simple: 'All the power for the people; all the means of production for the people; work obligatory on all. Down with private property!' You see, we are not rebels."

Pavel smiled, and the kindly fire of his blue eyes blazed forth more brilliantly.

"Please, more to the point!" said the presiding judge distinctly and aloud. He turned his chest to Pavel, and regarded him. It seemed to the mother that his dim left eye began to burn with a sinister, greedy fire. The look all the judges cast on her son made her uneasy for him. She fancied that their eyes clung to his face, stuck to his body, thirsted for his blood, by which they might reanimate their own worn-out bodies. And he, erect and tall, standing firmly and vigorously, stretched out his hand to them while he spoke distinctly:

"We are revolutionists, and will be such as long as private property exists, as long as some merely command, and as long as others merely work. We take stand against the society whose interests you are bidden to protect as your irreconcilable enemies, and reconciliation between us is impossible until we shall have been victorious. We will conquer—we workingmen! Your society is not at all so powerful as it thinks itself. That very property, for the production and preservation of which it sacrifices millions of people enslaved by it—that very force which gives it the power over us—stirs up discord within its own ranks, destroys them physically and morally. Property requires extremely great efforts for its protection; and in reality all of you, our rulers, are greater slaves than we—you are enslaved spiritually, we only physically. *You* cannot withdraw from under the weight of your prejudices and habits, the weight which deadens you spiritually; nothing hinders *us* from being inwardly free. The poisons with which you poison us are weaker than the antidote you unwittingly administer to our consciences. This antidote penetrates deeper and deeper into the body of workingmen; the flames mount higher and higher, sucking in the best forces, the spiritual powers, the healthy elements even from among you. Look! Not one of you can any longer fight for your power as an ideal! You have already expended all the arguments capable of guarding you against the pressure of historic justice. You can create nothing new in the domain of ideas; you are spiritually barren. Our ideas grow; they flare up ever more dazzling; they seize hold of the mass of the people, organizing them for the war of freedom. The consciousness of their great rôle unites all the workingmen of the world into one soul. You have no means whereby to hinder this renovating process in life except cruelty and cynicism. But your cynicism is very evident, your cruelty exasperates, and the hands with which you stifle us to-day will press our hands in comradeship to-morrow. Your energy, the mechanical energy of the increase of gold, separates you, too, into groups destined to devour one another. Our energy is a living power, founded on the ever-growing consciousness of the solidarity of all workingmen. Everything you do is criminal, for it is directed toward the enslavement of the people. Our work frees the world from the delusions and monsters which are produced by your malice and greed, and which intimidate the people. You have torn man away from life and disintegrated him. Socialism will unite the world, rent asunder by you, into one huge whole. And this will be!"

Pavel stopped for a second, and repeated in a lower tone, with greater emphasis, "This will be!"

The judges whispered to one another, making strange grimaces. And still their greedy looks were fastened on the body of Nilovna's son. The mother felt that their gaze tarnished this supple, vigorous body; that they envied its strength, power, freshness. The prisoners listened attentively to the speech of their comrade; their faces whitened, their eyes flashed joy. The mother drank in her son's words, which cut themselves into her memory in regular rows. The old judge stopped Pavel several times and explained something to him. Once he even smiled sadly. Pavel listened to him silently, and again began to speak in an austere but calm voice, compelling everybody to listen to him, subordinating the will of the judges to his will. This lasted for a long time. Finally, however, the old man shouted, extending his hand to Pavel, whose voice in response flowed on calmly, somewhat sarcastically.

"I am reaching my conclusion. To insult you personally was not my desire; on the contrary, as an involuntary witness to this comedy which you call a court trial, I feel almost compassion for you, I may say. You are human beings after all; and it is saddening to see human beings, even our enemies, so shamefully debased in the service of violence, debased to such a degree that they lose consciousness of their human dignity."

He sat down without looking at the judges.

Andrey, all radiant with joy, pressed his hand firmly; Samoylov, Mazin, and the rest animatedly stretched toward him. He smiled, a bit embarrassed by the transport of his comrades. He looked toward his mother, and nodded his head as if asking, "Is it so?"

She answered him all a-tremble, all suffused with warm joy.

"There, now the trial has begun!" whispered Sizov. "How he gave it to them! Eh, mother?"

CHAPTER XVI

She silently nodded her head and smiled, satisfied that her son had spoken so bravely, perhaps still more satisfied that he had finished. The thought darted through her mind that the speech was likely to increase the dangers threatening Pavel; but her heart palpitated with pride, and his words seemed to settle in her bosom.

Andrey arose, swung his body forward, looked at the judges sidewise, and said:

"Gentlemen of the defense———"

"The court is before you, and not the defense!" observed the judge of the sickly face angrily and loudly. By Andrey's expression the mother perceived that he wanted to tease them. His mustache quivered. A cunning, feline smirk familiar to her lighted up his eyes. He stroked his head with his long hands, and fetched a breath.

"Is that so?" he said, swinging his head. "I think not. That you are not the judges, but only the defendants———"

"I request you to adhere to what directly pertains to the case," remarked the old man dryly.

"To what directly pertains to the case? Very well! I've already compelled myself to think that you are in reality judges, independent people, honest———"

"The court has no need of your characterization."

"It has no need of *such* a characterization? Hey? Well, but after all I'm going to continue. You are men who make no distinction between your own and strangers. You are free people. Now, here two parties stand before you; one complains, 'He robbed me and did me up completely'; and the other answers, 'I have a right to rob and to do up because I have arms'———"

"Please don't tell anecdotes."

"Why, I've heard that old people like anecdotes—naughty ones in particular."

"I'll prohibit you from speaking. You may say something about what directly pertains to the case. Speak, but without buffoonery, without unbecoming sallies."

The Little Russian looked at the judges, silently rubbing his head.

"About what directly pertains to the case?" he asked seriously. "Yes; but why should I speak to you about what directly pertains to the case? What you need to know my comrade has told you. The rest will be told you; the time will come, by others———"

The old judge rose and declared:

"I forbid you to speak. Vasily Samoylov!"

Pressing his lips together firmly the Little Russian dropped down lazily on the bench, and Samoylov arose alongside of him, shaking his curly hair.

"The prosecuting attorney called my comrades and me 'savages,' 'enemies of civilization'———"

"You must speak only about that which pertains to your case."

"This pertains to the case. There's nothing which does not pertain to honest men, and I ask you not to interrupt me. I ask you what sort of a thing is your civilization?"

"We are not here for discussions with you. To the point!" said the old judge, showing his teeth.

Andrey's demeanor had evidently changed the conduct of the judges; his words seemed to have wiped something away from them. Stains appeared on their gray faces. Cold, green sparks burned in their eyes. Pavel's speech had excited but subdued them; it restrained their agitation by its force, which involuntarily inspired respect. The Little Russian broke away this restraint and easily bared what lay underneath. They looked at Samoylov, and whispered to one another with strange, wry faces. They also began to move extremely quickly for them. They gave the impression of desiring to seize him and howl while torturing his body with voluptuous ecstasy.

"You rear spies, you deprave women and girls, you put men in the position which forces them to thievery and murder; you corrupt them with whisky—international butchery, universal falsehood, depravity, and savagery—that's your civilization! Yes, we are enemies of this civilization!"

"Please!" shouted the old judge, shaking his chin; but Samoylov, all red, his eyes flashing, also shouted:

"But we respect and esteem another civilization, the creators of which you have persecuted, you have allowed to rot in dungeons, you have driven mad——"

"I forbid you to speak! Hm— Fedor Mazin!"

Little Mazin popped up like a cork from a champagne bottle, and said in a staccato voice:

"I—I swear!—I know you have convicted me——"

He lost breath and paled; his eyes seemed to devour his entire face. He stretched out his hand and shouted:

"I—upon my honest word! Wherever you send me—I'll escape—I'll return—I'll work always—all my life! Upon my honest word!"

Sizov quacked aloud. The entire public, overcome by the mounting wave of excitement, hummed strangely and dully. One woman cried, some one choked and coughed. The gendarmes regarded the prisoners with dull surprise, the public with a sinister look. The judges shook, the old man shouted in a thin voice:

"Ivan Gusev!"

"I don't want to speak."

"Vasily Gusev!"

"Don't want to."

"Fedor Bukin!"

The whitish, faded fellow lifted himself heavily, and shaking his head slowly said in a thick voice:

"You ought to be ashamed. I am a heavy man, and yet I understand—justice!" He raised his hand higher than his head and was silent, half-closing his eyes as if looking at something at a distance.

"What is it?" shouted the old judge in excited astonishment, dropping back in his armchair.

"Oh, well, what's the use?"

Bukin sullenly let himself down on the bench. There was something big and serious in his dark eyes, something somberly reproachful and naïve. Everybody felt it; even the judges listened, as if waiting for an echo clearer than his words. On the public benches all commotion died down immediately; only a low weeping swung in the air. Then the prosecuting attorney, shrugging his shoulders, grinned and said something to the marshal of the nobility, and whispers gradually buzzed again excitedly through the hall.

Weariness enveloped the mother's body with a stifling faintness. Small drops of perspiration stood on her forehead. Samoylov's mother stirred on the bench, nudging her with her shoulder and elbow, and said to her husband in a subdued whisper:

"How is this, now? Is it possible?"

"You see, it's possible."

"But what is going to happen to him, to Vasily?"

"Keep still. Stop."

The public was jarred by something it did not understand. All blinked in perplexity with blinded eyes, as if dazzled by the sudden blazing up of an object, indistinct in outline, of unknown meaning, but with horrible drawing power. And since the people did not comprehend this great thing dawning on them, they contracted its significance into something small, the meaning of which was evident and clear to them. The elder Bukin, therefore, whispered aloud without constraint:

"Say, please, why don't they permit them to talk? The prosecuting attorney can say everything, and as much as he wants to——"

A functionary stood at the benches, and waving his hands at the people, said in a half voice:

"Quiet, quiet!"

The father of Samoylov threw himself back, and ejaculated broken words behind his wife's ear:

"Of course—let us say they are guilty—but you'll let them explain. What is it they have gone against? Against everything—I wish to understand—I, too, have my interest." And suddenly: "Pavel says the truth, hey? I want to understand. Let them speak."

"Keep still!" exclaimed the functionary, shaking his finger at him.

Sizov nodded his head sullenly.

But the mother kept her gaze fastened unwaveringly on the judges, and saw that they got more and more excited, conversing with one another in indistinct voices. The sound of their words, cold and tickling, touched her face, puckering the skin on it, and filling her mouth with a sickly, disgusting taste. The mother somehow conceived that they were all speaking of the bodies of her son and his comrades, their vigorous bare bodies, their muscles, their youthful limbs full of hot blood, of living force. These bodies kindled in the judges the sinister, impotent envy of the rich by the poor, the unwholesome greed felt by wasted and sick people for the strength of the healthy. Their mouths watered regretfully for these bodies, capable of working and enriching, of rejoicing and creating. The youths produced in the old judges the revengeful, painful excitement of an enfeebled beast which sees the fresh prey, but no longer has the power to seize it, and howls dismally at its powerlessness.

This thought, rude and strange, grew more vivid the more attentively the mother scrutinized the judges. They seemed not to conceal their excited greed—the impotent vexation of the hungry who at one time had been able to consume in abundance. To her, a woman and a mother, to whom after all the body of her son is always dearer than that in him which is called a soul, to her it was horrible to see how these sticky, lightless eyes crept over his face, felt his chest, shoulders, hands, tore at the hot skin, as if seeking the possibility of taking fire, of warming the blood in their hardened brains and fatigued muscles—the brains and muscles of people already half dead, but now to some degree reanimated by the pricks of greed and envy of a young life that they presumed to sentence and remove to a distance from themselves. It seemed to her that her son, too, felt this damp, unpleasant tickling contact, and, shuddering, looked at her.

He looked into the mother's face with somewhat fatigued eyes, but calmly, kindly, and warmly. At times he nodded his head to her, and smiled—she understood the smile.

"Now quick!" she said.

Resting his hand on the table the oldest judge arose. His head sunk in the collar of his uniform, standing motionless, he began to read a paper in a droning voice.

"He's reading the sentence," said Sizov, listening.

It became quiet again, and everybody looked at the old man, small, dry, straight, resembling the stick held in his unseen hand. The other judges also stood up. The district elder inclined his head on one shoulder, and looked up to the ceiling; the mayor of the city crossed his hands over his chest; the marshal of the nobility stroked his beard. The judge with the sickly face, his puffy neighbor, and the prosecuting attorney regarded the prisoners sidewise. And behind the judges the Czar in a red military coat, with an indifferent white face looked down from his portrait over their heads. On his face some insect was creeping, or a cobweb was trembling.

"Exile!" Sizov said with a sigh of relief, dropping back on the bench. "Well, of course! Thank God! I heard that they were going to get hard labor. Never mind, mother, that's nothing."

Fatigued by her thoughts and her immobility, she understood the joy of the old man, which boldly raised the soul dragged down by hopelessness. But it didn't enliven her much.

"Why, I knew it," she answered.

"But, after all, it's certain now. Who could have told beforehand what the authorities would do? But Fedya is a fine fellow, dear soul."

They walked to the grill; the mother shed tears as she pressed the hand of her son. He and Fedya spoke kind words, smiled, and joked.

All were excited, but light and cheerful. The women wept; but, like Vlasova, more from habit than grief. They did not experience the stunning pain produced by an unexpected blow on the head, but only the sad consciousness that they must part with the children. But even this consciousness was dimmed by the impressions of the day. The fathers and the mothers looked at their children with mingled sensations, in which the skepticism of parents toward their children and the habitual sense of the superiority of elders over youth blended strangely with the feeling of sheer respect for them, with the persistent melancholy thought that life had now become dull, and with the curiosity aroused by the young men who so bravely and fearlessly spoke of the possibility of a new life, which the elders did not comprehend but which seemed to promise something good. The very novelty and unusualness of the feeling rendered expression impossible. Words were spoken in plenty, but they referred only to common matters. The relatives spoke of linen and clothes, and begged the comrades to take care of their health, and not to provoke the authorities uselessly.

"Everybody, brother, will grow weary, both we and they," said Samoylov to his son.

And Bukin's brother, waving his hand, assured the younger brother:

"Merely justice, and nothing else! That they cannot admit."

The younger Bukin answered:

"You look out for the starling. I love him."

"Come back home, and you'll find him in perfect trim."

"I've nothing to do there."

And Sizov held his nephew's hand, and slowly said:

"So, Fedor; so you've started on your trip. So."

Fedya bent over, and whispered something in his ear, smiling roguishly. The convoy soldier also smiled; but he immediately assumed a stern expression, and shouted, "Go!"

The mother spoke to Pavel, like the others, about the same things, about clothes, about his health, yet her breast was choked by a hundred questions concerning Sasha, concerning himself, and herself. Underneath all these emotions an almost burdensome feeling was slowly growing of the fullness of her love for her son—a strained desire to please him, to be near to his heart. The expectation of the terrible had died away, leaving behind it only a tremor at the recollection of the judges, and somewhere in a corner a dark impersonal thought regarding them.

"Young people ought to be tried by young judges, and not by old ones," she said to her son.

"It would be better to arrange life so that it should not force people to crime," answered Pavel.

The mother, seeing the Little Russian converse with everybody and realizing that he needed affection more than Pavel, spoke to him. Andrey answered her gratefully, smiling, joking kindly, as always a bit droll, supple, sinewy. Around her the talk went on, crossing and intertwining. She heard everything, understood everybody, and secretly marveled at the vastness of her own heart, which took in everything with an even joy, and gave back a clear reflection of it, like a bright image on a deep, placid lake.

Finally the prisoners were led away. The mother walked out of the court, and was surprised to see that night already hung over the city, with the lanterns alight in the streets, and the stars shining in the sky. Groups composed mainly of young men were crowding near the courthouse. The snow crunched in the frozen atmosphere; voices sounded. A man in a gray Caucasian cowl looked into Sizov's face and asked quickly:

"What was the sentence?"

"Exile."

"For all?"

"All."

"Thank you."

The man walked away.

"You see," said Sizov. "They inquire."

Suddenly they were surrounded by about ten men, youths, and girls, and explanations rained down, attracting still more people. The mother and Sizov stopped. They were questioned in regard to the sentence, as to how the prisoners behaved, who delivered the speeches, and what the speeches were about. All the voices rang with the same eager curiosity, sincere and warm, which aroused the desire to satisfy it.

"People! This is the mother of Pavel Vlasov!" somebody shouted, and presently all became silent.

"Permit me to shake your hand."

Somebody's firm hand pressed the mother's fingers, somebody's voice said excitedly:

"Your son will be an example of manhood for all of us."

"Long live the Russian workingman!" a resonant voice rang out.

"Long live the proletariat!"

"Long live the revolution!"

The shouts grew louder and increased in number, rising up on all sides. The people ran from every direction, pushing into the crowd around the mother and Sizov. The whistles of the police leaped through the air, but did not deafen the shouts. The old man smiled; and to the mother all this seemed like a pleasant dream. She smilingly pressed the hands extended to her and bowed, with joyous tears choking her throat. Near her somebody's clear voice said nervously:

"Comrades, friends, the autocracy, the monster which devours the Russian people to-day again gulped into its bottomless, greedy mouth———"

"However, mother, let's go," said Sizov. And at the same time Sasha appeared, caught the mother under her arm, and quickly dragged her away to the other side of the street.

"Come! They're going to make arrests. What? Exile? To Siberia?"

"Yes, yes."

"And how did he speak? I know without your telling me. He was more powerful than any of the others, and more simple. And of course, sterner than all the rest. He's sensitive and soft, only he's ashamed to expose himself. And he's direct, clear, firm, like truth itself. He's very great, and there's everything in him, everything! But he often constrains himself for nothing, lest he might hinder the cause. I know it." Her hot half-whisper, the words of her love, calmed the mother's agitation, and restored her exhausted strength.

"When will you go to him?" she asked Sasha, pressing her hand to her body. Looking confidently before her the girl answered:

"As soon as I find somebody to take over my work. I have the money already, but I might go *per étappe*. You know I am also awaiting a sentence. Evidently they are going to send me to Siberia, too. I will then declare that I desire to be exiled to the same locality that he will be."

Behind them was heard the voice of Sizov:

"Then give him regards from me, from Sizov. He will know. I'm Fedya Mazin's uncle."

Sasha stopped, turned around, extending her hand.

"I'm acquainted with Fedya. My name is Alexandra."

"And your patronymic?"

She looked at him and answered:

"I have no father."

"He's dead, you mean?"

"No, he's alive." Something stubborn, persistent, sounded in the girl's voice and appeared in her face. "He's a landowner, a chief of a country district. He robs the peasants and beats them. I cannot recognize him as my father."

"S-s-o-o!" Sizov was taken aback. After a pause he said, looking at the girl sidewise:

"Well, mother, good-by. I'm going off to the left. Stop in sometimes for a talk and a glass of tea. Good evening, lady. You're pretty hard on your father—of course, that's your business."

"If your son were an ugly man, obnoxious to people, disgusting to you, wouldn't you say the same about him?" Sasha shouted terribly.

"Well, I would," the old man answered after some hesitation.

"That is to say that justice is dearer to you than your son; and to me it's dearer than my father."

Sizov smiled, shaking his head; then he said with a sigh:

"Well, well, you're clever. Good-by. I wish you all good things, and be better to people. Hey? Well, God be with you. Good-by, Nilovna. When you see Pavel tell him I heard his speech. I couldn't understand every bit of it; some things even seemed horrible; but tell him it's true. They've found the truth, yes."

He raised his hat, and sedately turned around the corner of the street.

"He seems to be a good man," remarked Sasha, accompanying him with a smile of her large eyes. "Such people can be useful to the cause. It would be good to hide literature with them, for instance."

It seemed to the mother that to-day the girl's face was softer and kinder than usual, and hearing her remarks about Sizov, she thought:

"Always about the cause. Even to-day. It's burned into her heart."

CHAPTER XVII

At home they sat on the sofa closely pressed together, and the mother resting in the quiet again began to speak about Sasha's going to Pavel. Thoughtfully raising her thick eyebrows, the girl looked into the distance with her large, dreamy eyes. A contemplative expression rested on her pale face.

"Then, when children will be born to you, I will come to you and dandle them. We'll begin to live there no worse than here. Pasha will find work. He has golden hands."

"Yes," answered Sasha thoughtfully. "That's good—" And suddenly starting, as if throwing something away, she began to speak simply in a modulated voice. "He won't commence to live there. He'll go away, of course."

"And how will that be? Suppose, in case of children?"

"I don't know. We'll see when we are there. In such a case he oughtn't to reckon with me, and I cannot constrain him. He's free at any moment. I am his comrade—a wife, of course. But the conditions of his work are such that for years and years I cannot regard our bond as a usual one, like that of others. It will be hard, I know it, to part with him; but, of course, I'll manage to. He knows that I'm not capable of regarding a man as my possession. I'm not going to constrain him, no."

The mother understood her, felt that she believed what she said, that she was capable of carrying it out; and she was sorry for her. She embraced her.

"My dear girl, it will be hard for you."

Sasha smiled softly, nestling her body up to the mother's. Her voice sounded mild, but powerful. Red mounted to her face.

"It's a long time till then; but don't think that I—that it is hard for me now. I'm making no sacrifices. I know what I'm doing, I know what I may expect. I'll be happy if I can make him happy. My aim, my desire is to increase his energy, to give him as much happiness and love as I can—a great deal. I love him very much and he me—I know it—what I bring to him, he will give back to me—we will enrich each other by all in our power; and, if necessary, we will part as friends."

Sasha remained silent for a long time, during which the mother and the young woman sat in a corner of the room, tightly pressed against each other, thinking of the man whom they loved. It was quiet, melancholy, and warm.

Nikolay entered, exhausted, but brisk. He immediately announced:

"Well, Sashenka, betake yourself away from here, as long as you are sound. Two spies have been after me since this morning, and the attempt at concealment is so evident that it savors of an arrest. I feel it in my bones—somewhere something has happened. By the way, here I have the speech of Pavel. It's been decided to publish it at once. Take it to Liudmila. Pavel spoke well, Nilovna; and his speech will play a part. Look out for spies, Sasha. Wait a little while—hide these papers, too. You might give them to Ivan, for example."

While he spoke, he vigorously rubbed his frozen hands, and quickly pulled out the drawers of his table, picking out papers, some of which he tore up, others he laid aside. His manner was absorbed, and his appearance all upset.

"Do you suppose it was long ago that this place was cleared out? And look at this mass of stuff accumulated already! The devil! You see, Nilovna, it would be better for you, too, not to sleep here to-night. It's a sorry spectacle to witness, and they may arrest you, too. And you'll be needed for carrying Pavel's speech about from place to place."

"Hm, what do they want me for? Maybe you're mistaken."

Nikolay waved his forearm in front of his eyes, and said with conviction:

"I have a keen scent. Besides, you can be of great help to Liudmila. Flee far from evil."

The possibility of taking a part in the printing of her son's speech was pleasant to her, and she answered:

"If so, I'll go. But don't think I'm afraid."

"Very well. Now, tell me where my valise and my linen are. You've grabbed up everything into your rapacious hands, and I'm completely robbed of the possibility of disposing of my own private property. I'm making complete preparations—this will be unpleasant to them."

Sasha burned the papers in silence, and carefully mixed their ashes with the other cinders in the stove.

"Sasha, go," said Nikolay, putting out his hand to her. "Good-by. Don't forget books—if anything new and interesting appears. Well, good-by, dear comrade. Be more careful."

"Do you think it's for long?" asked Sasha.

"The devil knows them! Evidently. There's something against me. Nilovna, are you going with her? It's harder to track two people—all right?"

"I'm going." The mother went to dress herself, and it occurred to her how little these people who were striving for the freedom of all cared for their personal freedom. The simplicity and the businesslike manner of Nikolay in expecting the arrest both astonished and touched her. She tried to observe his face carefully; she detected nothing but his air of absorption, overshadowing the usual kindly soft expression of his eyes. There was no sign of agitation in this man, dearer to her than the others; he made no fuss. Equally attentive to all, alike kind to all, always calmly the same, he seemed to her just as much a stranger as before to everybody and everything except his cause. He seemed remote, living a secret life within himself and somewhere ahead of people. Yet she felt that he resembled her more than any of the others, and she loved him with a love that was carefully observing and, as it were, did not believe in itself. Now she felt painfully sorry for him; but she restrained her feelings, knowing that to show them would disconcert Nikolay, that he would become, as always under such circumstances, somewhat ridiculous.

When she returned to the room she found him pressing Sasha's hand and saying:

"Admirable! I'm convinced of it. It's very good for him and for you. A little personal happiness does not do any harm; but—a little, you know, so as not to make him lose his value. Are you ready, Nilovna?" He walked up to her, smiling and adjusting his glasses. "Well, good-by. I want to think that for three months, four months—well, at most half a year—half a year is a great deal of a man's life. In half a year one can do a lot of things. Take care of yourself, please, eh? Come, let's embrace." Lean and thin he clasped her neck in his powerful arms, looked into her eyes, and smiled. "It seems to me I've fallen in love with you. I keep embracing you all the time."

She was silent, kissing his forehead and cheeks, and her hands quivered. For fear he might notice it, she unclasped them.

"Go. Very well. Be careful to-morrow. This is what you should do—send the boy in the morning—Liudmila has a boy for the purpose—let him go to the house porter and ask him whether I'm home or not. I'll forewarn the porter; he's a good fellow, and I'm a friend of his. Well, good-by, comrades. I wish you all good."

On the street Sasha said quietly to the mother:

"He'll go as simply as this to his death, if necessary. And apparently he'll hurry up a little in just the same way; when death stares him in the face he'll adjust his eyeglasses, and will say 'admirable,' and will die."

"I love him," whispered the mother.

"I'm filled with astonishment; but love him—no. I respect him highly. He's sort of dry, although good and even, if you please, sometimes soft; but not sufficiently human—it seems to me we're being followed. Come, let's part. Don't enter Liudmila's place if you think a spy is after you."

"I know," said the mother. Sasha, however, persistently added: "Don't enter. In that case, come to me. Good-by for the present."

She quickly turned around and walked back. The mother called "Good-by" after her.

Within a few minutes she sat all frozen through at the stove in Liudmila's little room. Her hostess, Liudmila, in a black dress girded up with a strap, slowly paced up and down the room, filling it with a rustle and the sound of her commanding voice. A fire was crackling in the stove and drawing in the air from the room. The woman's voice sounded evenly.

"People are a great deal more stupid than bad. They can see only what's near to them, what it's possible to grasp immediately; but everything that's near is cheap; what's distant is dear. Why, in reality, it would be more convenient and pleasanter for all if life were different, were lighter, and the people were more sensible. But to attain the distant you must disturb yourself for the immediate present——"

Nilovna tried to guess where this woman did her printing. The room had three windows facing the street; there was a sofa and a bookcase, a table, chairs, a bed at the wall, in the corner near it a wash basin, in the other corner a stove; on the walls photographs and pictures. All was new, solid, clean; and over all the austere monastic figure of the mistress threw a cold shadow. Something concealed, something hidden, made itself felt; but where it lurked was incomprehensible. The mother looked at the doors; through one of them she had entered from the little antechamber. Near the stove was another door, narrow and high.

"I have come to you on business," she said in embarrassment, noticing that the hostess was regarding her.

"I know. Nobody comes to me for any other reason."

Something strange seemed to be in Liudmila's voice. The mother looked in her face. Liudmila smiled with the corners of her thin lips, her dull eyes gleamed behind her glasses. Turning her glance aside, the mother handed her the speech of Pavel.

"Here. They ask you to print it at once."

And she began to tell of Nikolay's preparations for the arrest.

Liudmila silently thrust the manuscript into her belt and sat down on a chair. A red gleam of the fire was reflected on her spectacles; its hot smile played on her motionless face.

"When they come to me I'm going to shoot at them," she said with determination in her moderated voice. "I have the right to protect myself against violence; and I must fight with them if I call upon others to fight. I cannot understand calmness; I don't like it."

The reflection of the fire glided across her face, and she again became austere, somewhat haughty.

"Your life is not very pleasant," the mother thought kindly.

Liudmila began to read Pavel's speech, at first reluctantly; then she bent lower and lower over the paper, quickly throwing aside the pages as she read them. When she had finished she rose, straightened herself, and walked up to the mother.

"That's good. That's what I like; although here, too, there's calmness. But the speech is the sepulchral beat of a drum, and the drummer is a powerful man."

She reflected a little while, lowering her head for a minute:

"I didn't want to speak with you about your son; I have never met him, and I don't like sad subjects of conversation. I know what it means to have a near one go into exile. But I want to say to you, nevertheless, that your son must be a splendid man. He's young—that's evident; but he is a great soul. It must be good and terrible to have such a son."

"Yes, it's good. And now it's no longer terrible."

Liudmila settled her smoothly combed hair with her tawny hand and sighed softly. A light, warm shadow trembled on her cheeks, the shadow of a suppressed smile.

"We are going to print it. Will you help me?"

"Of course."

"I'll set it up quickly. You lie down; you had a hard day; you're tired. Lie down here on the bed; I'm not going to sleep; and at night maybe I'll wake you up to help me. When you have lain down, put out the lamp."

She threw two logs of wood into the stove, straightened herself, and passed through the narrow door near the stove, firmly closing it after her. The mother followed her with her eyes, and began to undress herself, thinking reluctantly of her hostess: "A stern person; and yet her heart burns. She can't conceal it. Everyone loves. If you don't love you can't live."

Fatigue dizzied her brain; but her soul was strangely calm, and everything was illumined from within by a soft, kind light which quietly and evenly filled her breast. She was already acquainted with this calm; it had come to her after great agitation. At first it had slightly disturbed her; but now it only broadened her soul, strengthening it with a certain powerful but impalpable thought.

Before her all the time appeared and disappeared the faces of her son, Andrey, Nikolay, Sasha. She took delight in them; they passed by without arousing thought, and only lightly and sadly touching her heart. Then she extinguished the lamp, lay down in the cold bed, shriveled up under the bed coverings, and suddenly sank into a heavy sleep.

CHAPTER XVIII

When she opened her eyes the room was filled by the cold, white glimmer of a clear wintry day. The hostess, with a book in her hand, lay on the sofa, and smiling unlike herself looked into her face.

"Oh, father!" the mother exclaimed, for some reason embarrassed. "Just look! Have I been asleep a long time?"

"Good morning!" answered Liudmila. "It'll soon be ten o'clock. Get up and we'll have tea."

"Why didn't you wake me up?"

"I wanted to. I walked up to you; but you were so fast asleep and smiled so in your sleep!"

With a supple, powerful movement of her whole body she rose from the sofa, walked up to the bed, bent toward the face of the mother, and in her dull eyes the mother saw something dear, near, and comprehensible.

"I was sorry to disturb you. Maybe you were seeing a happy vision."

"I didn't see anything."

"All the same—but your smile pleased me. It was so calm, so good—so great." Liudmila laughed, and her laugh sounded velvety. "I thought of you, of your life—your life is a hard one, isn't it?"

The mother, moving her eyebrows, was silent and thoughtful.

"Of course it's hard!" exclaimed Liudmila.

"I don't know," said the mother carefully. "Sometimes it seems sort of hard; there's so much of all, it's all so serious, marvelous, and it moves along so quickly, one thing after the other—so quickly——"

The wave of bold excitement familiar to her overflowed her

breast, filling her heart with images and thoughts. She sat up in bed, quickly clothing her thoughts in words.

"It goes, it goes, it goes all to one thing, to one side, and like a fire, when a house begins to burn, upward! Here it shoots forth, there it blazes out, ever brighter, ever more powerful. There's a great deal of hardship, you know. People suffer; they are beaten, cruelly beaten; and everyone is oppressed and watched. They hide, live like monks, and many joys are closed to them; it's very hard. And when you look at them well you see that the hard things, the evil and difficult, are around them, on the outside, and not within."

Liudmila quickly threw up her head, looked at her with a deep, embracing look. The mother felt that her words did not exhaust her thoughts, which vexed and offended her.

"You're not speaking about yourself," said her hostess softly.

The mother looked at her, arose from the bed, and dressing asked:

"Not about myself? Yes; you see in this, in all that I live now, it's hard to think of oneself; how can you withdraw into yourself when you love this thing, and that thing is dear to you, and you are afraid for everybody and are sorry for everybody? Everything crowds into your heart and draws you to all people. How can you step to one side? It's hard."

Liudmila laughed, saying softly:

"And maybe it's not necessary."

"I don't know whether it's necessary or not; but this I do know—that people are becoming stronger than life, wiser than life; that's evident."

Standing in the middle of the room, half-dressed, she fell to reflecting for a moment. Her real self suddenly appeared not to exist—the one who lived in anxiety and fear for her son, in thoughts for the safekeeping of his body. Such a person in herself was no longer; she had gone off to a great distance, and perhaps was altogether burned up by the fire of agitation. This had lightened and cleansed her soul, and had renovated her heart with a new power. She communed with herself, desiring to take a look into her own heart, and fearing lest she awaken some anxiety there.

"What are you thinking about?" Liudmila asked kindly, walking up to her.

"I don't know."

The two women were silent, looking at each other. Both smiled; then Liudmila walked out of the room, saying:

"What is my samovar doing?"

The mother looked through the window. A cold, bracing day shone in the street; her breast, too, shone bright, but hot. She wanted to speak much about everything, joyfully, with a confused feeling of gratitude to somebody—she did not know whom—for all that came into her soul, and lighted it with a ruddy evening light. A desire to pray, which she had not felt for a long time, arose in her breast. Somebody's young face came to her memory, somebody's resonant voice shouted, "That's the mother of Pavel Vlasov!" Sasha's eyes flashed joyously and tenderly. Rybin's dark, tall figure loomed up, the bronzed, firm face of her son smiled. Nikolay blinked in embarrassment; and suddenly everything was stirred with a deep but light breath.

"Nikolay was right," said Liudmila, entering again. "He must surely have been arrested. I sent the boy there, as you told me to. He said policemen are hiding in the yard; he did not see the house porter; but he saw the policeman who was hiding behind the gates. And spies are sauntering about; the boy knows them."

"So?" The mother nodded her head. "Ah, poor fellow!"

And she sighed, but without sadness, and was quietly surprised at herself.

"Lately he's been reading a great deal to the city workingmen; and in general it was time for him to disappear," Liudmila said with a frown. "The comrades told him to go, but he didn't obey them. I think that in such cases you must compel and not try to persuade."

A dark-haired, red-faced boy with beautiful eyes and a hooked nose appeared in the doorway.

"Shall I bring in the samovar?" he asked in a ringing voice.

"Yes, please, Seryozha. This is my pupil; have you never met him before?"

"No."

"He used to go to Nikolay sometimes; I sent him."

Liudmila seemed to the mother to be different to-day—simpler and nearer to her. In the supple swaying of her stately figure there was much beauty and power; her sternness had mildened; the circles under her eyes had grown larger during the night, her face paler and leaner; her large eyes had deepened. One perceived a strained exertion in her, a tightly drawn chord in her soul.

The boy brought in the samovar.

"Let me introduce you: Seryozha—Pelagueya Nilovna, the mother of the workingman whom they sentenced yesterday."

Seryozha bowed silently and pressed the mother's hand. Then he brought in bread, and sat down to the table. Liudmila persuaded the mother not to go home until they found out whom the police were waiting for there.

"Maybe they are waiting for you. I'm sure they'll examine you."

"Let them. And if they arrest me, no great harm. Only I'd like to have Pasha's speech sent off."

"It's already in type. To-morrow it'll be possible to have it for the city and the suburb. We'll have some for the districts, too. Do you know Natasha?"

"Of course!"

"Then take it to her."

The boy read the newspaper, and seemed not to be listening to the conversation; but at times his eyes looked from the pages of the newspaper into the face of the mother; and when she met their animated glance she felt pleased and smiled. She reproached herself for these smiles. Liudmila again mentioned Nikolay without any expression of regret for his arrest and, to the mother, it seemed in perfectly natural tones. The time passed more quickly than on the other days. When they had done drinking tea it was already near midday.

"However!" exclaimed Liudmila, and at the same time a knock at the door was heard. The boy rose, looked inquiringly at Liudmila, prettily screwing up his eyes.

"Open the door, Seryozha. Who do you suppose it is?" And with a composed gesture she let her hand into the pocket of the skirt, saying to the mother: "If it is the gendarmes, you, Pelagueya Nilovna, stand here in this corner, and you, Ser———"

"I know. The dark passage," the little boy answered softly, disappearing.

The mother smiled. These preparations did not disturb her; she had no premonition of a misfortune.

The little physician walked in. He quickly said:

"First of all, Nikolay is arrested. Aha! You here, Nilovna? They're interested in you, too. Weren't you there when he was arrested?"

"He packed me off, and told me to come here."

"Hm! I don't think it will be of any use to you. Secondly, last night several young people made about five hundred hektograph copies of Pavel's speech—not badly done, plain and clear. They want to scatter them throughout the city at night. I'm against it. Printed sheets are better for the city, and the hektograph copies ought to be sent off somewhere."

"Here, I'll carry them to Natasha!" the mother exclaimed animatedly. "Give them to me."

She was seized with a great desire to sow them broadcast, to spread Pavel's speech as soon as possible. She would have bestrewn the whole earth with the words of her son, and she looked into the doctor's face with eyes ready to beg.

"The devil knows whether at this time you ought to take up this matter," the physician said irresolutely, and took out his watch. "It's now twelve minutes of twelve. The train leaves at 2.05, arrives there 5.15. You'll get there in the evening, but not sufficiently late—and that's not the point!"

"That's not the point," repeated Liudmila, frowning.

"What then?" asked the mother, drawing up to them. "The point is to do it well; and I'll do it all right."

Liudmila looked fixedly at her, and chafing her forehead, remarked:

"It's dangerous for you."

"Why?" the mother challenged hotly.

"That's why!" said the physician quickly and brokenly. "You disappeared from home an hour before Nikolay's arrest. You went away to the mill, where you are known as the teacher's aunt; after your arrival at the mill the naughty leaflets appear. All this will tie itself into a noose around your neck."

"They won't notice me there," the mother assured them, warming to her desire. "When I return they'll arrest me, and ask me where I was." After a moment's pause she exclaimed: "I know what I'll say. From there I'll go straight to the suburb; I have a friend there—Sizov. So I'll say that I went there straight from the trial; grief took me there; and he, too, had the same misfortune, his nephew was sentenced; and I spent the whole time with him. He'll uphold me, too. Do you see?"

The mother was aware that they were succumbing to the strength of her desire, and strove to induce them to give in as quickly as possible. She spoke more and more persistently, joy arising within her. And they yielded.

"Well, go," the physician reluctantly assented.

Liudmila was silent, pacing thoughtfully up and down the room. Her face clouded over and her cheeks fell in. The muscles of her neck stretched noticeably as if her head had suddenly grown heavy; it involuntarily dropped on her breast. The mother observed this. The physician's reluctant assent forced a sigh from her.

"You all take care of me," the mother said, smiling. "You don't take care of yourselves." And the wave of joy mounted higher and higher.

"It isn't true. We look out for ourselves. We ought to; and we very much upbraid those who uselessly waste their power. Ye-es. Now, this is the way you are to do. You will receive the speeches at the station." He explained to her how the matter would be arranged; then looking into her face, he said: "Well, I wish you success. You're happy, aren't you?" And he walked away still gloomy and dissatisfied. When the door closed behind him Liudmila walked up to the mother, smiling quietly.

"You're a fine woman! I understand you." Taking her by the arm, she again walked up and down the room. "I have a son, too. He's already thirteen years old; but he lives with his father. My husband is an assistant prosecuting attorney. Maybe he's already prosecuting attorney. And the boy's with him. What is he going to be? I often think." Her humid, powerful voice trembled. Then her speech flowed on again thoughtfully and quietly. "He's being brought up by a professed enemy of those people who are near me, whom I regard as the best people on earth; and maybe the boy will grow up to be my enemy. He cannot live with me; I live under a strange name. I have not seen him for eight years. That's a long time—eight years!"

Stopping at the window, she looked up at the pale, bleak sky, and continued: "If he were with me I would be stronger; I would not have this wound in my heart, the wound that always pains. And even if he were dead it would be easier for me—" She paused again, and added more firmly and loudly: "Then I would know he's merely dead, but not an enemy of that which is higher than the feeling of a mother, dearer and more necessary than life."

"My darling," said the mother quietly, feeling as if something powerful were burning her heart.

"Yes, you are happy," Liudmila said with a smile. "It's magnificent—the mother and the son side by side. It's rare!"

The mother unexpectedly to herself exclaimed:

"Yes, it is good!" and as if disclosing a secret, she continued in a lowered voice: "It is another life. All of you—Nikolay Ivanovich, all the people of the cause of truth—are also side by side. Suddenly people have become kin—I understand all—the words I don't understand; but everything else I understand, everything!"

"That's how it is," Liudmila said. "That's how."

The mother put her hand on Liudmila's breast, pressing her; she spoke almost in a whisper, as if herself meditating upon the words she spoke.

"Children go through the world; that's what I understand; children go into the world, over all the earth, from everywhere toward one thing. The best hearts go; people of honest minds; they relentlessly attack all evil, all darkness. They go, they trample falsehood with heavy feet, understanding everything, justifying everybody—justifying everybody, they go. Young, strong, they carry their power, their invincible power, all toward one thing—toward justice. They go to conquer all human misery, they arm themselves to wipe away misfortune from the face of the earth; they go to subdue what is monstrous, and they will subdue it. We will kindle a new sun, somebody told me; and they will kindle it. We will create one heart in life, we will unite all the severed hearts into one—and they will unite them. We will cleanse the whole of life—and they will cleanse it."

She waved her hand toward the sky.

"There's the sun."

And she struck her bosom.

"Here the most glorious heavenly sun of human happiness will be kindled, and it will light up the earth forever—the whole of it, and all that live upon it—with the light of love, the love of every man toward all, and toward everything."

The words of forgotten prayers recurred to her mind, inspiring a new faith. She threw them from her heart like sparks.

"The children walking along the road of truth and reason carry love to all; and they clothe everything in new skies; they illumine everything with an incorruptible fire issuing from the depths of the soul. Thus, a new life comes into being, born of the children's love for the entire world; and who will extinguish this love—who? What power is higher than this? Who will subdue it? The earth has brought it forth; and all life desires its victory—all life. Shed rivers of blood, nay, seas of blood, you'll never extinguish it."

She shook herself away from Liudmila, fatigued by her exaltation, and sat down, breathing heavily. Liudmila also withdrew from her, noiselessly, carefully, as if afraid of destroying something. With supple movement she walked about the room and looked in front of her with the deep gaze of her dim eyes. She seemed still taller, straighter, and thinner; her lean, stern face wore a concentrated expression, and her lips were nervously compressed. The stillness in the room soon calmed the mother, and noticing Liudmila's mood she asked guiltily and softly:

"Maybe I said something that wasn't quite right?"

Liudmila quickly turned around and looked at her as if in fright.

"It's all right," she said rapidly, stretching out her hand to the mother as if desiring to arrest something. "But we'll not speak about it any more. Let it remain as it was said; let it remain. Yes." And in a calmer tone she continued: "It's time for you to start soon; it's far."

"Yes, presently. I'm glad! Oh, how glad I am! If you only knew! I'm going to carry the word of my son, the word of my blood. Why, it's like one's own soul!"

She smiled; but her smile did not find a clear reflection in the face of Liudmila. The mother felt that Liudmila chilled her joy by her restraint; and the stubborn desire suddenly arose in her to pour into that obstinate soul enveloped in misery her own fire, to burn her, too, let her, too, sound in unison with her own heart full of joy. She took Liudmila's hands and pressed them powerfully.

"My dear, how good it is when you know that light for all the people already exists in life, and that there will be a time when they will begin to see it, when they will bathe their souls in it, and all, all, will take fire in its unquenchable flames."

Her good, large face quivered; her eyes smiled radiantly; and her eyebrows trembled over them as if pinioning their flash. The great thoughts intoxicated her; she put into them everything that burned her heart, everything she had lived through; and she compressed the thoughts into firm, capacious crystals of luminous words. They grew up ever more powerful in the autumn heart, illuminated by the creative force of the spring sun; they blossomed and reddened in it ever more brightly.

"Why, this is like a new god that's born to us, the people. Everything for all; all for everything; the whole of life in one, and the whole of life for everyone, and everyone for the whole of life! Thus I understand all of you; it is for this that you are on this earth, I see. You are in truth comrades all, kinsmen all, for you are all children of one mother, of truth. Truth has brought you forth; and by her power you live!"

Again overcome by the wave of agitation, she stopped, fetched breath, and spread out her arms as if for an embrace.

"And if I pronounce to myself that word 'comrades' then I hear with my heart—they are going! They are going from everywhere, the great multitude, all to one thing. I hear such a roaring, resonant and joyous, like the festive peal of the bells of all the churches of the world."

She had arrived at what she desired. Liudmila's face flashed in amazement. Her lips quivered; and one after the other large transparent tears dropped from her dull eyes and rolled down her cheeks.

The mother embraced her vigorously and laughed softly, lightly taking pride in the victory of her heart. When they took leave of each other Liudmila looked into the mother's face, and asked her softly:

"Do you know that it is well with you?" And herself supplied the answer: "Very well. Like a morning on a high mountain."

CHAPTER XIX

In the street the frozen atmosphere enveloped her body invigoratingly, penetrated into her throat, tickled her nose, and for a second suppressed the breathing in her bosom. The mother stopped and looked around. Near to her, at the corner of the empty street, stood a cabman in a shaggy hat; at a slight distance a man was walking, bent, his head sunk in his shoulders; and in front of him a soldier was running in a jump, rubbing his ears.

"The soldier must have been sent to the store," she thought, and walked off listening with satisfaction to the youthful crunching of the snow under her feet. She arrived at the station early; her train was not yet ready; but in the dirty waiting room of the third class, blackened with smoke, there were numerous people already. The cold drove in the railroad workmen; cabmen and some poorly dressed, homeless people came in to warm themselves; there were passengers, also a few peasants, a stout merchant in a raccoon overcoat, a priest and his daughter, a pockmarked girl, some five soldiers, and bustling tradesmen. The men smoked, talked, drank tea and whisky at the buffet; some one laughed boisterously; a wave of smoke was wafted overhead; the door squeaked as it opened, the windows rattled when the door was jammed to; the odor of tobacco, machine oil, and salt fish thickly beat into the nostrils.

The mother sat near the entrance and waited. When the door opened a whiff of fresh air struck her, which was pleasant to her, and she took in deep breaths. Heavily dressed people came in with bundles in their hands; they clumsily pushed through the door, swore, mumbled, threw their things on the bench or on the floor, shook off the dry rime from the collars of their overcoats and their sleeves and wiped it off their beards and mustaches, all the time puffing and blowing.

A young man entered with a yellow valise in his hand, quickly looked around, and walked straight to the mother.

"To Moscow, to your niece?" he asked in a low voice.

"Yes, to Tanya."

"Very well."

He put the valise on the bench near her, quickly whipped out a cigarette, lighted it, and raising his hat, silently walked toward the other door. The mother stroked the cold skin of the valise, leaned her elbows on it, and, satisfied, began again to look around at the people. In a few moments she arose and walked over to the other bench, nearer to the exit to the platform. She held the valise lightly in her hand; it was not large, and she walked with raised head, scanning the faces that flashed before her.

One man in a short overcoat and its collar raised jostled against her and jumped back, silently waving his hand toward his head. Something familiar about him struck her; she glanced around and saw that he was looking at her with one eye gleaming out of his collar. This attentive eye pricked her; the hand in which she held the valise trembled; she felt a dull pain in her shoulder, and the load suddenly grew heavy.

"I've seen him somewhere," she thought, and with the thought suppressed the unpleasant, confused feeling in her breast. She would not permit herself to define the cold sensation that already pressed her heart quietly but powerfully. It grew and rose in her throat, filling her mouth with a dry, bitter taste, and compelling her to turn around and look once more. As she turned he carefully shifted from one foot to the other, standing on the same spot; it seemed he wanted something, but could not decide what. His right hand was thrust between the buttons of his coat, the other he kept in his pocket. On account of this the right shoulder seemed higher than the left.

Without hastening, she walked to the bench and sat down carefully, slowly, as if afraid of tearing something in herself or on herself. Her memory, aroused by a sharp premonition of misfortune, quickly presented this man twice to her imagination—once in the field outside the city, after the escape of Rybin; a second time in the evening in the court. There at his side stood the constable to whom she had pointed out the false way taken by Rybin. They knew her; they were tracking her—this was evident.

"Am I caught?" she asked, and in the following second answered herself, starting: "Maybe there is still—" and immediately forcing herself with a great effort, she said sternly: "I'm caught. No use."

She looked around, and her thoughts flashed up in sparks and expired in her brain one after the other.

"Leave the valise? Go away?"

But at the same time another spark darted up more glaringly: "How much will be lost? Drop the son's word in such hands?"

She pressed the valise to herself trembling. "And to go away with it? Where? To run?"

These thoughts seemed to her those of a stranger, somebody from the outside, who was pushing them on her by main force. They burned her, and their burns chopped her brain painfully, lashed her heart like fiery whipcords. They were an insult to the mother; they seemed to be driving her away from her own self, from Pavel, and everything which had grown to her heart. She felt that a stubborn, hostile force oppressed her, squeezed her shoulder and breast, lowered her stature, plunging her into a fatal fear. The veins on her temples began to pulsate vigorously, and the roots of her hair grew warm.

Then with one great and sharp effort of her heart, which seemed to shake her entire being, she quenched all these cunning, petty, feeble little fires, saying sternly to herself: "Enough!"

She at once began to feel better, and she grew strengthened altogether, adding: "Don't disgrace your son. Nobody's afraid."

Several seconds of wavering seemed to have the effect of joining everything in her; her heart began to beat calmly.

"What's going to happen now? How will they go about it with me?" she thought, her senses strung to a keener observation.

The spy called a station guard, and whispered something to him, directing his look toward her. The guard glanced at him and moved back. Another guard came, listened, grinned, and lowered his brows. He was an old man, coarse-built, gray, unshaven. He nodded his head to the spy, and walked up to the bench where the mother sat. The spy quickly disappeared.

The old man strode leisurely toward the mother, intently thrusting his angry eyes into the mother's face. She sat farther back on the bench, trembling. "If they only don't beat me, if they only don't beat me!"

He stopped at her side; she raised her eyes to his face.

"What are you looking at?" he asked in a moderated voice.

"Nothing."

"Hm! Thief! So old and yet——"

It seemed to her that his words struck her face once, twice, rough and hoarse; they wounded her, as if they tore her cheeks, ripped out her eyes.

"I'm not a thief! You lie!" she shouted with all the power of her chest; and everything before her jumped and began to whirl in a whirlwind of revolt, intoxicating her heart with the bitterness of insult. She jerked the valise, and it opened.

"Look! look! All you people!" she shouted, standing up and waving the bundle of the proclamations she had quickly seized over her head. Through the noise in her ears she heard the exclamations of the people who came running up, and she saw them pouring in quickly from all directions.

"What is it?"

"There's a spy!"

"What's the matter?"

"She's a thief, they say!"

"She?"

"Would a thief shout?"

"Such a respectable one! My, my, my!"

"Whom did they catch?"

"I'm not a thief," said the mother in a full voice, somewhat calmed at the sight of the people who pressed closely upon her from all sides.

"Yesterday they tried the political prisoners; my son was one of them, Vlasov. He made a speech. Here it is. I'm carrying it to the people in order that they should read, think about the truth."

One paper was carefully pulled from her hands. She waved the papers in the air and flung them into the crowd.

"She won't get any praise for that, either!" somebody exclaimed in a frightened voice.

"Whee-ee-w!" was the response.

The mother saw that the papers were being snatched up, were being hidden in breasts and pockets. This again put her firmly on her feet; more composed than forceful, straining herself to her utmost, and feeling how agitated pride grew in her raising her high above the people, how subdued joy flamed up in her, she spoke, snatching bundles of papers from the valise and throwing them right and left into some person's quick, greedy hands.

"For this they sentenced my son and all with him. Do you know? I will tell you, and you believe the heart of a mother; believe her gray hair. Yesterday they sentenced them because they carried to you, to all the people, the honest, sacred truth. How do you live?"

The crowd grew silent in amazement, and noiselessly increased in size, pressing closer and closer together, surrounding the woman with a ring of living bodies.

"Poverty, hunger, and sickness—that's what work gives to the poor people. This order of things pushes us to theft and to corruption; and over us, satiated and calm, live the rich. In order that we should obey the police, the authorities, the soldiers, all are in their hands, all are against us, everything is against us. We perish all our lives day after day in toil, always in filth, in deceit. And others enjoy themselves and gormandize themselves with our labor; and they hold us like dogs on chains, in ignorance. We know nothing, and in terror we fear everything. Our life is night, a dark night; it is a terrible dream. They have poisoned us with strong intoxicating poison, and they drink our blood. They glut themselves to corpulence, to vomiting—the servants of the devil of greed. Is it not so?"

"It's so!" came a dull answer.

Back of the crowd the mother noticed the spy and two gendarmes. She hastened to give away the last bundles; but when her hand let itself down into the valise it met another strange hand.

"Take it, take it all!" she said, bending down.

A dirty face raised itself to hers, and a low whisper reached her: "Whom shall I tell? Whom inform?"

She did not answer.

"In order to change this life, in order to free all the people, to raise them from the dead, as I have been raised, some persons have already come who secretly saw the truth in life; secretly, because, you know, no one can say the truth aloud. They hunt you down, they stifle you; they make you rot in prison, they mutilate you. Wealth is a force, not a friend to truth. Thus far truth is the sworn enemy to the power of the rich, an irreconcilable enemy forever! Our children are carrying the truth into the world. Bright people, clean people are carrying it to you. Thus far there are few of them; they are not powerful; but they grow in number every day. They put their young hearts into free truth, they are making it an invincible power. Along the route of their hearts it will enter into our hard life; it will warm us, enliven us, emancipate us from the oppression of the rich and from all who have sold their souls. Believe this."

"Out of the way here!" shouted the gendarmes, pushing the people. They gave way to the jostling unwillingly, pressed the gendarmes with their mass, hindered them perhaps without desiring to do so. The gray-haired woman with the large, honest eyes in her kind face attracted them powerfully; and those whom life held asunder, whom it tore from one another, now blended into a whole, warmed by the fire of the fearless words which, perhaps, they had long been seeking and thirsting for in their hearts—their hearts insulted and revolted by the injustice of their severe life. Those who were near stood in silence. The mother saw their gloomy faces, their frowning brows, their eyes, and felt their warm breath on her face.

"Get up on the bench," they said.

"I'll be arrested immediately. It's not necessary."

"Speak quicker! They're coming!"

"Go to meet the honest people. Seek those who advise all the poor disinherited. Don't be reconciled, comrades, don't! Don't yield to the power of the powerful. Arise, you working people! you are the masters of life! All live by your labor; and only for your labor do they untie your hands. Behold! you are bound, and they have killed, robbed your soul. Unite with your heart and your mind into one power. It will overcome everything. You have no friends except yourselves. That's what their only friends say to the working people, their friends who go to them and perish on the road to prison. Not so would dishonest people speak, not so deceivers."

"Out of the way! Disperse!" the shouts of the gendarmes came nearer and nearer. There were more of them already; they pushed more forcibly; and the people in front of the mother swayed, catching hold of one another.

"Is that all you have in the valise?" whispered somebody.

"Take it! Take all!" said the mother aloud, feeling that the words disposed themselves into a song in her breast, and noticing with pain that her voice did not hold out, that it was hoarse, trembled, and broke.

"The word of my son is the honest word of a workingman, of an unsold soul. You will recognize its incorruptibility by its boldness. It is fearless, and if necessary it goes even against itself to meet the truth. It goes to you, working people, incorruptible, wise, fearless. Receive it with an open heart, feed on it; it will give you the power to understand everything, to fight against everything for the truth, for the freedom of mankind. Receive it, believe it, go with it toward the happiness of all the people, to a new life with great joy!"

She received a blow on the chest; she staggered and fell on the bench. The gendarmes' hands darted over the heads of the people, and seizing collars and shoulders, threw them aside, tore off hats, flung them far away. Everything grew dark and began to whirl before the eyes of the mother. But overcoming her fatigue, she again shouted with the remnants of her power:

"People, gather up your forces into one single force!"

A large gendarme caught her collar with his red hand and shook her.

"Keep quiet!"

The nape of her neck struck the wall; her heart was enveloped for a second in the stifling smoke of terror; but it blazed forth again clearly, dispelling the smoke.

"Go!" said the gendarme.

"Fear nothing! There are no tortures worse than those which you endure all your lives!"

"Silence, I say!" The gendarme took her by the arm and pulled her; another seized her by the other arm, and taking long steps, they led her away.

"There are no tortures more bitter than those which quietly gnaw at your heart every day, waste your breast, and drain your power."

The spy came running up, and shaking his fist in her face, shouted:

"Silence, you old hag!"

Her eyes widened, sparkled; her jaws quivered. Planting her feet firmly on the slippery stones of the floor, she shouted, gathering the last remnants of her strength:

"The resuscitated soul they will not kill."

"Dog!"

The spy struck her face with a short swing of his hand.

Something black and red blinded her eyes for a second. The salty taste of blood filled her mouth.

A clear outburst of shouts animated her:

"Don't dare to beat her!"

"Boys!"

"What is it?"

"Oh, you scoundrel!"

"Give it to him!"

"They will not drown reason in blood; they will not extinguish its truth!"

She was pushed in the neck and the back, beaten about the shoulders, on the head. Everything began to turn around, grow giddy in a dark whirlwind of shouts, howls, whistles. Something thick and deafening crept into her ear, beat in her throat, choked her. The floor under her feet began to shake, giving way. Her legs bent, her body trembled, burned with pain, grew heavy, and staggered powerless. But her eyes were not extinguished, and they saw many other eyes which flashed and gleamed with the bold sharp fire known to her, with the fire dear to her heart.

She was pushed somewhere into a door.

She snatched her hand away from the gendarmes and caught hold of the doorpost.

"You will not drown the truth in seas of blood———"

They struck her hand.

"You heap up only malice on yourself, you unwise ones! It will fall on you——"

Somebody seized her neck and began to choke her. There was a rattle in her throat.

"You poor, sorry creatures——"

Made in the USA
Monee, IL
03 May 2026

49438449R10225